Northern Sandlots
A Social History of Maritime Baseball

Northern Sandlots is the story of the rise and fall of regional baseball on the north-east coast of North America. Colin Howell writes about the social and economic influence of baseball on community life in the Maritimes and New England during the past century, from its earliest spread from cities and towns into the countryside, to the advent of television, and the withering of local semi-pro leagues after the Second World War.

The history of sport is an important feature of the 'new' social history. Howell discusses how baseball has been deeply implicated in debates about class and gender, race and ethnicity, regionalism and nationalism, work and play, and the commercialization of leisure. Baseball's often overlooked connection to medical and religious discourse is also explored.

Howell begins with the game's earliest days, when it was being moulded by progressive reformers to meet what they considered to be the needs of an emerging industrial society. He then turns to the interwar years, when baseball in the Maritimes was strictly amateur, revealing an emerging sense of community solidarity and regional identity. The game flourished at the community level after the Second World War, before it eventually succumbed to the new, commodified, and nationally marketed sporting culture that accompanied the development of the modern consumer society. Finally, Howell shows that fundamental changes in the nature of capitalism after the war, and in the economic and social reality of small towns and cities, hastened the death of a century-long tradition of competitive, community-level baseball.

Howell has written an informative and insightful social history that examines the transformation of Maritime community life from the 1860s to the mid-twentieth century.

COLIN HOWELL is a member of the Department of History, Saint Mary's University.

Northern Sandlots

A Social History of Maritime Baseball

COLIN D. HOWELL

UNIVERSITY OF TORONTO PRESS
Toronto Buffalo London

© University of Toronto Press Incorporated 1995
Toronto Buffalo London
Printed in Canada

ISBN 0-8020-5011-5 (cloth)
ISBN 0-8020-6942-8 (paper)

Printed on acid-free paper

Canadian Cataloguing in Publication Data

Howell, Colin D., 1944–
  Northern sandlots : a social history of Maritime baseball

  Includes bibliographical references and index.
  ISBN 0-8020-5011-5 (bound)   ISBN 0-8020-6942-8 (pbk.)

  1. Baseball – Maritime Provinces – History.
  2. Maritime Provinces – Social life and customs.
  I. Title.

  GV863.15.M37H6 1995   796.357'09715   C95-930193-3

University of Toronto Press acknowledges the financial assistance to its
publishing program of the Canada Council and the Ontario Arts Council.

This book has been published with the help of a grant from the Social
Science Federation of Canada, using funds provided by the Social Sciences
and Humanities Research Council of Canada.

To my father
in loving memory

Contents

Preface

Some time ago, when I first contemplated writing a social history of baseball in Atlantic Canada, a dear friend and colleague raised an initial challenge. 'Why baseball and not hockey?' she asked. What a strange question, I thought, akin to asking why someone writing a book about fish wasn't studying oil. It quickly dawned on me, however, that what had prompted her question was the assumption that baseball was an American sport, and that hockey was quintessentially Canadian. Ironically, this dichotomy is what attracted me to the topic in the first place. How was it that baseball, an American game, became the most popular summer sport in the Maritimes during the latter half of the nineteenth century? What social purposes did it serve, and what local conditions nurtured its growth? In short, how did the history of baseball in the north-eastern corner of the continent at once replicate and diverge from the patterns of its development elsewhere?

From the beginning, baseball appealed to me because of its connection to larger issues, issues that transcended regional and national boundaries, yet resonated within a local context. Clearly, baseball's development in the Maritimes derived much of its energy from the forces that drew the Maritimes and New England together over the years. At the same time, baseball developed at a time of significant social and economic transformation, when class and gender relations were in flux, when new ways of organizing work and play were being put into place, and when new assumptions about individual and social well-being and healthiness were being articulated. I was interested in the way that baseball was implicated in broader discourses involving respectable behaviour, masculinity and femininity, regionalism and nationalism, and class, ethnicity, and race. What follows is an attempt to unravel those discourses and their connection to the constantly shifting patterns of production, consumption, and commercialization that accompanied the transformation of capitalism and of sport over the past century.

Long before I thought seriously about questions of this sort, I had been a fan of baseball. Some of my earliest memories involve days with my father and grandfather at the ballpark in Kentville, a small town in Nova Scotia's Annapolis Valley, watching the semi-pro Wildcats play other teams in the Halifax and District Baseball League during the 1950s. Although these clubs were stocked mainly with American players from New England and the Carolinas, what seemed more important at the time was that the local ballpark served as a focal point of community identity and civic pride. Now and then there were those who questioned the reliance on American players and worried about the limited opportunity left for good local players to develop their talents, but in the friendly afterglow of the Second World War the links between the Maritimes and New England remained as strong as they had ever been.

In addition to the American imports, there were a number of local players good enough to compete and star in the various semi-pro leagues in the Maritimes. Although some of them, like Vern Handrahan of Charlottetown and Billy Harris of Dorchester, New Brunswick, went on to play major-league baseball, many equally talented athletes maintained a strong allegiance to the Maritime region, rejecting the blandishments of major-league clubs interested in recruiting them. One of the more prominent was Johnny Clark, a speedy outfielder from Pictou County whose daring exploits on the base paths earned him the nickname the 'Westville flash.' Then there was W.A. 'Buddy' Condy, generally regarded as the best natural hitter ever to play in the Maritimes, and a number of others who for their own reasons turned their backs on a pro career. At the end of the war Condy turned down a contract with the Montreal Royals, choosing to work towards a career in medicine rather than suiting up alongside Jackie Robinson and the other prospects on the Brooklyn Dodgers' top farm club. A couple of years later, after homesickness ended a short but successful stint in the semi-professional Quebec Provincial League, Johnny Clark rejected an offer from the Philadelphia Phillies and settled in to an eight-year career in the Halifax and District League.

When my friends and I weren't watching baseball in those days, we were playing it, making up in dedication what we lacked in proficiency. During the daytime it was pick-up baseball, often played from early morning to dusk. Evenings were set aside for organized competition from Little League up to Babe Ruth League and junior ball, or for cheering on the Wildcats at Memorial Park. There was a youthful masculine camaraderie in all of this, and when coaches like the old pro Eddie Gillis, now a regional scout for the St Louis Cardinals, drilled us in the fundamentals of the sport and the discipline it required, one got the feeling that we were also being instructed in the essentials of growing up. At the time we took the expectations of gender at face value; it seemed natural that baseball was a man's game and that women should watch from the sidelines as young men flaunted their physical abilities as an expression of their masculinity. No one thought much then about the socialization of gender roles; one simply experienced them as part of life.

Then came the announcement at the beginning of the 1960 season that the H&D league, the sole surviving semi-pro circuit in the region, had folded. I remember the mixture of disappointment and adolescent bewilderment that swept over me when I heard the news. It astonished me that the civic leaders of Kentville, Truro, Stellarton, Liverpool, Halifax, and Dartmouth could have let die something I considered so integral to community life and essential to my own growing up. What I failed to appreciate at the time was that the collapse of community-level baseball was a continent-wide phenomenon, related to the contraction of minor-league baseball during the fifties and sixties throughout North America. Nor did I understand then that small towns everywhere were being transformed. Gradually the development of the post-industrial capitalist economy was beginning to draw small towns out of their relative isolation and into a world of super-highways, consolidated schools, shopping centres, and industrial parks. At the same time, new patterns of leisure were emerging, influenced by the expanding numbers of people owning automobiles, summer cottages, and television sets.

If memories of my youth have prompted me to reflect upon the images of community, region, and adolescent masculinity that surrounded baseball in the fifties, my training as a historian alerts me to the fact that these concepts are themselves socially constructed. Obviously the discourses and images surrounding the game in the postwar years differ greatly from those of today. Contemporary baseball is characterized by the increasingly sophisticated marketing of sport and its ancillary operations as commodities in a consumer-oriented society. Mass-produced sporting wear makes the team logos of major-league clubs available across the continent, and major-league ballplayers some-times make as much in endorsements as they do in regular salary. In this context there is little space for the celebration of minor-league, let alone local community, baseball. Today's sporting culture, like the entertainment industry, has become a story of those currently in the public eye.

But what of the century of baseball history before the Second World War? In the nineteenth century baseball was enmeshed in the broad negotiation of class and gender relationships that accompanied the emerging industrial-capitalist order. Notions of bourgeois respectability, of gentlemanly amateurism, of skilful production, of worker solidarity, and of appropriate manliness were central to the discourse about base-ball's social purposes. Baseball's rise took place amidst the broader commercialization of leisure, and as such involved debates about the evils of gambling, of rowdy spectatorism, of irresponsible promoters and club owners, and of sharp and corrupt practices both on and off the field.

The game's early development was also shaped by those who saw sport as a tool for reform. Evangelical reformers attacked what they regarded as the unsavoury character of traditional recreations and saw organized sport as a vehicle for moral improvement. This attack on popular leisure pursuits, as Robert Malcolmson has pointed out, had begun long before the emergence of baseball.[1] By the beginning of the nineteenth century the cultural traditions of working people were meet-ing with greater contempt than ever before. Concerned about the rowdi-ness and drunkenness that accompanied traditional celebrations and carnivals, which satirized the existing social system, with charivaris, mummers' parades, and polymorphian processions, and with the unsa-voury influence of roughs and gamblers in such sports as horseracing, advocates of a more disciplined social order saw organized sporting activity as a civilizing force.[2] Increasingly, more genteel spectator sports displaced animal or blood sports such as cockfighting or bear baiting, revealing in the process a bourgeois concern for orderly behaviour and moral improvement. When placed in this context, the development of organized team sports such as baseball represents not merely a shift in fashionability, but suggests the negotiation and redefinition of class relations in an emerging capitalist order.

At the end of the nineteenth century the reform impulse assumed a less moralistic character. As urban populations swelled with the arrival of rural dwellers and immigrants in the second half of the century, a new professional élite, steeped in the language of science, promised social improvement and planned urban development through innovative forms of organization and professional management. In the vanguard of reform during the so-called progressive era were members of the various professions, particularly engineers, lawyers, journalists, educators, and medical practitioners, who responded to the social dislocations of urban life in such a way as to address some of its most obvious abuses. Emphasizing the need to reorganize modern society around the principles of efficiency, social justice, and expert management, progressive reformers took the lead in matters pertaining to sanitation and public health, inadequate housing, the proper ventilation of buildings and factories, improved inter- and intra-city transportation, the adulteration of food and drink, and the development of healthful forms of recreation, physical culture, and sport.[3]

In promoting a more 'scientific,' professional, and systematic approach to the physical environment, this group of professionals – which Harold Perkin described in the British context as 'the forgotten middle class' – played a crucial role in the rehabilitation of turn-of-the-century capitalism. When war came in 1914, most progressives responded to the bugler's call, seeing the war as an opportunity to apply principles of scientific management and human engineering to the remaking of the world order, just as they had tried to shape social relations at home through the medium of sport and organized recreation.[4]

By the 1920s the progressive dream of a world liberated through scientific understanding and technological advancement was in tatters. In the Maritimes the end of the war brought disillusionment: industrialization gave way to deindustrialization, markets for the region's primary products shrank, and large numbers of people left the area in search of employment elsewhere. Those who remained turned to images of the past as a form of consolation, celebrating the glories of the so-called Golden Age of sail and the integrity of the sturdy Maritime folk. Not surprisingly, one can discern a corresponding shift in the discourse surrounding baseball at this time, away from the imagery of class differentiation and social regeneration towards that of community identity and regional integrity. This postwar evacuation of the language of class, the idealization of local community life, and the invention of a Maritime folk tradition by Maritime writers and cultural anthropologists had a political counterpart in the Maritime Rights movement.[5]

For blacks, native peoples, and recent immigrants this idealization of the Maritime folk and local-community identity could only have served to reinforce their sense of isolation from mainstream society. Although minorities often turned to sports such as baseball as a way of encouraging self-respect and racial and ethnic identity, segregation on the basis of race was a continuing reality even on the supposedly 'democratic' field of play. Women, blacks, native people, and ethnic minorities were the 'other,' against whom standards of the 'normal' were erected. And, when barnstorming black baseball teams, or sectarian assemblages such as the 'House of David,' visited the region to play ball, the dramatization of their otherness was an important part of their appeal at the gate.

As for gender, there is no question that baseball had triumphed as a male sport by 1914. Despite the postwar celebration of the image of the 'athletic' woman in the advertising industry, and the growing involvement of women in sporting activity during the 1920s, the baseball park, like the workplace, would remain characterized by obvious gender segregation. Baseball was a 'manly' sport after all, serving as an obvious rite of passage from adolescence to manhood. There was little ideological room here for widespread female participation as ballplayers. To be sure, a few adventurous women did play the game, both in the nineteenth century and the twentieth, but the role of women in baseball was essentially that of spectators. By denying women an active role in the sport, baseball reinforced traditional stereotypes of women as consumers rather than producers. At the same time, the idealization of the 'lady' fan served the interests of promoters interested in attracting an expanded and 'respectable' audience.

What follows is a sweeping, some might say too sweeping, analysis not only of baseball's century and a half of development in the Maritimes, but its connection to broader social issues and processes. It touches upon significant theoretical debates about class formation, regionalism, community identity, gender, race, and ethnicity. At its most abstract level, it is a study of the cultural production and commodification of sport, and of the social dimensions of capitalist development in a hinterland region. Lay readers might find daunting some of the theoretical issues elaborated upon in the opening chapter, but they are intended to provide the analytical framework for the rest of the book. Even despite its theoretical content, however, this study is intended to be much more than an intellectual or scholarly exercise. My objective instead is to marry the insights derived from personal memory with those of recent scholarship, and to offer a sympathetic yet critical understanding of the making of the baseball world in the region by those who were part of its creation. It is hoped that both a scholarly audience and everyday enthusiasts of the game of baseball will find something in the following pages to maintain their interest.

In any work of this sort one becomes indebted to more people than one can adequately hope to repay. It is no exaggeration to say that this project simply could not have been completed without the generous assistance and support of the Social Sciences and Humanities Research Council of Canada. Without the Council's help I would have been unable to recover from the disastrous fire in November 1991 that burned my house to the ground. Fortunately, my SSHRCC research grant allowed me to take stock of what materials had been lost in the fire and, where possible, to replace them. A grant from the Senate Research Committee at Saint Mary's University also helped to recover lost data, and to photocopy smoke- and water-damaged material that eventually had to be destroyed.

It is in such difficult times that one realizes the value of true friendship. I am particularly indebted to the students and faculty in the Atlantic Canada Studies Program at Saint Mary's who gave so much of their time and effort to help me recover from my loss, organizing work parties, assisting in research, typing, and inputting material into the computer, and just providing moral support. Thanks to Jackie Logan at the Gorsebrook Research Institute, who is one of the most generous and helpful persons it is my pleasure to know; to Terry McLean, who has gone beyond the call of duty trying to make me computer-proficient; and to Susan Webber for assisting at a critical moment. Then there are the many research assistants who have worked with me on the project, and with whom I share a sense of collective effort. Lois Loewen developed an exhaustive card file on individual baseball players; Anne-Marie Smith scoured New Brunswick newspapers; Heidi Macdonald sorted through the religious press for stories relating to child-saving; Trudy Sable travelled far and wide interviewing native people about baseball; and Sheridan Hay helped sort out issues relating to community and race. I reserve a special mention for Gillian Allen, who took the post-fire mess and turned it into a filing system that testifies to her training in both history and law.

I am also indebted to my colleagues in the History Department at Saint Mary's, and to Marjorie Warren for responding so cheerfully to all that I have asked of her over the past few years. Fellow department members John Reid, Richard Twomey, and Michael Vance have all read and commented upon portions of the manuscript. So have a number of colleagues across the country. Thanks to Ian McKay, Sharon Tillotson,

John Thompson, Bryan Palmer, Alan Metcalfe, David Smith, Michael Smith, Peter Twohig, Chad Gaffield, and Sandy Young for their trenchant criticisms and their encouragement. I am particularly lucky to have friends like Rosemary Ommer and Phil Buckner, who can push you to clarify your thoughts and purposes, but always in a spirit of affection and concern. Thanks as well to my good friends at the University of Toronto Press, especially Gerry Hallowell, Rob Ferguson, and Laura Macleod, whose consummate professionalism has always been an inspiration. They can always play for my team.

Over the past few years I have been assisted at every turn by archivists, librarians, and university personnel. Carman Carroll, Allan Dunlop, and the staff at the Public Archives of Nova Scotia (PANS) have come to my relief in many a tight game, remaining dedicated to serving the historical profession despite serious funding cutbacks. Tom Sweet at the Nova Scotia Sports Heritage Centre is as gentle and helpful as his name implies, and Patti Hutchinson of the same institution cheerfully answered all my queries and made material available to me. It was with much sadness that I learned of the death of Robert 'Bun' Foley, a volunteer worker at the centre who spent hours regaling me with stories of Nova Scotia's sporting heritage. At Saint Mary's, Ken Clare kept alerting me to new publications and Sandra Hamm went out of her way to help secure interlibrary-loan material. During my work in the United States I received courteous assistance from the staff at the Bangor Public Library, the Fogler Library at the University of Maine, and the Maine State Archives in Augusta. And, finally, I would like to thank Tom Hecht, librarian at the Cooperstown National Baseball Library for his help, and for tickets to the Hall of Fame box in Oneonta.

Then there are my close friends and family who mean so much to me. To my wife, Sandi Galloway, to Heather and Kevin, Mike, Don, and Ken, thanks for helping me realize the important things in life. During the writing of this book, my father, Dennis Howell, passed away after a long struggle with cancer. With incredible dignity and courage, he showed all of us the nobility of fighting until the last out is recorded. It is to him, with all my love and affection, that this book is dedicated.

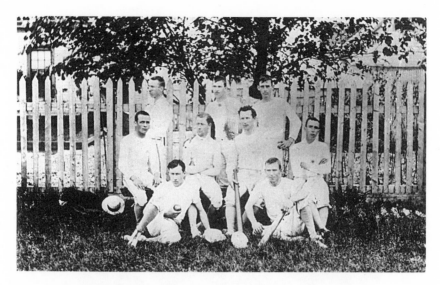

Atlantas Baseball Club, Halifax, 1878

Three players of the 1886 Young Men's Literacy Association team in Halifax.
From left: catcher Jack White, batter Jim Pender, and pitcher Michael Power

Socials Baseball Club, Halifax, 1887

The Chicago Blackstockings touring team in New Brunswick, 1891

Fredericton Tartars baseball team, 1899

Halifax Resolutes, 1900

Cover from *Tip Top Weekly* magazine, 1907

Halifax Crescents baseball team, 1916. Roy Isnor is seated third from the left, front row.

Baseball on the North Commons, Halifax, c. 1920

Baseball at the Wanderers Grounds, Halifax, in the 1920s. Note the preponderance of men in the audience.

Royals Baseball Club (Saint John, NB), Intermediate Champions, 1921

Halifax Coloured Diamonds, c. 1925

One of the finest pitchers of the interwar period, Sammy Lesser played for Halifax in the short-lived NS Professional Baseball League in 1924.

Charlie Paul, a Springhill native, played in the Boston Red Sox organization and for a number of teams throughout the Maritimes.

One of the few early photographs of native people playing baseball; the group poses after playing 'three catches and up' at Bear River, NS, in 1939.

Vince Ferguson accepts the good wishes of the mayor of Halifax (mid-1930s).

Babe Ruth, in street shoes, prepares to give a hitting exhibition at Wanderers Grounds, Halifax, in 1942.

Johnny Duarte, a right-handed pitcher of Latin American descent, played for the Dartmouth Arrows of the H&D League in the late 1940s.

Charles 'Bomber' Neal, one of the earliest black imports to the H&D League (1947)

Coach 'Peaches' Ruven and 'Bomber' Neal of the Dartmouth Arrows ham it up before the camera.

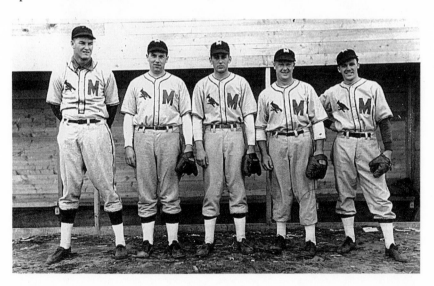

Middleton Cardinals (H&D League) pitching staff, 1947. Bucky Tanner is at extreme left.

Action from a game between the Halifax Shipyards and Dartmouth Arrows at the Halifax Wanderers Grounds, 1949

'Brother' Macdonald, Glace Bay Miners, slides into third base in a Cape Breton Colliery League match, 1949.

(PROCEEDS OF THESE PROGRAMS GO TO BOY SCOUTS)

Kentville

WILDCATS

vs

Truro

BEARCATS

Nº 2060

WATCH YOUR PROGRAM FOR LUCKY NUMBER . . . .

MEMORIAL PARK · · · · · · KENTVILLE, Nova Scotia

A scorecard from the H&D League, 1958

NORTHERN SANDLOTS

1

Laying Out the Field: Theoretical Approaches

Over the past decade or so the history of sport has established itself as one of the important concerns of the 'new' social history. To the early work of Peter Bailey on leisure in nineteenth-century Britain[1] and Robert Malcolmson's pathbreaking study of popular recreations in pre-industrial England,[2] scholars have added a number of useful studies that rescue sport history from the celebratory impulses of sports enthusiasts.[3] Much of this new work has focused upon the nineteenth century and the social and cultural transformation that accompanied the development of modern industrial capitalism. Two major approaches characterize recent work in this field. The first – the liberal or modernization approach – emphasizes the emergence of an organized sporting culture characterized by standardized rules, regularly scheduled games, organized league play, and provincial and national regulatory associations.[4] Some historians attribute the existence of this highly rationalized sporting edifice to the profound impact that urbanization and industrialization exercised upon leisure activity.[5] Others argue that the changes in the structure of sport began even before the emergence of the modern industrial order, and can be understood as part of a broader 'civilizing process' that began centuries before.[6]

A second approach, influenced by recent trends in social and labour history, suggests that the shaping of nineteenth-century sporting culture often pitted bourgeois reformers committed to 'rational' recreation – that is, recreation of a moral or improving character – against the very people they intended to reform. In this view, the changing nature of sport and popular recreation involved a continuing struggle about how recreational life should be reconstructed, about the social purposes of sport, the access to leisure time and space for people of different backgrounds, the relationship of work and play, and the appropriateness of different forms of recreational activity.[7] In this view, the sporting field was a 'contested' landscape upon which ethnic, gender, racial, class, and community rivalries abounded. These struggles, which had their roots in the economic and social inequities inherent in the capitalist mode of production, suggest that team sport offered a cultural resource to those who struggled against the bourgeoisie's desire to turn sport into an instrument of social control and domination.[8] Seen in this light, the development of sports such as baseball involve what Raymond Williams has called 'the social relations of cultural production,' the disparate and historically specific struggles, negotiations, and compromises among dominant, subordinate, and oppositional groups that are integral components of popular culture, indeed of the making of history itself.[9]

In both the Maritimes and New England the nineteenth-century baseball diamond provided a terrain upon which such battles were fought. From the game's earliest days in the 1860s and 1870s, in which baseball was being moulded by Evangelical reformers to inculcate appropriate notions of manliness and respectability amongst youthful members of the bourgeoisie, people from working-class backgrounds were being drawn to baseball for their own purposes. Among the well-to-do proponents of manly sport, the game soon acquired a reputation for rowdiness and roughness, suggesting that the bourgeois dream of creating a disciplined and 'gentlemanly' sporting culture across class lines was not always shared by those who played and watched the game. During the last two decades of the century, complaints about the sport's ungentlemanly associations were commonplace. 'Our experience with the national game of baseball,' read an editorial in the *New York Times* in November 1881, 'has been sufficiently thorough to convince us that it was in the beginning a sport unworthy of men, and that it is now, in its fully-developed state, unworthy of gentlemen.'[10] Yet, with the exception of a brief period at the beginning of the 1890s, baseball continued to grow in popularity, especially among working people.

If sport was an important ingredient of working-class culture in the late nineteenth century, it is also the case that ethnic, denominational, gender, and racial divisions occasionally fractured working-class homogeneity. Throughout the region – from Fall River, Massachusetts, Portsmouth, New Hampshire, and Portland, Maine, to Saint John, Moncton, and Halifax in the Maritimes – Englishmen, Irishmen, Catholics and Protestants, whites and blacks, men and women turned to the ball diamond for their own purposes, either as promoters, spectators, players, gamblers, or advocates of social reform. Their participation in the game reveals the social cleavages that were accented at the community level as capitalism was becoming transformed; it also sheds light upon the interconnections between class, community, gender, and ethnic identities throughout the region. Rarely were those identities independent of each other. As Mary Clawson notes, while 'identification based upon class, gender, race and ethnicity may appear as discrete alternatives, ... more commonly the density of historical experience intertwines them in intricate and consequential ways.'[11]

This history of baseball in the Atlantic Provinces and New England approaches sport as an aspect of cultural production, investigating the patterns of authority and resistance that derive from an unequal system of power relations within a patriarchally ordered capitalist system. These conflicts involved not only class but gender. Indeed, the marginalization of women as players was a product of a proscriptive patriarchal ideology that defined baseball as a manly sport, and a sexual division of labour that devalued women's work and consigned them to the domestic sphere. For young Victorian males, by contrast, baseball served as a rite of passage from boyhood to manhood. Just as women were socialized in many ways to accept the ideology of domesticity, so were men schooled in the supposedly masculine virtues of courage, strength, and physical robustness and those qualities that contributed to success in a competitive environment. Baseball defined and consolidated notions of manhood, provided a form of social bonding and brotherhood, and served to legitimize notions of male privilege.

The ideals of domesticity and manliness cut across class lines. Even for working-class women, many of whom were being drawn out of domestic service and into the factory workplace, the 'cult of domesticity' continued to influence their lives.[12] Despite their daytime work many women were expected to maintain a nurturing home environment, 'as the constructor of the place in which her husband might be humanized after the burdens of his labour and as the sustainer of the place in which he might leave for the re-creation of himself in the company of other men.' At the same time, while bourgeois reformers might define manly behaviour on the baseball diamond in terms of respect for one's opponents, deference to team officials, the acceptance of the authority of the umpire, and the avoidance of physical violence – all of which replicated an idealized bourgeois vision of appropriate social relations – working men often turned to baseball in order to demonstrate their physical ability and manly prowess in what appeared to be a more egalitarian environment than the workplace. On the baseball diamond, the aspirations among working men to demonstrate their masculine independence and respectability at the very time that artisanal skills were being devalued in the workplace meant that women would be cast as spectators rather than players – defending notions of respectability either in the stands or in the household.[13]

Baseball was much more than a vehicle for social reform or a crucible for developing masculinity, however. It was also a game that attracted promoters, entrepreneurs, and gamblers, those who recognized its potential as a marketable commodity, and whose interests diverged in many ways from those interested in moral rehabilitation through sport. Almost from its inception there was a tension between the reformers' veneration of baseball's civilizing character and its emergence as a marketable spectacle. Reformers lamented the commercialization and professionalization of baseball, and fretted about the unsavoury influences that surrounded the game. Wagering on games by spectators, players, and even umpires, rowdyism on the field and in the stands, and the potential violence that accompanied class and ethnic rivalries all raised doubts that the game could contribute to the moulding of true manliness, driving many to take refuge in an ideal of 'gentlemanly amateurism,' and its institutional expression, the amateur sport club. Ironically, therefore, while late-nineteenth-century progressive reformers venerated professional expertise as necessary for the solution of the problems that accompanied capitalist development, they often regarded professionalism among sportsmen with distaste because of its working-class associations.[14]

The debate over amateurism and professionalism in sport, which became particularly heated around the turn of the century, had its roots in an earlier concern about the relationship of work and play. As Warren Goldstein has observed, although baseball was about play and thus had a childish quality to it, it was never completely divorced from the world of work. Debates over the time devoted to practice and the development of essential skills, of 'playing for keeps' rather than for fun, suggested a tension between childish play and manly effort. Rooted in a mid-century work culture that venerated disciplined, productive craft labour, baseball was at once regarded as healthy exercise and amusement and as a skilful profession that demanded 'scientific' technique and productive efficiency.[15] Ironically, skilled craftsmanship was increasingly under assault in these years as new forms of capitalist enterprise began to emerge in the late nineteenth and early twentieth centuries.[16]

After the First World War, the debate about professionalism and amateurism would be recast in different language, reflecting among other things the degree to which baseball had attained respectability. Earlier, the objections to professionalism had been largely framed in class terms, revealing a bourgeois concern about the undisciplined nature of working-class culture. By the 1920s much had changed. Despite continuing class conflict in the Maritimes – especially in the coal fields of Cape Breton – baseball was no longer regarded so much as a class ritual as it was a symbol of community and regional identity, a contributor to civic loyalty in the small and medium-sized towns and cities of the Maritimes. Although this viewpoint reflected the postwar rise of regional political protest as an alternative to class politics, and the concomitant fragmentation of the working class in the Maritimes that accompanied regional deindustrialization, it also was part of a North American trend in which sport and other forms of commercialized entertainment served as unifying community enthusiasms that could transcend the boundaries of class. In the interwar period sport became a central element in the nurturing of local community allegiances and identity.

It is possible, of course, to idealize small-community life in the interwar period as a repository of family values and interdependence, a kind of Walton's Mountain world where the realities of poverty, class conflict, racism, and family violence magically dissolve in the face of universal good-heartedness. This romanticized notion of community, like the celebration of regional or national identity, carries obvious ideological intent, especially when accompanied by the assumption that shared interests and social solidarity have been more important in the past than class, ethnic, and gender conflict.[17] Not surprisingly, there is little agreement among academics as to the value of the concept. Some time ago, the sociologist George Hillery identified ninety-four different definitions of the meaning of community, and concluded that the only common ground for agreement was that a community consisted of 'persons in social interaction within a geographic area and having one or more additional common ties.'[18] This definition is so vague as to be meaningless.

Recently, the concept of community has been tied to anxieties about the social atomization and rootlessness that accompany modern technological society, and suggests a nostalgic longing for a more peaceful time.[19] Lamenting the the loss of an idealized past, contemporary conservatives imply that little can be done to alter modernity's course.

Similarly, in the 1920s and 1930s, the idealization of local community life and the promotion of Maritime regionalism that accompanied the collapse of the industrial hope served as a 'culture of consolation' that diverted attention from a more radical understanding of the process of capitalist underdevelopment. In this context of postwar antimodernism, baseball was reconceptualized as a fundamental constituent of community consensus. This new imagery by no means meant that class, gender, or racial conflicts had been resolved, only that the new discourse about baseball's civic utility disguised their importance.[20]

In its emphasis on small-town, amateur, or semi-professional baseball rather than on the professional game at the major-league level, this study offers an antidote to those who concentrate their attention on the main centres of organized sport in Canada and the United States such as Montreal, Toronto, Chicago, and New York.[21] Steven Riess has suggested that the bigger cities 'established models for smaller cities to emulate,' and that in 'cities of all sizes organized sports are structured pretty much the same way, with the same latent and manifest functions.'[22] The weakness of this argument is that while baseball has remained a fundamental constituent of the sporting culture of the large North American city, in smaller cities like Halifax, Saint John, Portland, Burlington, Vermont, or Manchester, New Hampshire, the game has withered and in some cases died. A half-century ago baseball flourished in each of these centres; indeed every small town and hamlet had its community team. By 1960, however, the game was virtually dead at the local-community level, gradually smothered by the mass-produced paraphernalia and marketing influence of major-league baseball. To understand this transition one must look beyond the history of the giant metropolis and of organized baseball and into the meaning and function of sport in hinterland regions such as northern New England and Atlantic Canada.

By the end of the nineteenth century a common baseball culture had emerged across the northeastern border of Canada and the United States.[23] Imported coaches and players from New England had a strong presence throughout the Maritimes, touring clubs played challenge games with Maritime teams, and towns on both sides of the border between Maine and New Brunswick organized international leagues with regularly scheduled games. Even during the economic depression of the 1920s and 1930s in the Maritimes, a period of introverted regionalism evident in both the Maritime Rights movement and the quest for a new Maritime folk identity,[24] New England teams were regular summer visitors to Maritime communities. It was only with the collapse of community-level baseball in the 1950s that the traditional sporting association between the Maritimes and New England was severed. Since then, new regional allegiances between the Maritimes and Newfoundland, fashioned in the political struggle to address regional disparity, have weakened the traditional connection of the Maritimes and New England.[25]

It has become fashionable in recent years to regard Atlantic Canada as a distinctive region with its own culture, identity, musical traditions, and social practices. Curiously enough, until recently Maritime historians have given little attention to the production of the region's culture, emphasizing instead the structural changes in the regional economy during the late nineteenth and early twentieth centuries, and the political and social responses to those changes. Most of the recent work of historians in the region has centred upon the process of regional industrialization and deindustrialization between Confederation and the First World War, and upon the sources and consequences of continuing regional disparity.[26] Unwittingly or not, historians of the region have tended to discount the significance of those social and cultural practices whose history does not on first glance contribute to an understanding of regional economic development.

This emphasis is beginning to change as historians in the region shift their attention from the broader regional economy to social and cultural relations at the level of the community, neighbourhood, and household.[27] Part of the explanation for this new perspective rests with the recognition of the importance of the largely ignored domestic or informal economy, an analysis of which does not fit comfortably into the urban-oriented model of regional industrialization and deindustrialization.[28] In addition, a growing interest in environmental issues has encouraged greater attention to rural spaces, primary production, and the cultural traditions of smaller communities.[29] There is much to be learned from an investigation of cultural change in these communities over time. For example, by placing the history of baseball in its community-level context, it is possible to inquire into the ways in which the sport contributed to a sense of community and regional identity in the Maritimes, how it reflected and encouraged, but also at times diffused, class, ethnic, and gender rivalries, and how it served and articulated the interests of city, small town, and rural regions in different ways at different times.

By the Second World War baseball had secured a central place in the local community life of the Maritimes. For the next two decades the game flourished in small-town New England and the Maritimes, encouraged by the pent-up demand for entertainment and the rising incomes that accompanied wartime and postwar production. Yet the 1940s and 1950s can be considered the 'Indian Summer' of Maritime baseball. While community baseball flourished after the war, it was virtually dead by 1960. Gradually detached from its roots in community and neighbourhood experience, the game was relentlessly drawn into the post-industrial consumer-oriented society, where it would be marketed as a commodity in the modern mass marketplace. Contemporary baseball has since become an integral component of 'the society of the spectacle,'[30] revealing all of the slickness, glitter, and seductive rationality of the modern capitalist world.

Baseball's absorption into an international marketplace of leisure and entertainment has, at the same time, elicited a yearning for a simpler and idealized past. Nostalgic critics of the seeming artificiality of modern baseball venerate the older game, played on real grass and in ball parks with 'character' or a touch of 'history.' Thus, Toronto's SkyDome, the epitome of the modern sporting palace, has been surpassed as the state-of-the-art ballpark by Baltimore's Camden Yards, where tactile images of the past merge with the reality of modern baseball.[31] The fascination with tangible – and notably marketable – icons of the past has served to inflate a burgeoning market for baseball cards and vintage baseball attire. Major-league teams have even taken to outfitting themselves in uniforms of earlier eras, as though the changes in the game over time – including its alienation from small-town life – are insignificant. Ironically, what is often overlooked in this flourishing of collective lament, is that the nostalgic image, like baseball itself, has become another commodity for consumption. Indeed, if Frederick Jamieson is right that the blend of nostalgia and novelty that characterizes postmodern society represents the ideology of advanced capitalism,[32] postmodernism serves to extend the reach of the market in new directions and in seemingly unobtrusive ways.

Amidst this celebration of the nostalgic imagination are the literary and academic testimonies to baseball's supposedly metaphysical character, evoking the virtues of the game that supposedly speak across – one might say at the expense of – history. The anthropologist Bradd Shore, for example, has linked the game's structure to enduring American ideals. Shore finds in baseball a kind of indeterminacy of possibility and open-endedness that sets an individual on a journey of endless opportunity but also of threatening obstacles. 'Baseball,' he writes, 'is our version of what Australian aborigines call a walk-about – a circular journey into alien territory, with the aim of returning home after making contact with sacred landmarks and braving hazards along the way.' Baseball, Shore argues, is a ritual that attempts 'to reconcile communal values with a tradition of heroic individualism and privatism.'[33]

The replacement of baseball history with allusions to its timelessness is a central characteristic of the writings of W.P. Kinsella, whose novels *Shoeless Joe*, *Box Socials*, and *The Iowa Baseball Confederacy* recount baseball lore in a quest for self-understanding. The denial of traditional forms of historical understanding can be found in each of these, but is most explicit in *The Iowa Baseball Confederacy*. In this novel, graduate student Matthew Clarke tries to write a history of this fictional league. After initially consulting sources that would confirm its existence, 'he quickly put them aside. He didn't *need* any confirmation from outside sources. The history of the Iowa Confederacy was carved on stone tablets in his memory. He couldn't know such things if they were not true.'[34] The problem was that Matthew's dissertation committee would not accept his lengthy manuscript as historical fact, despite its obvious literary merit. Tormented by the knowledge that he knew the truth, but that his detractors would never understand that timeless memory was as important as other historical sources, he ended his long struggle by putting his head in the way of a line drive off the bat of Billy Bruton during a game at Milwaukee's County Stadium.

These investigations of baseball's ritualistic character, which reduce the game to a vague set of social metaphors and sentimental remembrances, have a disturbingly chimerical quality to them. But there recently have been a number of critics who appear ready to join the doubters on Matthew Clarke's dissertation committee. 'Is nostalgia ruining baseball?' Nicholas Dawidoff asks in a recent article in *The New Republic*, and answers his own question by concluding that in an 'increasingly fractured and fracturing society, a national pastime that has existed for the near breadth of our history is being turned into a social balm – and is being embalmed at the same time. Indeed, America is so swamped in baseball nostalgia that the game threatens to be obscured by a cloud of kitsch.'[35] Rick Salutin, writing in the Toronto *Globe and Mail*, is also fed up with the overblown analogies of baseball to the mysterious secrets of life itself, noting that the result has been to obscure more down-to-earth, human issues, such as its 'massive commercialization, or even the role of women' within the game. Is it not time to ask, as Salutin does, what interests are being served by these gushes of metahistory? 'I don't mean all the hyperbolic baseballiana was intentionally devised,' Salutin writes, 'but when things get so far-fetched, it's legitimate to ask if other purposes are also being served.'[36]

What the dissolving of history into memory and metaphor obscures is both the way in which the game was produced, and how the social purposes of the game have altered over the past century. My argument is that in the half-century before the First World War the debates about baseball's character were framed largely in class terms, but that after the war baseball became attached to notions of regional identity and community self-awareness. Although this transition hardly meant that class, ethnic, and gender conflicts had been eradicated, it none the less allowed the game to sink deep roots at the local level. In turn, fundamental changes in the nature of capitalism after the Second World War and in the economic and social reality of small towns and cities in the Maritimes and northern New England hastened the death of local baseball and the triumph of a new, mass-produced baseball culture of Blue Jays caps and Montréal Expos sweatshirts.

2

First Innings:
Baseball, Cricket, and the
Bourgeois Ideal of Healthful Sport

On 7 May 1868 a group of about a dozen young Haligonians met at Doran's Hotel on Sackville Street and Bedford Row to organize the Halifax Baseball Club and prepare for the upcoming season.[1] Although this was not the first time that baseball had made an appearance in the Maritimes – nor was it the first incarnation of the Halifax Club – the meeting at Doran's Hotel was significant because it marked one of the earliest attempts to place baseball in Nova Scotia on an organized footing. Before this time, the game had been played sporadically amongst a random assortment of players and pick-up nines throughout the region, and had gained a certain amount of popularity amongst those who played it. One observer has suggested in fact that baseball was more popular in Halifax during the 1860s than the idea of Confederation, and that it did more for Canadian unity than any of the politicians of the day.[2] Although this is a gross exaggeration – even given the unpopularity of the idea of a union of the British North American colonies in the Maritimes – baseball was quickly emerging as a popular leisure activity that by the 1870s would rival other sports and appeal to reformers as a means to protect young middle-class men from idleness and indolence. A second club, the Independent Baseball Club, which had competed earlier against the Halifax Club, held its organizational meeting a couple of days later. The existence of these two baseball teams, not to mention the various cricket and lacrosse clubs in the city, caused the Halifax *Reporter* to predict 'a lively time in the "manly sports"' during the summer of 1868.[3]

The Halifax Club and the Independents had first organized early in the previous summer. 'It may not be generally known ... [but] Halifax has lately taken up the American game of Baseball,' the Halifax *Morning*

Chronicle reported, 'and as our American cousins last year came to Halifax to play us at our national game of Cricket, we will, I trust, be able next summer to show a very good front against them in their own game of baseball.' After a few months' practice, the two teams, whose players came mainly from the ranks of the middle class, had entered into a three-game series to test their abilities. The first meeting of the teams was a seven-inning affair on 27 July 1867 that had ended in a 77–55 triumph on the part of the Halifax Club, the high score reflecting the difficulties defensive teams had playing on poor fields with rudimentary equipment. The return match was held on 7 September, and the Independents, strengthened by their new pitcher and field captain, A.G.K. Keeling, beat Halifax 39–32 over the full nine innings. This set the stage for the rubber match on 28 September, in which the Independents prevailed by a score of 33–28.[4]

The early development of team sports such as baseball and cricket fell to an emerging middle class that regarded organized sporting activity as a social training ground for young men entering adulthood. Many bourgeois reformers believed that team sports inculcated respectable social values. The lessons learned on the gentlemanly field of play, it was hoped, would help young clerks, merchants, bankers, and professionals to provide future leadership and social refinement to their respective communities. In virtually every town of any size throughout the Maritimes and New England, middle-class reformers advocated a more disciplined and rational approach to leisure, seeking to replace irrational and often turbulent popular or working-class recreations with more genteel and improving leisure activities. At first, bourgeois sportsmen concentrated their attention on the improvement of middle-class youth. Later, as working men took up baseball in increasing numbers, they began to conceive of the baseball diamond as a place in which class and ethnic antipathies might dissolve in a setting of respectability, fair play, and democratic involvement. This proved to be a vain hope. In the long run, the bourgeois dream of cultivating respectability and class harmony met resistance from working people, especially skilled mechanics or artisans, who found in team sports such as baseball, and to a lesser extent cricket, a source of fraternal camaradie, and class and ethnic identity. Indeed, the debate over baseball's respectability and its continuing reputation for rowdiness throughout the nineteenth century suggest that bourgeois and working-class identity penetrated far beyond the workplace and shaped social and cultural life just as they did economic and productive activity.

Baseball in the nineteenth-century Maritimes and New England was both a social and an ideological phenomenon, rooted in class and gender relationships that were in a process of continuous renegotiation as industrial capitalism developed. On the social level one can trace baseball from its emergence as a bourgeois sport at mid-century to one that, after 1870, drew increasingly on a constituency of working people, particularly skilled workers or artisans. Baseball was also an ideological construct, however, and it is useful to investigate the various discourses that rationalized the game and other forms of sporting activity as socially valuable. In the period before the First World War those discourses centred around questions of class, gender, and nation. The imagery of baseball was connected to popular notions of physical, mental, and social degeneracy and disequilibrium, the elaboration of 'manly' character and fears of the 'feminization' of culture, and the concern for national vitality.

In the United States, baseball quickly established itself as the 'national game,' banishing cricket to the sidelines of American sporting life. Across the border, in the Maritimes, baseball's triumph was not so swift or complete, and nationalist imagery exerted a more tenuous influence. Rather, the debate over the relative virtues of cricket and baseball turned less on the question of nationality than upon issues of élitism, the sporting traditions of working-class communities, and urban boosterism. Ironically, the declining popularity of cricket in large urban centres in the Maritimes was related to its image as a game of the idle bourgeoisie, while its persistence in the coal-mining districts of eastern Nova Scotia and Cape Breton Island can be attributed both to the Scottish origins of the population and to working-class notions of 'manly' labour and hardy masculinity. As for baseball, a reform-minded bourgeoisie that regarded sport as a civilizing force provided the initial formulation of the game's social purpose.

Like many young middle-class men in the Victorian period, those who attended the organizational meeting at Edward Doran's old brick and granite hotel believed it important to establish a balance in their lives between physical and intellectual activity and to cultivate the so-called manly virtues.[5] Involvement in sports such as cricket or baseball allowed men like themselves to engage in what Evangelical reformers liked to call 'rational recreation,' physical activity that would prepare them to better carry out their occupational pursuits.[6] Drawn mainly from the professional and mercantile class, and thereby reflecting the pre-industrial and commercial character of the city, the newly elected officials of the Halifax Club included a physician, a dentist, two commission merchants, and an accountant.[7]

The president was Dr Alfred Chipman Cogswell, a 35-year-old dentist who advocated physical exercise as an antidote to sickness and debility. Born in 1834 near Cornwallis, Nova Scotia, Cogswell had entered Acadia University at the age of fifteen, and completed two years of study before ill health forced him to discontinue his education. At that point Cogswell moved with his family to Portland, Maine, where he worked on his father's farm for the next three years and in the process overcame his physical weakness. In 1854 Cogswell entered into the study of dentistry as an apprentice to Dr Edwin Parsons in Portland, and after four years of training in Portland and Boston, he opened an office in Wakefield, Massachusetts, where he married and began to contemplate a return to Nova Scotia. In 1859 he left Massachusetts for Halifax, where he formed a partnership in dentistry with Dr Lawrence Van Buskirk.[8]

It was during his sojourn in New England in the 1850s that Cogswell had first come into contact with the game of baseball. During that decade the game had been widely played in New England, especially among members of the middle class, and although there were great regional variations in the way the game was played, it gained rapidly in popularity. In Portland, where the Cogswell family had initially taken up residence, two clubs, the Portland and Forest City baseball nines, organized in 1858. In addition to local matches, the Portland club travelled to Boston for a match against the Tri-Mountain nine that summer, a trip that 'did much to remove the prejudices of many of the opponents of the game' and to consolidate its reputation as a respectable activity. Within two years the Sagamore and Putnam clubs had joined the roster of baseball clubs in Portland, and a home and home series between the Sagamores and a newly organized team in Augusta was a highlight of the 1860 season.[9]

The sixties witnessed a rapid expansion of the game in northern New England. In 1865 a tournament open to all clubs in Maine was held in Portland, with the Eons, the Howards, the Lincolns, and the Bowdoin College teams vying for the state championship. Although the Eons were edged 34–31 by Bowdoin in the championship match, they remained one of the more prominent teams in the state, along with the Androscoggins from the mill town of Lewiston, the Cushnocs from Augusta, and the Pine Tree Club of Kent Hill. In 1867 the baseball clubs of Maine formed the Maine State Association, whose member clubs would automatically qualify for a tournament held annually to crown the state champion. The association subsequently purchased a gold mounted rosewood bat and case, with a silver-plated ball, at the cost of $20, to serve as the championship trophy.[10]

By this time a friendly rivalry had developed between the Eons and the Kent Hill clubs, both of which prided themselves on their gentlemanly character. In addition to their polite manners, Kent Hill players had an excellent reputation on the field, 'having more practice than any other club in the state,' and they drew large crowds, including women as well as men, whenever they visited Portland. When the Kent Hill team played the Eons on 8 June 1867, the *Eastern Argus* made a special plea to ladies 'to be on the grounds early and occupy the seats, as no person except those seated and engaged in the game, will be allowed within the fence after the game commences.' The game itself created 'never known excitement,' and the Kent Hill players, who won the match 35–18, showed splendid deportment and behaved 'like gentlemen both on and off the field.'[11]

In June 1867 the Eons travelled to Boston to meet the powerful Philadelphia Athletics, one of the dominant teams of the decade, and subsequently the first champions of the National Association of Baseball Players in 1871. Billed as 'merely a friendly game played for the purpose of learning some of the fine points' of the sport, the Eons fell to the Athletics by an 88 to 23 score, playing before a crowd of 5000 on Boston Common. Despite the disappointing result, the *Eastern Argus* commended the Eons for their performance, pointing out that in 1866 the Philadelphians had won 23 of 24 games, scoring 1287 runs to only 350 for their opponents. The Eons had been told that they would 'not score six runs, and if they did the Athletics would throw up their hats for them.' The Eons surprised their opponents with their ability to score runs, but their pitching had not been able to subdue the Athletics, who 'made every blow tell on the game, and sometimes sent the ball spinning clean over the heads of the remotest spectators.'[12] Two weeks later, the Eons played another 'friendly' match, losing again to a strong nine from Lowell, Massachusetts, by a score of 52–29.[13]

In addition to its competitive first team, the Eons – like many of the more prominent early clubs – had a second and third nine that occasionally played each other in less serious 'muffin' games. In one of these 'muffin' matches in June 1867, the 'Noe' and the 'Eon' squared off before a friendly crowd. Seats were placed around the diamond, nearly all of which were occupied by ladies, whose presence demanded that the games be played in a gentlemanly way. No one cared too much about the result, one newspaper observed, for the game was full of fun, including good plays that brought applause and 'some horrid to offset them.' In addition to their muffin squads, many early baseball clubs also sported junior teams, such as the Dirigos of Augusta, who were state and New England junior champions in 1869, and the Unions of Lewiston.[14] Now and then, too, older veterans of the club would return to the field to play in 'old boy' matches. This was the case in August 1870 when the Old Portlanders, made up of those who played on the original Portland club in 1858, decided 'to try their hand again "just for the fun of the thing"' and invited the Iron Mills Club to play them. The game was 'very jolly,' but the 'lithe active young men' of the Iron Mills Club defeated the vets 37–27. The Portlanders 'exhibited some of the old fire, but time had laid its hand heavily upon them about the bowels,' said the *Eastern Argus*. 'They carried too much ballast. They had more bottom than speed!' At the end of the match the friendly feelings that characterized recreational play were evident. As was the custom, the Portland club gave three hearty cheers for their opponents, and 'were greatly obliged ... for their kindness in accommodating them with an opportunity to try their hand again.'[15]

The existence of muffin teams (known as such because of their tendency to muff chances in the field) served to restrain a win-at-all-costs attitude, and demonstrates that the purposes of many of the early clubs were as much social and recreational as they were athletic. Yet, as Warren Goldstein has pointed out, the social and fraternal character of these early clubs soon gave way to a new spirit of 'playing for keeps,' and an evaluation of play in the language of work and skilled production. Gradually the bourgeois vision of the game as a respectable and improving recreation for young gentlemen confronted another that regarded sport as an extension of the conflict between capital and labour, in which skilled workers cultivated and defended traditional skills in the face of the employer's introduction of new forms of scientific management and production. The growth of professionalism in baseball during the 1860s and 1870s gradually recast sport as work, and brought with it a greater emphasis on fundamental skills, increased specialization by position, and a fascination with measuring performance through the collection of statistics and the calculation of batting and fielding averages.

Goldstein sees two approaches to the game: the traditionalist, club, or fraternal ethic with its emphasis on pleasurable and healthful recreation, and the modernizing or reforming ethic that pushed beyond healthy exercise and fun to 'a serious application to practice, toward finer, more skillful play, and towards victories on the playing field.'[16] These two approaches also suggest that baseball was neither exclusively a middle- or working-class game. While the early clubs reflected an emerging middle-class concern for physical health through fresh air and exercise, and promoted individual self-control and manly character, they were not able to escape completely the influence of an artisan culture that defined respectability as a function of acquired skills and the dignity of labour. This is not to imply too sharp a division between these two traditions along class lines, for it is obvious that many working people were attracted to sport for its healthful benefits and the conviviality it engendered, just as many middle-class ballplayers were committed to the refinement of skilful play. Yet, if it is necessary to investigate the mutuality of class participation and the extent to which notions of respectability and manliness crossed class lines, it is also important to gauge how class allegiances shaped and were reinforced by involvement in the game as it developed over time.

The trend towards professionalism and more skilful play during the 1860s and 1870s had a dramatic impact upon the older social conventions of what had traditionally been a fraternally based and essentially middle-class sport. On 3 May 1879 the New York *Clipper* bemoaned the fact that the old veterans of the famous Knickerbocker Club, who 'could only play the regular, old-fashion muffer-game,' did not have a day of their own to follow their regular practice of choosing up sides and playing for the healthful pleasure and mere enjoyment of the exercise. Instead, they had to play 'side by side with the young experts of the club, who would persist in making swift and accurate throws, fine running catches, and all that kind of thing.'[17] In a similar lament, Harry McLean, a former ballplayer and occasional umpire, complained that the more competitive game had led to constant bickering and quarrelling. McLean recalled the 1850s and 1860s, an era of friendly sociability and fraternal respect, 'when no ill-feeling was engendered by reason of defeat, each nine under their captain's leadership giving a round of cheers at its conclusion, the representative of the unsuccessful nine presenting, with words of encouragement and praise, the ball which his nine had lost, and the captain of the victors receiving it with a most appropriate and graceful speech.' After these formalities, the banquet table was usually set, more toasts were offered, songs sung, and speeches made. 'Nothing was left undone to convince their sister club ... that we were of one brotherhood, fighting for a common cause, namely, that of promoting a game which is beyond question the noblest and grandest of all pastimes.'[18]

The first organized baseball club in the United States, the Knickerbocker Club of New York, was formed to provide its members with healthful recreation and fraternal cameraderie. The club, which came into existence on 23 September 1845, played its first game on 19 June 1846 at the Elysian Field in Hoboken, New Jersey. Made up of upwardly mobile members of the middle and professional classes, but by no means members of the city's élite,[19] the Knickerbockers had been playing ball on an unorganized basis since 1842. Eventually, a young bank clerk named Alexander Cartwright would suggest forming a permanent club with a constitution and written rules. Cartwright designed the diamond, diagrammed the playing positions and distances between the bases, and probably set the number of players at nine per side. Cartwright's diagrams, which set the distance between the bases at ninety feet and between home plate and the pitcher's mound at forty-five feet, became the basis for the developing American game. In 1858, the National Association of Baseball Players provided a number of refinements to the Knickerbocker rules, including the establishment of the pitcher's box, the standardization of the nine-inning rule, and the called strike, but even with those changes the essential elements of Cartwright's design remained intact.[20]

Henry Chadwick, the leading American sportswriter of the day, considered Cartwright and the Knickerbocker Club 'the pioneer[s] of the present game of baseball.'[21] Born in Exeter, England, in 1824, Chadwick came from a respected middle-class family that regarded healthful recreation as a necessary component of respectable civilization. Like his father James, a journalist, and brother Edwin, a leading British social reformer, Chadwick regarded sport as a way of civilizing youth. Excessive restraint of physical activity and an overemphasis on mental work in the school curriculum, they believed, encouraged mischief-making, delinquency, and mental and moral disorders of various sorts.[22] Like most Victorians, Henry Chadwick called for a balanced development of mind and body, believing that 'the spirit of the existing age undoubtedly favors the plan of a judicious combination of physical and recreative exercise with mental culture in order to attain the best results in our system of education.' He also believed that organized recreation was particularly important in urban areas, where the pressure of advancing civilization had created an effete and ennervated population. American city dwellers often lacked a healthy physique, Chadwick believed, and in the bustle of urban life their 'mental powers have been allowed to draw too largely on the nerve forces of their bodies,' resulting in premature illness and death.[23]

While Edwin Chadwick remained in Britain and became one of the leading sanitarians of the nineteenth century, Henry Chadwick emigrated to the United States in 1837 intent upon a career as a journalist. He began his sportwriting career with the *Long Island Star* in 1843, before accepting a position with the *New York Times* as a regular reporter on cricket and other sporting matters. In 1858 Chadwick joined the staff of the New York *Clipper*, where he soon gained the reputation as the most knowledgeable baseball journalist and statistician in the country.[24] For over six decades, the venerable reporter would lead the fight to keep baseball free from crookedness and dishonour, urging players – many of whom came from humble rural origins or from urban working-class backgrounds – to behave as 'gentlemen.' In addition to his denunciations of thrown games and the bribing of officials, Chadwick – who would never shrug off the effects of his bourgeois upbringing – remained especially critical of the rowdiness of those players who 'were without breeding or any knowledge of proper deportment in railroad stations, in hotels, on trains or on steamers.'[25]

If Chadwick's concerns about respectability reveal a preoccupation with the class question, he was also interested in baseball's relationship to national character. Although he was keenly aware that baseball had its origins in various English games involving a bat and ball, Chadwick eventually came to regard it as quintessentially an American sport. 'This invigorating exercise and manly pastime may now be justly termed the American Game of Ball,' he wrote in the 1867 edition of *Beadle's Dime Base-Ball Player*, 'for, though of English origin, it has been modified of its original features beyond the mere groundwork of the game.' The American game, Chadwick believed, derived from a children's game of the eighteenth century sometimes referred to as base-ball, but later as 'feeder' or 'rounders.' Rules for these games first appeared in England in 1829 under the name 'rounders,' and the identical rules, under the rubric 'base' or 'goal' ball were subsequently contained in the *Boy's and Girl's Book of Sports*, published at Providence, Rhode Island, in 1835. In rounders, the ball was softly tossed to a batter who was retired if he swung and missed three times. If the ball was struck, the batter and any baserunners proceeded in a clockwise direction to stones or posts placed from twelve to twenty yards apart. By the time of Cartwright's Knickerbocker rules the posts used in rounders had already been replaced by sand-filled bases, but the game continued to resemble a rather simple children's game when compared with the more sophisticated and 'scientific' sport of cricket.[26] 'When I first played base ball at Hoboken, N.J., in 1847,' Chadwick wrote, 'the game was little more than a mere schoolboy pastime, with the crudest rules to govern it.'[27]

Over the next half-century baseball would not only become increasingly sophisticated, but would establish itself as America's 'national pastime.' Many Americans, among them eventual Hall of Famers John Montgomery Ward and Albert G. Spalding, bridled at the assumption that baseball was little more than 'glorified rounders.' Ward argued vehemently that it was not rounders, but the American colonial game 'Old Cat' that was truly the forerunner of baseball. For years, too, Spalding would argue in friendly fashion with Chadwick about the origins of the sport, suggesting an American rather than British pedigree. Finally, in 1905, amid the nationalism that followed the Spanish American War and the muscle-flexing presidency of Theodore Roosevelt, Spalding moved to settle the controversy, setting up a committee to inquire into baseball's origins under the chairmanship of Colonel A.G. Mills, a former president of the National League. Upon the flimsiest of claims – evidence that Spalding had transmitted to the committee himself – the commissioners proceeded to accept the contention that baseball had originated with Abner Doubleday at Cooperstown, New York, in 1839.[28]

Despite the findings of the Mills commission, Chadwick's contention that baseball had an English origin remains a more convincing argument. In fact, even to credit Alexander Cartwright and the Knickerbocker Club with the creation of the American pastime is to obscure more than it reveals. As Stephen J. Gould has pointed out, creation myths are often more popular than evolutionary explanations in sport history, but they tend to divert attention from the variety of influences that affected baseball's emergence.[29] Outside of New York, different versions of the game continued to be played well beyond mid-century, suggesting other origins of the sport. In Philadelphia, a form of 'town ball' with marked similarities to baseball had been played as early as 1833 and would continue to be played until 1859. In Oxford County, Ontario, baseball was being played perhaps as early as the 1820s, and eleven-a-side baseball – the 'Canadian game,' as the New York *Clipper* called it – was being played as late as the 1860s.[30] In addition, for more than a decade after the introduction of the New York rules, ballplayers throughout New England and in some parts of the Maritimes followed the so-called Massachusetts rules, which drew heavily upon the game of rounders. The Olympic Club of Boston, established in 1854, for example, played a game where there were no foul lines, where bases were four-foot-high stakes, and where one hundred runs after a specified number of innings meant victory. As in Philadelphia 'town ball' and English rounders, base runners and batters were retired by 'plugging' or 'corking.' This tradition of retiring base runners by hitting them with a thrown ball persisted for years, especially in rural or hinterland communities.[31]

In Saint John, New Brunswick, a form of town ball or rounders was being played, possibly as early as the 1830s. Writing in his centennial essay on the history of Saint John in 1883, D.R. Jack noted that about 1840 it had been a common practice of the leading merchants of the city to assemble at a playground on the north side of King Square on summer afternoons for a game of cricket or baseball. The game achieved a more formal structure in 1853, when a group of Saint John's leading citizens met and organized the Saint John Baseball Club. Over the next fifteen years, games were played on a sporadic basis, either on the head of Courtenay Bay flats at low tide, or on a field opposite Kane's Corner on the Westmoreland Road when the Bay of Fundy tides rolled in. The rules were an amalgam of different elements, similar in some instances to the Massachusetts game, and in others to the Knickerbocker rules. As in the New England game, a batter was out when 'plugged' by an opponent, but the requirement for one hundred runs, which was a standard part of the Massachusetts game, was not followed. The Saint John club also followed the Knickerbocker model of nine players a side, but instead of nine innings and three outs, they played three innings, each of which lasted until all nine players had batted.[32]

By the early 1870s the modified Knickerbocker rules had become the standard for teams throughout the Maritimes and New England, as for most regions of the United States. The gradual standardization of the game's rules had been abetted by improvements in transportation and the development of frequent challenge matches between major urban centres. Just before the outbreak of the American Civil War, for example, the Brooklyn Excelsiors undertook the first extensive tour by a baseball club, meeting teams in Albany, Troy, Buffalo, Niagara Falls, and Rochester. Although the tour was confined to the state of New York, it was not long before lengthier tours were undertaken, such as the 3000-mile jaunt of the National Baseball Club of Washington in 1867. Tours of this sort necessitated agreement upon the rules of the game. By the time of the formation of the National Association of Professional Baseball Players in New York on 4 March 1871, baseball's regulations had gained universal acceptance.[33]

The major urban centres of the Maritimes quickly came to accept the rules and regulations of the National Association. The Saint John Baseball Club abandoned their modified 'New England'-style rules in 1872, and entered competition with the Mutuals and other local clubs who were now playing by Association rules.[34] In Halifax, New York rules had been in vogue for some time, so the transition was a smooth one. The development of intra-urban rivalries with other Nova Scotian teams, and the prospect of challenge games involving local players and visiting American teams such as the 'Undine' and 'Anchor' baseball clubs of the U.S. Naval Academy at Annapolis, Maryland, which arrived in Halifax on board the U.S.S. *Constellation* and U.S.S. *Saratoga* in July of 1871, meant an immediate acceptance of Association rules.[35]

With the completion of a railway connection between Bangor, Maine, and Saint John in 1873, challenge matches between Maritime and American teams became more frequent. In the summer of 1874, for example, an American cricket team from Philadelphia, on its way to an international cricket tournament in Halifax, accepted a challenge from a combined team of the Saint John's and Shamrocks baseball clubs to play a game in Saint John. Although the Philadelphians specialized in cricket, all of their team members were native-born Americans who had played amateur baseball around the city of Philadelphia.[36] Earlier in the year a number of them had played exhibition baseball and cricket matches at the club in Germantown, Pennsylvania, to prepare the celebrated American baseball eighteen, which included members of the Boston and Philadelphia baseball clubs, for its upcoming European tour. Upon arriving in Saint John, the Philadephians took the field for the challenge match, and drubbed their opponents by a score of 52–7. Thereafter, they concentrated solely on cricket, winning handily against the Canadian, British, and Halifax teams, and returned to Philadelphia with the 'Halifax Cup.'[37]

Although baseball was growing rapidly in popularity, cricket remained a popular sport throughout the nineteenth-century Maritimes, and whenever baseball's popularity waned – as it did in the early 1880s and again in the early 1890s – the noble English game took up the slack.[38] Cricket had been played at the British garrison in Halifax as early as 1786.[39] A half-century later, almost any community that boasted a church or tavern supported a team, especially if other towns nearby also had organized a club.[40] By 1845 there were daily cricket matches on the Halifax Commons, and in the years immediately following the Crimean War the cricket-playing abilities of soldiers of the 63rd Regiment garrisoned at the Citadel became legendary.[41] Cricket's popularity waned a bit in the 1870s, but the organization of amateur athletic associations in many Maritime communities in the last two decades of the century provided a further impetus to the game. Even after the turn of the century, a number of towns in the Maritimes still played it competitively. In 1912, for example, the Nova Scotia Cricket League, which sported teams in Truro, Stellarton, Sydney, and Halifax, played a complete summer schedule.[42] After the First World War, however, baseball supplanted cricket in virtually every Maritime town, although in Cape Breton the arrival in 1914 of a number of West Indian immigrants from Barbados seeking work in the steel plant ensured cricket's survival well into the postwar era.[43]

Cricket had always appealed to sports advocates as a way of instilling character among young members of the bourgeoisie.[44] In 1867, for example, Lewis Payzant provided a $20 prize for a cricket match between College and Academy students at Acadia College in Wolfville, Nova Scotia. Payzant had been distressed by the 'injurious consequences of students taking too little physical exercise, and sought ... to infuse more active exertion among them.' In a subsequent address to the graduates, Payzant's brother John reiterated this concern, noting the tendency of the male student to confine his attention to books at the expense of exercise, resulting in 'an injured or broken consitution, which shortened his life and rendered his work of preparation ... comparatively useless.' Involvement in the noble game of cricket, when combined with other gymnastic exercises, Payzant suggested, would assist in 'maintaining a proper equilibrium between physical and mental developments.'[45]

The need to develop an appropriate balance between mental labour and physical development was a common refrain in nineteenth-century thought. Adhering to the classical ideal of *mens sana in corpore sano*, Victorians of virtually every stripe believed that a healthy mind required a healthy body. Imbalance was unnatural, whether it stemmed from the undue excitement of the intellect or from the cultivation of physicality and sexual indulgence at the expense of the mental and moral faculties. It was the desirability of balanced development that the *Dominion Illustrated* was getting at when it contrasted 'a thin, delicate-visaged, studious-looking young man ... with a hulking giant, with cropped head, pointed obtruding ears, prominent jaw-bones and an exceptionally developed muscular system – the prize-fighter type.' The first of these characterizations represented the first-year 'broad-browed' undergraduate with a tendency to overstudy, the latter the college athlete at one of the 'faster sporting colleges,' whose narrow forehead and savage look reveal 'not a gleam of intellectual aspiration.'[46] Students who flouted Nature's requirement for balanced development were thought to face devastating consequences, as the death of A.C. MacKenzie, a young student at the Halifax Medical College seemed to suggest. MacKenzie's death in 1882 was attributed to brain fever, stemming from anxiety and overstudy in the summer heat of a Boston rooming-house.[47]

The desire to create the symmetrical development of body and mind was an essential component of the various physical-culture and dietary reform movements of the nineteenth century. Crusaders for health reform, such as William Alcott, Sylvester Graham, and Orson Fowler, were united by a belief in the need to acquire physical and mental equilibrium through a serious approach to diet, the avoidance of gluttony, a purposeful physical regimen, and the development of a hygienic environment. James Whorton has argued that nineteenth century health reformers preached 'physical Arminianism,' a form of healthful individualism in which each person was to 'assume responsibility for his physical salvation and earn it by physiological rectitude.'[48] Alcott regarded the cultivation of physical health as a project of Christian redemption, spurning meat eating and gluttony and advocating a hygienic, well-ventilated environment. Graham, the father of the Graham wafer, opposed excessive indulgence, advocated vegetarianism, and preached the virtues of fresh air and sunshine.[49] Fowler, a popular phrenologist from New England who made regular speaking tours throughout the Maritimes, stressed individual attention to mental, moral, and physical development and the need to create a sense of proportion, without which 'man can never be that finely developed and symmetrical creature that it is his privilege to be.'[50]

The emergence of this holistic idea of the interaction of mind and body was related to developing trends in physiological and psychological science, and to changing currents within the field of medicine. Nineteenth-century physiologists believed that the laws of human life could be understood by studying the human body scientifically, just as nature's laws could be understood by observing the natural universe in all its particularity. Michel Foucault has noted the emergence in the nineteenth century of a new and inquiring clinical orientation.[51] Under this new 'gaze' an interest in the working of discrete parts of the body gradually replaced an older set of rational principles relating to the action of disease. This empirical interest in the functioning of the body's parts led in turn to a better appreciation of the relationship between the body's various organs and the elaborate workings of the digestive, respiratory, and nervous systems. In addition, the transition from theoretical to empirical approaches to medical understanding and therapy encouraged a new emphasis on the 'healthy man' and allowed doctors 'to dictate the standards for physical and moral relations of the society in which he lives.'[52]

At the same time, a somatic tradition within psychology – growing out of nineteenth-century phrenology, which linked the physical contours of the skull to the nature of an individual's personality[53] – attempted to relate physiological 'imperfections' such as lesions of the brain, spinal cord, and reproductive organs to various forms of mental derangement.[54] Drawing upon the work of a generation of nineteenth-century medical theorists, including Thomas Laycock, W.B. Carpenter, and Weir Mitchell, Halifax asylum superintendent Alexander Reid believed that insanity derived from physical disorders 'of the higher ganglia of the nervous system ... most frequently in their minute structure,' the capillary vessels.[55] Reid's contemporary, Dr Richard M. Bucke of the London Asylum in Ontario believed that in many cases 'insanity rests upon utero-ovarian disease' and believed that ovariotomy provided an efficacious response to mental disorders in women.[56] Although somaticists such as Reid and Bucke often claimed more than they could prove, and engaged in questionable therapeutic practices as well, they none the less contributed to the growing appreciation in the nineteenth century of the symbiotic relationship of mind and body.

The last half of the nineteenth century also witnessed a shift in the orthodox medical profession's therapeutic orientation from interventionist, or 'heroic,' therapy to what was sometimes referred to as nature trusting or 'expectant treatment.' As traditional therapeutic techniques such as venesection and the use of strong purgatives such as calomel were called into question, doctors took refuge in a scepticism about the action of drugs, leaving healing to nature itself. In Halifax, Dr Daniel McNeil Parker noted in November 1873 that he was 'inclined to think that patients left without medication did as well as others,' and that doctors should only use drugs to build up the patient's natural recuperative powers. Increasingly, the orthodox profession's therapeutic regimen stressed appropriate nutrition, ventilation, and light; the use of tonics or stimulants such as alcohol to strengthen the constitution; and a reliance on hydrotherapy, massage, physical exercise, and other natural forms of treatment.[57]

This reverence for healthful nature understandably provoked concerns about the unnatural condition of modern urban life, and in particular the nervous stress that accompanied the rapid advance of modern civilization. As Morris Mott has pointed out in his study of urban reform in Winnipeg, sport was regarded as an antidote to the 'detrimental physical and moral effects of living in a congested urban environment.'[58] To many social critics, the rise of the city had created a weakened population, prone to nervous exhaustion and a loss of manliness. This was the argument of the American psychologist George Beard, who coined the term 'neurasthenia' to describe the nervous weakness that accompanied 'overcivilization.'[59] City life was considered artificial, unnatural, and debilitating. A naturally healthful life was more likely to emerge in the countryside. Nova Scotia's superintendent of education Alexander H. McKay argued that in rural communities boys and girls had the 'best opportunities of developing physical strength, manual dexterity, mechanical ingenuity and executive ability.' Farm labour provided for physical manliness, developed an appreciation of nature, and cultivated an interest in the sciences of botany, geology, and minerology. Urbanization, factory labour, and the 'less desirable class of immigrants,' by contrast, eroded 'manly characteristics.' Dr William Hattie, superintendent of the Nova Scotia Hospital, agreed with this assessment, noting that city-born and city-bred children – especially those of the poorer classes – were apt to suffer from bad hygiene and insufficient food, and as a result supplied a 'notoriously large percentage of our mental and moral defectives.'[60] Cheery classrooms, playgrounds, and organized sports such as cricket were thus necessary to stem the forces of degeneracy.[61]

Victorian reformers in the Maritimes such as McKay and the Payzants revered the game of cricket both for its mixture of 'scientific' play and physical exercise and for its identification with the attributes of the 'gentleman.' In early-nineteenth-century Britain cricket had been purged of its earlier unsavory associations with gambling, and by mid-century had risen to a state of prominence, endorsed by the Crown, the aristocracy, and the church.[62] Furthermore, its development within the public-school and university system in Britain associated it with the ruling class. The game's gentlemanly code of fair play, and its hostility to impropriety – implied in the phrase 'it's not cricket' – came to symbolize the legitimate authority of the fair-minded ruling class, and buttressed imperialist notions of racial and national superiority in the colonies. In a colonial community such as the Maritimes, the association of cricket with the British ruling class appealed to those whose allegiance to the Empire remained strong, but for many others – particularly working people – it was simply a game amongst games. When workingmen took up cricket they tended to do so in order to serve their own leisure needs, rather than the needs of those who attached improving motivations or national allegiances to the sport.

Whatever its attractions, cricket soon gave way to baseball as the Maritime region's primary summer sporting activity. There are a number of explanations for this transition. After witnessing the British tour of the American baseballists in 1874, Captain R.A. Fitzgerald of the prestigious Marylebone Cricket Club of London was convinced that baseball's short duration was perfectly suited to the North American character. Although from Fitzgerald's point of view there was little of the excitement caused by a fast bowler or quick wicket, baseball none the less demanded quickness of both foot and eye and precision in throwing. It was of no surprise to Fitzgerald that baseball was more popular in the United States than cricket. Cricket, he argued, had to contend against American materialism, its sharp business practices, and its attraction to money making. In America, time was money. Cricket was a luxury Americans couldn't afford. 'They will not give the time necessary for the game,' Fitzgerald wrote, 'they are not charmed with monotony even if it be high art.' Yet, if they chose to, Americans could learn much from Britain's noble game; 'if it inculcates one thing, it preaches and practices patience, it enforces self-control, it eliminates the irascible, it displays the excellence of discipline.' Baseball, by contrast 'encourages the two leading failings of the American character – ultra-rapidity, quicksilverosity, or whatever else of lightning proclivity you like to call it, and ardent speculation.'[63]

American commentators had different explanations for baseball's popularity. According to one columnist for the *Sporting News*, baseball created the ideal sportsman, a well-rounded, agile, physiologically and mentally balanced athlete. 'It is a fact that few all-round athletes are as perfectly developed physically as the typical league base ball player.' Other athletes, such as sprinters, oarsmen, or cyclists tended to develop only those muscles necessary for their specialties. The game of baseball demanded that the athlete bring into play all the groups of muscles necessary for success in any form of athletic endeavour. 'The professional baseball player is at once a sprinter, a thrower and a wrestler – hence his splendid physique ... He keeps the physiological balance, and that is nature's purpose.' Then, too, there was enough mental activity demanded by the game 'to preserve both physical and mental well-being and balance, two things absolutely essential in a perfect athlete.'[64] The key to baseball's success, then, was that it conformed to Nature's own design. No other sport so completely blended running, throwing, batting, and expert fielding 'in a constantly changing panorama that gratifies ... the passion for excitement.' The nearest in its approach to baseball was cricket, but this slow-moving game was 'hampered by a tediousness that utterly precludes its enjoyment except by a people who have abundant time to devote to a two or three days tournament that palls upon the senses from its own weight of anatomy.'[65]

Melvin Adelman has a more plausible explanation for the failure of cricket as an American game. In the period before 1840, Adelman argues, cricket in the United States remained a 'novelty sport, played almost exclusively by English immigrants,' and although it was the first ball game to respond to America's increasing urbanization and economic growth at mid-century, it would succumb to the challenge of baseball in the 1850s and 1860s. By the 1850s the attractiveness of cricket and baseball were linked to the question of national origin, and the fact that cricket tended to be run 'for and by' Englishmen gave it an image of snobbishness and exclusivity that undermined its popularity. Furthermore, baseball's 'more rapid interchange between offense and defense provide[d] ... [it] with an ebb and flow that ... [was] lacking in cricket,' and helps explain its emergence as a broad participatory sport.[66] While cricket remained a sport of the well-to-do, moreover, baseball would extend beyond the mercantile and professional classes to include working people. In the process social reformers who praised the 'uplifting' influence of 'manly' recreation transferred the social justification for cricket to baseball without missing a beat.

In the Maritimes, where imperial loyalty remained firm, the national-origin question was not as much an issue as it was in the United States. It is true, however, that in Halifax and Saint John cricket was most popular amongst the British troops garrisoned there, and among the merchant and professional élite of the two cities. As was the case in the United States, in the two largest cities in the Maritimes the game of cricket remained a middle-class pursuit, and had not extended to the working class. Throughout the 1860s, for example, the *Acadian Recorder* made continuous reference to the lack of 'healthful recreation' available to working people on the Saturday half-holiday. Aquatic sports, sailing regattas, and cricket matches were the pursuits of the well-off, but did little to meet the need for 'manly exercise' amongst the labouring classes. Working people were left to their own amusements, while the city's élite organized entertainment for itself. On 17 June 1867, the *Acadian Recorder* noted that Halifax city council had done little to provide Natal Day entertainment for the citizens of the town. 'The cream of the jest,' it noted, 'is that the Aldermen, instead of providing amusement for the million, purpose [sic] disbursing the paltry sum of an excursion in the *Neptune* with of course a grand feed for themselves.' Stung by the criticism, the city council at the last moment put in place a program for Natal Day, which included yachting races at the Royal Halifax Yacht Club and a cricket match at the Commons.[67] Neither of these events evoked great interest amongst working people in the city.

That cricket remained a sport of the élite and the garrison was evident in the response of the city of Halifax to the tour of the American Twelve in 1874. In the spring of 1874 Captain N.W. Wallace of the 60th Royal Rifles, stationed in Halifax, wrote many prominent cricketers in the United States, inviting them to an international cricket tournament in Halifax. It was hoped that all-star teams representing the United States, England, Canada, and Halifax would attend and compete for the Halifax Cup. Advertisements were placed in *Forest and Stream* and other American magazines, but the response from the United States was disappointing. When plans to get a combined American team fell through, the members of three Philadelphia cricket clubs, regarded as being among the premier squads in the United States, agreed to send a combined team to Nova Scotia.

Upon their first day in Halifax, the well-to-do Philadelphians left the Halifax Hotel and strolled through the 'dingy streets' of the little port town. Their meanderings evoked 'not much interest' from the general public, nor did they find much to interest themselves until they reached the imposing garrison at Citadel Hill, where they were hosted and toasted by the officers of the fort in a manner befitting 'gentlemen.' During the tournament, however, the Philadelphians were delighted by the attendance of the city's more wealthy citizens at the week's matches, and the ornate carriages that surrounded the cricket pitch. Cricket matches provided the urban bourgeoisie with an opportunity to display their fashionability, and in so doing to lay claim to an ascendancy over the social order. David Scobey has noted that throughout the mid-Victorian era, the bourgeois props of fashionability 'grew ever more elaborate: plush coaches, uniformed servants, thoroughbred horses, even heraldic devices ..., reflect[ing] a paradoxical ideal of sociability, at once elitist and expansive, exorbitant and regimented: a mix of heterosocial exhibitionism and "aristocratic" exclusiveness.'[68] One of the visitors wrote: 'It seemed as if everybody who is anybody in Halifax must keep a drag, or phaeton, or barouche, or tandem, or unicorn, or a carriage of some kind, and certainly the turnout of stylish equipages which appeared daily on the cricket fields was unexpected to the Philadelphians. The ladies as a rule remained in their carriages, and received visits from the swell-looking Englishmen, who to-day were off duty.' The chronicler also noted that some of the Philadelphians, who themselves were 'connoiseurs of feminine beauty' made a tour of inspection of the carriages and the high fashion that surrounded the games. 'It required but a glance to decide that all the wealth and fashion of Halifax was represented on the grounds.'[69]

Over the nine-day event the city's élite rolled out the red carpet for the visitors. Among the entertainments were yachting parties; balls at Government House and at private mansions; dinners by the mayor, the officers of the garrison, and citizens of Halifax; and lunches at private clubs and in the regimental messes.[70] At a closing reception, Captain A.A. Outerbridge thanked his hosts, and emphasized the social exclusiveness of the sport itself. Outerbridge toasted cricket as a 'game played by gentlemen, endorsed by dignitaries, and approved of and participated in by reverend gentlemen.'[71]

The visiting cricketers, made up of players from the Germantown, Young America, and Merion cricket clubs of Philadelphia, were the class of the tournament, winning handily over the Halifax, Canadian, and British elevens.[72] To commemorate their victory the mayor of Halifax presented each player with a small silver bat to be worn as a souvenir of the tournament. The Philadelphians also carried off all three silver cups offered for competition in the tournament, together with a prize silver ball, and several prize bats won by members of the team for individual scores over 50. Most important, they carried home the 'Halifax Cup,' which they subsequently presented for local competion for forty-six years, beginning in 1880, and which became 'a highlight of each sporting and social season in Philadelphia society.'[73] It is ironic that the Halifax tournament eventually spurred an American revival of cricket in the 1880s, for in Halifax the tournament marks the point at which baseball began to outstrip cricket as the most popular summer sport in the province, largely because of its growing appeal amongst working people. It is also worth noting that no baseball tournament in the history of Halifax – or any other community in the Maritimes for that matter – ever received the kind of attention that the city fathers lavished on the cricketers.

The experience of Halifax and Saint John seems to confirm Alan Metcalfe's argument that cricket in Canada was a game of the social élite, glorified initially by the British North American colonial aristocracy, and fostered by recent immigrants, by garrison teams, and by graduates from private schools that adhered to notions of British superiority.[74] In smaller communities throughout the region, however, this characterization does not hold completely true. In outlying districts, cricket had a broader appeal. In Pictou County, in eastern Nova Scotia, on Cape Breton, and on Prince Edward Island, cricket would rival baseball in popularity for much of the nineteenth century. What is striking in these areas is the popularity of the game among working people. In Stellarton, Pictou County, for example, cricket had been introduced during the 1820s by the officers of the General Mining Association, who made a cricket pitch available on the Mount Rundell estate for the use of the coalminers, many of whom were recent British immigrants. Even when the first baseball team in Stellarton was formed in 1889 cricket retained its appeal amongst the town's working class.[75]

Throughout the coalfields of the Maritimes cricket was a miner's game; indeed, as coalmining output increased so did cricket's popularity. Intense community rivalries throughout these areas were forged on the cricket pitch, nurtured by geographical propinquity and common occupational identities. Sport served to promote working-class solidarity, to be sure, but at times club and community allegiances stood in the way of larger forms of cooperation on the sporting field. When a suggestion was made in the Stellarton *Trades' Journal* that a Pictou County all-star team be established to travel to other places in the region, for example, it was rejected by Stellarton's Lansdowne Cricket Club as potentially disruptive of the existing clubs. Community clubs had their own identities, and they were already strong enough.[76] Stellarton cricketers thus chose to compete on their own, accepting challenges from the Halifax Wanderers, the garrison teams, the strong Sydney aggregation, and occasional touring teams from the United States, Great Britain, and the West Indies.[77]

Working-class involvement sustained interest in cricket in industrial towns such as Stellarton, Pictou, Londonderry, Oxford, Springhill, Amherst, Westville, Glace Bay, and Sydney until after the turn of the century, when baseball was being played as well. As late as 1906 the editor of the *Sydney Record* remained opposed to the introduction of professional baseball on the grounds that it encouraged spectatorism, and argued that cricket was a more appropriate game because it encouraged popular participation.[78] At the same time, smaller towns in more rural parts of the region – such as Truro in Colchester County, Windsor and Kentville in the Annapolis Valley, Milton, Shelburne, and Guysborough along the Atlantic coast, Digby and Yarmouth in south-western Nova Scotia, Sussex, a distributing centre in rural New Brunswick, and Charlottetown on Prince Edward Island – all had active cricket elevens. In most of these towns, industrial or otherwise, baseball was relatively late in developing. The Alpha Club of Westville was formed in May 1876; baseball teams in Pictou, Oxford, Bridgewater, and River Phillip organized in the same year; the strong Londonderry Ironclads formed in 1877; and in Kentville, Aubrey Davidson's Blue Stars of 1884 was the inaugural club in that town.[79]

Baseball came even later to Prince Edward Island, where the popular nineteenth-century sports were rugby, track and field, cycling, and cricket. During the 1860s and 1870s the Phoenix club of Charlottetown was the most prestigious cricket aggregation, and had often travelled throughout the Maritime provinces competing against the best clubs in the region. Baseball was an afterthought. It was the Park Cricket Club, in fact, that organized the first baseball club in Charlottetown in 1889. Three other teams organized that same year, the Tennis Club, the Diamond Baseball Club, and the Stars. Over the next couple of years baseball spread to other centres including Peakes Station, Tracadie, Stanhope, Baldwin's Road, and Roseneath, and in 1896 the first provincial championship match was organized, with Charlottetown prevailing over the Pisquid Club in the deciding game. But the roots of baseball remained shallow on the Island, and around the turn of the century cricket once again assumed the lead over its rival. It was not until 1903 that the vaunted Abegweit Amateur Athletic Association entered onto the provincial baseball scene,[80] and thereby revived a game that the Charlottetown *Patriot* described as 'defunct for some time in the city.'[81]

If cricket remained a widely played sport in the smaller towns of the Maritimes, particularly amongst Scottish miners in Cumberland, Pictou, and Cape Breton counties, it had a more tenuous hold in the larger urban communities of Halifax, Moncton, and Saint John. In Saint John, cricket had been introduced during the 1840s by British regiments in the city, each of whom sported a cricket eleven. As in Halifax, games between military and civilian teams did encourage some enthusiasm for the game, but not enough to offset the withdrawal of the garrison shortly after Confederation. Thereafter the game's popularity waned, and with the exception of rowing – in which Saint John's Paris crew gained an international reputation – baseball had no rival during the 1870s and 1880s as the pre-eminent summer sport in Saint John. This was also true of a number of New Brunswick towns close to the American border, where the influence of baseball was felt as early as the 1860s, and where cricket fell into disfavour.

Baseball had been played in Saint John as early as 1853, but during the 1860s it became dormant. Revived in the late 1860s through the efforts of newspaperman P.A. Melville, the game became extremely popular in the early 1870s. By 1874 a number of Saint John baseball teams, including the Invincibles, the Mutuals, the St John's, the Shamrocks, the Athletes, and the Royals, were playing each other and occasionally challenging teams from St Stephen, Carleton, Woodstock, St Croix, Fredericton, and Bangor, Maine. All across the region towns of any size were organizing baseball clubs, and the first attempts to establish an annual Maritime championship were being made. The first major interprovincial challenge occurred during the 1874 season, with the Atlantas of Halifax prevailing over the Moncton Excelsiors 55–29 in a game held in Truro. A more closely contested match between the Atlantas and the Shamrocks of Saint John took place in Halifax later in the season. This game, won by the Shamrocks by a score of 32 to 29, was apparently filled with excitement and superb fielding plays. Dan Cronan, the Atlantas pitcher, caught a line drive with one bare hand, 'right off the bat' of one of the Shamrocks, 'and was loudly cheered for it by the spectators,' while the Halifax shortstop's 'pickups and throws to first base were splendid.' For the Shamrocks, Dennis Costigan's catching and batting were superb, and Cain in left field 'took everything that came near him.'[82]

Interprovincial play became a regular feature of the baseball season in the years to follow. In 1875, the Halifax Atlantas travelled to Saint John and defeated the Mutuals 22–9, largely as a result of the excellent play of James Pender and Dan Cronan. In addition, the Atlantas avenged their defeat by the Shamrocks in 1874, emerging victorious in another exciting game in Halifax by a single run. In the following year, two new Moncton clubs, the Invincibles and the Redstockings, entered interprovincial competition and fared well. The Redstockings beat the Mutuals of Saint John in one match 36–14; but it was the Invincibles rather than the Redstockings that would establish themselves as Moncton's dominant team. In September the Invincibles squared off in a two-game series with the Atlantas to determine the Maritime championship. The Atlantas prepared for the opening match by enclosing their grounds and charging an admission fee, and before a large crowd they defeated Moncton 15–12.[83] In the following year, the Invincibles turned the tables on Halifax, defeating the Atlantas 36–27, and brought the Maritime championship to Moncton for the first time.[84]

By the end of the 1870s, baseball had become an integral component of the region's sporting culture, particularly in the larger urban centres. What is more, it had undergone a notable transformation over the previous decade. In its earliest stages baseball in the Maritimes had been a pursuit of young, upwardly mobile members of the commercial and professional classes of the region's urban centres. Gradually, however, the game would extend downward to the labouring classes, and it was there that its popularity would be secured. As the *Acadian Recorder* observed in August 1877, the fact that baseball was 'destined to be the standard game ... [was] acknowledged by all except some of the old enthusiastic cricketers, who are loath to admit that their noble game will ever occupy second place.' In order to recognize this fact it was only necessary 'to walk out to the Common any evening between six and eight o'clock where hundreds of men and boys are playing the game.'[85] Over the next dozen years, as the region began to experience the rapid growth of modern industry, the game would become even more deeply entrenched in the region's sporting life.

3

New Players: Baseball and Working-Class Culture

By 1875 baseball was firmly rooted in the sporting life of the larger urban communities of the Maritimes and New England. The sport prospered in Halifax, Moncton, Saint John, and Fredericton in the Maritimes, and in Bangor, Houlton, Lewiston, Portland, Portsmouth, and Manchester in northern New England, and was beginning to extend its reach into dozens of smaller communities. Improved railway communication between New Brunswick and Maine and, moreover, the completion of the Intercolonial Railway to Halifax by 1876 provided greater opportunity for inter-urban competition, facilitated regional championship play, and led to the development of an integrated Maritime and New England baseball culture. The next fifteen years witnessed even closer ties between these two regions, as Maritime teams began to import professional players and coaches from the United States, and international challenge matches became more frequent. In turn, baseball became a sport less confined to younger members of the mercantile and professional classes, extending its influence to the working class, both as a form of recreational exercise and as a spectator sport.

As baseball became a popular activity for the working class, the baseball diamond became a terrain increasingly ridden with ethnic, gender, religious, and class rivalries. In turn, bourgeois reformers who were initially attracted to the game because of its 'civilizing' qualities would often find themselves at odds with the promoters, gamblers, working people, athletes, and spectators, all of whom were attempting to shape the game to fulfil their own needs. During the 1880s reformers became increasingly uneasy about baseball's apparent rowdiness, fearing its unsavoury attachment to the betting world and the impact of professionalism on the ideal of 'gentlemany' amateurism. Their anxiety, rooted in class tensions that accompanied the industrial-capitalist penetration of the region, reveals much about the contested nature of the world of sport and leisure.

The extension of the game to the region's working class in the 1870s and 1880s accompanied the gradual remaking of the Maritime economy that followed the 'Panic of 1873' and the introduction of John A. Macdonald's 'National Policy' of 1879. At Confederation the economy of the Maritimes was largely mercantile and staples-based, centred about a prosperous wooden shipbuilding industry and the export of agricultural, lumber, and fish products. It was also an economy in flux. Already in 1866, in the wake of the abrogation of the Reciprocity Treaty of 1854, there was evidence that the regional prosperity of the Confederation era – artifically nurtured by the wars of the 1850s and 1860s and later mythologized as 'the Golden Age of Sail' – would not long endure.

The weaknesses of the old commercial economy became painfully evident during the 1870s. In 1873, a sharp financial panic announced the beginning of a major international depression that continued through the decade and beyond. American markets for Maritime lumber quickly collapsed and the wooden shipbuilding industry entered into a decline from which it would never really recover. The West Indian market for fish and the American market for foodstuffs also suffered, creating severe hardship for the region's rural inhabitants and forcing those on the margin to seek employment in the urban centres of the Maritimes or to leave in search of work in the 'Boston States.'[1]

It is tempting to regard the declining fortunes of the Maritime shipbuilding industry and the concomitant difficulties that farmers and fishermen experienced in the last quarter of the century as indications of a unilinear process in which an older pre-industrial order was giving way to a more industrial and modern society. Yet, as Johnathan Prude has pointed out, 'the coming of industrial order was not *only* a process by which economies moved from 'old' to 'new.' It was also a process by which old and new were bound together, by which old and new proceeded in one another's shadow.'[2] There was in fact no single industrial transition. Instead, the ways in which various communities and subregions experienced the coming of industrial capitalism differed in relation to their proximity to sea, railhead, or metropolis, and to the pre-existing configuration of economic production. In the towns and cities of the region, demography, geography, and the accessibility of capital, labour, and natural resources all played a part in shaping the particular character of the economic and cultural landscape of the industrial community.[3] Although the face and pace of industrialism differed in different locations, beginning at about mid-century and accelerating thereafter, it is possible to discern a significant increase in wage-labour and factory employment in communities strategically located along railway lines. Railway hubs like Saint John and Portland, for example, witnessed a minor boom in factory production during the 1860s and 1870s, especially in metal fabrication and the railway-supply industries, and in crucial consumer-goods industries such as textiles, boot and shoe manufacture, and leather goods.[4] By 1875 Saint John numbered over 600 manufacturing establishments employing 9500 workers.[5] Some 73 boot and shoe establishments in Saint John city and county employed 1071 men and women, and the city's ten foundries, besides its machine shops, over 400 hands.[6] In Moncton, the headquarters of the Intercolonial Railway, over 600 of the town's 5000 inhabitants in 1880 worked for the railway and the city was rapidly becoming an important distributing centre for the region.[7] Even Halifax, which retained its character as a commercial entrepôt and military and administrative centre, had begun to experience a growth in manufacturing during the 1870s, especially in the boot and shoe and confectionary industries.[8]

Industrialization, urbanization, and the factory system also brought with it a new relationship between work time and leisure time that replaced the more seasonal rhythms of rural life. In the industrializing towns of the Maritimes and New England, baseball became a particularly popular sport among working people. Although some historians have suggested that baseball's appeal lay in its ability to evoke images of rural simplicity in an age of industrial dislocation,[9] Steven Gelber argues that its growing appeal lay in its replication of the attitudes of the industrial workplace in its emphasis on organization, precision, and discipline.[10] Gelber is particularly suspicious of the pastoral image of the origins of baseball, especially the myth that the game was invented in a cow pasture by Abner Doubleday and his rural chums. Instead, Gelber argues, the game was essentially urban in outlook, appealing to working people not because it 'compensated for missing elements in the new work environment, but because it was congruent with business life.'[11] Baseball emulated business in its specialization of labour, its structural integration, its emphasis on speed and efficiency, its commitment to quantifiable production, and its rational and 'scientific' character. In addition, the sharper separation of work and non-work time that

TABLE 1
Occupation of Halifax Baseball Players, 1874–88

Occupation	Number	%
Clerks (including bookkeepers and accountants	29	21.8
Labourers (including teamsters, janitors, messengers, seamen, porters, stable boys)	32	24.0
Tradesmen	42	31.5
Students, merchants, and professionals	30	22.7

accompanied industrial production encouraged an emphasis on organized forms of recreation that would appeal to those young artisans, mechanics, and clerks who sought out ways to use their leisure time. Baseball, which could be played in a matter of a couple of hours, was a sport that suited the leisure needs of working people, while replicating the essential values of an emerging industrial system.[12]

A sample of players whose names appeared in newspaper box-scores in Halifax between 1874 and 1888 clearly demonstrates the extension of the game beyond youthful members of the mercantile and professional classes to include artisans and others of working-class origin. Of the 133 players whose occupation can be traced through census records and city directories, a large number came from working-class backgrounds. Labourers and unskilled workers made up 24 per cent of the sample; tradesmen such as cabinet-makers, carpenters, tailors, blacksmiths, machinists, brass finishers, gas-fitters, printers, bakers, plumbers, coopers and bricklayers comprised another 31.5%; the ubiquitous clerks (including bookkeepers and accountants) 21.8%; and merchants, students, and professionals made up the remaining 22.7% (see table 1).

Data relating to the ethnic origin and religious affiliation of 153 players gives a further indication of the game's popularity in working-class circles. In Halifax the game was particularly popular among Irish Catholics and black players, both of whom were overrepresented in working-class occupations. Irish and black players made up 59.4 per cent of the sample; those of English origin 20.9%; Scots and Germans 7.8% each. With respect to religious denominations, Catholics comprised 60.7 per cent of players (compared to slightly more than 40% of the total population), Anglicans 15.7%, Baptists (including African Baptists) 11.1%, and Presbyterians 7.8%.

A closer look at the composition of the teams that emerged during the 1870s, moreover, reveals a very sharp differentiation between teams along class, occupational, ethnic, and denominational lines. Most teams drew their players from similar class, ethnic, and religious backgrounds. For example, the successful Halifax Athletes club of 1874, captained by salesman Herman Cohn – an 'enthusiastic baseballist ... [who] has done more to create an interest in this fine American game than anyone in this city'[13] – drew its personnel exclusively from clerks and small merchants. The players, all of whom were Protestant except for Cohn, who was Jewish, included two soap manufacturers, a druggist, a salesman (Cohn), and five who identified themselves as clerks. The 1874 Atlantas, a team representing the Young Men's Literary Association, a self-improvement society for middle-class north-end youth, had a similar composition. Brothers Daniel, John, and William Cronan, employed in clerical jobs by their father John Cronan, a West Indian merchant with a warehouse on Cronan's Wharf on Halifax Harbour, were the nucleus of the club.[14] Others included Charles Crane, a bookkeeper and son of physician Chandler Crane; John Morton, a medical student at the Halifax Medical College; and confectioner Philip Ryan. The remaining team members were students.

The other competitive teams in Halifax during the 1874 season – the Resolutes and the White Stars – drew their players almost exclusively from the ranks of skilled tradesmen. The Resolutes – captained by saloon-keeper Isaac Cruse, a former cricket star recently returned from the United States where he had turned his talents to baseball – was a working-class team.[15] In addition to Cruse, the club's roster included two brass-finishers and shoemakers, a gas-fitter, a machinist, a cabinet-maker, and a printer. The White Stars, representing Richmond – a district in the industrializing north end of the city near and along Halifax Harbour – had a similar composition. Four club members were machinists, while the others that can be identified included a gas-fitter, a tinsmith, and a printer. The composition of these clubs would seem to confirm Warren Goldstein's point that skilled craftsmen who maintained craft traditions and were not yet reduced to sweated labour were prominent on baseball diamonds across the country.[16]

Over the next few years other clubs with working-class membership sprang up, revealing the growing interest and involvement in baseball not only of mechanics and artisans, but of unskilled labourers as well. The Actives, established in 1876, comprised mostly painters and cabinet-makers; the Greenstockings, a team of young Irish Catholics, emerged in the same year and included a mixture of shoemakers, truckmen, and labourers; and the Young Oxfords, the third new club organized in

1876, had a roster of young adolescents whose future occupations would range from blacksmith, butcher, mason, and cabinet-maker, to truckman, coachman, and common labourer. The Young Oxfords may well have been organized by one of the many advocates of sport as a form of child-saving, for they often competed against the boys of the Halifax Industrial School.

In addition to playing the game, working men – particularly skilled tradesmen or artisans – also made up a substantial portion of the audience. At the end of the 1877 season in Halifax, for example, Thomas Lambert, a well-known labour leader and employee at Taylor's Boot and Shoe Factory, presented a silver ball and bat to the city champion, Atlantas, on behalf of the mechanics of Halifax. (The *Acadian Recorder* emphasized that the prize was offered by the mechanics of the city alone, in recognition of their dedication to the game.)[17] As in numerous other cities and towns elsewhere in North America, it would appear that baseball provided skilled workers with a form of association that shaped and secured their class identity in a period of industrial capitalist development. 'It is possible, and even probable,' Bryan Palmer wrote of skilled workers in Hamilton, Ontario, 'that the associational life of skilled workers cultivated a sense of solidarity that strengthened the ability of the skilled to resist the encroachments of industrial-capitalist disciplines and development.' Furthermore, he suggests, 'historians who bypass this culture, denigrating its importance, miss a complex component of nineteenth- and early twentieth-century life.'[18]

Thomas Lambert's involvement in Halifax baseball is revealing in this regard. A major figure in the working-class movement, he had come to the city in 1865 with the 2nd Battalion of the Leicestershire regiment.[19] Soon after, he took up employment at Robert Taylor's shoe factory and became one of the first trade unionists in Halifax to attain international prominence. In 1869, he was elected an international officer of the Knights of St Crispin and became First Grand Trustee of the International Lodge in 1872.[20] The Knights were a particularly active and militant organization of shoemakers that drew on artisanal traditions to defend against disruptions that accompanied the development of factory production, and their history suggests a willingness to fight capitalist domination with whatever cultural resources were at their disposal.[21] Although there is no evidence that Lambert ever played baseball, he was instrumental in organizing a team at Taylor's after the company defeated the shoemakers in a bitter strike at the factory. Subsequently, in September 1877, Lambert appears as a scorekeeper in a game between the Crispin Club of Taylor & Co. and a team representing shoe-maker W.C. Brennan & Co. Later in the same month, two teams from Taylor's – Lambert's Nine and Baldwin's Nine – squared off, with the Lambert's playing to a 28–18 victory.[22]

If skilled workers were involved in the game as organizers and players, they also were there as spectators, apparently more than willing to pay the standard 25 cents admission fee for competitive club or inter-city matches. Although not much is yet known about the impact of industrialization on the real wages of working men and women in the urban centres of the Maritimes, or upon the family wage, it is likely that factory workers such as Lambert were enjoying an increasing real income, similar to skilled workers elsewhere in Britain and North America at this time.[23] The gradual tightening of workplace discipline, the growing separation of work and leisure, and the concomitant shortening of the workday, moreover, nurtured an increased demand for organized leisure by working people and bourgeois proponents of rational recreation alike.[24] At the same time, the movement of women into industrial and clerical work also led them to seek out ways to fill their leisure time, one of which was attendance at sporting events.[25] This is not to imply that women's non-work time was free of domestic responsibility. Several scholars have demonstrated that women, more than men, were expected to meet the needs of the home after they left their place of employment. Nevertheless, in the last quarter of the nineteenth century, the changes wrought by industrialization had engineered the basic prerequisite for the commercialization of baseball – the creation of an audience.

For spectators and players alike, class, ethnic, and community identities and rivalries provided an important impetus to the game. In Halifax, for example, challenge matches between the Mechanics and the Laborers, the Barkers and the Growlers, the Southends and the North-ends, the Young Atlantas and the Young Oxfords, the True Blues and the Greenstockings involved rivalries based upon occupation, religion, location, ethnicity, and age. In addition, teams representing various employers such as the Heralds, the Recorders, the Chronicles, and the Dolphins (for Dolphin's Factory) and Taylor Factory teams sometimes served to secure an identity to the firm and, in other cases, encouraged worker solidarity. While the Taylor Factory teams seem to have been made up exclusively of working men and revealed a continuing influence of the Knights of St Crispin, the Dolphins had a line-up that, in addition to factory hands, included manager Kellam J. Dolphin.[26] Sometimes referred to as Halifax's 'Baked Bean Man,' Dolphin ran a lobster cannery and distributed hermetically sealed goods from his Water Street factory and warehouse at the Steamboat Wharf. He was attracted to baseball both for its recreational value and its potential for encouraging workplace harmony, and remained active in the sport in Halifax until he left the city in 1882.[27]

Baseball also attracted social reformers who regarded sport as a means to protect youth from dissolute or criminal behaviour. This was the position of Dr Charles Cogswell – no relation to A.C. Cogswell of the Halifax Baseball Club – and of John Grierson, superintendent of the Halifax Protestant Boy's School. Cogswell, a long-time proponent of organized recreation in Halifax, believed that sport encouraged the 'manly virtues' of courage, strength, agility, teamwork, decision making. and foresight, and helped rescue working-class youth from 'gawking lazily at street corners to stare at passers-by, lounging about drinking saloons, smoking and guzzling' and partaking of 'other irrational modes of getting over life.'[28]

The eldest son of Hezekiah Cogswell, a wealthy Halifax merchant, Charles Cogswell was born in 1832 and grew up in the city. After completing his secondary schooling, Cogswell proceeded to study medicine, receiving a medical degree at the University of Edinburgh in the early 1850s. Although Cogswell returned to Halifax and later became an honorary member of the Medical Society of Nova Scotia, there is little evidence that he ever had a serious medical practice. Instead he seems to have used his inherited wealth to promote his land-speculation activities and to underwrite a number of reform ventures, including the initial establishment of the Halifax Ragged School for Boys and Girls with his sister Isabella Cogswell in the late 1850s. This school, a precursor of the Halifax Industrial School located on the city's rough and tumble Albemarle Street, provided care for neglected and friendless children, and offered training in paper-bag making, shoemaking, printing, tailoring, and other trades.[29]

Cogswell considered sport an important component of the community's physical, mental, and moral health, and over the years became one of the most prominent benefactors of sporting activity in the city. His efforts, the *Acadian Recorder* remarked upon his death in 1892, would 'among lovers of sport ... serve to keep his memory green.'[30] In 1858, for example, Cogswell created a championship rowing regatta on Halifax Harbour, and presented the Cogswell belt, 'a glittering band of ornately worked silver, about three inches wide, on a blue velvet ground,' as a prize to the victorious oarsman. In 1868 he added a 100 U.K. pound prize to the competition.[31] In the previous year, moreover, Cogswell sold two valuable water lots to the Royal Halifax Yacht Club to allow for the construction of a spacious new clubhouse, and in the process was made an honorary member of the club. If Cogswell's patronage was most obvious in cricket, rowing, and sailing, the summer and autumnal pursuits of the city's bourgeiosie, it also extended to baseball. Cogswell made available a large lot on the corner of Quinpool and Windsor streets, adjacent to the Commons, which became the home field of the Atlantas.[32]

In addition to his association with the so-called 'gentlemanly' sports – which he believed were important elements in the character formation of the ruling class – Cogswell also saw sport as a way to encourage respectability amongst working-class youth. Team sports were an integral part of the training program of the Industrial School, founded by Cogswell and later administered by John Grierson. The Halifax *Reporter* of 15 August 1867, for example, described the occupational, moral, and religious training of the forty boys at the school, and reported as well on the cricket match between the school team and the Rosebuds. 'The necessity of providing recreation for lads of this class,' wrote Grierson about the boys in his charge, 'is now universally admitted.'[33] In 1870 the school relocated on the old Forrestall property at the corner of Spring Garden Road and Carleton Street, allowing for the construction of a gymnasium and an athletic grounds for cricket and baseball. Throughout the 1870s and 1880s the boys competed in both cricket and baseball against teams such as the Young Atlantas and the Young Oxfords.[34]

As baseball emerged as a spectator as well as a recreational sport during the 1870s and 1880s, it lost some of its attractiveness to those who saw it as an antidote to crime, rowdiness, and class antagonism. The crowds that attended the regular Saturday afternoon matches at the Halifax Commons, or at the home grounds of the Atlantas, piqued the interest of promoters and speculators who were willing to pay for quality players and to provide financial guarantees for touring clubs in the hope of acquiring a profit. At first there was opposition to the importation of professional players. In February 1878 the Atlantas held an organizational meeting in which it was decided 'almost unanimously' not to import players and to prevent as far as possible other clubs from playing professionals. It was argued that the silver bat-and-ball trophy presented by the mechanics was intended to encourage native talent, otherwise 'the best semi-professional team shall win the bat and ball, not the best city club.'[35] Not long thereafter, however, Halifax's perpetual rivals, the Atlantas and Resolutes, both began to import professional players from the United States, among them Mertie Hackett from Cambridge, Massachusetts, who would play in the major leagues for Boston, Kansas City, and Indianapolis between 1883 and 1888, and John Bergh, who had played for the Philadelphia Athletics in 1876 and came to Halifax in 1879 after his Baltimore team disbanded. Bergh left Halifax the following year to join the Boston club of the National League.[36] Another paid import, catcher Thomas Donohue, field captain of the Resolutes in both 1878 and 1879, and a boarder at the Colonial Hotel, identified his occupation in the Halifax City Directory of 1879 simply as a 'base-ballist,' while his battery-mate, a pitcher named Lane, was described as 'being a whole team in himself.'[37] The importation of these professional players further intensified the rivalry existing between the highly competitive working-man's club, the Resolutes, and the Atlantas, whose players and supporters were drawn largely from the mercantile community. Although the standard of play improved with the imported players, it undermined the competitive position of amateur clubs like the True Blues, whose 'indefatigable efforts' were commended by the local press because they were 'unaided by imported stock.'[38]

In addition to importing professional players, the Atlantas made a number of improvements to their grounds. Their field had been fenced a couple of years before, and now a grandstand was erected for the accommodation of spectators. The *Acadian Recorder* judged the new facilities a success, noting that the umpire was now given a view of the whole field, and that reporters and scorers were provided with separate seating. The Atlantas also built a bridge across a ditch along the perimeter of the park, which earlier had been a 'threat to the timid' and 'almost impassable to the ladies.' A second grandstand for the 'special use of the fair sex' and their escorts also made the game more attractive to spectators.[39]

Although little evidence is available to identify the promoters who underwrote the importation of professional players and the cost of improved facilities, it is possible to provide some educated guesses as to who was involved. Kellam Dolphin, in addition to organizing his own factory club, served as president of the Atlantas in 1878, the same year that the club began to hire professionals. In addition to his support for the Atlantas, Dolphin was also involved in the organization of several exhibition games that bordered on the burlesque. One such match was played in July 1878 between the Fat Men – all of whom were to weigh in excess of 200 pounds – and the Atlantas. In order to give their obese opponents a chance at victory the Atlantas agreed to pitch, bat, and throw left-handed. The Fat Men's line-up included not only Dolphin but a 'ringer' named Morris who weighed less than 200 pounds. When Morris's involvement was disclosed it was agreed that he should be handicapped by carrying a number of cans of 'Boston Baked Beans' supplied from Dolphin's factory. 'The match ... was a complete success,' reported the *Acadian Recorder*, 'and the crowd assembled, numbering nearly 500 persons, was kept in continual roars of laughter by the blunders and exertions of the Fat Men' and by the rulings of Umpire Fultz, a three-foot-six-inches-tall midget weighing about 80 pounds. A few weeks later Dolphin's 'Fat Men' appeared once more in a novelty game against a team of Mi'kmaq Indians.[40]

Isaac Cruse was also involved in the promotion of novelty attractions. The custodian of the Resolutes club in 1878, Cruse operated a saloon at 47 North Park Street in Halifax where players and club supporters congregated. Largely patronized by young skilled workingmen and sports buffs, Cruse's tavern provided a locus for male fraternalism and conviviality, where games were replayed over a pint of beer and where wagers could be laid on upcoming matches. In June 1879 the *Acadian Recorder* reported that the agent of the California Antique Burlesque Baseball Combination had made arrangements with Cruse 'to give the first of their unrivalled outdoor entertainments on the Resolute Grounds.' Each member of the team would appear on the field in the 'most ridiculous of costumes.' They were reputed to be excellent players. Cruse may have been supported in this promotion by Resolute club president Arthur Renner, who had a grocery and liquor business and stood to gain from the growing popularity of baseball and the connections that existed between working-class sportsmen and tavern life. So may have John Morton of the Standards, whose baseball and sporting-goods shop was one of only two establishments in the city that dealt in baseball equipment.[41] Games such as those organized by Dolphin and Cruse were commonplace in the nineteenth century, complementing an emerging leisure world of music halls, minstrel shows, vaudeville houses, public lectures, and circuses. Beverly Williams has pointed out that 'throughout these decades a steady stream of panoramas, circuses, magicians, minstrels, human freaks, astrologists, ventriloquists, scientific wonders and carnivals poured into Halifax.'[42] To a credulous public fascinated with the claims of science and susceptible to unscrupulous entepreneurs who played upon the public's thirst for organized leisure, science, sensationalism, popular education, the theatre, and sport all became part of the world of entertainment.

Evangelical reformers may have intended to develop moral and educational leisure activities that would rescue working people from destructive habits, yet their hopes were often dashed as a result of the public's desire for simple entertainment. Martin Hewitt has shown that, while Saint John's reform-minded élite in the first half of the nineteenth century saw lectures and scientific displays as a way to inculcate the values of respectability among working people, the response of the audience was to turn science into an entertainment spectacle, undermining the improving motivations inherent in the Victorian bourgeoisie's social philosophy. 'Science,' writes Hewitt, 'became just one element in the range of leisure opportunities which Saint John developed in the 1830s and 1840s, during which time the traditional motifs of the rational recreation ideal were appropriated and diluted by a wide spectrum of popular entertainments.'[43]

The relationship between sport and theatre was much more intimate in the nineteenth century than it is today. Periodicals such as the New York *Clipper*, *The Sporting News*, and *The Sporting Life* regularly mixed articles on sport with those pertaining to theatrical or vaudeville productions, and frequently reported on burlesque baseball matches. In May of 1881, for example, the *Clipper* announced that a team of overweight Canadians, none weighing less than 200 pounds, had organized a tour through New York State. 'Fat men of New York state, to the rescue,' it urged. 'Organize your nines at once.'[44] Other such exhibitions included games between married and single men, or homeopathic and allopathic practitioners, games on ice or roller skates, and at the Worcester Insane Asylum the well-known comedian Tony Hart umpired games between the physicians and attendants. In what ranks as the most tasteless of these exhibitions, two teams of one-legged Civil War veterans from Philadelphia and Trenton, NJ, the Crips and the Hoppers, squared off against each other in a couple of matches.[45]

Baseball's emergence as a spectator sport coincided with a significant transformation of the theatre in the last half of the nineteenth century. In *Highbrow/Lowbrow: The Emergence of Cultural Hierarchy in America*, Lawrence W. Levine traces the growing nineteenth-century distinction between popular and high culture by looking at the theatre, the opera house, and the fine arts. Levine finds that for much of that century, theatrical audiences were drawn from across the social spectrum, and that consequently most theatre companies offered their diverse audiences a blend of Shakespearean drama, popular farces or melodrama, and various novelty acts. By our standards, the nineteenth century audience was unruly and undisciplined, registering its approval or displeasure with the performance as it proceeded and at times pelting those on stage with fruit and vegetables to express its annoyance. 'The theatre,' Levine writes, 'was one of those houses of refuge in the nineteenth century where the normative restrictions of the society were relaxed and both players and audience were allowed "to act themselves" with much less inner and outer restraint than prevailed in society.' Audiences operated with a degree of freedom of action that has since been denied to theatre-goers.[46]

The traditional acceptance of unruly and desultory audience behaviour also provided an opportunity for working-class patrons in the cheaper balcony seats to direct their derision at wealthier theatre-goers beneath them. When a correspondent of the Halifax *Morning Herald* decided to witness a performance from the perspective of the 'gods' – as the spectators in the balcony's cheap seats were called – he was appalled by the sarcasm directed towards the wealthy patrons below. 'A particularly dignified old gentleman was spoken of as the "old boy,"' he reported. 'A young man handsomely "got up" ... pronounced to look as drawn through a knot hole ... An aristocratic old lady who sailed majestically in was declared to have a "whole flower garden" on her head.'[47] Given this mockery of class pretensions, it is understandable that the genteel assault on popular traditions and rowdy recreation that had contributed to the development of an organized and disciplined sporting culture would be extended to the arts. By the beginning of the twentieth century a division had been created between legitimate theatre, including drama and stage plays, and the slapstick, acrobatic, and equestrian acts, which had been integral appendages of drama in nineteenth-century theatres. The latter now were seen to be the preserve of vaudeville, burlesque houses, and the circus. In the process of distinguishing between high and low culture, the theatre-going audience would be subjected to greater discipline and the characteristic 'unreserve' of earlier audiences would increasingly become a thing of the past.

Sporting audiences, of course, could also become unruly, and it should not be surprising that the attempt by social reformers to discipline spectators would extend to the football pitch, the hockey rink, and the baseball diamond. Many of the doctors, educators, ministers, and journalists who actively promoted organized sport hoped that the sporting field would create a common culture that transcended class divisions, and they dreamed of a world of play where class distinctions would be eradicated. Baseball was to be a 'gentleman's game' played before a respectable audience. At the park, however, the reality was quite different. Genteel patrons might be protected from rowdiness by purchasing a grandstand ticket, but as the *Acadian Recorder* pointed out, 'hoodlums,' 'toughs,' and 'persons of similar character' often sneaked into the grandstands and took the seats of ticket holders. Alcohol abuse, cigar and cigarette smoking, offensive comments, and occasional fist fights also offended more sedate spectators, as did the widespread open gambling that often took place on the grounds. Drinking and gambling both tended to increase conflict and precipitate disturbances in the crowd, yet both were associated with the game until after the turn of the century.[48]

Gambling on the outcome of matches became increasingly evident as baseball rivalries intensified and spectator interest grew. 'The constant rivalry existing between the ... [Resolutes and Atlantas] has originated an energy and enterprise heretofore dormant,' the *Acadian Recorder* observed on 9 September 1878. 'Professional players were imported, and though this act displeased many, yet the result has been beneficial to baseball in Halifax. It lent to it additional interest, drew out the finer points, and to use a cant expression, showed our boys the wrinkle.'[49]

Nevertheless, the newspaper warned, if the sport was to prosper, promoters would have to keep gambling in check. Neither the umpires nor the players should be allowed to bet on the outcome of the matches. The need for impartiality became particularly evident after a dispute about the score of a game between the Resolutes and Atlantas on 25 September resulted in both teams refusing to complete the game. The umpire declared the match a draw, much to the chagrin of those who had wagered money on the game.[50]

Reformers were increasingly concerned about the relationship between professionalism and the influence that betting men seemed to exercise upon the sport. Critics of professionalism noted the greater likelihood of corruption, gambling, and match-fixing among professional players, no doubt sympathizing with the Toronto *Mail*'s description of a professional as a 'double cross athlete who would cut his throat to keep his reputation as crooked if he thought that anyone was betting that he would live.'[51] Indeed, gambling was widespread amongst Maritimers during the Victorian period, and substantial sums of money could change hands in matches involving urban rivals or barnstorming clubs from the United States. Players were by no means immune from the lure of quick money and, when the odds warranted, occasionally had friends place bets against them. The rivalries that attracted the greatest interest among spectators, gamblers, and promoters, however, were those between teams representing various towns and cities throughout the Maritimes and New England. By 1880 improved railway service made it easier for barnstorming New England club and college teams to tour the region, while telegraph communication – which had existed for over two decades – allowed promoters to schedule games with touring teams in return for expenses and a guaranteed portion of the gate. During the 1880s inter-urban and cross-border contests had become regular fare. When pioneer baseball player James Pender announced his retirement in 1888 after fourteen years on the most competitive Halifax teams, therefore, he could count among his appearances victories over the Saint John Mutuals and Shamrocks, the Moncton Redstockings, and various other teams from Londonderry, Fredericton, Houlton, St Stephen, Bangor, and Boston.[52] Pender had started his career as a catcher for the Atlantas in 1875, at a time when there were no gloves, masks, or chest protectors, and when games between communities were restricted to the Maritimes. By the time of his retirement the baseball culture of the Maritimes was becoming more intimately linked with that of New England, a hardly surprising development considering the significant exodus of young Maritimers during the seventies and eighties to the 'Boston States.'[53]

The gradual integration of Maritime and New England baseball brought a number of changes in the nature of the sport in the region. Along the Canadian-American border, towns such as St Stephen, St Croix, Eastport, Calais, Houlton, Presque Isle, Caribou, Carleton, and Woodstock all sported teams during the 1870s and 1880s. Friendly matches between teams in Calais and St Stephen, in fact, had been played as early as 1871. In that year the Frontier Club of Calais won a pair of games over the Oscerla and Wide Awake teams from St Stephen.[54] Two years later the Frontiers overwhelmed the Saint John Mutuals by a score of 32–13. Soon after that, international play came to involve teams from southern Maine and Massachusetts on the American side of the border and the larger towns in New Brunswick and Nova Scotia. The connection between the Maritime teams and those in New Hampshire, however, remained tenuous. In mill towns such as Manchester, an influx of French-Canadian immigrants from the province of

Quebec created different allegiances.[55] Indeed, while teams from Maine and Massachusetts were regular visitors to the Maritimes, touring teams from Quebec or New Hampshire made only the rarest forays into New Brunswick or Nova Scotia.

During the 1870s Saint John emerged as the leading baseball centre in New Brunswick. A city of slightly more than 40,000 inhabitants in 1871, Saint John's economy rested upon a mixture of mercantile, handicraft, and industrial enterprises. Throughout the first half of the nineteenth century Saint John prospered as a commercial rather than a manufacturing city, its economic life centred about the wooden ship-building industry and the export of lumber, fish, and agricultural goods. Although the conservative nature of the city's merchant élite may have retarded the transition to a manufacturing economy,[56] the city had experienced significant industrial growth in the 1860s and 1870s. T.W. Acheson has noted, moreover, that 'as the economy expanded and became more diversified it produced a more stratified society – one in which the extremes of great wealth and abject poverty became increasingly obvious.'[57] The city became increasingly divided along class, ethnic, and denominational lines, and the city's poorer inhabitants, many of them of Irish extraction, congregated in the three- and four-storey tenements in the city's north end. Not surprisingly, these divisions would reveal themselves in the sporting life of the community.

Baseball in Saint John followed a similar pattern to that of Halifax, beginning around mid-century as a form of recreation for the bourgeoisie and subsequently becoming the favoured game of the city's working class during the 1870s and 1880s. The early Saint John Baseball Club – which through its sporadic history had played the 'New England' variant of baseball until its acceptance of the Knickerbocker rules in 1872 – had recruited its members from the city's leading mercantile and professional families. The more prominent players included William and Chiptain Olive, from a family prominent in shipbuilding and the hardware business; Milton Barnes, keeper of the Marine Hospital; physicians James Christie and Peter Inches; and Francis Collins, a commission merchant who dealt in leather and rubber goods and manufactured cut nails of all kinds. Of the thirty-four players from this era whose occupations can be established, nine were grocers or flour merchants, eight were hardware, stationery, or general merchants, and seven were clerks. There were two druggists, two physicians, two customs officers, one hospital administrator, a jeweller, a law student, and a shipbuilder.

The Saint John Baseball Club operated throughout most of the 1840s and 1850s, but went into hibernation during the 1860s. Through the influence of Saint John newspaperman P.A. Melville, the game was revived in 1869 and grew rapidly in popularity over the next half-dozen years. Even the venerable Saint John Cricket Club succumbed to the attractions of the game, reorganizing in April 1874 as the Saint John Cricket and Baseball Club.[58] Some people, however, had little time for the sport. The *New Dominion* of Saint John, for example, erroneously attributed the introduction of the game in the city to a clergyman from Guelph, Ontario, and pronounced it 'the wickedest game we ever knew a minister of the gospel to engage in. We don't think the reverend gentleman can have any regard for his character and profession, when he rolls up his sleeves to engage in such [a] dirty pastime.'[59]

Despite concerns of this sort, baseball thrived in and around Saint John. In May 1874 the amateur clubs in the city and surrounding area organized the Saint John County Baseball Association composed of the Saint John, Mutual, Athlete, Shamrock, and Royal clubs in Saint John city; the Invincible, Modoc, Resolute, and Northern Star clubs of Port-land; and the Eastern Star club of Fairville. A constitution and by-laws for the association were drawn up and rules governing a league cham-pionship were adopted. The games were scheduled to be played on the barrack green, and for the first time an admission fee was to be charged for spectators. Unfortunately, soon after the league began play, the Modoc, Invincible, Northern Star, Resolute, and Eastern Star teams were forced to withdraw from the association. The federal government, which controlled the grounds, would only agree to six teams using the facili-ties during the summer.

As was true elsewhere, moreover, class, ethnic, and community loyalties invigorated local rivalries, and at times encouraged outright hostility. The intense emotions that attached themselves to the sport also spilled over into contests with visiting teams. When the Halifax Atlantas arrived in Saint John in August 1875 to challenge the Mutuals and the Shamrocks, for example, they were greeted by a 'rowdy element' of Shamrock supporters who shouted indignities at the visitors and threw stones at their horse-drawn cab. Nor did the Atlantas receive the $75 purse that had been promised them for their victory over the Mutuals by a 22–8 score.[60] Incidents of this sort lent the game a rather unruly reputation and gave pause to social reformers who believed that sport would help 'uplift' the working classes from their seemingly rude behaviour.

As the name indicates, the Shamrocks were a team of Irish Catholic working men who represented Saint John's north-end tenement district of York Point. Over the years the club operated with the support of Irish businessmen such as Dennis Costigan, John L. Carleton, John J. O'Hearn, A.H. Gorman, John Keefe, and others, all of whom recognized the importance of sport both as a way of developing a sense of community and ethnic solidarity, and as a potentially profitable business pursuit. Keefe, who was one of the officers of the Irish Literary and Benevolent Society, even served as the baseball club's manager in 1889 and 1890.

The Irish of Saint John had come to the city in two waves of immigration, the first before 1840 and the latter as part of the famine migration between 1845 and 1849. Although many of the thirty thousand people who arrived in the city in the latter migration did not remain there, those who stayed became heavily concentrated in labouring jobs, and contributed to a society rigidly stratified along class, ethnic, and denominational lines.[61] Given the concentration of the Irish Catholic population in the tenements of the York Point district, and the relatively disadvantaged occupational situation that they experienced, it is hardly surprising that the Irish of Saint John regarded baseball as a means to express their ethnic identity and self-worth. Nor is it surprising that in Saint John, as was true in Halifax, Irishmen and Catholics both were more heavily represented on the ballfield than in the general population.

Although the popularity of the game in Saint John grew during the early seventies, it received a setback in June 1877 when a calamitous fire swept across the main peninsula of the city. Aided by brisk summer winds, the fire raged for nine hours, levelling 1600 buildings in an area covering 200 acres.[62] For many of the city's residents, the fire meant a loss of employment and the need to leave the city in search of jobs. For others the task of rebuilding meant that there was little time for recreational pursuits for the rest of the summer. Sport in Saint John suffered greatly in the wake of the fire, and for the next few summers there was little competitive baseball played. By the early eighties the game would revive in Saint John, but the hiatus affected the calibre of play in the city. This would ultimately lead to a reliance on imported players and the beginning of professional baseball in New Brunswick.

4

'Throw 'em Out': Rowdyism, Respectability, and the Yankee Baseballist

In November of 1885 W.A. Frost wrote to the editor of *The Varsity* at the University of Toronto to protest the formation of a baseball club at the college. He warned Toronto's students of the unfortunate class of people associated with the game, including a local saloon-keeper 'who is notorious for his love of baseball and his generosity in bailing out of prison disreputable characters who are unfortunate enough to be placed under the restraints of the law.' Frost purported not to be opposed to baseball as a sport – for intrinsically it 'may be as good as either cricket or football' – but worried none the less about its unsavoury associations. 'The associations of the game are ... of the very lowest and most repugnant character,' he wrote. 'It has been degraded by Yankee professionalism until the name of baseball cannot fail to suggest a tobacco-chewing, loud-voiced, twang-nosed bar-tender, with a large diamond pin and elaborately oiled hair.' Nor did Frost believe it advisable for undergraduates to take up the game in order to elevate it, for in so doing they would be more likely to 'lower themselves.' Instead, Frost advised the college to restrict its sporting endeavours to football and cricket in order that it might not only defeat all Canadian opponents, but its American and overseas competitors as well.[1]

Lurking beneath Frost's attack on American professionalism was the question of the relationship of the classes. During the 1870s and 1880s baseball had taken on a unique character in Canadian sporting culture. Although the game had originated as a game for youthful members of the advancing middle class, after 1870 baseball became predominantly a working-class sport, encouraging fraternal feelings among skilled workingmen. As Bryan Palmer has noted in his study of Hamilton, Ontario, baseball served – along with mechanics' festivals, parades, picnics, and union balls – to enhance working-class solidarity and consciousness and to illuminate and dramatize class inequalities. This was clearly the case in Saint John and Halifax, where teams such as the Shamrocks and Resolutes carried the hopes of working people onto the diamond, and where games involving printers, shoemakers, and other tradesmen maintained a loyalty to the craft. Little wonder that amidst the growing class antagonism that accompanied the late-nineteenth-century development of industrial capitalism, bourgeois reformers were disturbed by the seeming rowdiness and working-class associations that accompanied the sport's development.

During the 1885 season baseball promoters in Saint John contracted with Christopher Toole, manager of the Queen City team of Bangor, Maine, to play a home and home series. A hotelier and tavern-keeper, Toole was an avid sportsman. As a boy he had worked in the summers as a lumberman on the Penobscot River, where he developed a reputation as 'one of the best men on a log' ever to work the area. In the late 1870s Toole took up the sport of pedestrianism - a form of long-distance walk racing – and became known as one of the finest athletes in the north-east. He was also a proficient horse trainer with a subtle appreciation of quality horseflesh. But his greatest love was baseball. For over a quarter of a century Toole was a major promoter of semi-pro baseball in Bangor, stocking his teams with the best college players from the north-east, and often putting his hotel business in jeopardy in the process.[2]

In assembling the club that would meet Saint John, Toole had a considerable reservoir of talent to draw upon. Baseball had flourished in Maine during the 1870s and 80s. Virtually all towns of more than a thousand people fielded competitive amateur or semi-pro nines. In 1877, for example, semi-pro baseball was being played in Augusta, Bath, Lewiston, Wiscasset, Gardiner, Gorham, Biddeford, Fryeburg, and Belfast, as well as in the larger centres in the state. In the same year the Portland Resolutes met the National League champion Boston club in a match in Portland. The Bostons, led by manager Harry Wright – whom Henry Chadwick called the 'father of pro baseball' – and his brother George Wright, a slick infielder, beat the Resolutes 15–3, but the Portland club's commendable play demonstrated the growing sophistication of baseball in Maine.

Baseball interest in Maine grew significantly in the 1880s, with the teams in the southern half of the state securing closer ties with clubs in New Hampshire and Massachusetts, and those in the north cultivating a connection with teams in the Maritimes. In the early eighties, Portland regularly fielded a team of professionals that played teams in Fall River, Lowell, Haverford, Brockton, Lynn, and Lawrence, Massachusetts, as well as teams in its home state. During the 1885 season, two Maine teams, Portland and Biddeford, joined with Haverhill, Brockton, and Lawrence to form the Eastern New England League. In 1888, an all-Maine League was established comprising clubs in South Portland, Augusta, Lewiston, Bath, and Cumberland Mills. They were joined the following year by teams in Hallowell and Gardiner. By the end of the decade Portland, Biddeford, Lewiston, and Augusta were members of the professional New England League, which had operated since 1877.

In addition to the semi-pro and community-based amateur clubs that emerged in the 1870s and 1880s, various commercial, industrial, and workingmen's teams developed in the larger cities. In Portland the boot and shoe industry, the railroad, the town's boiler-makers, the machinists, the clothing and hat trade, and Bradley's Commercial Street all had baseball nines. This was also the case in the larger towns in the state, such as Augusta and Bangor. The *Bangor Commercial* reported in July 1889, for example, that 'some great games of baseball are being played on the Boston and Bangor Steamship Wharf between the "Sun Downs" and the "Wharf Rats."'[3] Then there were the college nines. The Maine State Intercollegiate Association, which included Bates, Bowdoin, Colby, and Maine State colleges, had particularly strong teams who were competitive with the better university nines in the east, such as Harvard, Cambridge, Amherst, and Brown.

In the first match with the Saint Johns in 1885 the Bangor club showed its decisive superiority, mauling its opponent by a 26–1 score. A headline in the Bangor press the next day announced 'the Provincials [to be] Not Very Well Versed in Modern Baseball Warfare – They Couldn't Get on to the Curves and Didn't Happen to Get on to Much of Anything Else.'[4] Despite the disappointing result in the opening game in Bangor, the return game in Saint John attracted an expectant crowd of 3000 people to the Saint John barrack grounds. Although this was an error-filled match (17 errors on one side and 28 on the other), owing in part to the poor condition of the grounds, the lopsided 17–5 victory for Bangor clearly demonstrated the superiority of baseball in Maine and provided an impetus for Maritime teams to import coaches and players from the United States. As baseball revived in Saint John, competition with teams in Maine became a routine affair in the years to follow. In 1887 the Saint John Nationals played two games with the

University of Maine at Orono, losing the first 9–8 and winning the second 3–2. In the following year the Nationals beat the collegians 12–8 and 10–1, handing Maine its only two defeats of the year. Earlier Maine had won 10 straight games against its conference opponents at Colby, Bates, and Bowdoin colleges.[5]

Ironically, the victories of the Saint John club over Maine were secured in part by college players from the United States who sought to earn a little money over the summer months. During the 1888 summer season the Nationals imported two college ball players, A.P. Wagg and William Larabee, from Colby College, and thereby ushered in a period of professional baseball. The following year, three more imports, pitcher Frank Small, catcher Dan Rogers, and third baseman Billy 'Whit' Parsons, were added to the team. Parsons, *The Sporting Life* reported, could 'see a flea at one hundred yards. He is a big favorite and everyone, girls and all go to see 'Whit' smack the sphere.'[6] The Shamrocks secured the services of Edward Kelly of Portland and William Donovan of Bangor. Kelly lasted a mere two weeks before being released. An unsavoury character who had played for Chris Toole's Bangor club in the 1885 home and home series with Saint John, Kelly would subsequently become involved in a scandal involving a prostitution ring in Saint John. Kelly's 'release,' the Bangor press reported, 'is a cautious term meaning "bounced". Kelly has been hitting the bottle too hard to suit the Shamrocks. He cared for nothing and nobody and drank hard.'[7]

As baseball re-established itself in Saint John in the late 1880s its popularity also rose in Moncton, a rapidly growing industrial and railway town that the Saint John press dubbed derisively 'the smoky city.' Baseball was first played in Moncton almost two decades before with the organization of the powerful Invincibles and Red-Stockings clubs in the summer of 1874. The Invincibles were quick to carry Moncton's banner forward in competitive matches with teams in Saint John and Halifax, and along with the Red-Stockings competed against the Atlantas of Halifax for the Maritime championship between 1875 and 1877.

By that time a lively rivalry was emerging between Moncton and Halifax on the baseball diamond. In late April 1878 an impatient columnist for the *Moncton Times* noted that the Halifax ball clubs had been organized for some time and warned that 'if Moncton's oldest and best club the Invincibles have any notion of again trying their luck with the Maritime provincial champs, it is about time for their reorganization.'[8] Shortly thereafter W.B. McDonald, secretary of the Atlantas, invited the

Invincibles to 'toss the leather' once again for the 'continuance of friend-ly relations.' A challenge was also received from the Resolutes, who were described in the press as 'practically professionals.' For some unexplained reason, however, the Invincibles appear to have disbanded in mid-summer, and were not revived in the future. 'All efforts to reorganize the old Invincible Baseball Club on a "war footing" have been unavailable,' the *Moncton Times* reported in May 1879, 'and some of the old players have joined the cricket club.' Other players joined the newly formed Moncton Nine, which subsequently accepted a challenge to play 'the once far-famed' baseball club the Shamrocks of Saint John to celebrate a visit of the Governor-General to New Brunswick.

In addition to the Invincibles, other Moncton clubs such as the Reso-lutes, the Moncton Nine, and the junior Mayflowers Navy Blue and Silver Stars received or accepted challenges from the Newcastle Maple Leafs, the Fear Nots from Hopewell Corner, the Hardly Evers from Campbellton, and teams from Hillsboro, Salisbury, Rivière du Loup, and Portland, Maine. Games involving Moncton and the Crescents of Rivière du Loup on the New Brunswick–Quebec border are particularly interesting and suggest the involvement of those of Acadian descent in baseball's emergence in Moncton. Indeed, contests involving teams from Quebec were almost unheard of in most other towns in the Maritimes. While touring teams from New England regularly criss-crossed the region, the most remarkable aspect of baseball in the Maritimes before the Second World War was its isolation from the baseball world of francophone Quebec.

It would be easy to exaggerate the significance of the matches be-tween the Moncton and Rivière du Loup nines. A look at the rosters of both clubs reveals little involvement by those of Acadian heritage. Of the eighteen players from these teams whose names appeared in news-paper box-scores only Marchessault, the Crescents star pitcher, had an identifiable French name. Moncton's club included players by the name of Anderson, Magee, McHaffie, McCormack, Cook, Spence, Wier, Clark, and Wright, while the remaining Crescents included Lyons, Burke, Collins, Waddell, King, and Arthur and two players named Scott. Still, baseball had its following in Acadian communities. During the summer of 1880, for example, the *Moniteur Acadien* announced the formation of a team in the Acadian community of Shediac, and over the following decade teams would emerge in French-speaking communities from Tracadie to Bathurst and along the province's Acadian north shore. Elsewhere in Albert County, towns like Hopewell were succumbing to the baseball craze. 'The baseball mania has reached Albert County,' the *Moncton Times* reported, 'and judging from appearances at present of a most infectious character that nothing but severe cold weather will check ... The almost entire absence of any other kind of recreation gives these games about as much importance as they deserve.'[9]

Like any other town of pretension, Moncton established an amateur athletic association to promote various athletic and recreational pursuits in May 1888. Although the Moncton Cricket and Amateur Athletic Association ostensibly encouraged all kinds of athletic activity, baseball very quickly became its central focus. Cricket would continue to be played until after the turn of the century, but in 1895 the MC & AAA became the MAAA.[10] The initial objective of the association was to find and purchase a suitable ground for the ball club, a task that monopolized the efforts of club officials during the 1888 season. Community bazaars supplemented the investment of local businessmen in the development of the association, and a field and clubhouse emerged. But the popularity of baseball as a spectator sport undercut the founders' original intention of promoting a wide range of sporting activity for amateur athletes. The problem, said columnist Geoffrey Cuthbert Strange, was that the club executive 'like the eastern potentates who wonder that Europeans who can afford it don't hire someone to do their dancing for them,'[11] committed itself to professional baseball rather than amateur athletics. They found it amusing to pay 'seven giants of the profession' from $15–20 per week and to sit contentedly in the grandstand smoking cigars and chatting with lady friends 'and thought what a lovely thing it was to belong to an athletic club.'[12]

During the 1889 season a number of towns in New Brunswick were importing American players in order to remain competitive with the Saint John clubs and with towns on the other side of the border such as Houlton, 'a remarkably lively baseball town' with its own 'breezy' little sporting sheet 'the Baseball News,' which appeared twenty minutes after every ball game.[13] Fredericton reportedly gave a catcher named Call from Bates College a 'sizeable sum' to play for them, and signed his teammate Graves who had been released by the Augusta club. Moncton signed pitcher Fred Doe of the Waltham club and Oliver Burns, a fine little catcher who caught for Toole's Bangor club in 1887. Doe would later distinguish himself as a player and manager for several professional clubs in New England.

The development of professional baseball in New Brunswick during the late 1880s contributed to the sharpening of metropolitan rivalries that accompanied the coming of industrial capitalism to the province. One such rivalry involved the region's two largest urban centres, Saint John and Halifax, both intent upon becoming the major Canadian eastern railway terminus and winter port, but neither of which could establish a commercial or industrial hegemony over the entire region. Whenever it could, the Saint John press contrasted the bustling exuberance of the New Brunswick centre to that of somnolent Halifax. A dispatch from the Saint John *Telegraph*, carried in Halifax newspapers on 31 July 1888, described games between the Nationals of Saint John and the Atlantas of Halifax as a 'very easy contract' and suggested that if Halifax remained uncompetitive the Nats would have to go south of the border to find better competition. 'The Atlantas play good ball in the quiet town of Halifax,' the *Telegraph* concluded, 'but when they come to a great city like Saint John, the noise and bustle and excitement seem to unnerve them.'[14] In the following year, when the Socials travelled to Saint John to play a challenge match during the Saint John city carnival, they were treated to a city parade that routinely burlesqued Halifax. One float was a replica of the mail steamer *Atlas* detained in fog eighty hours outside Halifax Harbour. Another was adorned with a banner reading 'Little Sister Halifax. Haligonian Specialities. Fog in Summer, Harbour Skating in Winter.' When the Socials were subsequently defeated by the Saint John Club, one newspaper wrote that 'bright, active, energetic Saint John scored one against her old and unprogressive rival yesterday, and she did not require the assistance of ... [the umpire] to make that score either.'[15]

Halifax held its own summer carnival in early August 1889. The roster of activities included a match between a New York cricket team and the garrison team, single scull races, a Labrador whaler-boat challenge, fencing and gymnastic displays, wrestling, and even a mock military battle at Point Pleasant Park. The highlight of the carnival, however, was a series of baseball games between the Halifax Socials and the John P. Lovell Arms Company and the Woven Hose teams of Boston. These teams were made up of players signed and paid to advertise the companies' wares, especially their sporting-goods lines, and were reputedly among the strongest teams in the United States outside of organized baseball. Toby Lyons, the twenty-two-year-old pitcher of the Lovells from Cambridge, Massachusetts, would play the next season for the major-league Syracuse club.

The Socials had been one of the premier teams in Halifax during the 1880s, and became even stronger near the end of the 1888 season when club officials decided to amalgamate with the Atlantas, the Socials retaining the team name. This merger, it was hoped, would place the club 'in a position to cope with any foreign teams which might visit Halifax.' It was also decided to hire a professional player-coach, and the new club executive turned to John 'Jocko' Flynn, a diminutive Irishman from Lawrence, Massachusetts. Flynn, who had won twenty-four games for Chicago when they won the National League pennant in 1886, was reportedly hired 'to coach and alternate in the box, at a salary exceeding that of any professional player in this country.' The Socials also secured the services of John White, the star catcher of the city, Richard Fitzgerald, a third baseman and outfielder, and James Pender's brother Michael, who was noted for his speed on the basepaths. In addition, James Doyle, who had previously been induced to go to Gardiner, Maine, to play professional ball, returned to the club to play second base. The other members of the team were pitcher Robie Davison, team captain and 'as good as any in the provinces,' third baseman Howard Smith, and outfielders John Graham and John O'Brien.[16]

During the 1889 season, the Socials played twenty-one matches against teams from other cities, winning eleven. In addition to the two teams from Boston, their opponents in 1889 included Portland, Bath, Gardiner, Lewiston, Augusta, and Bangor, Maine; Colby College and Bates College – as 'gentlemanly a set of fellows as ever graced a diamond' – and the Boston St Stephens. 'Jocko' Flynn led the Socials in both pitching and batting, hitting .324 and winning 9 of 14 decisions on the mound, while the change or back-up pitcher Robie Davison had a 2 and 5 record with an earned run average of 1.71.[17] In the following season, the Holy Cross Collegians, the Worcester professionals, and a regular assortment of teams from Maritime centres provided Halifax with stiff competition.[18]

As baseball grew in popularity during the 1880s many sports reformers hoped that the game would encourage cultivated behaviour and respect for authority. Players were expected to approach the game in a mannerly and respectful fashion, playing for the love of the sport and avoiding disparaging remarks about their opponents. But the importation of professional players from the United States during the late 1880s raised concerns that the values of sportsmanship and fair play would give way to Yankee showmanship and commercialism. In July 1888, a crowd of 1200 Haligonians, including a 'large gathering of the fair sex,'[19] turned out to see the Saint John Nationals and their star import player named A.P. Wagg, whose reputation as an ostentatious and garrulous player had preceded him. A pitcher from Colby College, Wagg struck one newspaperman as resembling 'the lecturer outside a side-show at the circus.' In the sixth inning, a number of 'hoodlums' tried to stop Wagg's 'continual prattle by endeavouring to irritate him ... , but it was useless.' The same reporter criticized William Pickering, the second baseman, for loud and uncontrolled language and chided Richard Fitzgerald of the Atlantas for talking too much while guarding his base.[20]

The concern of most sports reformers was that undisciplined behaviour by the players would encourage similar rowdiness amongst the audience. Promoters of the game especially feared the effect of unruly behaviour and 'bad manners' upon women spectators. Women, of course, were important to the future of the game, not only as patrons, but also as symbols of respectability; their attendance provided the game with the hallmark of gentility that reformers wished to establish. Boorish behaviour by male spectators, of course, undermined the respectable image baseball's proponents were eager to promote. Aware of this, the Saint John *Progress* of 11 August 1888 apologized for the behaviour of a few rowdies who crowded into the press box and smoked persistently, even though ladies were present. The columnist took further pains to assure female spectators that the perpetrators of this 'crudeness' were not members of the press.[21]

Reformers also were concerned that the commercialization and professionalization of baseball would attract as players less dignified members of the working class, who put financial reward above the values of self-discipline, self-sacrifice, and teamwork, and who would indulge in various forms of desultory and unsavoury behaviour. These attitudes were no doubt confirmed when the off-field activities of two of the early imports to Saint John, Jack Guthrie and Edward Kelly, blossomed into a public scandal in September 1889. These two Irish-American ball players had arrived in Saint John from Maine in the summer of 1889, accompanied by a number of young girls destined for employment in a bordello run by Mattie Perry, sometimes known as 'French Mattie.' One of the girls was a young teenager from Bangor named Annie Tuttle who had been recruited by Guthrie's companion Lizzie Duffy. When Annie Tuttle's mother travelled to Saint John in search of her daughter and reported her disappearance to the authorities, the police raided Mattie's Brittain Street house and found the girl there. Mattie was told to leave the city at once and, accompanied by Kelly, 'one of her boon companions in Saint John for some weeks,' left that night on the American Express for Presque Isle, Maine. Guthrie, also 'well known in base-ball circles' in both Bangor and Saint John, left on the same train with Lizzie Duffy.[22]

While the establishment of professional baseball served to elevate the calibre of competition in the Maritimes, then, it also raised questions about the essential purpose of sport itself. Initially, sport advocates hoped that baseball would serve, as cricket and rugby had done, to enhance 'gentlemanly' values.[23] Bedecked in uniforms that occasionally included high sneakers and bow-ties, players were often admonished against uttering derogatory remarks about their opponents and the umpire. Newspaper accounts of games regularly criticized the practice of 'kicking,' or disputing an umpire's decision, and derided those players who would not accede to the arbiter's authority. Protests of calls were seen to be the responsibility of the team captain, and individual players were urged to defer to the captain's authority. The extent to which 'kicking' was criticized, however, reveals that the players themselves did not conform easily to the 'gentlemanly code' that others wished to bring to the game.

Nor were umpires always the neutral officials that they were supposed to be. Poorly trained, often not completely cognizant of the rules, and prone to betting on the games that they officiated, umpires were frequently biased in favour of their home teams during inter-urban matches. At the opening match of the 1890 season in Fredericton, a correspondent of the Saint John *Progress* noted the unprofessionalism of Umpire Allen, who officiated the game in 'a black cutaway and Oxford,' rather than in proper uniform. This improper garb, the newspaperman mused, may also throw light on why he had at one point 'mistaken three strikes for two.'[24]

Disputes about the competence and neutrality of umpires were a recurring theme of these years, and upon closer scrutiny often reveal the deep class, ethnic, and community rivalries that accompanied the development of the sport. After a game between the Saint John Nationals and the Halifax Socials in 1888, for example, the Saint John press charged umpire William Pickering, who regularly played second base with the Socials, with 'bare-faced cheating,' and also alleged that Fred Robinson, a Halifax gambler, had bribed the umpire. 'All that Pickering needs is a dark lantern and a jimmy to make a first-class burglar,' said the Saint John *Progress*. 'Rather than play with such a gang, we might wisely get up a series with a convict nine from Dorchester' penitentiary.[25] Robinson admitted boasting to friends in a local hotel that he had bought Pickering, but subsequently denied having done so even though he won a sizeable amount on the game's outcome.[26] In the following year, Pickering was again the subject of criticism for his partisanship during a doubleheader between the Socials and a team from South Portland, Maine. Both games, said the Halifax *Acadian Recorder*, featured obviously partisan umpiring and, in the second, Pickering was calling strikes against Portland batters that were nowhere near the plate.[27]

Despite these instances of favouritism, it was generally conceded that the authority of the umpire was an essential component of the game. This was a common theme in the columns of Frank J. Power, part-time sporting columnist for the *Acadian Recorder* and the Halifax *Daily Echo*. Power's columns often lauded the work of his namesake, James 'Shorty' Power, a highly respected umpire whose career behind the plate spanned four decades. 'Shorty' Power's baseball career began during the 1870s as a player for the Atlantas, but in the 1880s he turned to umpiring on a regular basis. Power was an authoritarian figure, respected for his integrity and decisiveness in dealing both with players and unruly fans. Even spectators were subject to his authority. At one game, for example, Power demanded the ejection of a spectator for joking that the umpire had a glass eye. 'He simply raised his arm,' said the *Acadian Recorder*, 'and a big policeman escorted ... [the fan] out.'[28]

In Saint John, umpire Morton Harrison cut a commanding presence behind the plate, similar to that of 'Shorty' Power in Halifax. A colourful figure, whose trademark was to chew on a lemon while umpiring the game, Harrison had the respect of the fans, players, and the press as well.[29] 'I never had any other opinion but that Harrison was as honest as the sun,' said one newspaper columnist. 'Some of his decisions may have been wrong, but that can be said of the best of umpires.'[30] By the end of the 1889 season, however, Harrison had had enough, and decided to devote his time to business and the city orchestra. The problem was that the home-plate umpire was the only official on the field, with responsibility not only for calling balls and strikes, but also for making all the other decisions that were required. Mistakes could easily be made, and in the highly charged atmosphere that surrounded competitive matches the umpire received considerable abuse.

In 1890, Fredericton and Moncton established professional teams, and a four-team New Brunswick professional league was set up that relied heavily upon imported players. The Nationals (now called the Saint John Athletic Association) discarded Dan Rogers – the club's catcher in the previous year who had upset management by leaving town with all of the team's catching gear – and signed Jack Priest, Billy Pushor, Billy Merritt, and pitcher E.C. Howe of Harvard University. The Shamrocks cut Kelly and added brothers Jim and Joe Sullivan of Charlestown, and John T. Griffin of Brockport, Massachusetts, Abel Lezotte a feisty, young, bullet-armed catcher and first baseman from Lewiston, Maine, and Saint John native John 'Chewing Gum' O'Brien.[31] The two Sullivans, Merritt, Lezotte, and O'Brien would all subsequently play major-league baseball. Fredericton engaged the services of Wagg and Larabee, the two imports who had introduced professional ball to New Brunswick, and filled out the roster with a number of other paid players, including Edward Thayer, a pitcher from Yale University, and the battery of Neil Stynes and McCormack, who had starred for Rockport in the Massachusetts State League the year before. (Late in the same season Stynes would jump to the Cleveland club of the newly formed Players' League.) Moncton had seven professionals on its club, including Nova Scotia native Fred Lake as player manager, pitchers Roach and Farrell, and big Jim Richardson the star first baseman from Maine State College. A twenty-four-year-old catcher who could play every other position on the diamond except pitcher, Lake would play for the Boston club in the National League in 1891. Known as a fine baseball mind, Lake ended his major-league career as a player and manager of the same Boston club in 1910.

The 1890 season opened on the 24 May holiday with what the *Progress* called 'undoubtedly the biggest baseball day in the province.' The Saint Johns and Shamrocks played a two-game series, the first on the Shamrocks' field, the latter on the AA grounds. Everybody got their money's worth, the press reported, 'except perhaps those in the back row of the solid wall that encircled the AA club diamond.' Club receipt books showed 1700 paid admissions to the Shamrock grounds and 4,000 to the Saint John AA Club. With a general-admission fee of 25 cents, and an additional ten-cent charge for the grandstand, the gate for the two matches exceeded $2000. Considering that weekly player salaries ran approximately $250 per team, the promoters had turned a tidy profit.[32]

The 1890 season had been awaited with anticipation by fans across the province, and the large crowds attending the season opener in Saint John stimulated interest even more. Everywhere people were asking, 'How much is Parsons getting? What is Whitenect being paid per week? How are Priest and Pushor paid?' In 1889 the Saint Johns had spent $2260.72 in player salaries over the season, but this figure increased substantially during the 1890 campaign.[33] Before the 1890 season the executive committee of the Saint John AAC had set a salary cap of $90 per month per player, but gave a 'power to increase' to the baseball club management in the event that the team could not compete on equal terms with Fredericton and Moncton, both of which had made a profit on their operation in 1889.[34] The Shamrocks also increased player salaries, improved field maintenance, and outfitted the team in new bluish-gray uniforms trimmed in green and with green stockings 'as usual.'[35] In order to cover these expenses the club held a large bazaar to supplement the investment of several local businessmen. 'The guarantee fund is looming up in great shape,' said the *Progress*, predicting that 'the season will be so prosperous that the signers will have nothing to do but guarantee.'[36]

By the end of June it was becoming clear to the Saint John AAC executive that the team would have to be strengthened if the Spalding pennant was to fly from the club's flagstaff during the 1890 season. Unhappy with the seemingly indifferent efforts of one of its first-string pitchers, Frank Small, the club began negotiations with Amos Alonzo Stagg, the great Yale pitcher, to come and finish out the season.[37] When Stagg refused to leave Yale, fearing that his amateur standing might be threatened, the club sent its agent, Thomas Bell, to Marlboro, Massachusetts, to induce E.C. Howe of Harvard, considered 'the best amateur college pitcher, excepting Stagg,' to come to Saint John. Like Stagg, Howe was an amateur and did not wish to turn pro, but Bell eventually convinced him to spend his summer vacation in New Brunswick and pitch for the Saint Johns.[38]

As the season progressed the Shamrocks did handsomely at the gate, allowing the club to meet its obligations to the players, cover travelling expenses, maintain the grounds, and amass a tidy profit. Their success at the gate owed a great deal to the bitter rivalry that existed between the Shamrocks and the Saint Johns. Jack Griffin, the Shamrocks' import shortstop from Brockton, Massachusetts, who like a number of his teammates was also an accomplished professional boxer, commented on the source of that rivalry in a letter to the *Police News*. 'This is a great place,' he wrote, 'and baseball is all the craze. The team I am playing for is backed by Catholic Irishmen, and the St. Johns are backed by Orangemen.' In one July match the Shamrocks found their grounds heavily patronized by visiting Orangemen who were attending a convention in the city, and who cheered lustily for the Fredericton Celestials in their game against their Irish Catholic opponents.[39]

The intensity of the Saint Johns and Shamrocks rivalry carried over into a contest organized by the Saint John *Progress* to determine the most popular player in the city. For weeks in August the newspaper ran contest ballots in its pages. By the time the polls closed on 4 September, the floor of the *Progress* office was heaped with ballots. Eventually the contest became a race between two players, catcher Billy Pushor of the Saint Johns and catcher William Donovan of the Shamrocks. The interest in the contest was so great that the *Progress* was forced to print extra copies to supply the demand for ballots, and the editors were amazed to receive votes from Moncton, Halifax, Fredericton, St Stephen, Houlton, Cambridgeport, Massachusetts, and as far away as Columbus, Ohio. When the votes were counted Pushor emerged the victor by a count of 25,905 to 16,507. The remaining 5200 votes were divided among sixteen other players.

Although the Shamrocks–Saint Johns rivalry was without question the most vociferous of all, games between other metropolitan centres often created intense feelings. On 7 June 1890, for example, the *Progress* reported upon the 'vitriolic reception' of the Saint Johns in Fredericton, and the failure of the umpire to control the crowd. 'The sneers and epithets hurled at them were more than a sufficient excuse for the visitors to lose their temper, which I am glad to say did not happen. A dazed umpire at the plate set the grand stand going in a short time, and between the jibes from both quarters he also had a tough time of it.'[40]

Given the intensity of ethnic and metropolitan loyalties, disputes involving umpires' decisions were inevitable on the ball field. In the sixth inning of a game between the Saint Johns and the Shamrocks on 30 June, for example, a rhubarb erupted over the decisions of umpire Jimmy Christie, after the official scorer had announced that one of his rulings had been incorrect. Christie was at a loss to know what to do. The sports columnist of the Saint John *Globe* was particularly critical of Christie's indecisiveness. 'Blundering by an umpire inevitably creates an uproar among the excited patrons sitting in the grand stand,' he wrote, 'and there was a capital representation of bedlam for a while this morning.' For the Shamrocks, the issue was not so much one of incompetence, but of unfairness, because Christie was the umpire chosen by the Saint John AA Club.

In an attempt to deal with charges of favouritism on the part of officials, the New Brunswick League adopted the 'double umpire' system that had been followed by the new Player's League in the United States, and that was under consideration by the National League as well. This system, which allowed each competing club to have an umpire of its choice who would rotate behind the plate with his opposite number from game to game, was intended, said one sportswriter, to protect umpires in order that they might 'get their life insurance premiums reduced about one half.'[41]

Unfortunately, even the double-umpire system could not overcome the suspicion and antagonism that accompanied matches between the Saint Johns and the Shamrocks. On 19 July 1890 the two teams met at the Shamrock grounds before an assembled crowd of over 1500 people, but the game was scrubbed because of a dispute over umpires. The Saint Johns had just acquired 'Harvard' Howe and the club management wanted every advantage for him as he faced the arch-rival Shamrocks. Concerned that the Shamrocks' umpire Dan Connolly would rob them of the game, the Saint Johns' manager asked the Shamrocks to agree to a system whereby their umpire Jimmie Christie would call balls and strikes for Howe, while Connolly would umpire Joe Sullivan of the Shamrocks. When manager John Keefe of the Shamrocks refused, the Saint Johns decided to forfeit the game, much to the annoyance of the Saturday afternoon crowd.

The game was tentatively rescheduled for the following Tuesday evening, but doubts emerged that the dispute would be resolved in time. Keefe, the Shamrock manager, announced that his club would be on hand to play, but doubted that the game would be played as one member of the Saint John AAC executive committee intimated that the club might disband. Another official told him that the Shamrocks would only get into the grounds if they changed their position on the umpiring rotation, or if they climbed the fences, as the gates would be closed to them. President A.O. Skinner of the Saint Johns also felt that the executive would stick to their contention of Saturday, and if the Shamrocks failed to give way there would be no game. Eventually a compromise was reached and the game went on, avoiding an early break-up of the league.[42]

Over the next month the rivalry heated up, and finally came to a boil on 21 August 1890 during a game at the Shamrocks' grounds. There was already trouble in the air when umpire Dan Connolly called 'play ball.' Rumours were flying thick and fast that some sort of violence was likely. Problems began when Connolly awarded captain Donovan of the Shamrocks a base on balls, and Billy Pushor of the Saint Johns turned in amazement and expostulated to the crowd, at which point Shamrock supporters began to shout themselves hoarse. 'Fueled by a little rum, and spurred on by the Shamrocks' captain,' the home crowd edged closer and closer to the foul lines, shouting epithets at the Saint John players, raising their fists and threatening them with bodily harm. 'Some of the remarks from the grandstand were fearful,' the *Progress* reported, 'calling up all the differences of race and creed.' The menacing crowd upset the Saint John players and threw their ace pitcher Howe off his game, allowing the Shamrocks to capitalize on their anxiety. The Irishmen, who had been unable to score a run during the first five innings, took advantage of Howe's nervousness, scoring seven runs in the sixth inning and three in the seventh on their way to a 12–8 victory.

The prospect of ethnic and class violence could no longer be disregarded, and had a sobering effect upon the promoters of the game. 'Professional baseball received a heavy blow Thursday,' the Saint John *Globe* commented, 'owing to the unruly action of the spectators and supporters of both teams ... Good lovers of the game say Thursday's exhibition was the most disgraceful they ever saw.'[43] Fearful that the rivalry was getting out of hand, the executive of the Saint John AAC met on the morning of 22nd August and decided not to play any further matches with the Shamrocks, and after their scheduled game with Moncton the following night the club disbanded.[44] 'The death of professional ball is a matter of rejoicing,' said the *Globe*, 'but regret must be felt at the nature of the death.'[45]

While the Shamrocks continued to play out their schedule and won the championship of the New Brunswick league when the Moncton club also disbanded, the Saint Johns prepared for a pair of September doubleheaders against the Halifax Socials, which they regarded as an unofficial Maritime championship series. What transpired, however, delivered the *coup de grace* to professional baseball in the region. Beginning in the third inning of the second game in Halifax, a number of curious incidents led the crowd of over 1000 to believe that a fix was on. It was in that inning that a Saint John man whose money was being wagered on the Socials walked across the field to the Saint John players' bench. Shortly thereafter, the umpire, himself from Saint John, began to make calls that favoured Halifax, giving bases on balls to the Socials on obvious strikes. The Saint John players were also involved, making little attempt to disguise their complicity. For Saint John, Jack Priest the pitcher struck out by swinging at balls nowhere near the plate, and third baseman Parsons, after hitting safely, removed his hand from the base and allowed a Socials player to tag him out.[46] This transparently fixed match, said the *Daily Echo*, provided an indication of the depth that professional players could sink to when betting men were interested.[47]

A number of reasons were given to explain the fix. In the first place, the Socials were going to Saint John the following week and a victory for the Halifax team, which had lost its opening game, would ensure Saint John promoters a big crowd. It was also widely believed that revenge was the motive, because the bettor who had fixed the match had been taken advantage of by Halifax gambler Frank Robinson, who bet $300 on the Saint John team at two-to-one odds during the first game of the series, and would double his money if the Saint Johns won the second game as well.

That the outcome of the game could turn on the involvement of gamblers once again brought the respectability of the sport into question. Haligonians were especially outraged when a correspondent of the Moncton *Times* reported that a banquet was held for the Saint John players when they returned home, despite their acknowledged throwing of the game. Seven of the nine men, the *Times* correspondent reported, were involved in the fix and they 'openly avow and boast of it.' At the dinner, an MPP from Saint John chaired the festivities, which included a succession of speeches glorifying the players. 'This barefaced outrage on public morals,' the correspondent concluded, 'will perhaps bring a gulled public to some sense of the honour involved in professional baseball.'[48]

Even the Saint John *Progress*, which had supported the Saint Johns throughout the season and had taken their side against the Shamrocks, was disgusted by the behaviour of its players. 'Nothing can excuse the rank and dishonest game they worked in the second contest at Halifax,' wrote its sports columnist. 'I care not whether Robinson got left or not, the simple fact remains that they did not play ball. They lost the game purposely because Robinson had money on them. The actions of a gambler should not affect the playing of the team.' The Saint John *Globe* called the game 'a miserable game of playing' and noted that the decision of the Saint Johns to throw the game to gain revenge on Robinson 'shows to what a low state professional ball has got.'[49] The *Progress* also reported that the executive of the Saint John AAC would refuse the team access to the grounds for the return visit of the Halifax club to Saint John unless the players could clear themselves of the charge of selling the game in Halifax. Unable to do so, and without a field to play on, the Saint Johns cancelled the remainder of the series.

The thrown match at the end of the 1890 season had a devastating impact upon professional baseball in the region. Before that time, the elevated standard of play that accompanied the importation and payment of athletes had attracted a growing clientele. Players were performing before crowds that averaged about 1200 in Halifax and Moncton, and about twice that number in Saint John. In the latter city, fan interest was so great that the King Street merchants had installed a telephone at the baseball grounds in August 1888, so that after each inning the score of the game in progress could be telephoned to the DeForrest and March store, at the corner of King and Germane streets, and placed on a large blackboard that could be seen from a considerable distance.[50]

During the 1890s fan interest waned. Amid questions about the game's integrity, the Halifax Socials tried to carry on, but disbanded in mid-summer 1891 when declining support and forfeited games became the rule. In a last-ditch attempt to revive the game the Socials arranged games with a touring women's team in August 1891, only to be attacked for promoting a disreputable spectacle. Thereafter baseball in Halifax was played on a strictly amateur basis. Rivalries between employees at manufacturing or commercial establishments, between ethnic groups or recreational clubs, provided the community with interesting but not outstanding baseball. Matches with other city clubs or touring teams were rare, and although there were sporadic attempts to revive competitive baseball in the city, there was little enthusiasm for the professional game through much of the decade.

In Saint John professional baseball's popularity also nosedived. The threat of ethnic and class violence that lurked beneath the surface in bitterly contested matches between the Shamrocks and the Saint Johns, and the unsavoury characteristics attached to professionalism, resulted in a cry for a return to amateur play. In a post-season retrospective the *Progress* reminisced about the previous three seasons of baseball, and the unhappy state to which it had fallen. When professional baseball arrived in 1888 'we were all enthusiastic ... We could not see another club win without a pang of jealousy or hatred. We were pleased ... with the wiles of Wagg and plucky Larabee. They were to us what Clarkson and Kelly were to the Bostonians.' In those early years college teams that were evenly matched with local clubs crossed the border to win or be beaten. But gradually the fans wanted more. With thorough-going Yankee professionalism came gambling and the erosion of a sense of fair play. The result was the end of professional ball, and no one seemed to mind. 'Is any body sorry?' the *Progress* asked. 'Did I hear a complaint? Not one. There are no mourners, save, perhaps, the expectant and ambitious collegians of Maine, who have looked forward to New Brunswick as a Vacation Bonanza where gold and sunshine abounded and there was no work. Amen to all that.'

In the short space of two decades, then, the baseball culture of the region had undergone a significant transformation. Organized initially as a manly pursuit for youthful members of the bourgeoisie, the game gradually found a significant constituency amongst working-class youth. Unlike curling, tennis, or golf – sports that appealed almost exclusively to members of the urban élite – baseball attracted the support of virtually all social classes. Rather more than other sports, therefore, baseball gave vent to class, ethnic, and community rivalries. As a result, the game became associated with rowdyism, and proponents of 'respectable' recreation remained ambivalent about it. Although they would never completely relinquish the hope that baseball could contribute to manly character and rescue young men from vicious and degenerate pastimes, sport reformers worried about the unsavoury influence of gamblers and speculators, the commercialization of sport, and the ungentlemanly behaviour of both players and spectators alike. During the 1890s, as women and blacks took up the game throughout the region, and as the antagonism between capital and labour sharpened, the debate over baseball's place in modern sporting culture took on a new intensity.

5

Gendered Baselines: The Tour of the Chicago Blackstockings

Early in August 1891 two baseball promoters, M.J. Raymond and William Burtnett, arrived in Saint John from Boston and registered at the Hotel Stanley. What made their visit different from that of the advanced agents of most barnstorming baseball clubs was that they represented a female nine, the Chicago Young Ladies' Baseball Club, known as the Blackstockings, and were interested in arranging a tour of the Maritime provinces. Their hope was to have the club, which was at that time playing a series of games in Portland, Old Orchard, and Bangor, Maine, spend a month in the Maritimes, appearing in Fredericton, Saint John, Sussex, Moncton, Amherst, Truro, Halifax, and Yarmouth, and any other towns along the way that might be interested in hosting them. The thought of young women intruding on what was regarded traditionally as male leisure terrain caused great excitement and considerable consternation throughout the Maritimes. The ensuing tour brought into sharp relief the question of the relationship of the sexes, the prevailing notions of respectable behaviour, and the ways in which baseball served to delineate and shape existing definitions of masculinity and femininity.[1]

It is hardly a novel insight to point out that the development of baseball, like other forms of organized team sport, was a gendered process. Yet most accounts of baseball have taken its masculine character for granted, seemingly satisfied that the game had little to do with the female sex. In fact, the general exclusion of women from organized sporting activity – except as spectators who were thought of as a civilizing force, restraining rowdyism and thereby consolidating notions of respectable masculinity – should alert us to the centrality of the gender question to the making of the nineteenth-century leisure world. It also invites inquiry into the relationship between leisure activity and work. Sonya Rose has demonstrated the many ways in which gender differentiation was connected to the production and reproduction of the emerging industrial-capitalist order, noting at the same time that the engendering of the labour process was only one aspect, albeit a vital one, of the 'cultural process distinguishing females and males in all social relations.'[2] Indeed, although the separation of leisure and work accelerated with the emergence of modern industrial capitalism, the relationship between work, leisure, and capitalism was a symbiotic one in which common class and gender issues can be perceived. This symbiosis deepened, moreover, as leisure itself increasingly fell under the disciplining influence of the capitalist market-place, where play was reconstituted as work, and games were presented as commodities to be purchased and consumed.

This chapter addresses three separate yet related issues pertaining to the laying down of baseball's gendered baselines. In the first place, it deals with the relegation of women to the role of the spectator – to that of a consumer rather than producer of sporting entertainment – and the concomitant use of an idealized image of the 'lady' spectator, an ideological construct that served at once to constrain class rowdiness and promote a conformist definition of respectable behaviour that transcended class lines. Related to this is the way in which the differentiated gender roles in baseball, and in other sports, were part of the broader social construction of masculinity and femininity, at once shaping and shaped by a set of discursive relations involving human biology and psychology, which drew upon ideologically constructed images of both the body natural and body politic. And finally, by concentrating upon the Blackstockings' tour – and that of other women's teams at the end of the nineteenth century – it is possible to show how the development of baseball as a marketable product resulted in the commercialization and marketing of women as spectacle. This process contributed in turn to the consolidation of gender and class hierarchies, the exploitation of women baseball 'workers,' and a reaffirmation of notions of male hardiness and female frailty.

Although women had been playing baseball in the United States since the early 1860s, their involvement in the sport was largely confined to spectatorism. Despite the interest of both moral reformers and sport entepreneurs in attracting women to baseball in order to enhance its respectability and profitability, however, women made up only a minor part of the nineteenth-century baseball audience. Ironically, during the

1850s and 1860s, when baseball was still a fraternal, club-based, recreational sport for young men of the advancing middle class, women often
attended the matches, dinners, dances, and other social functions that
were associated with the game. But female patronage declined as baseball became increasingly popular with workingmen. 'When photographs
of the crowd show men in caps more numerous than men in hats,'
Allen Guttmann observes, 'few women are to be seen.'[3] Middle-class
women apparently feared damage to their reputations if they patronized
a sport associated with gambling, alcoholism, tobacco-chewing, and
other disreputable forms of behaviour.

One might have expected young working-class women to respond to
the growing interest in the game evinced by their brothers, boyfriends,
and fathers, but they did not flood the parks either. Not only did many
young girls have domestic responsibilities that left them little time for
leisure, but as Kathy Peiss has pointed out, leisure was experienced in
different ways by men and women of working-class backgrounds. For
workingmen, who asserted their independence from their employers in
the public space of the saloon, lodge, or ball diamond, control over their
own leisure time involved not only resistance against capitalist control,
'but a system of male privilege in which workers' self-determination,
solidarity, and mutual assistance were understood as "manliness".' The
leisure activities of nineteenth-century women, by contrast, tended to be
segregated from the public realm and remained 'sinuously intertwined
with the rhythms of household labor and the relations of kinship.' As
the nineteenth century drew to a close, however, womens' leisure
patterns were beginning to change. Employed more frequently as wage-
earners outside the home, young women came to regard organized
leisure as a distinct realm of activity to which they could demand
access. Yet young women's pursuit of pleasure led them not to the
traditional leisure domain of workingmen, but to the new commercialized forms of recreation, such as dancehalls, amusement parks, excursion boats, and vaudeville theatres.[4]

Baseball promoters none the less took pains to encourage female
attendance in order to counteract baseball's reputation for attracting
'drunken rowdies, unwashed loafers, and arrant blacklegs.'[5] Women in
the stands, it was hoped, would have a civilizing effect. The 'presence
of an assemblage of ladies purifies the moral atmosphere of a baseball
gathering,' said an article in the *Baseball Chronicle*, 'repressing as it does,
all the outburst of intemperate language which the excitement of a
contest so frequently induces.'[6] Warren Goldstein has pointed out that

there was always a tension in baseball between the notion of manly self-control and the excitement that the game produced, and because rules-makers and promoters of the game alike recognized that the players and audiences might lose control in the heat of the fray, women were regarded as 'agents of control' whose presence restrained 'potentially unregulated passion.'

Baseball clubs tried to attract women in a number of different ways. The provision of grandstand seating separated women from the unruli-ness of the crowds that stood along the foul lines, where a rope barrier was often the only thing restraining the crowd from spilling onto the field. Most clubs admitted women to the grandstand free of charge, so long as they had a male escort. The cost of purchasing a grandstand ticket also meant that those in close proximity to women spectators would likely be less inclined to offensive behaviour than the general ticket holder. The press also encouraged the attendance of women, and often criticized the foul language and smoking habits of male patrons as offensive to women spectators. Indeed, the impulse towards genteel behaviour that had led to the disciplining of theatrical audiences was evident at the ballpark, where promoters, reformers, and journalists found the idealized notion of the 'lady-like' spectator a useful ideologi-cal construct in their struggle against 'rowdyism.'

One of the most successful inducements to female attendance was ladies' day; not only were women admitted to the park free, but also in coming to the park a woman would likely find a number of her sisters in attendance. Most semi-pro teams routinely admitted women without charge. At the professional level, where a number of games were played weekly, ladies' days were usually restricted to one or two days per week. Club owners often came up with additional incentives to ensure a good turn-out on ladies' day. In Minneapolis, women were not only admitted to the grounds free, but had the privilege of being included in a group photograph of the patrons of the grandstand, and subsequently receiving a copy from the management.[7] By the end of the century, in fact, regularly scheduled ladies' days had become so effec-tive in attracting female spectators that they had begun to outlive their usefulness. In Pittsburgh, where for years Tuesdays and Fridays had been ladies' days at the park, male patrons complained bitterly that women were crowding into the grandstands and taking the best seats even though they paid no admission. 'There is no doubt but that the ladies have abused our kindness at the park in years past,' said Presi-dent Kerr of the Pittsburgh club at the beginning of the 1896 baseball season. There were almost a thousand of them in the grand stand every Tuesday and Friday last season, and they, of course, took the best seats ... When a man pays 75 cents ... he wants a good seat.'[8]

Whatever the merits of this case, by the time of the Chicago women's team tour of the Maritimes during the summer of 1891 the role of women within baseball had been firmly established. Women were spectators rather than players, and as such were expected to serve as agents of respectability and control. When women played the game, they contradicted the image of feminine decorum that promoters and social reformers employed for their own purposes. Even worse was playing the game for money, which placed women baseballists on the same level as bawdy theatrical performers, or even prostitutes, willing to barter their femininity for filty lucre. As women barnstorming teams toured the country, the press routinely referred to women ballplayers as 'Amazons,' 'freaks,' or 'frauds,' while at the ballpark women players had to put up with verbal and physical assaults that belittled and degraded them.

The Chicago team, known as the Blackstockings, was the brainchild of W.S. Franklin, a rather unsavoury New York speculator and dramatic agent who had been involved in women's baseball since 1879 and considered himself – in something of an exaggeration – to be 'the father, founder and originator of baseball playing by young ladies in America.'[9] In August 1890 Franklin had advertised in the New York *Clipper* for fifty girls, 'young, not over 20, good looking and good figure,' to stock a female baseball league of four to six clubs. Applicants from outside of New York who were unable to appear in person were asked to send a photograph with their application. The successful girls were promised a salary of five to fifteen dollars a week plus expenses, plus an extended engagement to travel. Franklin's Dramatic Agency at 1162 Broadway was immediately besieged with interested candidates, and scores of letters flowed in from across the country. Five clubs were organized for the 1891 season, representing Chicago, Cincinnati, Boston, New York, and Philadelphia, but by the end of that summer only three remained. One of those was on tour in Massachusetts, another headed west to California, and the third came north to Maine and the Maritimes.[10]

In establishing his teams, Franklin was keenly aware of the objections that were usually raised against women on the sporting diamond, and he took steps to assure the public that the exhibitions were 'free from all objectionable features.'[11] Club rules strictly regulated conduct, and

provided hefty fines for breaches of etiquette. Any quarrelling or de-
monstrative complaints while travelling, or about the quality of hotel
rooms, would result in a twenty-five-cent fine for each offence. No team
member would be allowed to enter, either day or night, any saloon or
bar where intoxicating drinks were sold, or face a fifty-cent to one-
dollar fine. 'Flirting,' 'mashing,' or making the acquaintance of men on
trains or steamboats, in depots or hotels, 'or permitting the least famil-
iarity,' carried a fine of twenty-five cents to a dollar depending on the
seriousness of the incident, and hotel clerks were instructed not to
forward notes to the girls from 'dudes' or would-be seducers.

If Franklin had had his way, the girls would have had little time for
'mashing,' lounging around bar-rooms, or loafing in hotel offices. Franklin wanted his girls to learn lacrosse, polo, bicycle riding, and fencing,
how to play the cornet and trombone, beat a snare drum, and play the
fife, so that they could parade before the game and attract more paying
customers. In fact the procession to the ballpark was often as entertain-
ing as the game itself. Outfitted in red and black striped jockey caps,
light-coloured flannel blouses, red and black striped dresses reaching to
the knees, and black stockings, the Chicago girls would march to the
park, often accompanied by the town band. In Halifax, for example, the
girls drove through the city in open carriages, attired in their uniforms,
carrying banners and flags, and headed by a brass band.[12] Playing for
a club such as this, the Saint John *Progress* concluded, was 'a grand
opening for girls who are "quick to learn", and have mastered the art
of never getting past twenty years of age.'[13]

Although women's baseball was relatively new to the Maritimes,[14]
women had been playing the game for some time in the United States,
where their participation usually met with formidable opposition.
Moralistic denunciations from the clergy, prevailing notions of biology
that emphasized woman's nurturing character and physical frailty,
genteel assumptions about the feminine personality, and an idealized
notion of the family that identified the young girl as 'the quintessential
angel in the house,' all combined to discourage participation in competitive sports.[15] When women did play, they usually did so 'only within
limited behavioural boundaries which confirmed the separate spheres
of the sexes and the superiority of men.'[16]

The medical profession provided a powerful biological rationale for
restricting women's activity in sport. Contemporary medical wisdom
suggested that women's bodies were fundamentally unhealthy, placing
them at a distinct disadvantage when compared to or competing against

men. Wendy Mitchinson has argued that medical doctors regarded men's bodies as the biological norm; in those areas where womens' bodies deviated from mens' they were considered problematic. Fascinated by a woman's gynaecology, most practitioners saw women as prisoners of their reproductive systems, predisposed to weakness, ill health, and nervous disorders of various sorts.[17] Dr Andrew Halliday, of Stewiacke, Nova Scotia, for example, noted the importance of understanding 'the more weakly organized physical constitution of the female sex, and ... the important series of phenomena which occur at the period of puberty, when extra demands are being made on what is perhaps an already weak constitution and while ... a nerve storm is raging both in the cerebro-spinal and sympathetic systems.'[18] Given womens' physiological weakness and nervous instability, it followed that neither their bodies nor their minds should be placed under too great a strain. 'A woman who lived 'unphysiologically' – and she could do so by reading or studying in excess, by wearing improper clothing, by long hours of factory work, or by a sedentary, luxurious life,' threatened her own future well-being and that of her offspring.[19] Doctors thus counselled moderate forms of exercise for women, while popular magazines such as *Good Housekeeping*, *Ladies Home Journal*, *Woman's Home Companion*, and *Godey's Ladies Book* extolled the virtues of physical culture. Competitive sports such as baseball, however, were believed to be 'unnatural' activities that could have debilitating consequences.

The rhetorical emphasis on the declining health of nineteenth-century women was connected to notions of degeneracy and nervous depletion and to anxieties about the development of a highly industrialized and urban society. Although fears about declining vigour involved people of either sex, women were considered especially prone to debility. Worried that women were becoming less hardy than their grandmothers, especially those who had academic or intellectual aspirations, newspapers, magazines, and health manuals warned of the deleterious consequences of maternal weakness. Those who aspired to higher education were considered susceptible to all sorts of maladies, and in their desire to emulate men lost their sexual attractiveness and femininity. 'Very intellectual women,' the *Christian Guardian* suggested in 1872, 'are seldom beautiful; their features and particularly their foreheads, are more or less masculine.'[20] At the same time, hereditarians warned that because women had a special influence over heredity and the reproduction of the race, they were more likely than men to pass on any constitutional weakness, or diathesis, to their offspring. As a result, women's physical well-being became of increasing concern to those interested in combating degeneracy.[21]

Although most Victorians regarded competitive sport as inappropriate activity for those of the so-called weaker sex, women had begun to play baseball as early as the 1860s. In taking to the diamond, women challenged the prevailing myth of female weakness, an ubiquitous assumption in a society characterized by notions of male superiority. At the same time, however, new conceptions of female beauty that encouraged a growing attention to physical exercise were emerging in the context of national expansion and rapid industrialization. As Lois Banner has suggested, 'the post–Civil War years were a confusing period, when varying types of beauty vied with each other.' Although most nineteenth-century fashion magazines portrayed the ideal woman as thin and pale, a more buxom ideal emerged in the third quarter of the century, followed by a more athletic look in the 1890s and after 1900.[22]

The changing conception of the ideal body type was also related to the medical profession's struggle to assert its legitimacy and maintain professional influence in the face of challenges from its competitors. During the 1860s and early 1870s orthodox practitioners had begun to lose confidence in an earlier 'heroic' therapy, which depended upon brisk purgatives, the regulation of secretions through leeching or vene-section, and counter-irritant therapy such as blistering to reduce inflammation in engorged bodily organs. Increasingly sceptical of traditional drug therapy – the dosing of patients with cathartics (that is, purgatives, laxatives, or 'drastics'), expectorants such as iodine or the carbonate of ammonia, and anodynes or stimulants such as opium, codeia, chloral hydrate, and alcohol – the profession increasingly came to rely on the healing power of nature. The result was a new emphasis on a strong and healthy female form, suited to child-bearing. 'The vogue among medical men for supporting the ideal of plump and voluptuous women after the Civil War was, in part, an effort to regain control of women by devaluing their minds and re-emphasizing their bodies,' Patricia Vertinsky has argued. 'Large bosoms and swelling hips were extolled as a visual manifestation of woman's only purposeful role – maternity.'[23]

During the last quarter of the nineteenth century the emphasis on physical regeneration through appropriate exercise became a standard element in the therapeutic orientation of the orthodox medical profession. As doctors increasingly preached the virtues of physical culture they began to bridge the gap between medical orthodoxy and a larger health-reform movement that urged people to engage actively in their own physical purification through regular exercise and good eating habits. Like their counterparts in the Maritimes, American physicians prominent in the physical culture movement, such as Dan Sargeant, Edward Hitchcock, Dioclesian Lewis, Charles McIntyre, and William Anderson, stressed the need for exercise programs in the public schools to reduce mental strain, counteract the evils of sedentary work, and correct physical imperfections resulting from poor posture. To do nothing to counteract the physical weakness of many young schoolgirls, argued Dr Clara Olding of Saint John, was to place stress upon the bright young mind 'with a body physically incapable of sustaining it.' At the same time, however, most doctors remained committed to a dualistic vision of the sexual relation. Stressing the fundamental biological differences between women and men, doctors believed that physical training for women should be undertaken in such a way as to enhance the essential characteristics of womanhood – her domesticity, passivity, moral refinement, and nurturing nature.

Employers of female domestic and factory labour also began to question the virtue of feminine weakness. On the one hand, the belief in female frailty served to legitimize patriarchal dominance and promoted notions of passivity and feminine subservience; on the other, it impeded the employer in his desire for more efficient production. It was hard to idealize the weak and frail female, when her weakness meant absenteeism and unproductive work. Employers wanted healthy, yet docile, workers. 'Public opinion,' said the editor of the *Acadian Recorder* in August 1875, 'seems to be setting in favor of strong and healthy girls. Pale faces are not thought to be as interesting now-a-days as they used to be. A sneer goes round at the inefficiency of the women who work for a living and ask for good wages.'[24]

Attitudes towards womens' involvement in competitive sports such as baseball met with a similar ambivalence. Reflecting the growing acceptance of a more physically active womanhood in the post-bellum period, a newspaper editor from western New York in 1867 urged women to play ball, contending that baseball was 'worth twice as much as this insipid, Amanda-Arabella game called "Crow-K", which is nothing but a mighty poor kind of billiards on grass.'[25] More commonplace, however, were suggestions that baseball was a man's game, and that women were not suited to playing such a physical sport. 'A woman may be able to throw a rolling pin at the object of her undying affections with grace and accuracy, but she never can learn to throw a ball,' said one misogynistic student from Columbia University. 'Up shoots the arm, back bends the body; her toes dig convulsively in the ground, and then suddenly she shuts up like a jack-knife; while her arm, without bending a joint, flies over like the paddle-wheel of a mud-scow; and away the ball goes – about six or seven feet – in just the direction she had the least idea of throwing it.'

Women none the less threw baseballs, swung bats, and ran the bases. At Vassar College in Poughkeepsie, New York, founded in 1861 by wealthy brewer Matthew Vassar, women were playing baseball as early as 1866, just seven years after the first men's intercollegiate match between Amherst and Williams in June 1859.[26] Although he rejected the notion that female weakness was inherent in women, Vassar felt that the flower of feminine beauty 'too often blooms but palely for a languid or a suffering life, if not for an early tomb,' and advocated vigorous physical exercise for young women.[27] Women also played baseball at Smith College in Northampton and at Mount Holyoke in South Hadley, Massachusetts. That womens' colleges provided a setting in which young women could play baseball is understandable, given the controversial nature of women's involvement in higher education, and the likelihood that those women who enrolled in these colleges were more willing than most of their sex to confront the prevailing assumptions of a patriarchal society. Female colleges were important aspects of the women's rights movement, concerned not only with developing the intellectual capacities of women, but also with their right to develop and control their own bodies. As Kate McCrone has argued in her excellent study of sport at the Oxbridge women's colleges, early women athletes spearheaded a movement towards greater female autonomy and provided extremely valuable role models for other women. 'Every sphere of university life women penetrated, whether it was the lecture hall, the honours examinations or the sports field,' she writes, 'told in favour of opening up new spheres and conceding to women rights to personal and public liberty.'[28]

Yet, while women's colleges encouraged changing beliefs about appropriate activity for women, the importance of physical exercise, and the unhealthy character of restrictive dress, they did not mount a fundamental challenge against the sexual division of labour. Nor did they subvert conventional concepts of femininity and well-entrenched notions of ladylike behaviour. Instead, most of these colleges attempted to turn out '"refined" ladies of leisure.'[29] At Mount Allison University in Sackville, New Brunswick, the first institution to grant a bachelor's degree to a woman in the entire British Empire, tension between the academic and 'ornamental' traditions in women's education remained largely unresolved before the First World War.[30] Although the college continued to emphasize the need for a rigorous academic education for women, many of those well-to-do Maritimers who sent their daughters to Mount Allison regarded it as a finishing school. Most would have agreed with David Allison, an early president of the college, that 'any woman's best and highest sphere [was in] ... aiding some good, honest, faithful man in discharging the duties of life.'[31]

The involvement of women in physical education on campus, which touched upon deeper uncertainties about the relationship between the sexes, also took place amidst a debate about the impact of higher education on the nervous systems of men and women alike. It was commonly understood that the individual's vital life force, both physical and intellectual, was limited, and that excessive indulgence in either physical – including sexual – or intellectual activity would result in enfeeblement of the body or mind.[32] In a speech in Saint John in 1882, for example, the Hon. John Boyd (MP) criticized the competitive, high-pressure educational system that 'shattered or partially destroyed the health of so many young men and women.'[33] Advocates of the theory of vitalism attacked the overstimulation of the intellectual capacities of young children, of working people whose 'dull' minds supposedly limited their capacity to think deeply, and, of course, of women, who were regarded to have a fragile nervous system that could not withstand the demands of intellectual development. In these cases, said one turn-of-the-century alienist, the attempt to broaden the mind beyond its limits of expansion was 'far too often, a direct offence to physiological law.'[34]

Edward H. Clarke's *Sex in Education or a Fair Chance for the Girls* (1873) drew heavily upon vitalism in its attack on higher education for women. Clarke was convinced that an educational system that treated men and women equally was responsible for the 'grievous maladies' of womanhood, sapping her vitality, taxing her delicate nervous system, and creating 'crowds of pale, bloodless female faces, that suggest consumption, scrofula, anemeia, and neuralgia.' The 'female organization,' Clarke argued, predisposed women to the bearing and raising of children. An overemphasis on education placed a great physiological burden on the constitution of the female, whose natural role was that of procreation. Women were endowed with a set of reproductive organs 'whose complexity, delicacy, sympathies, and force are among the marvels of creation.' If those organs were properly cared for, they would be the source of strength, but if neglected would 'retaliate upon their possessor with weakness and disease, as well of the mind as of the body.' The contemporary fascination with women's education, Clarke believed, meant neglect of 'the temple God built for her,' and explained why in the nineteenth century each succeeding generation had become feebler than its predecessor.[35]

In order to clinch his point, Clarke drew upon a comparison between New England and Nova Scotian girls offered by a recent traveller to the Maritime provinces. Clarke's anonymous female commentator provided a highly romanticized account of an idyllic Nova Scotian world, whose people lived close to nature and remained unspoiled by the demands of excessive education. In the town of Wolfville, 'just beyond the meadows of the Grand Pré, where lived Gabriel Lajeunesse, and Benedict Bellefontaine, and the rest of the "simple Acadian farmers,"' she came upon a Sunday School whose services had just ended. Thirty or forty boys and girls emerged, all with 'fair skins, red cheeks, and clear eyes; ... all broad-shouldered, straight and sturdy.' She was struck not only by the robust healthiness of the children but of their parents, who 'were broad-shouldered, tall, and straight, *especially the women.*' In Halifax, during the celebration of the anniversary of the Province, Clarke's traveller saw a similar sight: hundreds of children marched in the day's parades, but she counted 'just eleven sickly children.' She attributed the difference between the blooming youth of Nova Scotia and the unnatural weakness and premature decay of young girls in New England to the fact that until recently 'there have been in Nova Scotia no public schools, comparatively few private ones; and in these there is no severe pressure brought to bear on the pupils.'[36]

Ironically, women's college administrators and students were able to use Clarke's arguments to their advantage, emphasizing the necessity for physical recreation and sport as an antidote to mental strain and female weakness. Everywhere, advocates of physical education used the critique of women's mental frailty to legitimize entry into a sporting terrain that was regarded as a male preserve. For example, Dr Grace Ritchie, a well-known Halifax feminist, spoke at the annual conference of the National Women of Canada in 1895, and made an earnest plea for physical training for young women. Ritchie noted the increased strain that accompanied the cultivation of the female intellect. 'Their nervous systems are apt to be overworked,' she said, 'and we must counteract this. The best way ... is by giving them healthy exercise in some form or another.'[37]

These arguments were directed more to young college students, however, than to the young women who played for the Chicago Black-stockings, most of whom were working-class girls still in their teens who had left home to find employment. Unlike college women, who played in the protected preserve of the campus and outside of the derisive gaze of male spectators, the lady barnstormers challenged the gender apartheid of nineteenth-century sporting culture without any elaborate intellectual defence. As would be the case with black barnstorming teams in the twentieth century, these women's teams were tolerated because of their 'novelty' or 'entertainment' value rather than from a sense of the legitimacy of their involvement in a more egalitarian social order. They were also subject to ridicule and abuse. Nevertheless, by pressing into a field of activity that had been closed to them, even if they could not escape the indignities, exploitation, and stereotyping that accompanied their involvement, women and black baseball players – like others of their race and gender in the emerging entertainment industry – resisted those who would deny their full humanity.

The earliest barnstorming teams were organized in June 1879 as a money-making speculation by theatrical agents W.F. Franklin of New York and William J. Gilmore of Philadelphia. The Reds, who hailed from and represented New York, and the Blues from Philadelphia first played in public on 4 July in Oakdale Park, Pennsylvania. After that they left on an eastern tour through Maryland, Massachussetts, and New Hampshire. The tour started out splendidly, to the delight of both the promoters and the players. On 7 and 8 July they played a two-game series in Baltimore and amassed gate receipts of $1450. Games followed in Boston, Lowell, and Manchester, New Hampshire, and the New York *Clipper* reported that the women 'conducted themselves in an unexceptionable manner on and off the ball-field.'[38] Then things went awry. On 5 August, after an exhibition game in Worcester, one of the managers absconded with the team's funds, leaving the players penniless.

Within two weeks the teams were reorganized, and the women began a western road trip through Ohio and Kentucky. This tour was even more disastrous than the previous one. At Louisville, on 25 August, they played before a noisy and boisterous crowd that insulted and pelted them with stones when they tried to leave the ground. A couple of days later a number of the girls were arrested in Cincinnati. As a result, when the women arrived in Springfield, Ohio, there were only eleven players available to play. Trouble soon arose between a group that the *Clipper* described as 'hoodlums' and 'some negroes,' apparently because the black spectators had yelled insults at the women, a privilege presumably restricted to whites. 'Hot words led to blows, and the upshot was that one of the negroes was fatally wounded by being hit on the head with a piece of board.' After the game, the team manager took the gate receipts of $250, and left for Columbus for the ostensible purpose of arranging a game there. The girls, who were already ticketed, followed by train, but upon reaching the city they found that the manager had once again left them high and dry.[39] They would not play again that season, nor in the following year.

After another brief and unsuccessful effort in 1881, Franklin tried to resuscitate the experiment during the 1883 season. The Reds and the Blues, now also known as the Blondes and the Brunettes, were revived, with Harry H. Freeman and W.F. Phillips as team managers. (Phillips would later manage the Chicago Blackstockings and accompany them on their tour of the Maritimes.) Once more the teams faced frequent insults and legal difficulties. After a game in Pittsburgh against the Alleghany club, Freeman and Phillips were arrested and subsequently released on payment of a licence and costs. Freeman, it would appear, was frequently in trouble with the law. Reports circulated that he recruited his women not only as ballplayers, but also as prostitutes. After several complaints that he had convinced young girls to run away from home against their parents' wishes, Freeman was eventually arraigned in May 1886 as a 'dangerous and suspicious character.'[40] Similar claims were made about Sylvester F. Wilson, a one-time backer of the Reds, described in the press as 'female baseball manager, ticket scalper, all-around swindler, and professional debaucher of female morals.' In October 1891 Wilson was convicted, sentenced to a five-year term at Sing Sing prison, and fined $1000 for having abducted Libbie Sutherland, who played on one of his female clubs.[41]

Part of the problem that the women faced while on tour was that they were amateurish players, assembled merely as a speculative venture that would attract fans because of the novelty of their participation. In addition to the insults that came their way as a result of their 'unladylike' behaviour, they were ridiculed for their inept play. After a game at the grounds of the Manhattan Athletic Club that attracted about a thousand spectators, the New York *Clipper* observed that 'there were just four of the eighteen who could handle the ball at all, and but one of these four was even approaching expertness.' Newspaper reports from city after city echoed these sentiments. Finally, the reputation of their poor – some might even say fraudulent – performances caught up with the clubs in the middle of a southern tour. At the end of November they were stranded and out of money in St Louis. The experiment 'deserved no better fate,' said the *Clipper*. 'It was from the first nothing but a sensation.'

In early December thirteen of the girls, the oldest of whom was only seventeen, had made it to Chicago, where they hoped to raise enough money to be sent home, but a benefit on their behalf raised only thirty-five dollars. At this point the *Clipper* interviewed Miss Temple, the pitcher of the 'Reds.' She was asked:

Are any of them tired of the fun?

Yes, I guess they are; I know I am.

You don't mind it, do you, in warm weather, when you are in good luck?'

Oh, no. It's all right then, but we made a mistake in starting out on this last trip. It was too late in the season.

Do any of the girls ever get their teeth knocked out or anything during the progress of a game?

No, we don't throw as hard as the men do, and if a ball comes too fast for us we look out for No. 1 and dodge it you know.

Where did the girls of the company come from? Were any of them ever on the stage?

They're mostly from Philadelphia. Only two of them have ever been on the stage – one as Topsy and the other as Eva in a juvenile 'Uncle Tom' party a year or two ago. The rest are working-girls and school-girls who like the fun and the travel.

Harold Seymour believed that the girls were mostly normal-school or Sunday-school graduates, seeking to emulate their Ivy League counterparts, but this benign characterization hardly conforms with Miss Temple's description of her teammates.[42]

The 1891 tour of the Chicago Blackstockings was much better organized than those of earlier years, and perhaps because of this the players avoided some of the violence, theft, and exploitation that had surrounded the previous ventures. Better equipped than before, the team carried with it a 300-foot canvas fence that could be erected on any suitable field if they were denied access to regular club grounds. In addition, though they were by no means adroit players, the women were athletic and enthusiastic, and unlike earlier tours when they played mainly against a rival women's team, they now competed against community men's teams. William Burtnett, the team's advance agent, described the women as excellent players, with a 'fast pitcher, dandy batters and quick fielders and baserunners,' and suggested that they were the equal of the best amateur teams in the country.[43]

The reality was somewhat different. After the first game in Fredericton, a reporter noted that 'while the girls were more agile than might have been expected,' they were really not proficient players. Most people were disappointed with what they saw, especially after Burtnett's pre-game hype. When May Howard, the team's catcher and captain, came to the plate, the *Daily Gleaner* reported, the crowd was 'breathless' with anticipation. The Fredericton pitcher opened the game with a couple of swift curveballs, but immediately 'the truth flashed across every mind when she offered faintly at two or three and finally struck out ... [The girls] could not bat, catch, throw or pitch.' In particular, their pitcher had great difficulty finding the plate, and the centre fielder 'had to make two or three throws in order to get the ball to second base.'[44]

This was a common refrain as the tour continued. The Saint John *Progress* called the Blackstockings team a 'grand fake,' adding sarcastically that 'there were two frisky members ... that could actually pick up a ball from the ground.'[45] After a game in Moncton, played in a downpour, the local *Transcript* found them 'quite active, and with fine weather their attempts to bat, field and throw balls and run bases, in all of which they show amusing awkwardness, would be interesting.' A report of a game in Amherst between the Amherstians and Amazons, in the Halifax *Morning Herald*, observed that the locals 'treated them gallantly and took no undue advantages either by a large display of science or in indulging in the usual wordy rows that generally characterize baseball matches.' Still, the town had been excited by their visit. After the game, a jovial crowd, including a 'large number of ladies' who 'were bound to have a look at the departing girls base ball players,' accompanied the girls to the Amherst railway station. It was generally felt, said one newspaper report, 'that a large number of our citizens would go to see them play again, and there was just a whisper that they will probably come again.'[46]

As the Blackstockings' tour continued, considerable opposition to their visit developed. The Truro *Daily News* reported that a clergyman in New Glasgow had spoken strongly against the tour at a local prayer meeting, while in Truro a delegation of citizens unsuccessfully lobbied the mayor to prevent the team from playing.[47] On the day of the game, the Truro newspaper noted that 'many people, doubtless, will be there to witness the antics of the girls, but if all reports be true, the propriety of attending is very questionable.'[48] After the games in Truro and New Glasgow, the local press criticized the women as frauds who could not compete on equal terms with men although they presumed to do so.[49] 'They are nothing better than a lot of hoodlums from a crowded city,' said the New Glasgow *Eastern Chronicle*, 'and any boys from 10–14 years of age could knock them out, throw them out, or catch them out every day of the week. They are frauds of the first water.'[50]

The Blackstockings received mixed reviews in the three largest cities in the Maritimes. In both Moncton and Saint John the women were refused access to the local amateur athletic association grounds. As a result, no game was played in Saint John; in Moncton the girls had to erect their portable canvas fence for the game. After the match in Moncton, however, the local *Transcript* announced the intention of local officials to invite the women to play another match in the city on their return trip from Nova Scotia. In Halifax there was considerable support for the girls. The game was such a topic of conversation in the week or so before their arrival that an overflow crowd was expected, and when Herbert Harris of the Law and Order League petitioned the mayor of Halifax to prevent the girls from playing on moral grounds, James Pender, manager of the Socials, denounced this as an attack on the respectability of all 'gentlemanly' baseball players in the city. He observed that the managers and players 'have reputations to sustain and they look upon the petition as an insult.' Pender and the manager of the Mutuals had made the arrangements to bring the Blackstockings to Halifax, and they did so believing baseball to be 'just as modest and pretty a recreation or sport as lawn tennis, or cricket; all of which are played by respectable ladies.' They also felt that 'nobody has either right or reason to object to those young ladies playing here until they have seen or heard something detrimental to their character.'[51]

Before the game in Halifax, the *Acadian Recorder* predicted that the novelty of seeing the young women play baseball would attract an immense crowd.[52] On game day over three thousand people jammed the Wanderers' Grounds in Halifax. Outside the park young boys scaled electric-light poles and trees to get a look at the game, and a large crowd of men and women congregated on Citadel Hill overlooking the grounds as well. A full half-hour before the match, the entire 550-seat grandstand, including 'more than the usual number of ladies present for an outdoor event,' had been completely sold out. The *Morning Herald* noted that many in attendance were witnessing baseball for the first time, having heard of the 'technicalities of the great American game' without ever attending a match. 'Old and young, rich and poor, bald heads and well-covered craniums – all were represented.' In addition, many women in the audience seem to have considered this a perfect opportunity to introduce themselves to the sport. 'The game is spoken of as being too exciting and accompanied with some rough play and a little danger. When one of the teams was composed of ladies there could be no fear of those disagreeable episodes.'[53]

As usual, the game itself was disappointing. The Halifax team had great trouble to keep from scoring runs and had to give what assistance they could to their opponents in order to keep the score close. 'The girls are not baseball players,' said the *Morning Herald*. 'Their battery was "girlish", and their fielding was just good enough to stop the balls which the gentle batting of the men treated them to; running was the best of their play.'[54] The *Acadian Recorder* observed that the spectators were not long in becoming tired, and were disappointed when they observed that many of the girls were young and small, an appearance that was emphasized by their short skirts. At the same time, 'there was nothing indecorous in their conduct, and the crowd contented themselves with loudly applauding the few long hits by members of the visiting team, and two catches of foul flies by the backstop.' The game was called after two hours, with the score 18 to 15 in favour of the women, although under the circumstances the result had little meaning.[55]

In retrospect, the Blackstockings' tour revealed the serious constraints that women laboured under in trying to legitimize their involvement in what was considered a 'manly' sport. Many of the young women who signed on to play were no doubt attracted by the prospect of seeing the country and having fun, while some may have taken the opportunity to escape unfortunate circumstances at home. Nevertheless, the conditions that they worked under were both difficult and demeaning and the price they paid for their involvement was high. At the mercy of employers who demanded their obedience and docility, and of unscrupulous managers who sometimes preyed upon them, touring women's teams were always one step away from abandonment and even imprisonment. If the advance agents reneged on paying field rent or licence fees, the women might find their belongings seized, leaving them with only the clothes they had on their backs.[56] If their managers ordered them to play on Sundays in violation of the local by-laws, they faced the prospect of legal action.

On the field the women had to contend with the hoots of derision from male spectators and the prospect of violence and physical assault or being accosted by unwanted 'admirers' at the end of the match. Just defending themselves from such advances risked further abuse. The *Acadian Recorder* reported an incident of this sort in Halifax. When the women returned to their hotel after attending a performance at the Lyceum theatre, a number of 'young lads' were waiting for them on the street and blocked their way. Apparently they were angry about an incident at the theatre, in which a young man about eighteen had caught hold of one of the girls by the hair. She had advised him to stop, but when he refused, she struck him on the face and he fell to the floor. Their masculine pride seemingly injured, the group proceeded to make known their feelings about the 'unladylike' character of the girls.[57]

The assumption that women who played baseball could not be 'ladies' dogged the girls throughout their travels. President Byrne of the Brooklyn baseball club, for example, called the womens' teams 'a disgrace to baseball.' Byrne refused to lease his grounds for 'such a disgusting exhibition,' and called upon all other managers to follow his example.[58] Just as often it was other women who objected to the female baseballists. In Freeport, New York, for example, the women of the town, upon hearing of a proposed match, 'rallied in righteous wrath and let their husbands know that attendance at the game would constitute grounds for divorce.'[59]

Critics of women in sport argued that involvement in 'manly' pursuits undermined femininity and created a more masculine womanhood. Helen Lenskyj has observed recently that over the past century of women's participation in organized sport, 'femininity and heterosexuality have been seen as incompatible with sporting excellence: either sport made women masculine, or sportswomen were masculine at the outset.'[60] Nineteenth-century degeneracy theorists such as R. von Krafft-Ebing believed that involvement in competitive sporting activity revealed the atavistic character of those women who participated and, furthermore, that the preference for playing masculine sports was a symptom of lesbianism. Opposition to women's involvement in competitive sport on these grounds suggested a fear of the potential anarchy of uncontrolled female sexuality.[61] Indeed, for women to attack the bastions of male sport was to bring into question all of the assumptions of women's passivity and sexual passionlessness that Victorian moralists had erected into the 'archetype of human morality.'[62] If women were to compete as men, what impact would this have on the 'natural' evolution of 'true womanhood?' Cesare Lombroso had distinguished modern women from 'savage peoples' by their attention to those maternal functions that 'neutralize her moral and physical inferiority.' In modern society, he believed, lofty sentiments accompanied motherhood, pity replaced cruelty, and maternal love counteracted sexual passionlessness. Would women competing with men not mean an end to womankind's nurturing sensibilities and 'a desire for license, idleness, and indecency?' Would not a rejection of her traditional maternal role lead to the degeneration of the race?[63]

The fact that the women who toured the Maritimes, like other barnstorming female clubs, could not compete on equal terms with competitive men's teams meant that the challenge to masculine authority was not as threatening to men as it might have been. Had they been more proficient athletes it is likely that they would have been regarded as women who were traitors to their sex, aggressive, unfeminine, obtrusive, and dangerous radicals thrusting themselves into activity that they had no right to enter. However, their inability to play well – understandable as it may have been considering their young age and their limited experience in the game – made them appear as frauds and subjected them to uncommon abuse. When the American Female Baseball Club visited Cuba in the spring of 1893 a crowd in Alamendares became so upset at having paid to see women who could not play ball that they attempted to attack the players. 'Horrible confusion ensued,' said the *Sporting News*, 'and the shrieks of the frightened young women could be heard mingled with the execrations of the mob.' The players, including the men of the Cuban club, took refuge in a house, but the mob pursued them, obtained entrance, and pillaged the residence. Only the valiant efforts of the Cuban players and the quick arrival of the police saved the girls from being more seriously hurt.[64]

Notwithstanding their limitations as ballplayers, and the controversy surrounding their involvement in such a 'manly' sport, the Chicago team's tour of the Maritimes provided an important impetus to the organization of women's baseball teams throughout the region. Women played baseball in several urban communities in the Maritimes and New England before 1900, and even in smaller communities such as Bocabec, Chatham, and Newcastle in New Brunswick and Oxford, Nova Scotia, teams of women baseballists risked the wrath of the churches as they pushed into a formerly male sporting domain. In addition to baseball, the 1890s witnessed the involvement of women in several new forms of leisure activity, from competitive swimming to cycling and even ice hockey. In Prince Edward Island married women took the ice against single women in 1893. The Alpha hockey club of Charlottetown, formed in 1895, was perhaps the finest women's team of the day. The Alphas also organized a baseball club in 1905.[65] After the turn of the century, women's ice hockey gained a foothold in the colleges, and teams like the Kanenites of New Glasgow gained a reputation for aggressive and skilful play.

Nothing contributed more to the growing physical emancipation of women than the cycling craze of the mid-nineties. The development of a bicycle safe enough for female use, was an important catalyst of social change. Middle- and working-class women alike turned to the bicycle as a form of physical exercise, but also as an instrument of liberation from the constraints of Victorianism. Cycling affected courtship patterns, dress and fashion, and attitudes towards women's physical development, and contributed to new systems of credit, advertising, and consumption.[66] Some critics worried that the bicycle offered young girls too much freedom in their courtship practices, and others that riding created sexual excitement and 'a distinct orgasm in women.'[67] Cycling was also believed to be the source of a number of maladies, including bicycle 'hump,' 'arm' and 'knee,' and some believed that it could lead to insanity.[68]

All of these fears reflected the concern that by proceeding beyond her 'proper sphere' a woman faced a number of disabling consequences to her femininity.[69] In her study of women and sport in the Maritimes, Michael Smith has argued that the development of more aggressive feminine sporting activity at the turn of the century raised fears that competitive sports and strenuous exercise programs were exerting a masculinizing effect on those women who participated in them. Advocates of sport and exercise for women cautioned against immoderation in physical activity, and feminized rules in sports such as basketball and ice hockey in order to curb destructive competition. 'Fearful of the "masculinizing" tendencies of the manly sports and concerned that the "new women" threatened the stability of the existing order,' Smith writes, 'male and female reformers worked to develop a feminine sporting tradition distinct from that of male athletics.'[70]

Those occasions on which women and men competed against each other were infrequent, and often popular because of their novelty. In 1905, the Boston Bloomer Girls, a barnstorming baseball team that had begun operations in 1897 and had toured all across the United States from Maine to California, took a swing through the Maritimes. The star of the club was Maud Nelson, a twenty-four-year-old pitcher and third baseman, and fine all-around ball-player, who was a dominant figure in women's baseball and softball until the Second World War. As with many of the touring teams after the turn of the century, the Bloomer Girls' roster, though made up mostly of women, was supplemented by two or three men known as 'toppers' who occasionally wore wigs and skirts in order to pass as women. Most often the teams carried a male catcher, infielder, and outfielder. Sometimes playing under assumed names, the male players were usually first-rate athletes: indeed, eventual Hall of Famers Rogers Hornsby and Smokey Joe Wood both toured with Bloomer Girls teams at the beginning of their careers.

As the First World War approached, women were becoming increasingly active in team sports such as baseball, but they were none the less urged to compete amongst themselves and in such a way as to keep their athletic prowess within the bounds of feminine propriety. Accordingly, in June 1910, when the Halifax *Morning Herald* encouraged girls to play ball and not allow their brothers to monopolize the game, it could not help but note that 'bloomers and gym jackets make dandy suits for the diamond – and the boys may be requested to remain away.'[71] As women took a prominent role in organizing the home front during the First World War, however, criticism of their involvement diminished and prevailing notions of female frailty came under assault. 'For tens of centuries man had pictured woman as a lovely, but inferior being whose glory was merely the reflection of his own superior light,' wrote F.M. Bell in *A Romance of the Halifax Disaster*, published in 1918. 'And then came the war, and ... she rose to her full height ... In the brighter light ... she towered above him, a new idol, a new ideal, the woman who could work as well as play, who could fight as well as love, who could be silent under sorrow and cheerful in the face of tragedy.' Yet if this realization made it less difficult for women to engage in athletic endeavours, women would continue to face considerable opposition in their struggle for physical emancipation.

As more women played the game after the war, some became proficient enough to compete with and now and then play for competitive men's teams, while others joined various Bloomer Girls aggregations. One of these was Edna Lockhart, from Avonport, Nova Scotia, a fine all-around athlete who starred in basketball, softball, swimming, and bowling, and played for two years with Margaret R. Nabel's New York Bloomer Girls as a pitcher and third baseman in the mid-1930s.[72] Another was Elizabeth 'Lizzie' Murphy, a Rhode Island native who was 'known as the "Queen of Baseball" throughout New England and eastern Canada' during the interwar years.[73] A slick-fielding and hard-hitting first baseman who once played for a New England All Star team in a match with the Boston Red Sox, Murphy toured the postwar Maritimes as a member of Ed Carr's Auburn All-Stars, a team made up mostly of college and semi-pro players from the Boston area.

What is most striking, however, is that despite the attempts of women to breach the male monopoly over competitive baseball, the game remained essentially a masculine sport. Although it became increasingly acceptable for women to play the game as the force of Victorian moralism weakened during the twenties and thirties, it was assumed that only the unusual woman would be able to do so with proficiency. Indeed, this was one of the ironies of teams such as the Chicago Blackstockings that challenged baseball's gender divide. In their attempt to penetrate what was regarded as a male leisure space, these women also helped confirm and reinforce notions of masculine superiority. Subject to exploitation by their employers who sought to extract a profit from their performances, off the field they submitted to a series of regulations that required them to behave like 'ladies.' In addition, because the early promoters were more interested in profit than in quality of performance, stereotypes of the physically untalented and awkward female athlete continued to abound. Even in the postwar years, as a new and more physically athletic feminine ideal began to emerge, women were regarded as inferior to their male counterparts. Cast in the role of spectator or cheerleader, where they could offer support to the more 'productive' male, women at the ballpark were expected to replicate their role at home, providing sustenance and support to the male provider. At the same time, young boys participated freely in a game that most people believed moulded masculine character and turned youth into men.

6

A Manly Sport: Baseball and the Social Construction of Masculinity

'Baseball is a red-blooded sport for red-blooded men,' observed the immortal Ty Cobb. 'It's no pink tea, and mollycoddles had better stay out. It's ... a struggle for supremacy, a survival of the fittest.'[1] For Cobb, like many young boys who came of age at the turn of the century, the baseball diamond was a testing ground for manhood, offering boys a chance to prove their masculinity to their peers. Yet Cobb's Darwinian sentiments were at odds with the ideals of many Victorian and progressive reformers when it came to defining the appropriate elements of manly character. Cobb regarded baseball as an athletic equivalent of war, playing with unregulated passion, sliding into base with spikes high, ready to bowl over and wound opposing fielders who got in his way, and willing to use all the tricks available to him whether they fell within the rules of the game or not.[2] In the opinion of many observers, however, Cobb's personal search for self-affirmation through fierce competition typified the rough and rowdy character of a sport that prior to the First World War had yet to acquire an unquestioned reputation of respectability. Although a generation of journalists, medical doctors, churchmen, child-savers, physical culturists, and educators might agree that baseball was a crucible in which manly character could be moulded, they tended to believe that the game should balance competitiveness and individualism with a sense of teamwork and cooperation, aggressive play with respect for one's opponents, and the desire to win with a gracious acceptance of defeat. While baseball was none the less to be played with 'ginger,' that is with energy and passionate intensity, it was also a game that, in true Victorian spirit, should involve the regulation of individual passion.

In the past half-dozen years or so, historians have begun to turn their

attention to the ways in which notions of manhood have been constructed, just as feminist historians have been concerned with the social
definition of femininity.[3] Like femininity, masculinity is culturally
defined, shaped by the larger context of gender relationships and the
distribution of male authority and power within the larger social order.[4]
In the nineteenth century, as in our own time, there were many ways
for youths to absorb what society deemed to be the appropriate standards of manly behaviour.[5] At sea, young sailors were taught to forfeit
a female world of nurture for a world of social brotherhood.[6] In the
workplace, apprentices were schooled in the skills of what were considered essentially male occupations, and in the process developed a
respect for craft and professional traditions. In the home, young men
were sometimes prematurely thrust into the role of provider upon the
death of the male head of household. On the battlefield young men
faced death realizing that their actions affected directly the well-being
of those who fought alongside them.[7] And, finally, there was the sporting ground, where reformers sought to instil in young men the values
of courage, individual initiative, teamwork, and social responsibility.

Victorian assumptions about baseball's cultivation of manly virtue
developed amidst a reconceptualization of American masculinity in the
nineteenth century. In his insightful work on the social construction of
American middle-class manhood, Anthony Rotundo has traced the
shifting contours of a discourse about masculinity from the eighteenth
century into the post–Civil War era.[8] In the early republican period, he
suggests, the comfortable classes defined manliness in social and spiritual rather than in physical terms. Manly virtue came to be identified with
social usefulness and spiritual dedication. 'The good man of the eighteenth century,' Rotundo notes, 'was the one who devoted himself to
the good of the community while he "lived a life of piety" and "mild
religion."' Thus, when Johnathan Scott, an Old Light minister from
Yarmouth, Nova Scotia, eulogized his late father-in-law, George Ring,
he described 'a humble, serene, affectionate Christian ... and constant
attendant on the Gospel and ordinances of Christ, and consequently an
unspeakably *useful* member of the Church,' who was also 'an unspeakably *useful* member of society,' and whose successful shipping business
was the means by which 'a number of poor people were *usefully* employed' (italics mine).

This identification of manliness and the useful life gave way after the
turn of the century to an emerging language of individual or self-improvement. The first half of the nineteenth century venerated the self-

made man, and idealized the sturdy, independent, and self-reliant head of the household.[9] In British North America this was an age of self-improvement societies, of mechanics institutes that tried to provide a context in which workingmen might attain greater self-understanding and government savings banks that hoped to encourage self-reliance and thriftiness among the poorer classes. In the United States, the ante-bellum reform impulse revealed a Christian concern with individual salvation and social improvement, and was imbued with perfectionist assumptions. In its most romantic and anti-institutional form, perfectionism cast off Christian notions of the redeemed and embraced transcendentalism, which saw all men and women capable of heroic achievement; by their work and example individuals could sweep away the obstacles to human progress. In this context, true manliness demanded a dedication to self-improvement and personal regeneration, and history itself became the product of the lives of great men.[10]

Throughout the nineteenth century these spiritual definitions of manliness increasingly gave way to a veneration of physical hardiness, so that by the time of the Civil War bodily vigour was coming to be regarded as 'the wellspring of true manhood.'[11] There are several explanations for this reconceptualization of masculinity in physical terms. In part, it was facilitated by a growing admiration of martial valour and physical courage that accompanied the Civil War and the subsequent age of imperial expansion. It was also a reaction to what Ann Douglas has referred to as the 'feminization of American culture,' which fed concerns that woman's influence in the church and the schoolroom, and in the authority they exerted over their sons at home, was contributing to social debilitation.[12] Late-nineteenth-century reformers feared the decline of society into muscular flabbiness, nervous weakness, and 'effeminacy,' and worried that in seeking out the comforts of life American men had become increasingly unable to withstand pain or live a virile life.[13] Distinguishing between the sexes on the basis of physical differences, these reformers ensured that 'the meaning of being masculine shifted from being the opposite of childish to being the opposite of feminine.'[14]

Roberta Park has recently drawn attention to the way in which images of the body became a central element in Victorian attempts to distinguish gender. The popularity of pictorial representations of the ideal male physique contributed to the consolidation of notions of male power and female softness and enhanced patriarchal dominance.[15] This preoccupation with the bodies of both sexes revealed itself particularly in the cult of physical measurement. Physical anthropologists measured the cranial capacity of female and male skulls – as well of those of various races – in order to confirm their Eurocentric and patriarchal assumptions about the mental superiority of Caucasian males.[16] Others used measurement to establish definitions of the ideal body type for both men and women. The Venus-like female was to measure five feet five inches and weigh 138 pounds. Her waist was to measure twenty-four inches, her bust thirty-four, her wrists and ankles six and eight inches respectively, and her thighs and calves twenty-five and fourteen and a half inches in turn. For those who did not conform to these guidelines, the symmetrical development of the body's parts was the objective. In James McKay's Halifax gymnasium, for example, careful body measurements accompanied McKay's exercise programs for young men which, he believed, would compensate for the overdevelopment of muscles on the right side of the body occasioned by the repetitive movements required in factory work.[17]

In this fascination for measurement there was an assumption that ideal physical development – which could be encouraged through physical-culture programs or involvement in organized sports – contributed to manly character and a healthy mental state. Arguing the importance of anthropolgical data in the investigation of 'all classes of men,' the American criminologist Arthur MacDonald undertook a study of the physical characteristics of American baseball players. The application of 'scientific' principles of measurement to baseball, MacDonald argued, would improve the game, enhance gate receipts, and encourage youth to play it, thereby 'developing sound bodies and sound minds, which will make them better citizens.' The result of Macdonald's measurements of 140 leading major-league players, however, was nothing more than an averaging of players by height, weight and position. The average height and weight, of these players was 5 feet 9½ inches and 174 pounds. The tallest by position were pitchers at 5 feet 11¾ inches and 175 pounds; the smallest were shortstops, who measured 5 feet 9⅖ inches and averaged 167 pounds in weight. Nor were any specific conclusions drawn from these findings, except that those players 'less than 5'11" were in general better batters and fielders than their taller counterparts.' What remained unstated was MacDonald's apparent presumption that mathematical averaging had identified the ideal baseball physique.[18]

More revealing of MacDonald's purposes were subjective judgments accompanying his published results that bore no clear relation to the statistical evidence he had amassed. MacDonald began his study by noting that criminologists were interested in baseball because it is one of the 'greatest moral tonics for boys and young men,' directing physical and mental energy into the 'right channels,' providing healthy recreation, and promoting the values of cooperation and teamwork. If the game had a weakness, however, it was the specialization of players by position, which placed fielding skills above batting. Among other things, specialization had developed 'a tribe of catchers who are clumsy on their feet, usually weak at bat, poor base runners and of very little value when sent to other positions.' This conclusion derived from MacDonald's belief that although specialization of labour contributed to technological advancement and material progress in the industrial state, it also encouraged mental monotony and unbalanced physical development in individuals, thus contributing to social degeneracy and mental weakness. Influenced by a generation of degeneracy theorists from Morel, Lombroso, and Maudsley to Havelock Ellis and Krafft-Ebing,[19] MacDonald became fascinated by the apparent physical, mental, and moral stigmata that branded as degenerate the 'abnormal or atypical man.'[20] MacDonald saw baseball as a metaphor of the larger world, where progressive and regenerative forces warred against those degenerative influences – both environmental and hereditary – that contributed to 'the criminal, pauper and defective classes.'[21]

Like many of his contemporaries, MacDonald applied a biological model both to the definition of appropriate masculinity, and to an understanding of society itself. Ideal manhood involved physical symmetry, mental acuity, and moral uprightness, and could only be achieved by cultivating body, mind and soul. Abnormal manhood, by contrast, bore the 'bodily landmarks called stigmata.'[22] Accepting this premiss, William Krauss, a medical doctor from Buffalo, New York, identified eleven types of cranial deformity, twenty-three malformations of the ear, seven abnormalities of the teeth, nine of the extremities, and twenty-six conditions of the eyes that reflected stigmatic degeneracy, as well as hairy moles, 'neurotic' fingers and toe-nails, deformities of the pelvis and genitalia, and malformations of the brain.[23] Physical imperfections were also thought to accompany 'moral stigmata' such as acquired sexual perversions or a proclivity for degenerate pastimes, and were thought to be found more regularly in immigrants than in the native American population. In an article in the *Alienist and Neurologist*, Eugene S. Talbot, professor of dental and oral surgery in the Woman's Medical College in Chicago, reported that of 128 men that he had observed in a billiard hall, 82 possessed marked signs of degeneracy. In a larger survey of 8614 people, Talbot reported that 'as compared with most foreigners, Americans exhibit the fewest signs of degeneracy,' and that 'the most marked degenerated types found here are imported individuals.'[24]

The turn-of-the-century discourse about gender thus was connected to notions of physical and moral degeneracy, and to analogies between the natural body and the body politic. In an essay entitled 'The Republic of the Body,' Woods Hutchinson suggested that 'the triumphs of democracy have been as signal in biology as they have been in politics.' In biology, he argued, 'the sturdy little citizen-cells have steadily ... fought their way to recognition as the controlling power of the entire body-politic, have forced the ganglion-oligarchy to admit that they are but delegates, and even the tyrant mind to concede that he rules by their sufferance alone.' If the individual cell, like the individual citizen of a republic, was the source of life and strength, it could also be the source of degeneracy, for the 'normal activities of any cell carried to excess may constitute disease, by disturbing the balance of the organism.'[25] Hutchinson pointed to numerous instances of degeneracy and moral weakness in the United States, arguing that 'American lawlessness, American disrespect for authority, the dishonesty of our business, the corruption of our politics, the looseness of our marriage tie – are all matters of world-wide notoriety.' Crime rates, he concluded, were higher in the United States than in Europe 'except in certain trivial eccentricities such as wife-beating, burglary, ill treating children, thieving, [and] drunkenness.'[26]

In their assault on degeneracy a generation of progressive intellectuals in the United States, from E.L. Godkin to William James, came to regard sport as 'a social technology designed to generate and direct human energy' towards the revitalization of American republicanism and manly character. Yet, as Mark Dyerson has suggested, there was no real consensus on whether the energy that derived from the strenuous life or the field of play would lead naturally to social renewal. Although most progressives believed that sport might counteract the feminization of American culture, some felt that it might do so only by encouraging masculine pugnacity. Dirty tricks, a lack of respect for authority, and unbridled individualism were often as much in evidence on the ball field as social cooperation, fair play, and civic responsibility. Like any other technology, sport needed to be directed towards progressive ends. Architects of a new progressive social order believed that the appropriate direction of young men towards responsible adulthood, in a regulated sporting environment, would counteract the degenerative impact of selfish individualism.[27]

The discourse about degeneracy and national weakness extended far beyond the borders of the United States. In his study of the concept of national decline in *fin-de-siècle* France, Robert Nye has demonstrated that 'a language of national pathology which regarded crime, mental illness, or alcoholism as signs of national debility' was shared not only by medical practitioners, asylum superintendents, and criminologists, but also by the lay public. As in America, concern about the deteriorating health of the nation meant that sport would become a force for social and individual regeneration: in this context the body 'became an ideological variable in the first burst of modern sportive nationalism.'[28] The harnessing of sport to national renewal – institutionalized in the revival of the modern Olympic Games at the end of the nineteenth century – was a recurring motif in late-nineteenth-century Europe and North America.

At the same time, defeat in international competition could heighten concerns about the decline of manhood and national virility. John Nauright has shown that the defeats suffered by British rugby and cricket teams at the hands of colonial New Zealanders, Australians, and South Africans reinforced middle-class conceptions of physical decline in Britain, and raised fears about the 'feminization of a British male imperial culture.' Colonials in turn were lauded for their virility and robust nature. 'In an increasingly competitive world the masculine qualities ascribed to colonial men were ... qualities which British men were now believed to be sadly lacking.'[29]

In Canada the notion of physical degeneracy was widespread. The editor of the *Canada Lancet* saw signs of moral degeneration everywhere: in sexual aberration, neurasthenia, and in the movement to remove 'barriers hampering "down-trodden woman," making pleas, not for the elevation of man's morals to a higher standard, but license for woman to lower hers to man's.'[30] Dr. William Bayard of Saint John thought that neurasthenia and insanity were increasing rapidly because of excessive competition, worry, compulsory education, the availability of sensational novels, and the migration from countryside to city, where the striving for existence was exhausting and sanitary surroundings unfortunate.[31] The Canadian Medical Association *Journal* attributed physical deterioration to the replacement of muscular work by machinery as industrialization proceeded. In addition, crowded streets and school-yards deprived children of natural physical outlets. School boards were therefore encouraged to provide 'properly supervised play in spaces reserved as play-grounds in the crowded districts of the city' so that 'inevitable physical degeneration might be avoided.'[32]

In Fredericton, New Brunswick, Dr A.B. Atherton wrote extensively on the causes of degeneracy and the virtue of sports such as baseball in bringing about social regeneration and a more vigorous manhood. This was the topic of his presidential address to the Maritime Medical Association in July 1907. Atherton attributed degeneracy to the character of modern life and to unscientific approaches to marriage and reproduction. In the former category he identified the herding of people together in large cities, poorly ventillated schools and workplaces, the lack of playgrounds around city schools that would allow children to play cricket, football, and baseball, and the impact of 'overstudy' on those of nervous temperament or delicate constitutions. Atherton also called for the 'better breeding of the race,' suggesting the need to discourage and prevent the marriage 'of those who are defective in physical or mental or perhaps even moral qualities; for it is more than probable that these last are also handed down to their progeny.'[33] P.C. Murphy, a Charlottetown physician and Atherton's successor as president of the Maritime Medical Association, continued in a similar vein, suggesting a program of mating the weak and strong, the tall and short, blond and brunette, stout and slight. Such a principle, Murphy believed, would create a physically balanced and symmetrical population 'without any dislocation of our social system.'[34]

By the end of the century, most medical doctors, asylum superintendents, social workers, and criminologists – even those who regarded degeneracy as a hereditary taint – advocated sport and exercise as a way to promote vigorous manliness and social regeneration.[35] Otis McCulley, a Saint John practitioner who shared the popular interest in the physical characteristics of degenerate manhood, was an avid sportsman and one-time president of the Maritime Provinces Amateur Athletic Association who considered sport a social tonic. His colleague Dr William F. Roberts, who would later become the first minister of health in the British Empire, wrote extensively about building manly character and physical robustness in the Canadian boy, and was the major financial backer of the Saint John Roses baseball team, one of the most competitive teams in the region during the 1890s and first decade of the twentieth century.[36] In Charlottetown, the city health officer, Dr H.D. Johnson, promoted a cleaner environment and improved athletic facilities as a way to protect young men from dissipation. A long-time member of the Abegweit Amateur Athletic Association, Johnson was elected president of the Maritime Provinces Amateur Athletic Association in 1909.

In addition to the medical profession, the churches played a critical role in the fostering of physical notions of manhood. At first, many churchmen were suspicious of baseball and were reluctant to have anything to do with it. The emergence of the 'social gospel' and the tendency of the churches to subordinate theology to social regeneration resulted in a more approving attitude. Baseball seemed to be one possible solution to what social gospellers called 'the young boy problem' and the declining involvement of young males in the work of the church. As sports such as baseball were increasingly seen as contributing to Christian manliness, moreover, ministers were finding it useful to employ baseball analogies in their sermons, warning their congregations not to become stranded on the third base of life. 'There is no heaven, not even a newspaper notice for the player who freezes on third base,' said the Reverend James W. Kramer. 'Young men, it will take manhood to reach the home plate.'[37] This was a common theme. 'There is an analogy between a game of baseball and the game of life,' another churchman wrote. 'In each game there is a race to be run; and it is made by stages and beset with difficulties at every point. It would be an easy matter to get around the bases and make a home run if there were not some one at every available point to hinder you and put you out.'[38] At times it seemed hard to know where traditional religion stopped and where the religion of baseball began. 'To doubt the utility of the game because we ourselves cannot take part in it as we did in the simpler sport of our boyhood, is to beg the question,' said one Saint John columnist who relied upon a religious metaphor to clinch his point. 'Few of us feel ourselves able to occupy a pulpit, yet we do not, for that reason, cease to attend church.'[39]

As Victorians became enamoured of 'muscular Christianity' and genuflected at the altar of robust physicality, baseball gradually assumed the status of a civil religion for both players and spectators, for young and old, for rich and poor. The doctrine of muscular Christianity, which replaced earlier more pietistic and spiritual assumptions with a tradition of sturdy manliness and religious dedication, drew heavily upon the writings of Englishmen Charles Kingsley and Thomas Hughes, who insisted upon the 'connections between a vigorously human Christ and a vigorously humane Christianity.'[40] In Britain, advocates of this more physical approach to the gospel sought to merge a tradition of moral manliness with the more secular traditions of the English gentleman. In *Tom Brown's Schooldays* (1857) and its sequel *Tom Brown at Oxford* (1861), Hughes idealized public-school sturdiness and physical manliness. A blend of sports such as cricket, rowing, and rugby and appropriate Christian instruction were the fundamental ingredients in moulding gentlemanly character, and helped to counteract an earlier spiritualism that smacked of effeminacy. Norman Vance has argued that the term 'muscular Christianity' is an unfortunate rendering of the Kingsleyan gospel, because it draws more attention to 'muscularity' than to Christianity. While Hughes and Kingsley evoked an ideal of physical manliness, they were equally concerned about the development of Christian and gentlemanly character.[41] Their pleas for balance were not always listened to: many Victorians remained less attentive to spiritual matters than to the promotion of physical well-being.

In North America at the turn of the century the idealization of physicality became a veritable religion of its own, attached to notions of Anglo-Saxon superiority, nativist concerns about immigration from eastern and southern Europe, and a rising tide of nationalism and imperialism. In *Our Country: Its Possible Future and Present Crisis* (1885) Congregational minister Josiah Strong expressed a commonplace fear that Anglo-Saxon manhood was losing its virility, and that the greater fecundity of the lower classes and immigrant populations was leading to racial decline. Theodore Roosevelt, who came to epitomize the values of the strenuous life, having himself overcome childhood weakness through vigorous exercise, warned of the 'danger of placing too little stress upon the more virile virtues – upon the virtues which go to make up a race of statesmen and soldiers, of pioneers and explorers.'[42] Roosevelt advocated a physical regimen that included manly out-of-door sports such as baseball, football, boxing, wrestling, running, rowing, shooting, horseback riding, and mountain climbing. 'The whole test of the worth of any sport,' he declared, 'should be the demand that sport makes upon those qualities of mind and body which in their sum we call manliness.'[43]

This was also the message of the famous dime novels celebrating Frank Merriwell, the fictional Yale hero whose exploits on the baseball field and gridiron enthralled a generation of readers at the turn of the century. The author of the Merriwell series, writing under the name Burt L. Standish, was Gilbert Patten, a native of Corrine, Maine, whose family's pacifism and uncompromising Adventist beliefs had moulded 'a shrinking lad with a sense of inferiority.' As a youngster, despite his lack of physical coordination, Patten had a passion for baseball, but was discouraged from playing the game by his parents. In making Merriwell 'a paragon of manly strenth and muscular coordination,' Patten was compensating for his own clumsiness as a youth. In addition, Merriwell provided Patten with the chance 'to preach – by example – the doctrine of a clean mind in a clean and healthy body.'[44] After his marriage, Patten moved to Camden, Maine, and, having now escaped parental influence, became involved in the game that he had earlier followed from afar. During the early 1890s Patten managed the local semi-pro ball team in Maine's Knox County League, where he came into contact with a number of talented young players including eventual major leaguers William 'Rough' Carrigan, Louis Sockalexis, and Mike Powers, as well as hard-bitten old pros such as 'Old Nick' Nickerson and 'Gramp' Morse, who threw at opponents' heads with little remorse. Patten's experiences here provided him with valuable information and anecdotes that he later incorporated in the Merriwell series.[45]

Patten introduced Frank Merriwell to American readers on 18 April 1896. After that his hero reappeared on a weekly basis in Street and Smith's *Tip Top Weekly* until the series was discontinued in 1916. The epitome of youthful masculinity, as his name implied, Merriwell blended physical ability with moral courage. 'For my hero I took the given name of Frank to express one of his characteristics – open, on the level, above board, frank,' Patten wrote in his autobiography. 'Merriwell was formed by a combination of two words, Merry – expressive of a jolly high-spirited lad – and well, suggesting abounding physical health.'[46] In many of these stories the theme was the same: Frank was engaged in a struggle against criminals and gamblers, whose evil intent often led to his being abducted before the most important game of the season.[47] At the very last moment he would escape, returning in the nick of time to lead his team to victory. In this sense Frank was an archetypical hero of the Progressive era, steadfastly opposing the corrupt practices of gamblers and speculators in a spirit reminiscent of muckraking journalists and moral reformers. Resourceful masculinity and moral toughness were also recurring elements in Patten's tales of the Maine lumberwoods, where 'Bainbridge of Bangor' unravelled various timberland intrigues while on the trail of unscrupulous land grabbers.

On college campuses across the land, proponents of manly vigour tried to live out the Merriwell ideal, establishing daily regimens that included strenuous recreation and participation in manly sports.[48] In

March 1903 a student at the Anglican Prince of Wales College in Charlottetown complained about the lack of gymnasium facilities at the
college, pointing out that the college had an empty garret that could be
used for the purpose of manly exercise. This would be a welcome
alternative to the Hillsborough Rink and YMCA gymnasium in the
town, and would be far less expensive than involvement in games such
as hockey that required equipment and ice rental. A teacher at the
college, Professor E.E. Jordan, was capable and willing to put the students through gymnasium drill and to promote the balance of mind and
body. Physical exercise, he believed, helped to 'nerve a man, make him
manly and give him physical strength in order that he may be able to
use his mind to better advantage than if his body were weak ... Feed the
one excessively, nourish its support moderately and compensation has
less power to exhaust the body for the mind. The mind has a principle
of growth within itself, it has a natural power of self-development ...
Athletics is a process artificially applied to the body, as something is
artificially done to the brain, the two they call education.'[49]

Manliness was also a central preoccupation of the Canadian novelist
Charles William Gordon, writing under the pseudonym Ralph Connor.
A Presbyterian minister, Connor saw Anglo-Saxonism, Christianity, and
a robust Canadian nationality secured by a manly population who
confronted the 'ever rising surge of immigrants, many of whom he
thought did not share those virtues as readily as they might.'[50] Connor's
The Man from Glengarry (1901) tells the story of the sturdy Scottish
woodsmen of Glegarry County, Ontario, who 'carried the marks of their
blood in their fierce passion, their courage, their loyalty; and of the
forest in their patience, their resourcefulness, their self reliance.' Deep
within the souls of these mighty lumbermen, whose confrontation with
stern nature had bred in them hardiness of frame, remarkable endurance, and an alertness of the senses, 'dwelt the fear of God.' It was this
combination of physical manliness and Christian humility that ensured
national greatness. 'For not wealth, not enterprise, not energy, can build
a nation into sure greatness,' wrote Connor, 'but men, and only men
with the fear of God in their hearts, and with no other.'

The theme of many of Connor's novels was that men who made their
living in this harsh northern country needed a masculine rather than a
highly intellectualized and pious form of Christianity. In *The Sky Pilot*,
a young minister just out of divinity school comes to a cattle camp in
the foothills of the Canadian Rockies to set up his church. The initial
response of the camp's brawny cowboys to this 'blankety-blank, pink-

and-white complected nursery kid' was lukewarm at best. Most of the ranch hands 'despised, ignored, or laughed at him, according to their mood and disposition.' For one thing, holding Sunday service conflicted with the weekly baseball match. One Sunday, however, the team's pitcher failed to show up, and the young minister agreed to fill in, amidst undisguised mockery and hoots of derision. What they did not know was that he was a fine athlete, having played ball for Princeton. By the end of the game it was clear that he was 'the best all-around man on the field.' Having now won the respect of his parishioners, he could bring them the kind of manly Christianity that appealed to 'young lads, freed from the restraints of custom and surrounding,' and who 'stood forth in the naked simplicity of their native manhood.'

Another turn-of-the-century Canadian churchman who embodied the gentleness of Christianity and the manliness associated with competitive sports was the Methodist minister Edwin Pearson, whose son Lester would later become the prime minister of Canada. Extremely popular amongst his parishioners in small-town Ontario, Ed Pearson believed that the church, the school, and the playing field all served the cause of Christianity and temperance, and rejected those who either 'would crush out all amusement ..., [or] pursue everything from which pleasure is derived.'[51] Pearson's approach was a compromise, John English has observed, leading 'straight to the ball field and away from the tavern.'[52] The Pearson boys, Duke, Vaughan, and Lester, followed their father's lead to the baseball diamond. To Lester, whose baby-face, mildly lisping speech, and religious family background may have suggested a wimpish milk-sop, exploits on the sporting field as football quarterback, Oxford rugby star, and semi-pro baseball player stood as an assertion of his masculinity.

The desire to strike a balance between physical vigour and moral sensibility in young boys and men was a recurring theme in the religious press in Canada. The *Presbyterian Witness* believed that most young boys recognized the virtue 'of bodily exercises, of ... the gymnasium, of the ball field, of outdoor and indoor sports in general,' but whatever strength was gained through rational exercise 'will be impaired or lost by an unhealthy, morbid, impure mind.' The young boy was admonished to show respect for his mother, to avoid wasting time instead of 'striking with all his might,' to associate with reputable companions, to avoid tobacco and alcohol, but above all to work vigorously, for hard work and early self-denial was the key to successful manhood. For its part the church had to present a gospel that 'appeals to the manly man,' faithful to the teachings of Christ, but 'a live religion that expects to grow, a robust religion that is meant for work, of a virile type that is neither weak-eyed nor maudlin.'[53]

The main concern of the Protestant denominations was to win young middle-class boys to the church. At an Anglican conference on 'The Church, The Child and the Home,' held in Halifax in September 1910, Hubert Carleton, editor of the *St. Andrew's Cross*, stressed that it was the duty of the church and parents to 'win the boy,' particularly 'the big boy,' or adolescent, who was 'conspicuous by his absence, both at the services of the church and in Sunday School.'[54] Many of the churches established athletic and reading clubs for adult men, young men, and boys, and though church reformers were sometimes criticized for merely providing an alternative to 'worse places,' such as the saloon or billiard hall,[55] athletic and reading clubs did provide an institutional framework for child-saving. Other churches established Boy's Brigades, an idea brought to North America from Scotland in the early 1890s. In the *Canadian Magazine*, J. Castell Hopkins saw these brigades as a catalyst of a disciplined, orderly, and manly society. 'We require all the discipline and habits of order which can possibly be encouraged and taught amongst the youth of our land,' Hopkins opined.[56] Capitalizing upon the 'martial spirit' of this period, and on what the *Presbyterian Witness* believed was the boy's 'natural love of militarism,' boy's brigades actively promoted military drill as a way to turn boys into men. 'They come into the hall boys,' said one editorial, 'and the moment the company is formed they are soldiers.'[57]

Although the most successful of these character-building institutions was the Young Men's Christian Association (YMCA), its reach, like that of most of these child-saving clubs and organizations, usually did not extend beyond the middle class. David MacLeod has seen character-building organizations as institutions that imposed middle-class values not upon the working class, but 'upon itself, or rather upon its own young people.'[58] Those involved in the YMCA, the Boy's Brigades, and the Boy Scout movement might admire 'the tough virtues of the old-style, work-bound boyhood ... and admire the vigour of sturdy street boys,' but they feared the contaminating influence of lower-class delinquency. The social programs of these organizations, therefore, were 'directed against the bogy of the hooligan, against working-class loafers and shirkers, and against the possibility of lower middle-class boys joining the degenerate in their idleness.'[59] In turn, the rougher lads of the street, accustomed to a working-class culture of masculinity that venerated toughness and a resistance to middle-class notions of social improvement, responded to parades of scouts and uniformed members of boy's brigades with 'ribald jeers, derisive songs and occasional stone-throwing.'[60]

The YMCA's fourfold plan of mental, physical, social, and religious development was aimed primarily at middle-class teenagers from good families, who were thought to be susceptible to the temptations of tobacco, alcohol, and sex, and could easily be led astray by falling in with the 'wrong crowd.' This middle-class fear of youthful wayward-ness by no means implied the waning influence of the family as a moulding force of appropriate manliness. Rather it revealed a new form of adolescent dependency within the middle-class family, reflected in an extended duration of family residence, lengthier schooling, and an elevated age of entry into the workforce.[61] Within and without the middle-class family in the nineteenth century, adolescence was receiving more attention than it ever had before. YMCA gymnasiums, swimming pools, and reading rooms were thus not meant to 'rival the home,' said clergyman Calvin Dill Wilson, but only 'to fight perilous resorts. The young men will gather together somewhere ... Many of them will meet in the pool room if no better place is provided as a rendezvous.'[62]

Within the Y's program of physical activity, baseball did not always play a prominent role. In the cities and towns of the Maritimes and New England, the emphasis was usually upon gymnastic exercise and swimming, while in the Y-sponsored summer camps, swimming and hiking usually took precedence over ball games. There were two fac-tions within the organization, both espousing muscular Christianity, but divided upon the virtues of baseball. One faction supported baseball as a form of manly exercise, while the other saw it as inefficient in devel-oping physical fitness. Because of the emphasis on the confrontation of batter and pitcher, others on the field simply stood waiting and those on the bench sat idle until their turn at bat. Gymnasium exercise, by contrast, was physically demanding work that built healthy bodies and moral character. This debate was never fully resolved, however, and YMCA baseball leagues and teams were a commonplace reality throughout the region before the First World War.[63]

The idea of organizing children's play was a commonplace element in the intellectual armament of turn-of-the-century progressive reform-ers such as John Dewey, Jane Addams, Lester Ward, and G. Stanley Hall. Hall drew heavily upon notions of atavism in degeneracy theory, regarding childhood behaviour as an acting out of primitive impulses and instincts. He argued that the development of the individual organism, or 'ontogeny,' recapitulated 'phylogeny,' or the evolutionary process, so that a child's interest in tree climbing and swinging from branches was a vestige of his primitive ancestral origins. He proceeded to argue that playgrounds were important because through supervised play 'what was morally valuable in our primitive heritage was preserved and what was inappropriate, unnecessary or disruptive was weakened or modified.'[64]

By the first decade of the twentieth century, most of the major urban centres of New England and the Maritimes had supervised playgrounds. Following the lead of larger centres such as Boston and New York, civic officials in several towns in Maine and the Maritimes developed playgrounds as an alternative to street play or the use of city parks for baseball. Portland established a supervised playground at Deering's Oaks, Lewiston set up a playground in its city park, and similar plans were inaugurated in Auburn during the summer of 1908. Urban reformers, businessmen, and reform organizations such as the Local Council of Women in Halifax and Saint John or the Twentieth Century Club in Bangor, Maine, saw playgrounds as providing a healthy and safe environment for children, 'free from the moral and physical dangers of the street and questionable companions,' where they would be 'incidentally taught to be ladies and gentlemen and learn how to handle themselves, acquiring grace and agility.'[65] In Amherst, land provided by the late Senator Dickey was turned into a playground where, the *Daily News* reported, young men and boys could 'congregate and indulge in those healthy sports that go to build up a sturdy and upright race of men.'[66]

The fact that most of the character-building institutions of the late nineteenth century were preoccupied with elaborating an ideal of manliness to middle-class males suggests that the discourse surrounding the manly sports was part of the contested terrain of both class and gender. Unfortunately, when one begins to probe the existing literature for a discussion of working-class dimensions of the making of masculinity, both on the baseball diamond and off, one is faced with a profound silence. Most of the work on the social construction of masculinity reveals a strong preoccupation with articulate, white middle-class reformers and their prescriptions for turning youth into men. When historians have ventured beyond this mainstream constituency, they have done so, more often than not, to address issues of racial exclusivity or ethnic assimilation. As a result, we know much more about the exclusion of blacks from the game, or the extent to which ethnic minorities found sport an avenue to social mobility, than we do about how class impinged upon and shaped both baseball and the culture of masculinity of which it was a part.

In his critique of the social history of leisure, Gareth Stedman Jones warned against the tendency to elevate the study of workers' recreational time to 'a subject in its own right.' Concerned that writing on leisure either tended towards a 'social control' interpretation that denied agency to the subordinate classes, or to a position that celebrated the victories of workers in struggles over recreation while they lost the more important war in the workplace, Stedman Jones called for an understanding of leisure as an escape from the harsher realities of the workaday world. Such an interpretation, however, overlooks the important discourse about manly labour that connected the worlds of work and play and that was rooted in changes in the labour process and the concomitant de-skilling of workers. 'Manliness' was an ideal constructed within a society characterized by continuing class antagonism, a shifting relationship between capital and labour, and the emergence of new standards of gentility and ethical conduct. In this context, notions of manly behaviour carried considerable ideological force, depending upon who was employing them.

What makes this discourse difficult to unravel is the fact that the language of masculinity often transcended class divisions. On the ball field, teams drawn from different class backgrounds often employed similar nicknames, identifying themselves as exemplars of manly virtue. Team names were often chosen to indicate the essential characteristics of manliness: courage, physical alertness, and fraternal loyalty. A quick glance at the sporting press reveals the prominence of names such as the Actives, the Athletics, the Fear Nots, the Intrepids, the Invincibles, the Mutuals, the Resolutes, the Socials, and the Unions. Sportswriters lavished praise on players for their 'pluckiness' and endurance, especially those like Michael Pender, catcher of the Halifax Socials, who refused to let a badly mashed hand send him to the sidelines in an important match.[67] Ballplayers were expected to bear injury 'manfully,' and to approach hard-hit grounders and fly balls barehanded, without any visible indication of fear. In his description of the introduction of the fly-ball rule and the elimination of the one bound out during the 1860s, for example, Warren Goldstein has demonstrated how sportswriters praised attempts to catch the ball on the fly and scorned 'unmanly' players who waited to play the ball on the bounce. 'No manly or skillful player will ever be guilty,' said the *Clipper*, 'of sacrificing the catch on the fly to the more simple effort on the bound.'[68]

Although these elaborations on masculine courage seem to have had a universal appeal, bourgeois reformers and workingmen often employed the rhetoric of manliness to serve different purposes. As we have seen, the Victorian middle class regarded strenuous athleticism, physical dexterity, and symmetrical muscularity as essential to the development of national virility and Christian manliness, and an antidote to the 'feminization' of middle-class culture. Despite the ballplayers' physical prowess, however, the behaviour of athletes of 'lesser rank' often offended middle-class commentators. The usual bourgeois stereotype of working-class masculinity dramatized a culture of brawny physicality, heavy drinking, rough language, and sexual indulgence, which carried with it the implication of limited intellectual acumen or moral refinement. The notion that working-class athletes lacked the self-restraint to control their passions – similar to the depiction of black men as slaves to their sexual impulses[69] – was a common theme in the parables of dissipation that graced the pages of the sporting press.

Alcohol, tobacco, and illicit sexuality made up the unholy trinity of dissipation that destroyed the bourgeois ideal of true manliness and undermined the athlete's physical talents. The sporting magazines were full of references to those who had 'disgraced themselves,' damaged their health, and brought disrepute to the game. Editorial after editorial worried that 'lushing,' or heavy drinking, was doing the game 'a great deal of harm,' or that rowdyism and ungentlemanly behaviour was lowering 'the tone of the sport' and driving respectable patrons from the parks.[70] To be sure, training rules prohibited smoking, drinking, and profane language – some clubs even required players to forfeit their salary for contracting 'disease through misconduct' – but enforcement of these regulations was often lax, especially for those whose skills made them indispensable to their clubs. Outfielder Jocko Fields, a hard-living Irishman and star of the Pittsburgh club, for example, was famous for smoking cigarettes during the game. While playing for the Memphis club in the Southern League in 1895 Fields had a clause in his contract allowing him to smoke while the game was in progress.[71] Horrified by the extent of cigarette smoking, the *Sporting News* reported that 'an average of three players per nine' were hooked on a habit 'that shatters the nerves, debilitates the heart and the eyes, and cripples the wind apparatus.' The same journal attributed the physical deterioration and death at age thirty-seven of Boston star Mike 'King' Kelly to his dissolute habits. 'Kelly was a cigarette fiend of the most confirmed stripe,' the *Sporting News* reported, 'such a slave to the habit that he would awake from a profound slumber and puff the ennervating, enticing roll of paper.'[72] Kelly was also a frequent presence in the taverns and saloons of Chicago's Clark Street. When club owner Albert Spalding hired a Pinkerton detective to inquire into the after-hours exploits of his players, and presented his report to the players, Kelly offered the following amendment. 'In that place where the detective reports me as taking a lemonade at 3 a.m. he's off. It was straight whiskey: I never drank a lemonade at 3 a.m. in my life.'[73]

While the inability of players to restrain themselves from engaging in 'degenerate pastimes' was often used to explain poor play, managers also were criticized for their inability to control their players. The *Sporting News* castigated Patsy Tebeau of the Cleveland club for his profanity and argumentative demeanour on the field, which set a bad example for his players and contributed to rowdyness and 'ruffianism on the diamond.'[74] It also took Bill 'Scrappy' Joyce, manager of the Washington club, to task for his inability to teach players self-restraint. At issue was an incident involving Senators pitcher Win Mercer. Annoyed that his second baseman, New Brunswick native John 'Chewing Gum' O'Brien, had failed to cover the bag on a double-play ball, Mercer intentionally threw the ball into centre-field to embarrass his teammate, allowing the Reds to score several runs in the process.[75] On the other hand, the *Sporting News* no doubt would have commended manager Wreath of the Augusta ball club for witholding cheques to his players on 1 July 1907 so that they would not buy too much liquor over the July 4th holiday.[76]

These parables about manly self-restraint, managerial discipline, and respectable living not only involved concerns about appropriate standards of personal behaviour, but were connected as well to the larger issue of labour-management relations and the commercialization of sport. Although baseball, like any other game, could be merely a form of amusement and healthful recreation, in its professional and semi-professional guise it was reconstituted as work. Very early in the history of the game, promoters had seen an opportunity to turn sport into a commodity, fencing grounds, erecting grandstands, charging admission to spectators, and seeking out skilful players who would attract an audience. In the larger urban centres of North America, baseball became a big business operation, often connected to urban political machines. Owners sought out the support of municipal politicians, street-railway companies, and other utilities in an attempt to reduce operating costs and increase profit margins. Even in smaller towns such as Fall River, Salem, and Brockton, Massachusetts, Dover, New Hampshire, and Lewiston, Maine, street-railway companies provided support to the clubs in the form of free grounds and cash subsidies.[77]

As baseball developed as a profitable business enterprise, the interests of players and owners often diverged. For the most part, players hoped to sell their skills in a relatively unregulated labour market, while owners attempted to keep salaries down by binding the players to their clubs contractually. The players were particularly opposed to the 're-serve rule' that bound a player to a single club, and in 1885 organized a Brotherhood of Professional Baseball Players in order to protect themselves from the exploitative practices of the owners. The leader of the Brotherhood was John Montgomery Ward, a star pitcher and shortstop for the New York team in the National League, whose legal training had allowed him to draft the Brotherhood charter in 1885. Hardly a militant labour leader – Ward had spurned affiliation of the players with the Knights of Labor – he none the less was a vigorous critic of the reserve rule, attacking it as a modern 'fugitive slave law' that 'carries [the player] back, bound and shackled, to the club from which he attempted to escape.'[78] In 1889 the owners, led by John Brush of the Indianapolis club, tried to consolidate and extend their authority by establishing a classification scheme that included salary limitations, and even assigned marginal players such menial tasks as tending the turnstile or sweeping out the parks after the game.[79] Ward argued that although ballplayers earned larger salaries and had shorter work hours than most skilled workers, the relationship with the owners 'leaves us none the less workingmen.' When the owners failed to soften their stance on the reserve clause and on salary limits, the Brotherhood established a rival Players' League, which operated during the 1890 season before collapsing before the 1891 campaign.

In confronting the owners, baseball workers appealed to a broader discourse about manly work, skilful production, and working-class independence that accompanied the development of late-nineteenth-century industrial capitalism. In the last quarter of the century workers on all fronts confronted employers interested in implementing new notions of scientific management and efficiency, which tended to reduce skilled to sweated labour. A number of historians, such as David Montgomery, Alan Dawley, Paul Faler, Greg Kealey, Wally Seccombe, Bryan Palmer, and Sonya Rose, have drawn attention to the attachment of the 'manly' ideal to work, particularly to skilled craftsmanship. Appeals to sturdy manliness, especially in confronting unscrupulous capitalists and unmanly scab labour, was a crucial component of the artisans' attempt to defend their livelihoods. Joy Parr has argued that in the mid-nineteenth-century a generation of craft-absorbed managers also asserted their masculinity through skilled work, and by so doing 'obscured the differences between masters and men behind a veil of craft fraternity.'[80] With mass production and scientific management, however, that relationship was altered and 'the gauze of common gender identity began to tear.'[81] No longer as dependent upon traditional craft skills, the new industrialist denied the notion that virility was rooted in skill and physical effort. Workingmen fought in turn to defend those traditions of skilled craftsmanship that were essential to their conception of manliness, and asserted their right to a 'manly' wage. In choosing the ideal of manliness as a way of defending their class interests, however, skilled workers also contributed to the engenderment of work and the subordination of women in the workplace. As Keith McClelland has pointed out, while the foundations of the working class 'rested on ... [labour's] subjection to capital and competition within the labour market ... they also rested on the exclusion from or subordination of women' in the workplace and their dependency within the household.[82]

As baseball developed as commercialized entertainment – both at the semi-pro and professional levels – the relationship of the player/worker to the owner/club was characterized by increasing tension and antagonism. But if the relationship of capital and labour within the baseball business was similar in many ways to that in other emerging industries in the late nineteenth century, there were some significant differences. Unlike in many factory settings where mechanization undermined traditional skills, on the baseball diamond the game was dependent upon the development and refinement of the skills that players employed. The skills of ballplayers and other athletes were more likely to be endangered by injury and advancing age than by technological or managerial assaults on their craftsmanship. The erosion of athletic skills, moreover, was readily measurable. Given baseball's fascination with statistical measurement of player performance, and because athletic skill was as much a function of age and sharp relexes as it was of experience or strength, players knew that their careers could end quickly. As a result they often resisted the attempts of owners and managers to restrict their mobility and to control their off-field activities.

For their part, profit-seeking owners wanted to employ the most skilful players for the least amount of money and, in the hope of fielding a competitive team, to keep better players under contract and management control. The owners also realized that baseball's reputation for rowdiness hurt them at the gate. Control over the extracurricular activities of players, therefore, served to enhance baseball's respectability while encouraging players to perform to the best of their abilities. Even owners like Albert Spalding and Connie Mack, who had graduated from the player ranks, demanded that players maintain a respectable and gentlemanly demeanour and defer to their authority. Having grown up in the shoemaking town of Braintree, Massachusetts, Mack turned to the ball diamond as an escape from his working-class origins.

On the issue of player autonomy and owner control, the sporting press was ambivalent. The *Sporting Life* was cautiously supportive of the players' cause, and often criticized the exploitive practices of the owners. Arguing for a reformed relationship between players and owners based upon mutual respect, it took the position that exploitation of the players made it less likely for 'gentlemen' to play the game. At first it had been uncomfortable with the decision of the players to form their own league; later it saw benefits. The Players' League had undermined the monopolistic control that owners exercized, elevated salaries, and, it argued, counteracted the degradation that used to characterize baseball. High salaries put an end to the 'toughs' who played the game; increasingly, players were being recruited from the 'ranks of the educated, refined and well-to-do.' The 'toughs' had cultivated only their 'animal tendencies,' said the *Sporting Life*, but the bums and drunkards were being weeded out quickly. 'Today questions of character are almost as potent as records of ability in securing engagement, and respectable young men may now enter the profession without feeling that they are inviting the suspicion and contempt of their friends and the general public.'[83]

The *Sporting News* was not so easily convinced that high salaries would naturally result in the uplifting of the sport to respectability. For the most part it took the side of the owners, arguing for greater managerial discipline, defending the reserve clause, and attacking players for any breaches of club regulations. In so doing it believed itself to be protecting the game from those who put their own needs before those of the club. Contract jumpers, known as 'revolvers,' were regarded as selfish and unmanly, and were berated for being ungrateful for the opportunity that baseball had provided them to play and make a living at the same time. Revolving, The *Sporting News* argued, destroyed the stability of franchises, and undermined the attachment of fans to their

local team. Without the reserve rule, it argued, the players would demand excessive salaries, and 'kill the goose that laid the golden egg.'
How many players, it asked rhetorically, would succeed in careers
outside of baseball? The implication was that few had any other real
talent. 'The majority of them go into the saloon business after their
careers are over and most of them never save a cent of their earnings.'[84]

The tug-of-war between owners and players, the issue of rowdiness
on and off the field, and the continuing influence that gamblers exerted
on the game all continued to plague baseball at the turn of the century.
For some the solution was a return to the traditions of gentlemanly
amateurism and the concomitant assumption that professional play
debased the sport. For others the answer was to reform the professional
game so that players and owners might exert 'an earnest effort to work
together harmoniously as a whole.'[85] Whatever the solution, in the two
decades prior to the First World War, the discourse surrounding baseball's development continued to turn upon the class question and the
need to uplift the game to respectability. Gradually, however, baseball
would reform itself; and as the issue of respectability carried increasingly less weight, images of class conflict that had surrounded the game
gradually gave way to those of national purpose, regional loyalty, and
civic pride.

7

Reforming the Game:
Baseball in the Progressive Era

By the end of the nineteenth century, baseball was routinely accepted as the 'National Game' in the United States, and vied with lacrosse for a similar status in Canada.[1] Not just a playful escape from the frantic momentum of industrialization and burgeoning urbanization, baseball instead responded to the central concerns of the day. From its origins the game was quickly enmeshed in debates about respectable behaviour, the appropriate relationship between the sexes, how to balance individualism and collective enterprise, and the interactions between the white Anglo-Saxon majority and ethnic and racial minorities. At the same time, as a marketable commodity, baseball could hardly escape the larger questions associated with the maturation and transformation of the industrial-capitalist economy. Indeed, its attractiveness to a public audience willing to pay to be entertained made it equally attractive to speculators who sought to profit from it. For those who had regarded sport as a potentially uplifting force, the attachment of baseball to the market-place subverted the social purposes that the game was supposed to achieve. Could baseball create respectability and contribute to community identity, or did its commercialization imply its degradation? Could baseball serve as an antidote to class antagonism, or did it merely contribute a forum in which those conflicts could endure? These issues found expression in the debate over amateurism and professionalization, in the attack on gambling and its corrupting influence, and in the frequently contested relationship between capitalist owners and professional or semi-professional athletes.

In the two decades before the First World War, the discussion in the Maritimes and New England about baseball's social value took place within the context of a broad movement for social reform generally referred to as progressivism. In both Canada and the United States, progressive reformers sought to address the ills of a rapidly changing industrial-capitalist order, blending Christian principles of social justice to a faith in technological efficiency and scientific management. Yet, if progressives looked to the future, they were also unable to escape their past. Many of the earlier debates about rowdyness and respectability, about sport as an alternative to social and individual degeneracy, and about the need to protect children from the destructive influences of an urban environment carried over into the pre-war decades. At the same time, the discourse surrounding baseball increasingly turned upon the 'scientific' character of the game, the rationalization of professional baseball as a business enterprise, the relationship of professional, semi-professional, and college baseball, and the resolution of labour-management disputes in 'the interest of the game.'

In his path-breaking work on baseball in the progressive era, Stephen Riess has noted the dichotomy between the values the game was supposed to express – individualism, honesty, competitiveness, and fair-mindedness – and its links to machine politics in large urban centres.[2] One of the first historians to place the game in its broader social context, Riess was interested in demythologizing baseball. His work demolished the notion that 'sports constituted one of the most democratic indigenous institutions since participants were ... recruited solely on the basis of their talent and skill.'[3] Carefully studying social mobility among major-league baseball players around the turn of the century, he concluded that 'baseball was not a valuable source of vertical mobility for the newer ethnics at the bottom of the social ladder' (except for the Irish, whose pre-eminence continued well into the twentieth century), and that the vast majority of players were drawn from the ranks of skilled and white-collar workers.[4] During the first quarter of the twentieth century, baseball began to attract an increasing number of college graduates as a result of its elevated social prestige and improved player salaries. In the two decades before the First World War, a declining percentage of those players who made it to the major leagues came from the social margins; it was in these years, moreover, that baseball came to be regarded as a respectable sport.

As baseball entered the 1890s, however, it continued to suffer from its reputation for roughness, its association with gamblers, the unsavoury reputation of both players and its robber-baron owners, and the labour strife surrounding the reserve clause and declining player salaries. The *Boston Advertiser* attributed the depressed state of the game to the disputes between the National League and the American Association in the 1880s and, later, between the League and the Brotherhood. 'The people wearied by the constant bickerings, the great multitude of clubs, and a general dissatisfaction resulting from many grievances,' said one editorial, 'stayed away from the games, and the capitalists who had formerly reaped great profits, from base ball were compelled to undergo heavy losses.'[5] All of this demonstrated the need for reform: clubs had to be made more equal in strength, a more 'rational' salary structure had to be put in place, and brutal and offensive play had to be regulated and controlled.

In the Maritimes the game experienced a similar malaise. The thrown game between the Socials and the Saint John team at the end of the 1890 season ended the experiment with professional baseball in the major cities of the region, and led to a revival of interest in cricket, especially in the newer amateur athletic clubs such as the Halifax Wanderers AAC, which had been established in 1884 but flourished during the nineties. The decline of baseball in Halifax was precipitous. Although an eight-team city league was established in 1891, including the Mutuals, Socials, Acadia, Crescents, Metas, Excelsiors, Blue Stockings, and Clippers, attendance at the games was abysmal. There were only about one hundred fans at the games held at Wanderers Grounds on the 24 May holiday. Even the old rivalry between the Socials and Mutuals failed to draw a substantial crowd on Natal Day the following month. After a subsequent match between the two clubs the *Acadian Recorder* reported that 'not more than 150 spectators were present. Baseball seems to have lost its interest for Halifax sporting men in common with the decline in popularity elsewhere.'[6] When the Crescents failed to show up for a scheduled match with the Clippers in early August, the league folded and the season came to an abrupt end. 'Baseball seems to have received a death blow in the city,' the *Morning Herald* reported. 'At the opening games of the season good crowds wended their way to the ball field, but owing to rank games which recently have been played, a small number now attend the games. Baseball has few supporters now in Halifax and cricket is in the ascendant.'[7]

Baseball remained in the doldrums in Halifax for the next five years. There were occasional attempts to revive the sport, but even though the Crescents organized each year, not enough interest could be sustained to organize a competitive league. The situation improved a bit in the spring of 1895. On 13 May, the *Acadian Recorder* reported that Sam Milligan, a Saint John ballplayer, was arranging a game between the old

Saint John Nationals and the Halifax Socials in order to promote interest in baseball in Saint John and especially in Halifax, where it was 'dead.' Players from the old teams, before the days of professionalism, were sought after to play, and games were held in both cities.[8] Then in June a four-team league including the Crescents, St Mary's, Chebuctos, and Wanderers was formed in Halifax. The league secured the services of George W. Barnum, a member of the touring Harkins Dramatic Company and one of the better umpires in the old National League and American Association between 1887 and 1892, to umpire its opening games. 'What he don't know about baseball isn't worth noting,' said one columnist. 'Mr. Barnum is here there and everywhere and his work yesterday was highly complimented by both teams.'[9]

By the end of the century, baseball's revival in Halifax was complete. The old Resolutes and Standards, dormant for almost a decade, resumed operations in 1899, and within a year were again importing professional players. In addition to city league play, Halifax teams once again took to the road to play against their rivals in Moncton, Fredericton, and Saint John. A visit to Halifax by the powerful Saint John Roses in August 1898 contributed greatly to the revived interest in the game. Backed by Dr William F. Roberts, a reform-minded medical doctor who would later serve as minister of health in the New Brunswick legislature, the Roses were arguably the finest team in the region at the time. On the field, their leaders were the eighteen-year-old phenom, William 'Tip' O'Neill, a slick fielder and speedy base runner who later played left field for the World Series champion Chicago White Sox in 1906, and big Jim Whelly, a left-handed pitcher with a wicked curve ball who had refused offers from big-league clubs in order to work his way up in the coal and wood business in Saint John.[10]

In addition to competitive clubs of this sort, company and workingmen's clubs became increasingly active in the late 1890s. Between 1898 and 1900, Halifax's Printers, Plasterers, Lathers, and the Rough and Ready (a team of labourers), as well as dock workers at Jones Wharf and Plant Wharf, played each other in friendly rivalries based upon occupation and craft.[11] Over the next few years local teams were sponsored by a number of industrial establishments in Halifax, such as Power & Company, Crump and Perrier, and C.R. Hoben & Co., all of which were involved in plumbing, gas-fitting, and hot-water-heater construction; merchant houses such as George Boak & Company, Smith Bros., and H.R. Silver; clothing manufacturers such as Robert Taylor's Shoe Factory, Clayton & Sons, and W.F. Page; and confectioners and grocers such as Wilson and Sullivan, the Dominion Molasses Company, and Moirs Limited. It is impossible to know in many cases whether these teams emerged spontaneously among workers, or whether employers like H.R. Silver, who not only owned his own import/export business but served as vice-president of Dominion Molasses, provided equipment and uniforms to their players as a form of corporate paternalism. Whatever the case, the rapid expansion of industrial and merchant baseball clubs revealed not only the impressive revival of baseball's popularity in Halifax, but indicated its emerging credibility among the mercantile and industrial leadership of the city.

Even as the game secured its place once again as the public's summer sport of choice, the discourse about its respectability continued in the popular press. The concerns were the same as they had always been: 'kicking' by the players, rowdyness on the field and in the stands, and the suspicion that players were throwing games for money. 'Baseball is an exciting game,' said the Saint John *Globe*, 'but lovers of it should insist on its moral improvement. There seems to be no other game where players will in such a barefaced way attempt to cheat ... to cut bases when the umpire isn't looking ... [and to] kick against the umpire's decisions even when they are beyond all doubt correct.'[12] Another concern was that of contract jumping or 'revolving.' Although there was a relatively successful effort to control this practice within organized baseball during the 1890s, semi-pro clubs like those in Halifax, Saint John, Fredericton, Moncton, Houlton, and Bangor could do little to deter athletes from selling their services on a game-by-game basis or permanently joining another team where salaries were higher. In a game between the Saint John Roses and Fredericton Tartars in August 1900, for example, the Roses were without four of their regular players. Friars and Shannon abandoned the club to play a game for Eastport against Calais, Maine. Cunningham was in Houlton playing for the Alerts, while Bill O'Neill was at Black River training for a race for a money purse.[13]

The inability or unwillingness of clubs to enforce player contracts encouraged widespread player raiding between teams in the region. During the 1901 season, for example, trainer John J. Mack, a professional athletic coach of the Wanderers AAC in Halifax, was implicated in an attempt to induce the star battery of the Saint John Alerts (Webber and Dolan) to jump the club and sign with the Halifax Resolutes. The Saint John *Globe* noted that Mack and manager P.A. Neville of the Resolutes club offered the players salaries higher than those currently offered in the New England League. 'All of this goes to show,' said the *Globe*, 'how the baseball craze is taking hold of Halifax: how the ring of sporting men, whose sole idea of sport is to gamble on it, are getting in their fine work and are turning the game into a money making speculation, robbing it of all that is genuine and lowering its standard to those of cock-fighting or pugilism.'[14] Mack denied allegations of unfair practice, but admitted writing to Webber, who was 'under his care in the University of Maine all last winter and spring,' and who had subsequently contacted Mack and expressed his desire to play in Halifax.[15]

As semi-pro clubs in the region sought out the best players, salaries often exceeded those for players within organized baseball. In addition to the supposedly handsome offers to Webber and Dolan, the press in the region often noted the ability of local clubs to outbid their rivals within organized baseball. In August 1907, for example, the team in Presque Isle, Maine, offered Stone, a catcher from Biddeford who had been sought after by several professional clubs, a salary of $45 per week plus room and board, more than most catchers in the professional New England League. Similarly, Bangor players Collins and Gardner refused flattering offers from the Boston Americans. Collins chose instead to protect his eligibility for college ball, making a comfortable summer living selling his services to clubs on a game-by-game basis. For example, the team in Caribou, Maine, enlisted Collins to pitch a particularly important game against Houlton, which he won 1–0, striking out thirteen and allowing only two hits. After the game Collins was offered a salary 'that would cause most any man to jump a contract,' but he chose instead to remain a free agent, selling his talent to the highest bidder.[16]

Before the turn of the century most clubs in the region purported to be strictly amateur, but few of the better players played without remuneration of some sort.[17] In August 1897 the Fredericton Tartars arranged a money stake game with Saint John, but later chose not to play for a purse fearing that some of their players who played in other sports would lose their amateur standing.[18] It was well known that the Fredericton club had a substantial payroll and that a number of its players were imports from New England. Third baseman Tommy Howe was a journeyman ballplayer who played for almost two decades for semi-pro teams in Saint John, Halifax, Moncton, Sydney, Glace Bay, and Lewiston, as well as for Montreal in the International League and Lowell in the New England League; shortstop Art Finnamore, one of several ball-playing brothers from Fredericton, was also a veteran of organized baseball; pitcher Harvey Cushman, a native of Rockland, Maine, eventually played for Pittsburgh in the National League; and the Tibbitts brothers, Adie and James, would play for several teams in New Brunswick and Maine over the next decade and in the professional New England and Tri-State leagues. To accept publicly a money purse, however, would seriously compromise those players on the team who wished to be considered amateurs. 'We do not think that there are more than three bona fide amateurs in the Tartars,' said one Saint John newspaper, 'but if there were only one his wish should be respected.'[19]

Baseball in New Brunswick followed a similar course to that of Nova Scotia, falling on hard times in the early 1890s, but regaining popularity and flourishing by the end of the decade. After the collapse of the New Brunswick League in 1890, amateur athletic associations in Saint John, Fredericton, and Moncton moved to develop a broader base of sporting activity, encouraging cricket, lacrosse, and track and field in addition to baseball. In Saint John, the highlight of the 1891 season was not baseball, but the provincial tour of a Massachusetts cricket eleven, arranged by A.O. Skinner of the Saint John Amateur Athletic Association. Lacrosse had also captured the public's imagination, owing to the efforts of Adam Bell, who organized the Union Lacrosse Club in 1889 and arranged for a series against the vaunted Caughnawaga Indian Lacrosse Club. During the early 1890s, with baseball in eclipse, lacrosse teams were formed in Moncton, Springhill, Pictou, Truro, and Halifax, and each fall they vied for the Maritime championship and the Nelson Cup. Baseball's fall from grace was evident in the decision of the management committee of the Saint John AAA to institute the following schedule for use of its field: baseball was given access to the grounds on Monday and Thursday; lacrosse would be played on Wednesday and Friday; and cricket matches were to be scheduled on Tuesday and the highly desirable Saturday half-holiday.[20]

As for baseball, some observers welcomed the end of importing professional players as a chance to concentrate on the development of skilful home-brews. In Moncton, sporting columnist Geoffrey Cuthbert Strange had carried on a continual denunciation of professional baseball on the grounds that it encouraged spectatorism, while in Fredericton it had often been argued that the town's baseball club should be composed of locals rather than be paying to 'increase the skill of American players.'[21] In Saint John, the YMCA baseball club, which laid claim to the Maritime Championship in 1891 after defeating the Halifax Orients, blended seasoned local veterans, like Frank White, Charles Kearns, and

George Whitenecht who had played regularly for the professional Saint John clubs in the two previous years, and talented younger players such as Thomas Bell, Harry DeForrest, and Andy Tufts. Saint John had a four-team league, including the Shamrocks, Thistles, Lansdownes, and YMCA clubs, but in many other centres league play gave way to exhibition matches and irregular games. Whatever the virtue of pure amateurism, there is no doubt that both the calibre of baseball and spectator interest in it declined in the early 1890s.[22] Occasionally a particulary talented player, such as Pat Hanifin of Halifax, could rise above the level of local competition and proceed to a professional career. Hanifin, a young Halifax tailor who played for the amateur Metas in 1891, left the Maritimes for a baseball career in the United States, and appeared briefly in a Brooklyn Bridegrooms uniform during the 1897 National League season.[23]

Baseball began to revive in Saint John in 1895, evident both in expanded newspaper coverage and the inauguration of a six-team South End League, including the Starlights, Franklins, Thistles, LaTours, Acadias, and Portlands. The league drew such solid support that Allie Dunbrack, 'a shrewd young sporting man,' decided to lease the ball grounds and run the games on a business basis. Dunbrack made arrangements with the clubs that he supply playing equipment, and in return charged a five-cent admission to defray his costs. The Starlights and Franklins were the class of the South End League. The Franklins defeated both the Bangor club and the Colby College nine during the 1895 season, while the Starlights played so well in defeat against the semi-pro Fredericton Tartars, the strongest team in the province at the time, that they were invited to join the Tartars, the Monctons, and the Saint John AA Club in a four-team New Brunswick league the following season. When over a thousand spectators turned out to watch Jimmy Tibbitts, Jack Doran, and Tommy Howe lead the Tartars to the provincial crown, disposing of the Starlights 12–2 in the championship game at the old Shamrock grounds, baseball's resurgence in New Brunswick was all but assured.

The 1896 season also witnessed the inauguration of a vigorous rivalry in Saint John between the Alerts, a team drawn from the south and east ends of the city, and the Roses from the working-class district of the north end. Initially there was concern with the proliferation of ball clubs in Saint John, and it was frequently suggested that an all–Saint John team be formed to play town clubs from Halifax, Moncton, Fredericton, Houlton, Eastport, Bangor, and Portland. The strength of Saint John teams was further sapped by the loss of local players to clubs across the border and even to clubs in the Canadian West.[24] At the beginning of the 1897 season, Charlie Kearns signed with the Bangor club, Tommy Hayes left to play with Rockland, Maine, and Pete Burns hooked on with Paris of the West Texas League. The Roses also lost two of their starters. Later that same year, after a four-game series involving the Alerts and the Roses and Portland of the New England League, second baseman Tip O'Neill signed with the Portland team, beginning a professional career that led ultimately to the major leagues. Another Saint John native, John 'Chewing Gum' O'Brien, who had played on the old professional Shamrock club in 1890, was already playing for Washington in the National League. O'Brien, who had moved to Lewiston, Maine, as a teenager, was considered a model ballplayer, clean-living and respectable to a fault. 'When O'Brien played in Saint John,' said the *Globe*, 'he was not only a teetotaler but used to walk a couple of miles every day to drink from a certain spring.' In a six-year major-league career comprising 501 games, O'Brien batted .254 and stole 45 bases.

Keeping in touch with the careers of those who once played in the region was a favourite pastime of local newspapers. The *Globe* carried the following story of one of 'Chewing Gum' O'Brien's team-mates on the old Shamrocks, catcher Billy Merritt, of Lowell, Massachusetts. In the middle of the 1891 season, the infamous Cap Anson, manager of the Chicago club, was passing through the lobby of a Boston hotel, when a boyish-looking young fellow dressed raggedly and in bare feet came up and asked, 'Are you Anson?' When Anson replied in the affirmative, the young fellow said, 'Well, I see you need a ketcher and I walked here all the way from Providence to see if you'd give me a chance. I'm a ketcher and I think I'll do.' Anson gave him a try-out, liked what he saw, and put him in the line-up. Two games were played by Anson's club that day, and Merritt caught in both, handling the pitchers without a passed ball and hitting the ball on the nose. After the game Merritt was signed to a formal contract, thus beginning an eight-year major-league career with five different clubs.

The drain of potential baseball stars from the region was made worse by the widespread outmigration of Maritimers to the 'Boston States' during the last quarter of the nineteenth century. Several players who were born in the Maritimes and eventually graduated to the major leagues actually left the region at a very early age as their parents sought stable employment elsewhere. Pitcher Gene Ford was born in Milton, Nova Scotia, in April 1881, but before his second birthday was living in Brandon, Manitoba. His brother, Russ Ford, went on to win 99 games in the major leagues. Charles 'Pop' Smith, a twelve-year veteran of the major leagues, who holds the dubious distinction of being the only player to commit five errors in a single inning, was born in Digby, Nova Scotia, but moved with his family to Boston as a young child. The same was true of Bill Phillips, born in Saint John in 1857, who began a decade-long career in the majors with Cleveland and Brooklyn in 1879. Other players with family roots in the Maritimes included eventual Hall of Famers Harry Hooper and Harold 'Pie' Traynor, and Jack 'Stuffy' McInnis, first baseman in Philadelphia's famous $100,000 infield. Hooper's father was a ship's captain from Charlottetown, PEI, who emigrated to California in the 1870s; Traynor's father, Jimmie Traynor, lived and worked in Halifax during the 1890s; and 'Stuffy' McInnis had family roots in Cape Breton. McInnis returned briefly to Nova Scotia after the Second World War to coach in the mining towns of Westville and Stellarton during the heyday of Maritime community baseball.

The revival of semi-professional baseball in Saint John, Fredericton, Moncton, and Halifax, and in the mining districts of Cape Breton at the turn of the century reversed an earlier trend, as local clubs sought to hold onto the better local players and to attract available players from south of the border. Unable to beat the rival Roses with any degree of consistency, the Alerts were the first Saint John club at the time to turn to imported professionals, bringing in several college players in 1899. Catcher Harry Jope and pitcher Jack Kennedy, likely playing under assumed names in order to protect their eligibility for collegiate competition, provided the Alerts with a crackerjack battery. 'Happy' Iott, a twenty-three-year-old outfielder from Houlton, Maine, who had played for Woodstock, NB, the previous season, was also induced to join the club, as was another catcher named Kelly from Manchester, New Hampshire. In the following year, both the Alerts and Roses were relying upon a blend of imported players and local stars such as Dan Britt, a hard-hitting first baseman. The Alerts added two new imports, a young pitcher named Foster from Tufts College, and Frederick Francis Yapp, a six-foot tall, 195-pound first baseman and pitcher from Cambridge, Massachusetts. The Roses, who had already reacquired Tip O'Neill after a season with Worcester in the Eastern League, added pitcher Frank Sexton, the ace of the Brown University pitching staff, and a hulking catcher named Larry 'Jack' McLean, who had played for Fredericton the year before. Iott, Sexton, and McLean later went on to play in the major leagues. So did Yapp, who played under the name

Fred Mitchell, winning thirty-one games as a pitcher from 1901 to 1905 for Boston, Philadelphia, and Brooklyn.

Of all the players to play in the region in these years, none was more colourful than big Jack McLean. A hard-drinking, fast-living youth, McLean was also a gifted athlete who stretched 195 pounds over a six foot five inch frame. Behind the plate McLean was a steadying influence on pitchers, his large presence giving them a good target, and his cannon-like arm demanding respect from base runners. The *Baseball Encyclopaedia* gives his birthplace as Cambridge, Massachetts, but it seems that he spent much of his adolescence in and around the Fredericton area. Between 1899 and 1901 McLean played for the Tartars, the Roses, and the Halifax Standards, often jumping from one club to another when he received a better offer. After a brief stint with the Boston club of the American League in 1901, McLean returned to the Maritimes and played for the Roses for the next couple of years.

McLean's weakness was alcohol, and he often found himself in trouble as a result of his tendency to 'neglect training,' as the press euphemistically put it. In May 1903 'Big Jack' and his brother Charles were arrested in Saint John on suspicion of stealing $318 from a Bathust businessman after a night of drinking at the Grand Union Hotel. There was not enough evidence to lay a formal charge, however, and they were set free.[25] A year later, McLean was playing regularly in the National League. A potent force in Clarke Griffith's Cincinnati club from 1906 to 1912, McLean hit .298 in 128 games in 1910 and .285 in 107 games the next year.

In an age when baseball was attempting to divest itself of its rough image, McLean was something of a rebel. On 11 April 1910 the Halifax *Herald* ran a story on Big Jack under the headline 'Baseball's Largest Player Is Not Strong on Headwork.' Although McLean had been laid up for part of the previous season with a leg injury, the *Herald* revealed, the Reds kept him under contract and paid his full salary. When he went to spring training in 1910 Griffith offered him the chance to captain the team. In return, McLean promised to stay on the 'water wagon.' It was promise he couldn't keep. After an initial flare-up with Griffith over his tendency to break training, he apologized and was taken back. When McLean was again caught coming in at 5 a.m., he was suspended for a month and stripped of his captaincy.[26] Some who knew him were not surprised to learn, in March 1921, that McLean had been shot dead crawling across a bar to get at a disagreeable bartender during a Boston saloon brawl.[27]

During the first decade of this century, competitive semi-pro leagues, drawing heavily upon imported talent, were a commonplace in the Maritimes and in border towns in Maine, but the limited size of many of the region's urban centres and the cost of travel made it difficult to sustain regular operations over an extended period. When leagues folded as a result of the defection of one or more teams, the remaining teams usually carried on with exhibition matches. Promoters were quick to cut their losses when things began to go bad for them, and players had always to be ready to market their skills in other locations or fight for back wages. In July 1903, the Bangor *Daily Commercial* reported that, because of poor attendance, Saint John's professional clubs might suspend operations. If so, it noted, the following American ballplayers would be out of work: Frank Goode, William McDermott, William Connors, and Nicholas Taylor, all of Roxbury, Massachusetts; future major-league star John 'Colby Jack' Coombs and his team-mate from Colby College William Cowing; Joseph Walsh of Salem, George O'Hearn of Pittsfield, and Frank Willis and John Phelan of Boston, Massachusetts; and Lou Sockalexis, a native Penobscot from Old Town, Maine, who had starred in the outfield for the Cleveland Spiders a few years before.[28] Fortunately, the league carried on and the players received their promised salaries, although the Alerts' franchise, including stars such as Saint John native Dan Britt and Jack Coombs, was shifted to Waterville, Maine. The Alerts would be much luckier than the players of the 1907 Lewiston club, who were forced to take legal action to get their salaries, attaching 'the grandstand and fence through their attorney ... for the back pay now amounting to about $900.'[29]

The ability of any community or sub-region to maintain semi-professional baseball was not just a function of fan support, but was affected by the existence of other leagues that competed for players. When semi-pro clubs folded in one part of the region, therefore, they often emerged nearby. Rarely did professional teams prosper in all of the major centres in the Maritimes and Maine at the same time. During the 1890s, when baseball had languished in the Maritimes, for example, it had flourished in Maine. Beginning in the 1880s and through the next decade, teams from Portland, Biddeford, Lewiston, Bangor, and Rockland were often included in the fast New England League, which had first been organized in 1877 and which survived until after the Second World War. Although membership in a league affiliated with organized baseball may suggest a greater likelihood of stability, the fact was that even those franchises were continually collapsing and shifting, and many of the players who found themselves out of employment overnight would play throughout the region on various semi-pro teams. There was thus very little difference in quality between minor-league baseball and the independent clubs that predominated throughout the Maritimes and northern New England; as often as not these independent teams came out on top in exhibition games with their rivals within organized baseball's minor leagues. According to Neil Sullivan, 'Minor league baseball in the late nineteenth century was a different game from that we have come to know ... Many excellent ball players performed for teams and leagues in an era that was too unstable to permit comparisons of the quality of the different leagues' or of local club teams.[30]

Given the instability of baseball franchises before 1900, it is perhaps not surprising that, when semi-pro baseball returned to the Maritimes in the late 1890s, it did so at the expense of competitive baseball in Maine. In 1897 the New England League temporarily abandoned Maine, and a newly formed Maine State League with teams in Augusta, Bangor, Belfast, Lewiston, Portland, and Rockland quickly fell on hard times.[31] For almost a decade after that, it was the Maritimes rather than Maine that would be the locus of semi-pro baseball in the region. There were a few exceptions to this rule, particularly in the border towns of Houlton, Caribou, and Presque Isle, whose proximity to Saint John, Fredericton, and Woodstock allowed them to play lucrative matches with their cross border rivals. Over the years, former or eventual major leaguers Lou Sockalexis, Mike Powers, George 'Squanto' Wilson, Chet Chadbourne, Ralph Good, 'Happy' Iott, and William 'Rough' Carrigan all suited up for the Houlton nine.

Of these, Carrigan had the most illustrious career. A native of Lewiston, Maine, Carrigan began his professional career as an eighteen-year-old infielder for the Houlton club during the 1901 season, and entered Holy Cross University the following year. His manager at Holy Cross, Tommy McCarthy, converted him into a catcher, where his skills at handling pitchers and blocking the plate attracted the attention of the Boston Red Sox, who signed him to a major-league contract. 'Rough' Carrigan, as he was known, played for ten years for the Red Sox, and for the last four was the team's playing manager. As a student of the game, and a tough disciplinarian, Carrigan was noted for his ability to control the various explosive forces forever popping out along his bench, winning three World Series in four years. His 1915 Bosox, with Tris Speaker, Harry Hooper, Smokey Joe Wood, Dutch Leonard, and a youthful Babe Ruth won 101 games and lost only 50 in winning the

American League pennant. Ruth later called him the best manager he had ever had.

The opening decade of the twentieth century also witnessed the first connections between professional baseball on the mainland and on Cape Breton Island. Baseball had been slow to arrive in Cape Breton, but by 1905 teams in Sydney, Sydney Mines, Reserve Mines, and Glace Bay were importing players. The Dominion No. 1 team was the only team in this colliery district league that chose not to import players. The Sydney *Record* of 21 August 1905 reported that better baseball than had ever been witnessed on the Island was now being played, 'though the results are getting to depend too much on which team can import the most and best men.'[32] Glace Bay, managed by Fredericton draughtsman 'Dick' Malloy, was the class of the league, and their victory in the league championship resulted in a boisterous celebration in the centre of town.[33] Crowds of eight hundred per game were common in Cape Breton during the 1905 season, and seeing the potential for even more profitable gates, sport promoters like M.J. 'Mike' Dryden of Sydney and George McSweeney of Reserve Mines began to prepare for a strictly professional baseball operation for the 1906 season. The Sydney *Daily Post* reported that McSweeney was 'scouring the provinces' for first-class talent, and that the lucrative salaries being offered by the various clubs had resulted in the hiring of several players from Moncton and Saint John.[34] The Glace Bay AAA club hired journeyman Tommy Howe and the Finnamore brothers, George, Art, and Bert; New Aberdeen signed Jack Norris, Jack Woods, and George Malcolm 'at a fancy figure and ... [with] considerable dickering ... before they could be induced to come to the island'; Dominion No. 1 signed Breen, Paris, Daley, and Eddie Ramsay, all of Saint John, and Jimmy Trott, a cagey right-hander from Springhill whose sharp-breaking curve was his bread-and-butter pitch; and McSweeney's Reserve club imported Haligonians Billy Rawley and Bert Messervey, both of whom rejected offers from teams within organized baseball to come to Cape Breton. Two veterans of baseball in Saint John, big Dan Britt and Charles 'Slasher' McCormick also played briefly in the league that year. A member of the New Brunswick champion Saint John Alerts in 1903, Britt had most recently played for New Haven of the Eastern League, while the peripatetic McCormick spent the 1905 season playing in the outfield for San Francisco of the Pacific Coast League, Vancouver of the Western League, and then Canmore, Alberta, 'where he joined with the team that won baseball's Western Canada League trophy.'[35]

Although there were those who regarded the provision of recreation to the colliers of Cape Breton as a valuable antidote to class antagonism, not everyone supported the introduction of professional baseball. The editor of the Sydney *Record* regarded it warily, thinking it a scheme of unscrupulous promoters who, in preying upon the mining districts, would encourage idle habits amongst the working class. The summer months, the editor continued, were already busy with sports, picnics, excursions, and holidays that took people away from the workplace. 'We should be the last to deny to anybody a reasonable amount of recreation and a reasonable amount of holidays,' the editor wrote, 'but this taking a day or a half day off at frequent intervals disorganizes the working man. England today is suffering from an excess of the sporting and holidaying spirit and she is in consequence feeling the competition of the steadier and more industrious continental nations.'[36] In taking this stand, the newspaper was echoing the position of the operators of the Dominion Coal Company, who complained that the scheduling of games before 5 o'clock resulted in 'a considerable number leaving work early in the day, three or four times a week,' and diminished output. 'Picnics have also contributed their share of adverse influence,' said the Halifax *Acadian Recorder*, 'but baseball is the principal sinner.'[37] The company prevailed upon the league to move the starting time to 5 o'clock from 3:30 p.m., but this proved inconvenient. The company also proposed that all games be held on Sunday, but the miners refused this interference by the company in their leisure activities and opposed Sunday baseball on religious grounds.[38]

While semi-pro baseball gained popularity in industrial Cape Breton, the amateur game established itself elsewhere in the Maritimes. In Pictou and Cumberland counties, where cricket had held sway among coalminers of British origin, baseball flourished during the 1890s. In the coal towns of Joggins, Westville, and Springhill, baseball was an important cultural component of worker solidarity, as it was in 'busy Amherst,' one of the fastest-growing industrial towns in the region. 'The baseball craze has struck Springhill,' said the Springhill *News and Advertiser* of 13 August 1896, 'there are about three teams on Herritt road and two or three in town.'[39] Within a few years, a four-team Pictou County Baseball League was operating with teams in Westville, Stellarton, New Glasgow, and Trenton.[40] Rivalries based both upon propinquity and shared occupational and cultural identities also invigorated matches between Joggins, Springhill, and Westville. At the same time, towns from Truro to Annapolis were playing each other and accepting American challenges. Similar rivalries emerged in the north-western counties of Nova Scotia between Windsor, Kentville, and Middleton; to the south-west in Digby and Yarmouth; and across the Bay of Fundy in Macadam, Woodstock, and Carleton.

The relationship between amateur and professional baseball became an especially contentious issue after 1907, when the Maritime Provinces Amateur Athletic Association (MPAAA) became affiliated with the Canadian Amateur Athletic Union (CAAU), rather than its rival organization the Amateur Athletic Federation of Canada (AAFC). For over two years the CAAU and the AAFC were involved in a jurisdictional struggle for the control of amateur sport in Canada, eventually resolved by the amalgamation of the two organizations into the AAU of Canada in September 1909. This struggle, Don Morrow has argued, 'served to embalm and enshrine an outmoded amateur ideal' in an age when the commercialization of sporting activity made professionalism ubiquitous.[41] For baseball, like other team sports, the crucial concern was the prohibition against amateurs from competing with or against professionals without losing their amateur status. For years the MPAAA had turned a blind eye to the fact that amateurs had played alongside professionals, thus allowing the development of semi-professional baseball in the Maritimes, both in the late 1880s and after 1895. Beginning with the 1907 baseball season, however, the refusal of the MPAAA to tolerate the mixing of amateurs and professionals on the ball diamond seriously undermined those clubs committed to semi-pro competition.

In Cape Breton, the implementation of a definition of strict amateurism meant the end to its two-year experiment with semi-pro baseball. In 1906 the MPAAA had followed a less restrictive position. Recognizing the public demand for semi-pro ball, the MPAAA agreed to allow amateurs and professionals to play together where gate money was collected, but not for a trophy or other prize. In addition, any amateur who accepted money for playing would be suspended pending an investigation by the MPAAA.[42] This ruling had permitted teams in the Cape Breton County League to import professionals, and allowed amateur clubs such as the Glace Bay AAA to engage in the ironic practice of fielding teams made up almost exclusively of professional baseball players.[43] In 1907, with the MPAAA taking a hard-line stance prohibiting the mixing of pros and amateurs, the Cape Breton County League required all of its players to hold amateur cards with the CBAAU before turning out on the diamond.[44]

Over the next few years an energetic debate about amateurism and professionalism took place in the regional press, culminating in a series of articles on the issue in the Halifax *Herald* in January and February of 1910. Much of the debate centred upon the rapid growth of professionalism in hockey, but baseball was also a matter of lively concern. The *Herald*'s position was clear. The main evil was not playing for pay, but the system of amateurs and professionals playing alongside each other. What justification was there for promoters paying one athlete while exploiting another? This inequality of treatment encouraged amateurs to turn professional, many of whom would still be playing for the love of the game, except that someone was 'getting the green on the side.'[45] At the same time, the *Herald* admitted that working-class athletes needed compensation for lost wages and the sacrifice of time, noting the argument of a well-known Maritime catcher who pointed out that he could not afford to play ball on a Saturday afternoon without compensation for docked wages. But the same player's suggestion that the MPAAA give up its jurisdiction over baseball and let amateurs and pros play side by side was given a hasty rejection. 'Amateurs and Pros Mix,' said a headline of 25 February, 'No! No! Say All in Chorus!'[46]

The growing support for a clearer demarcation of amateur and professional sport led James G. Lithgow to resign as president of the MPAAA in 1909, to be replaced by Dr H.D. Johnson of Charlottetown. Lithgow, actively involved in sporting organization in the region and at one time president of the Nova Scotia Amateur Hockey League, had often turned a blind eye to violations of amateur standing. He must have been naïve, the Halifax *Herald* concluded, not to know that professionalism was widespread, especially after a lawsuit involving a Fredericton hockey club revealed that all its players, in the 1908 season, were under salary and that many of them were playing in Nova Scotia during the 1909–10 season. In fact, Lithgow was opposed to the extension of the ideal of strict amateurism to team sports such as baseball and hockey, and had resigned because of more stringent requirements ordained by the AAU of Canada. As incoming president of the MPAAA, Johnson strongly advocated the separation of amateur and professional play and instituted a tighter transfer rule to discourage player raiding in both hockey and baseball. Johnson's position on amateurism was to let bygones be bygones; if a player had played professionally in the past but was henceforth willing to declare himself an amateur, he would receive an amateur card. Subsequent violations of amateur standing, however, would be severely dealt with; beginning in

1910, the ruling maxim of the MPAAA would be 'once a professional, always a professional.'

The desire to separate amateurs and professionals was rooted in a traditional assumption that sporting professionals were people of low breeding who would sell their 'athletic talent to the highest bidder, fix the outcome of contests and generally dupe the public for personal profit.'[47] As such, the revival of the amateur ideal was connected to the bourgeois attack upon the idle and dissolute life, and was part of the progressive impulse towards the supposed moral reclamation of the working class. To middle-class reformers there seemed to be something 'unmanly' about relying on sport to make a living; it was considered analagous in a way to prostitution and gambling. Professional athletes, the Halifax *Herald* argued, should have an honest 'position' in order to qualify for any team sport. Holding a steady job in the community would also establish real residency, and act as a break upon contract jumping. 'As for put up jobs and games sold, the press could soon remedy these proceedings, and when the players are once detected in doing the "false act" such as some have been guilty of this season – throw them out of maritime sport forever.'[48]

Before the First World War, in fact, gambling on sporting events was widespread. Newspapers in the region are filled with references to betting on games, both by spectators and players, and poor play on the field often raised suspicions that matches were fixed. When Halifax turned to professional baseball in 1911, there were many who felt that this would mean heavy gambling and thrown matches. 'It is to be hoped that when the professional baseball league starts in Halifax, those who witness the contests and those who hear about them will be more sportsmanlike than to say the games are "fixed,"' said the Halifax *Herald*. 'There was enough of this kind of scandalous and unfair chatter concerning the pro hockey last winter.'[49] Paul Voisey has noted a similar preoccupation with gambling on baseball in turn-of-the-century Alberta, attributing its appeal to the speculative character of frontier society. Immensely popular in Alberta, baseball was surrounded by heavy betting, sometimes involving wagers of hundreds of dollars or even a quarter-section of land.[50] In fact, gambling was deeply imbedded in Victorian North America and Britain, and its connection to sport was by no means confined to frontier regions. The *Acadian Recorder* reported, for instance, that, during a game between Saint John and Halifax teams in September 1888, over $4000 was wagered, and a group of Saint John men lost 'several thousands.'[51]

In addition to large sums such as this, smaller wagers were often placed with bettors, like the notorious Halifax gambler Frank Robinson, who usually gave odds on the game. Petty betting was particularly popular amongst working-class consumers of sport, serving to invigorate loyalty to one's team while offering a chance for a little extra pocket money.[52] In the British context, Ross McKibbon has described popular betting on sporting matches as the most successful example of working-class self-help in the modern era. It was at every stage a proletarian institution and bore all the characteristics of the British working class.[53] Not surprisingly, working-class betting met with criticism from bourgeois reformers, who considered it an irrational activity on the part of those who couldn't afford it, but such criticism was muted by the fact that the love of risk and the longing for commercial expansion were also regarded as virtues by the middle class.[54] Thus, while newspaper articles about baseball often denounced the unsavoury influence of gamblers, they routinely commented upon the amount of money changing hands and the odds that had been established by those who took the bets.[55]

By the middle of the first decade of this century, then, the contradictions that baseball presented to the dream of recreational respectability were abundantly evident. Rather than encouraging a unity of sentiment that transcended class lines, the development of baseball seemed to reveal the worst influences of commercialism, a flagrant disrespect for the sanctity of contract, an encouragement of reckless gambling, and unruly crowd activity. Professional baseball also undermined the participatory character of amateur athletics. Rather than playing themselves, spectators preferred 'to watch a few experts whose business it is to play for the public amusement,' and in turn, while neighbouring provinces were scoured for ballplayers in return for 'a good salary, a lazy time and the small boys' idol,' local amateur sport did not receive the attention it deserved.[56]

There were other concerns. On the field of play, the working men who played alongside college students seemed not to be uplifted to respectability, but, in the eyes of sports reformers, posed a threat to the respectable character of young college men. This concern was by no means confined to critics of professionalism in the Maritimes. Dr E.H. Nichols of Harvard University opposed college students playing alongside professionals in summer leagues and voiced the increasingly widespread belief that the longer a person stays in pro ball 'the worse he becomes.'[57]

In the United States the NCAA struck a committee in 1913 to rid college baseball of objectionable practices. Reporting in the following year, it recommended the following:

1. Strict adherence to base-coaching rules, especially those prohibiting coaches from inciting or gesticulating to the crowd or using defamatory language
2. Enforcement of rules against blocking the runner, prying runners off base, or other forms of trickery
3. Prohibition of verbal coaching from the bench
4. Prohibition of encouragement of the pitcher from outfielders. 'Remarks of endless iteration' were deemed disagreeable to spectators, thus encouragement should only come from the infield.
5. Prohibition of catchers talking to batters
6. Restriction of indecorous or unseemly behaviour of any sort

The report concluded that 'a college baseball game is a splendid contest of skill between two opposing nines before an academic throng of spectators. It is not a contest between a visiting team and a local team assisted by a disorderly rabble.'[58]

The supposed confrontation between amateur collegians and professionals, not to mention the destructive influence of gamblers and other unsavoury characters on the sport, became a recurring morality play in the Frank Merriwell dime novels of Burt Standish. Time after time Merriwell would fall into the clutches of gamblers and others who refused to play by accepted standards of fair play. In this sense Merriwell epitomized the 'gentleman' amateur, a college-educated athlete who played for the love and honour of the game rather than for financial reward. Yet this appeal to virtuous amateurism was an increasingly dated ideal. As the First World War approached, professional baseball was shedding its disreputable image. Baseball was just one of a number of big businesses that had come under the disciplining influence of progressive reformers, whose attacks on robber-baron capitalism had served to rehabilitate the image of the responsible big-business enterprise. Benjamin Rader has pointed out that major-league baseball enjoyed unparalleled popularity in the first two decades of the twentieth century. Attendance doubled, women were attending games in greater numbers, and William Howard Taft lent official sanction to the sport by establishing the precedent of the President of the United States throwing out the first ball at the beginning of each new baseball season.[59]

Ironically, the regulations aimed at separating amateurs from professionals did not encourage the development of competitive amateur baseball in the Maritimes, but led to a more thorough-going system of importing professionals. In 1911, a professional New Brunswick–Maine baseball league was formed through the hard work and perseverence of Saint John businessman D.B. Donald, Fredericton mayor C.H. Thomas, and Joe Page, a well-known baseball buff and scout for the Chicago White Sox. Though not part of organized baseball, the league relied heavily on players from major-league organizations, especially the White Sox. The six-team loop had two teams in Saint John and one each in Fredericton, St Stephen, Woodstock, and Calais. The Marathons of Saint John were the class of the league, led by ex–major leaguer and team captain George Winter. Rounding out the squad were Al Sweet, Jack Nelson, and Leo Callahan, all three of whom were the property of the Chicago club; Larry Conley, Ray Tarbell, and a third baseman named Williams from the University of Vermont; and locals Sullivan, Fraser, Riley, and Eddie Ramsay.

Other teams also sported impressive line-ups. The Fredericton Pets placed second in the league, fielding a fast and aggressive squad of ballplayers, many on loan from the Lowell club of the New England League. The roster included player manager Joe Dugan, pitchers Ray Tift and Bill Duval, and Bob Ganley, late of the Pittsburgh club in the National League. St Stephen's line-up sported two Maritimers who would eventually play major-league ball, Halifax native Shorty Dee and Saint John–born Art McGovern. The St Stephen roster also included journeyman shortstop Art Finnamore, second baseman C.H. Callahan, and outfielder M.J. Butler from the reserve list of the White Sox. Saint John had a starry battery in pitcher Cecil Ferguson, a six-year veteran of the major leagues, and catcher Pat Donahue, who had played three years in the American League. Donahue was on loan to Saint John subject to recall by the Boston Red Sox. Woodstock had two mainstays in pitchers Marvin Peasley, who grew up in Maine and New Brunswick and had played for the Detroit Tigers the previous season, and Joe Wehquart, who later joined the Philadelphia Athletics organization. Although Calais had no particularly bright stars, manager 'Happy' Iott had a competitive club that finished third in the league behind the Marathons and Fredericton.

The highlight of the 1911 season was a three-game series in September between Lowell, the champions of the New England League, and the Marathons, winners of the regular season in the New Bruns wick–Maine circuit. The Marathons started strongly, winning the first game 3–1 behind George Winter's sparkling five-hit pitching performance, then faltered badly, losing the second match by a score of 8–1. The final game was an exciting one, and until the ninth inning the Marathons seemed poised to win. On the mound for the Marathons, Jack Callahan pitched eight scoreless innings and his mates played errorless ball behind him. The Saint John club entered the ninth inning leading 3–0. Three hits and a couple of costly errors, however, allowed Lowell to send the game into extra innings. Two more runs in the tenth inning sealed the fate of the Marathons and sent Lowell on to victory and the championship of northern New England and the Maritimes.

The 1911 season also witnessed the return of professional baseball to Nova Scotia. In Halifax, the Socials and the Standards declared themselves professional, and organized the Halifax City Pro League, with Robie Davison, once a star pitcher of the Socials during the 1880s, as league president. The two clubs entered into a nineteen-game series, and played several games with touring clubs as well. The Socials won the local series ten games to nine. In exhibition matches, Halifax won 12 of 17 games against professional teams from Westville, Stellarton, Saint John, Moncton, Andover, and Dorchester, Massachusetts. In a league dominated by pitchers Roy Isnor and Jack Cogan, batting averages were low. The exceptions were infielders Lee McElwee, who led the league with a .409 average and would later play for Connie Mack's Philadelphia Athletics, and Haligonian Charley Foley, who hit .333 over the nineteen-game schedule.[60]

Outside of Halifax, independent clubs in Springhill, Cape Breton, Truro, Middleton, and Yarmouth, and the Pictou County League, with teams in Stellarton, Westville, and New Glasgow, also turned to imported professionals during the 1911 season. The Yarmouth club fielded a team of New Englanders supplemented by a single home-brew, while Stellarton's line-up was made up largely of players from Massachusetts.[61] At first Stellarton tried to maintain its designation as an amateur club.[62] Later they described themselves as semi-professionals, implying that there were both amateurs and pros on their rosters. Under the MPAAA's definition of amateur standing, of course, those who played alongside professionals were no longer amateurs. The designation semi-professional was thus only a euphemism. 'Westville, New Glasgow and Stellarton call their teams semi-professionals,' said the *Halifax Herald*. 'Doesn't this make you smile ...? The Pictou County leaguers are professional and nothing else. A dog cannot be a cat.'[63]

The extension of professional baseball throughout Nova Scotia in 1911 was due in large part to the success of professional hockey in the province during the preceding winter. Truro, Halifax, New Glasgow, and Amherst all had pro hockey clubs during the 1910–11 season. In addition, the decision of the South Shore Hockey League to renounce its amateur status paved the way for the transformation of the Western Baseball League to professional play. As Nova Scotia moved in a seemingly relentless way towards professionalism in hockey and baseball, moreover, earlier concerns about the respectability of professional sport seemed to be put aside. Increasingly, commentators seemed to regard professionalization as an inevitable attribute of a society intent upon casting off tradition and embracing modernity. 'Amateur baseball like amateur hockey is a thing of the past in the Maritime provinces,' said one columnist. 'It's either got to be professional or none. The "tourist" brand is all right for a little while but it's bound to culminate into out and out professional sooner or later.'[64] Gradually, it seems, baseball had been transformed from a cultural struggle involving the rough and the respectable to a marketable spectacle and an increasingly commercialized form of organized leisure.

The baseball careers of brothers Roy and Gordon Isnor reveal the changing perception of the virtues of amateur versus professional baseball. The Isnors were prominent figures on the Halifax baseball scene before and after the First World War. Of the two, Roy Isnor was perhaps the more accomplished. A hard-throwing right-hander, Isnor grew up haunting the baseball diamonds of the city, and served as batboy for the amateur Crescents 'almost as soon as I could walk.'[65] By 1910 he was a star on the mound for the same club, and during the season was offered a chance to tour with a New England team as it circled through the Maritimes. Isnor chose not to accept the offer, the Acadian Recorder observed, because 'he might have to play with a pro or two and he objects to that as he likes the sport for sport sake.'[66] When professional baseball returned to Halifax the following year, however, it was the Isnor brothers who were its strongest proponents. Roy Isnor became field manager of the Socials, and Gordon Isnor assumed the position of secretary-treasurer of the new league. Gordon Isnor, the Halifax Herald noted, was 'to a large extent responsible for the Halifax pro league ... [and] is determined to see professional baseball popular in most of Nova Scotia's baseball towns.'[67] Clearly, there was no hint here that professional baseball was a disreputable pastime. Nor would there be the following year when Gordon Isnor and fellow professional baseball promoter John T. Murphy threw their hats into the ring in an aldermanic contest in Halifax. On the contrary, Isnor would draw upon his reputation as a successful businessman and sports enthusiast in pursuing a political career that ultimately led to his appointment to the Canadian Senate.[68] In 1912 Stellarton and Westville joined the two Halifax clubs in the Nova Scotia Professional Baseball League, bringing the highest calibre ball to the province since the turn of the century. Enthusiasm ran particularly high in Stellarton, where public donations, private support, and the proceeds of benefit performances at the local Star theatre raised money to attract a squad of fine athletes. On the mound for the Stellarton team was Jack Cogan from Cambridge, Massachusetts, who had starred for the Halifax Standards the previous year. Behind the plate was a twenty-one-year-old catcher from Saint John named Tom Daly. One of the classiest players in the league, Daly hit close to .400 during the season and sparkled defensively. He deserved, said one Halifax sportswriter, to be 'in faster company.'[69] Daly's talent did not escape the notice of Joe Page, the regional scout of the Chicago White Sox, who signed him to a contract for the following year. Daly later played eight years in the Windy City, with a .239 career batting average.

The New Brunswick–Maine League also flourished in 1912, increasing its salary limit from $1000 to $1150 per month in order to keep many of the stars from the previous year under contract, while attracting new players. Tip O'Neill returned to Saint John to play for the Marathons, but, having lost much of his old-time speed, had a mediocre season. The Marathons signed pitcher Casey Hageman, formerly of the Boston Red Sox, to back up George Winter; while the arch-rival Fredericton Pets picked up right-hander Andy Harrington, a native of Wakefield, Massachusetts, who would later play for the Cincinnati Reds. During the season there was a hot three-way race between Fredericton, the Marathons, and the new Houlton club, with the Pets coming out on top. Fredericton would later play a three-game series with the Halifax Standards for the Maritime championship.

At the end of the season, the New England League champions once again came north to play the Marathons in a best-two-out-of-three series. In the first game the Marathons pulled off a 4–1 victory, thanks to a bases-loaded triple by Marathon shortstop Eddie Ramsay. For the next match, almost 4000 fans jammed the park and witnessed one of the most exciting games the city had ever seen. The Marathons sent the crafty old pro George Winter to the mound to lock horns with Lynn's

Andy Harrington, who had started the year with the Fredericton Pets. The game was a pitchers' duel, with Winter and the Marathons coming out on top with a 2–1 victory in twelve innings. After the game the fans mobbed the field, took Winter on their shoulders, tossed him in the air, and carried him to his hotel, while local traffic and streetcars waited for the crowd to pass.[70] In the meantime the Fredericton Pets had travelled to Halifax, where they defeated the Halifax Standards two games to one for the Maritime baseball championship.

The success of professional ball in Nova Scotia and New Brunswick – in August 1912 over 8000 spectators attended a game between the Saint John Marathons and Houlton, Maine – quickly attracted the attention of promoters such as Frank J. Leonard of the Lynn Baseball Club of the New England League, who envisaged a prosperous new league in Maine and the Maritimes.[71] Leonard advocated the affiliation of professional baseball leagues in the Maritimes with organized baseball, arguing that it created a more stable operation and protected against contract jumping. Besides, the victory of the Marathons over his club in two straight games made it clear that the New Brunswick–Maine League was on a par with the New England League. Joe Page, manager of the Saint John Marathons, who doubled as a scout for the Chicago White Sox and sports agent for the Canadian Pacific Railway, also believed that the New Brunswick–Maine League and the Nova Scotia Professional League should seek the protection of organized baseball and together become one league.

Among other things, affiliation with organized baseball would provide some protection against player raiding and contract jumping, an issue that flared up after an independent professional club from Dorchester, Massachusetts, toured the Maritimes in July 1912. For a number of the Dorchester players, including ex–major leaguers Howard Wakefield and Jack Coffey, the tour provided an opportunity to showcase their talent and sell their services to local clubs, who could use them in their drive towards the league championship. On 15 August, the day after Roy Isnor of the Standards had pitched a three-hitter to beat Dorchester 4–2 in the final game of its tour, the Halifax Socials signed catcher Wakefield and his battery-mate Warwick, who had pitched effectively for the Lowell team that had played in Saint John in 1911. Less than a week later it was reported that Warwick and Wakefield had been offered $200 per month to play for Reserve Mines in the Cape Breton League. Wakefield was the only one to take the offer, but he was met up the line on the train to Cape Breton and induced to return to

Halifax. The *Acadian Recorder* vented its frustration: 'Since the season opened Finnamore has gone to Houlton, Doherty to Woodstock, Maloney and Chisholm have had offers from Houlton and Warwick is said to have an offer from Fredericton. If such is continued another year it means the end of professional baseball in Nova Scotia.'[72] What was needed, it argued, was an agreement between the various leagues not to take players without the consent of their existing clubs.

Frank Leonard's initial attempt to solve this problem by creating a regional professional league within organized baseball failed to bear fruit in the 1913 season, but was taken up once again in the spring of 1914 by Joe Page. Operating on behalf of officials of the Saint John baseball teams, Page hoped to spearhead a new professional league in the Maritimes. This league, slated to operate as a Class 'D' circuit within organized baseball, was to include teams in Halifax, Saint John, Moncton, New Glasgow, and Stellarton. Page also secured several name players for the new circuit, including former Boston, Detroit, and Cleveland player Cy Ferry. Unfortunately, when Moncton and New Glasgow demanded guarantees of $2745 for thirty-eight appearances in Halifax and an equal amount from Saint John, yet offered none in return to the other clubs, the scheme was scuttled.[73]

Had the war in Europe not broken out, it seems likely that the integration of Maritime baseball into the larger framework of organized baseball would eventually have taken place. After the war, however, baseball in the Maritimes took a different turn. Influenced by an emerging sense of regional identity and a concomitant veneration of the hardy Maritime 'folk,' Maritime baseball became less reliant on imported professionals from New England. Between the wars there would be a few experiments with professional baseball, including the Cape Breton Colliery League, which operated for three years within organized baseball, but by and large baseball in the Maritimes operated on a strictly amateur basis. In these years, the MPAAA maintained its rigid separation of amateurs and professionals. What is interesting, however, is that the rationale for this delineation changed. Earlier the discussion of amateur and professional baseball had been connected to a discourse about respectability and gentlemanly character and as such was connected to the class question. During the 1920s and 1930s, the emphasis on strict amateurism grew out of a desire on the part of Maritime communities to create a level playing field for all who sought to compete for the Maritime championship.

8

Baseball as Civic Accomplishment: Regionalism, Nationalism, and Community Identity

By the First World War professional baseball had established a credibility that it lacked twenty years before. Through much of the nineteenth century, promoters of the game lamented the characterization of baseball as a rough and rowdy sport, tainted by gamblers, disreputable owners, and players who cared only about their own selfish interests. Beginning around the turn of the century, organized baseball entered into a process of reform, reining in irresponsible owners, establishing a more equitable relationship between the clubs and the players, raising player salaries, limiting gambling and rowdyism, and emphasizing the 'scientific' character of the game. Part of the broader progressive reform movement that swept North America in these years, this reform impulse altered the prevailing discourse about baseball. In the decade or so before the First World War, the imagery of business efficiency, scientific management, and social responsibility began to supplant the earlier preoccupation with respectability and roughness, and notions of national service and civic accomplishment assumed more prominence than the question of class relations.

This new imagery accompanied a movement for reform that helped secure the legitimacy of the modern business corporation. In *The Corporate Ideal in the Liberal State: 1900–1918* James Weinstein has charted the shift from laissez-faire liberalism, during the age of robber-baron capitalism, to a new more socially responsible 'corporate liberalism' that emerged during the Progressive Era in the United States. Incorporating notions of social efficiency and social engineering, and a more 'business-like' approach to labour-management relations, progressives in both the United States and Canada sought 'to bring together "thoughtful men of all classes" in "a vanguard for the building of the good community."'

In general, progressive reformers demanded a more responsible capitalist system and a less destructive relationship between capital and labour, seeking class peace and social efficiency. These ideals, 'formulated and developed under the aegis of those who ... enjoyed ideological and political hegemony,' offered an ideological alternative to populists on the right and socialists on the left, and helped to consolidate the authority of big-business interests throughout the United States and Canada.[1]

The reform of major-league baseball mirrored the larger movement to address the growing uneasiness about too-rapid industrialization and large scale monopoly capitalism, a concern that had been prompted by labour militancy and continuing public antipathy to the rapacious practices of trusts, rings, and combines. As the 1890s opened, baseball faced a serious labour revolt, occasioned largely by the controversial 'reserve clause,' which bound players to their respective clubs. Unsuccessful in rescinding what they regarded as baseball's 'fugitive slave law,' the players established their own Players' League in 1890 as a rival to the National League. The new league lasted only a single season before collapsing, however, and with the absorption of the rival American Association the following year, the National League emerged without peer or rival. Almost immediately the baseball monolith attracted the ire of antimonopolistic reformers. There was, as one editor put it in 1894, 'probably no business – unless it is the gas office – that is conducted more in the Vanderbilt public-be-damned principle than baseball.'[2]

Although the collapse of the Players' League had given the magnates the power to keep players under their thumbs, they continued to have their actions subjected to close scrutiny in the sporting press. The *Sporting News*, for example, carried on a vigorous assault on the St Louis Browns' owner, Chris Von der Ahe, because of his attachment to liquor, gambling, and horse-racing interests. A controversial figure to say the least, the bulbous-nosed, mustachioed Von der Ahe had made a sizeable fortune on his St Louis ball club during the 1880s, only to lose it as a result of his profligate living. In a desperate attempt to recoup his losses, Von der Ahe planned a racetrack at Sportsman's Park. The association of baseball and horse-racing riled the editor of The *Sporting News*, as did his private life. 'Von der Ahe's private life is an affront to the community,' said one editorial. 'He consorts with courtesans and lives in open adultery. His baseball career has been discreditable and is rounded out by incapacity ... His reputation as a bulldozer is national. His financial standing has become so impaired through dissipation and mismanagement that he is without the necessary means to strengthen his team.'[3]

It would be wrong to single out Von der Ahe for criticism, for many of his fellow owners behaved in equally irresponsible ways. Owners bet for and against their teams, tampered with players on other clubs, cheated each other on gate receipts, slashed player salaries, violated their contracts, and levied fines against them in order to avoid paying them their full salary. Writing at the turn of the century, journalist Frank Richter observed that baseball was characterized by the owners' 'gross individual and collective mismanagement, their fierce factional fights, their cynical disregard of decency and honor, their open spoliation of each other, their deliberate alienation of press and public, their flagrant disloyalty to friends and supporters and their tyrannical treatment of the players.'[4] In short, the baseball magnates revealed all of the characteristics of irresponsible 'robber baron' capitalism.

Harold Seymour has argued that, although the National League had 'always desired a monopoly of baseball, ... [it] did not know how to handle it once it achieved it,' making the owners vulnerable to the challenge of the American League, which began operations in 1901. The existence of the new league forced a more conciliatory attitude towards the players, and a recognition of the legitimacy of the newly formed Players' Protective Association. Faced with the defection of its players to the new league, and the urging of leading sporting periodicals that they meet the players in 'a spirit of friendship ... for the good of the game,'[5] the old owners found it necessary to proceed in a spirit of greater responsibility. Over the next decade, major-league baseball experienced greater stability, and with improved salaries the clubs were able to recruit an increasing number of college players. All of this brought a new respectability to the sport.

As baseball entered the twentieth century, then, it benefited from the popular acceptance of big business as an essential component of the modern order. '$30,000,000 or Maybe More Is Invested in the Game of Baseball,' announced a story in the Halifax *Herald* in August 1909, which noted that the game was rapidly becoming one of the world's great industries, revealing an attachment to principles of rational management and efficient organization. 'Businessmen have systematized baseball until the organization compares with a Harriman railroad.' As baseball became an efficient business, moreover, it also attained respectability and a broad audience. Unlike tennis, golf, hockey, lacrosse, and football, which had 'class followings,' the *Herald* observed, 'baseball has acquired a mass following.' Furthermore, as the 'rough edges of the game' were 'knocked away,' baseball extended its appeal across the social spectrum. Fans of the game, the article continued, no longer looked upon it with suspicion as they did fifteen years before.[6]

Articles of this sort played upon the public's somewhat exaggerated faith in business efficiency and the progressive effect of technological advancement. Increasingly, baseball imagery involved allusions to scientific management, technical expertise, and strategic play. Newspapers carried instructional articles on the 'science' of hitting or fielding, popular magazines wrote of the 'grooves of attack,' applying geometrical equations to explain the game,[7] and scientific periodicals applied Bernoulli's principle to explain the curving of the baseball.[8] 'In the scientific development of baseball,' wrote Hugh Fullerton in the *American Magazine* in 1912, 'it probably will become necessary within a generation or two for the manager to be a post graduate in physics and for him to maintain a barometer, a wind pressure gauge and other scientific apparatus in connection with the bench. Already, in such crude ways as testing winds, studying the weight of the atmosphere, and the chemical composition of balls, the managers are commencing to recognize this.'[9] Yet, Fullerton and others argued, scientific management did not by itself ensure a winning team. Success only came by marrying scientific understanding with individual execution and innovation, or what was generally referred to as 'inside baseball.' 'Inside ball must not be confused with scientific ball,' wrote Edward Lyell Fox. 'The former is necessitated by the latter. The big managers, McGraw, Mack, Chance, Jennings, and Clarke, never employ players who cannot think for themselves, who have not the knack of guessing.'[10]

The imagery of sport as a social technology that, in the right hands, could bring about liberating results was commonplace among a generation of progressive intellectuals from John Dewey to William James. Sports like baseball were not seen as an affirmation of Darwinian notions of 'survival of the fittest,' but as exercises that drew upon modern science, individual initiative, and appropriate management in order to promote the interest of the team, the public, and the nation. James had described sport as 'the moral equivalent of war,' one of those 'human inspired technologies' that directed individual energy and competitive instinct into a stable system of morals and civic honour. Although repelled by war, James saw strenuous competition as an important component of progress; sport thus represented a positive alternative to destructive combat. Yet as war came to Europe, the notion of sport as a force for national renewal was quickly turned into a justification for war itself.[11]

With the outbreak of the First World War, the language of managerial efficiency, technological sophistication, and social responsibility responded obediently to the call for national sacrifice. It was easy enough to turn images of sport to military purposes, rousing the spirits of enlisted men and encouraging others to volunteer for military service. Halifax newspapers, for example, carried photos of notable 'Halifax Athletes in the Big Game,' or 'Crack Athletes Who Are Now on the Firing Line,' emphasizing that sport had prepared them physically and morally for carrying on the fight.[12] For those who had not yet volunteered, columns like Herbert Kaufman's 'Play Ball' sought to inspire youth to military service and sacrifice through the use of baseball analogies. The message was that of wartime progressivism: selfish individualism was the characteristic of the bush leaguer; the true sportsman, by contrast, was one who was willing to sacrifice and put the team or nation's interest before his own. Kaufman wrote:

> Without practice, proficiency and will finally disappear.
> The Big League is continually drafting pennant timber out of the minors.
> Play the game. Deliver the goods and your average will travel.
> But if you insist upon sticking to your own base and merely take care of what comes your way, you'll remain a busher to the finish.
> The winning spirit asserts itself over the entire field.
> The whole world is scouting for lads who count a personal record secondary to the team's race.[13]

Paul Fussell has outlined the wartime construction of an apologetic language that euphemistically turned blackened and dismembered corpses into the 'fallen,' transformed soldiers into 'warriors, and rendered the blood of the dead and wounded into 'the sweet, red wine of youth.'[14] Sporting analogies served to mask the horror of war in similar ways. If baseball was analogous to war, did it not follow that war was just a more serious form of sport? Indeed, as the slaughter in Europe continued, sportswriters on the home front found that battlefield language provided 'colour' to their prose and gave expression to their patriotic sensibilities. Baseball managers became 'field generals,' catchers donned their 'armour,' pitchers threw 'bullets,' visiting teams became 'invading combinations,' and home clubs fought with 'desperate resistance.' At some point in the game, one of the 'combatants' might bring out the 'heavy artillery' and begin the 'fusilade' that would result in the 'enemy' breaking 'under the strain of the conflict.'[15]

Ironically, while the militarization of baseball language served to romanticize war, the war seriously interrupted baseball's development throughout the Maritimes. Not only were there more immediate concerns to address than the organization of sporting activity, but the loss of young men to overseas service, the shortages of sporting equipment, and the use of sporting grounds for military purposes meant that in most localities baseball became an ad hoc affair. Only a week after the outbreak of the conflict, the Sydney *Record* reported that the war was playing havoc with sports events, and observed that 'the very flower of Canada's athletes will go to the front from the president of the Amateur Athletic Union of Canada down.'[16] Virtually all coverage of local baseball was discontinued and sport news tended to deal only with national and international events. In Halifax, the military took over the Commons, the centre of baseball activity for a half-century, erected military barracks, and drilled troops where ballplayers usually played.

Initially, there were many who regarded sporting activity as frivolous and inappropriate when so many young men were risking their lives on the battlefield. Demands grew for the cancellation of athletic events on both moral and fiscal grounds. Not everyone considered this wise, however. In a letter to the *Acadian Recorder* in August 1915, Stuart McCawley of Glace Bay complained that in 'the upper provinces' nearly all amateur athletic tournaments were cancelled or postponed because of the war, and now 'the Maritime Province Executives are bitten and are sending out postponement notices.I think they are wrong. War, if it is anything good, nearly resembles a great feat of strength, where the last game after munitions, money and transportation are exhausted, must be won by the men who are most physically fit, who are the best sports, and who know how to, and who will, play "the game" with strength brain and cunning.' McCawley observed that almost the entire Glace Bay baseball team was at Valcartier, six ex-captains and twenty-eight players of the Glace Bay football club were on the firing line, and the Caledonia football club had sent all its members overseas, with the exception of two who were turned down because of leg injuries suffered last season. 'If Canada is determined to maintain her present splendid record for producing men of good physique who have learned how to fight and "play the game" in football, hockey, baseball, golf or tennis, then for goodness sake let the sporting executives "boost" not kill sport.'[17]

When baseball was played during the war, it often served wartime ends. The game provided a convenient vehicle for raising money and equipment for troops at the front,[18] and wartime leagues such as the professional Halifax Army & City League supplied useful recreation for troops awaiting overseas transport. Established in 1916 and operating until war's end, the Army & City League was made up of the Composite and 219th regiments, the Crescents, and the Socials. All monies raised by these teams either went to patriotic funds or to various charities in the city.[19] Elsewhere, baseball served as a prod to productivity in essential industries. A baseball league representing the various departments at the Dominion Steel mills at Sydney operated in 1918, with teams from the office, blast furnace, open hearth, wire mills, and coke ovens. Employers no doubt hoped that the rivalries on the baseball field would stimulate one department's desire to out-produce another in the workplace.[20] At one match in July 1918, when the Coke Ovens defeated a U.S. Army club, girl guides collected $60 for the Red Cross and a community band furnished music free of charge.[21]

Baseball was also a popular pastime among troops overseas, in both Britain and France. In 1915, the Toronto City Council sent seven cases of baseball equipment to troops in France, noting that the 'boys at the front desire to play ball when taken back from the firing line to "rest" or when in reserve.'[22] In a despatch from Canadian Military Headquarters in France in 1917, Stewart Lyon observed that 'baseball and concerts are the supreme delights of our Canadians.' He reported that he recently 'saw a hotly contested ball game on a bit of land subject to frequent gun fire and on which the enemy airmen were liable at any moment to drop bombs. Sports has done almost as much as patriotic ardor to steady the nerves of the Empire's sons for the great ordeal of war.'[23] Some time later, Harry Stringer of the U.S. War Department's Commission on Training Camp Activities surveyed recreational and relief facilities among American overseas forces and noted the popularity of baseball among the soldiers. 'I saw our boys playing from London to Paris right up to the front line trenches ... Rivalry is keen and men take as much interest in their respective nines as they do in the big league races at home.'[24]

Upon the arrival of the American Expeditionary Force in 1917, a baseball rivalry between Canadian and American servicemen quickly developed. In 1918 the Anglo American League was organized in London, with three army and one navy team from the American forces and four Canadian teams from London headquarters. One of the top teams was the U.S. 342nd Field Artillery, AEF club, with Grover Cleveland Alexander on the mound.[25] Even though most American teams had four or five players with major-league experience, the Canadian teams more than held their own against the Yanks.[26] In one particularly notable match, Halifax native W.R. 'Tee' Doyle locked horns in a pitching duel with Hall of Famer Herb Pennock, who was then at the pinnacle of a baseball career that saw him win 240 games in the major leagues in 22 seasons. On this day at least, Doyle was the better man, holding the Americans to a handful of hits, and leading the Canadians to victory.[27]

When the war ended, the returning veterans were ready to pick up where they had left off before the war, but this was sometimes difficult. 'Gee' Ahern, a sports columnist in Halifax, lamented the altered condition of the Commons, the centre of sporting activity in Halifax for a century or more, which now had buildings spread from end to end. 'When the majority of the boys sailed for overseas,' he noted, 'the Common was as level as the best ball diamonds in the country, and one could stand at one end and look to the other and could see ball players, footballists, cricket players.' Now all that remained of the playing fields were a couple of small spots, neither of which was fit for baseball. 'Alas, the Common is now gone for many years to come. Should the buildings be removed during the next few years, it will be many years before the diamonds can be put in proper shape.'[28]

Inadequate facilities did not interfere for long with the determination of returning veterans to play ball. During the 1919 season, five competitive leagues, the Halifax City, Dartmouth, Intermediate, Military, and Commercial circuits were established, and league officials, besieged with applications, had to refuse several teams who wished to join.[29] The Commercial League, with teams representing Moirs Ltd., Stairs Son & Morrow, United Banks, and the Shipyards, seemed the most popular with local fans, and received the lion's share of press coverage. At the end of the season a city championship tournament between the winners of the five league titles was held, with Saint Patrick's of the Intermediate League defeating the Technical College of the Military League in the final match. In addition to the city championship, an All-Halifax club, drawn mainly from the Socials and Standards of the City League, won the Nova Scotia championship in a series of tightly played games against Stellarton, Springhill, and Westville. All-Halifax also played a three-game series with a Saint John club in 1919, that drew over 6000 fans.[30]

By 1920, the Maritime Provinces branch of the Canadian Amateur

Athletic Association, which had been practically inactive during the war, reasserted its control over amateur athletics in the region. Almost immediately disputes arose over the amateur standing of those who had played professionally before and during the First World War. The MPAAA addressed the question of the reinstatement of wartime professionals first, agreeing to their reinstatement in May 1920. When it came to those who had played professionally before 1914, the MPAAA registration committee refused to recommend amateur status for Dave Keeler, Steve Whelan, and the irrepressible Roy Isnor. Isnor, along with his brother Gordon, had spearheaded professional baseball in the province a decade before, and continued to promote it during the war. Incensed by his exclusion, Isnor responded with a series of open letters in local newspapers, asking G.G. Thompson, the chairman of the local committee, why he, Whelan, and Keeler were not recommended for reinstatement when 'dozens who played with me previous to that date, and ... many who were playing professional ball, when I was carrying bats' had received their cards.[31] The CAAU national office subsequently reinstated Steve Whelan and Dave Keeler, but Isnor was forced to sit out the season.

For Steve Whelan, difficulties with the MPAAA continued. Early in the season Whelan had agreed to suit up with Reg Buckler's Annapolis Royal club of the Valley Baseball League, but had not been able to play without his card. After gaining his release from Annapolis on 26 June, Whelan signed with the Halifax Crescents. Unfortunately, Whelan had neglected to communicate his release to the secretary of the Valley League. When the Crescents proceeded to the provincial playdowns in August, defeating the Amherst club in the opening game of the series, Amherst protested the use of Whelan, who was technically still property of the Annapolis club. They also protested his team-mate Walsh, who had gained his release from the Great War Veterans Association club just at the 1 July deadline for registration. The executive of the Nova Scotia Baseball Association, operating under the MPAAA guidelines, upheld the protest, declaring Whelan and Walsh ineligible, and awarding the game to Amherst. To the Halifax *Herald*, always a staunch supporter of amateur play, decisions that allowed provincial titles to be decided on minor technicalities rather than on the ball field, would simply 'open the way for professionalism to creep in.'

Already in Cape Breton and New Brunswick promoters were experimenting with semi-professional baseball, mixing amateurs and pros. Cape Breton County League teams in Reserve Mines, New Waterford, and Dominion were dotted with imports from mainland Nova Scotia, New Brunswick, Ontario, and the United States.[32] In Saint John, the Alerts of the City League broke with the MPAAA, dissatisfied with the way President A.W. Covey of the NBABA was running the operation. The Alerts favoured the mixing of pros and amateurs, but Covey adhered strictly to the CAAU's definition of amateurism. The Alerts proceeded to import American players and challenged all comers in Nova Scotia, New Brunswick, and Maine. 'But who will they play down in Nova Scotia,' asked the Halifax *Herald*, 'where all the towns and cities are supporting amateur ball with the exception of a few towns in Cape Breton county?'[33]

One possibility was that the Crescents, angered at the protest against Whelan and Walsh, would break away and play as an independent team, if not in 1920 at least the following year. There were rumours as well that a Class D circuit would operate in the Maritimes during the 1921 season, financed by American baseball promoters. The Halifax *Herald* was sceptical about the prospect of full-fledged professionalism, however. Promoters of professional baseball in Halifax would have to address the fact that the Wanderers Amateur Athletic Club controlled the only decent ball field in the city, and that they were opposed to any more professional baseball being played on their grounds. 'If arrangements could be made with the CAAU,' the *Herald* suggested, 'semi-pro would be the brand, and the crowd would be sure to come.'[34]

Over the next decade, teams from the Nova Scotian mainland adhered to the amateur code, except for one brief experiment with professional baseball in 1924. The Nova Scotia Professional League, with teams in Halifax, Kentville, Middleton, and Yarmouth, attracted American imports such as 'Jersey Joe' Stripp, a lithe third baseman who later amassed a .294 career batting average during an eleven-year stint in the major leagues; strong-armed left-hander Phil Page, who was also destined for the majors; and a mysterious slick-fielding shortstop named Ozer, who, it was later rumoured, was really Leo Durocher playing under an assumed name. Although this has never been confirmed, it is at least possible. Durocher began his professional career the following year with Hartford of the Eastern League.

In addition to the imports, local stars played a prominent role in the Nova Scotia Professional League. Among the most prominent were two left-handed pitchers, Sammy Lesser of Halifax, and Stellarton native Billie Richardson, who played for the Middleton club. A student of the game, Lesser was one of the best pitchers in the Maritimes, with a blazing fastball and tricky change-up, but like many of the better players in the region with major-league potential, he was discovered too late in his career by major-league scouts. Billie Richardson started his baseball career as an outfielder with the senior team in Westville in 1917. After the war he took to the mound. In 1921 the wiry left-hander struck out twenty-two batters in a game against Stellarton. Richardson moved to the Bear River club in 1923, leading it to the provincial finals, and then to Middleton for the 1924 campaign. The mainstay on the mound for the Middleton pros, Richardson was one of the top pitchers in the league, chalking up a couple of one-hit games during the season.[35]

In New Brunswick, Saint John clubs chafed under the amateur requirements of the MPAAA and experimented with professional baseball between 1922 and 1924, as did Moncton and Fredericton. Similarly, the town of St Stephen, attracted by the prospect of competing with clubs on the other side of the American border, had a semi-pro aggregation led by a right-handed submarine-delivery pitcher named Vince Shields from Plaster Rock, New Brunswick. Shields later played for the St Louis Cardinals. In 1930 Saint John took a final fling with semi-pro ball, entering the Boston Twilight League, which included teams from Quincy, Dorchester, Malden, South Boston, and Roslindale, Massachusetts.

Although the question of amateurism and professionalism was in some ways an extension of an issue that had originated in the nineteenth century, the current debate differed in one significant respect. Earlier, the separation of amateur and professional play had turned on the question of respectability and the relationship of the classes. The roots of the nineteenth-century amateur ideal were entwined in the debate about appropriate 'gentlemanly' behaviour; the branches, by contrast, were in the amateur athletic clubs. In an insightful essay on amateur athletic clubs in New York City, Joe Willis and Richard Wettan have argued that after 1880 these clubs took on the characteristics of social clubs with an exclusionist mentality. Many instituted membership policies directed at keeping out 'undesirables,' and had provisions for screening spectators at athletic events or admitting them by invitation only.[36] Although the amateur clubs in the Maritimes tended to be less exclusive, they none the less had a membership that was essentially middle-class in character. With the exception of the Caledonia Amateur Athletic Club in Glace Bay and certain municipal clubs in Nova Scotia's Cumberland and Pictou counties, few club members came the ranks of the working class.[37]

What is most striking about the discourse surrounding baseball's social purpose after the First World War, is the evacuation of both the language of class and of progressive allusions to scientific management and national sacrifice. Baseball was now regarded as community entertainment, rather than a vehicle for social regeneration. When proponents of baseball alluded to seemingly more noble purposes, more often than not they spoke of the cultivation of regional or community allegiance and civic pride. The baseball diamond was envisioned no longer as a field of class, gender, and ethnic rivalry, but as a unifying community enthusiasm that transcended social cleavages and brought employer and employee, young and old, male and female together in a common civic pursuit. After a novelty contest between the fat and lean men of Amherst in July 1919, for example, the local *News and Sentinel* observed that when businessmen forget their dignity and get out and 'create fun and amusement,' the town will 'forge ahead.' The game suggested 'the revival of the clannish spirit of Amherst' and indicated 'a brighter future for our town.'[38] Similarly, the Halifax *Herald* of 31 July 1920 praised the strong community identity of fans in Yarmouth and Middleton, where 'young and old, men and women, know baseball, and did not sit dumb in the grandstands like our fans ... Rooters clubs, megaphones, and hundreds of noisy instruments put the old pep in the game, not to speak of the organized band of young ladies, who braved the sideline to give the town yell.'

During the twenties and thirties the provincial and Maritime baseball championships assumed a greater importance than ever before, and even small communities like Milton, Hantsport, Annapolis Royal, and Berwick in Nova Scotia and Hopewell, Shediac, and Devon in New Brunswick entered teams in county or district leagues in order to prepare themselves for the provincial playdowns. Now and then teams would sign American players to improve their competitiveness, but these players would have to be dropped when the playoffs began. In 1922, the Clark's Harbour team of the Nova Scotia South Shore League signed Boston schoolboy sensation Danny MacFayden, whose family regularly spent its summers in Nova Scotia. MacFayden later pitched seventeen years in the major leagues, and after his retirement coached baseball at Bowdoin College in Brunswick, Maine. A few years later, Westville signed Bobby Brown of Dorchester, Massachusetts, who played a season in Nova Scotia before joining the Boston Braves of the National League the following year. Brown and MacFayden played on the 1935 Braves team that travelled to Yarmouth to play the Maritime champion Gateways, the only time that a major-league club played in Nova Scotia during the regular baseball season. The year before the Braves had travelled to St Stephen, New Brunswick, to play the mighty Kinsman club, scoring nine runs in the first two innings off a nervous sixteen-year-old Kenny Kallenberg on their way to an 11–3 victory.[39]

The prominence given to provincial and regional championships in the interwar period accompanied the development of a new regional sensibility that had its political expression in the postwar Maritime Rights movement. The flourishing of Maritime regionalism accompanied continuing deindustrialization and the disillusionment with national crusades that followed the war. Ernie Forbes has attributed the growth of a Maritime consciousness after 1900 to the declining influence of the region in federal politics, the dismantling of a regionally oriented transportation system, and the failure of the federal government to provide a fair adjustment of the subsidy question. During the 1920s shipping declined, business failures increased, wholesale warehousers lost customers, and workers lost jobs. As a result, feelings of regional grievance and betrayal mingled with working-class and agrarian discontent in a volatile and potentially radical political culture. Facing growing labour unrest and the rise of class-based political movements such as the Farmer-Labour alliance, the Maritime business and political élite attached themselves to the cause of Maritime Rights, diverting attention from their own failures and blaming the difficulties of the region on the inequitable policies of the federal government.[40]

Maritime regionalism also permeated postwar cultural and intellectual life. The 1920s and 1930s, Ian McKay argues, witnessed a reconceptualization of the region's identity. The earlier progressive fascination with industrial development and productive efficiency gave way, after the war, to an antimodern ideology that celebrated a traditional Maritime folk essence. McKay has demonstrated how during the 1930s Nova Scotia Premier Angus L. Macdonald promoted a vision of Nova Scotia as a land of simple Scottish folk. Macdonald, he writes, 'took a general Nova Scotia sense of regional grievance, merged it with a doctrine of the Scottish essence, and thereby helped transform regional protest from a form of "progressivism" into something that was more like the "conservatism" many scholars have diagnosed.'[41]

This postwar ideology of the folk, promoted by folklorist Helen Creighton and a generation of writers including Frank Parker Day, Thomas Raddall, Charles Bruce, and Ernest Buckler, presented an image of a simple, but essentially virtuous Maritime community that struggled to avoid the corrupting influences of modernity. The 'golden age' of this generation was rooted in a mythologized pre-industrial past, rather than in a vision of future prosperity, and as such had more to do with those who worked the soil or fished inshore waters than with those who laboured in factories or coalfields. There was, McKay notes, little in this mythology about the bitter conflict pitting coalminers and steelworkers against their bosses, or of their attachment to radical causes. The romanticized ideology of the folk, consoling both to those who fashioned it and to proponents of Maritime Rights who derided the treatment of a virtuous and innocent people by the slick and powerful mandarins of Ottawa, essentially ignored the lives of working people struggling in poverty or against the exactions of capital. In short, postwar regionalism, as an intellectual tradition, was essentially conservative: it provided an alternative analysis from those on the left who protested the unequal social relations that characterized modern capitalist society.[42]

The altered discourse about baseball's social value in the interwar period reveals the same avoidance of the imagery of class conflict that can be observed in Maritime literature and folklore. Discussions of baseball no longer centred upon questions of class and status, on respectability and rowdyism, or even upon scientific management and technically efficient play, but rather upon images of community identity and regional allegiance. Baseball flourished at the community level, and the inter-urban rivalries that developed throughout the region helped swell attendance at the park. One game at Liverpool attracted so many visiting fans from Yarmouth that local hotels were overflowing and many had to seek lodging in private homes. 'Never in the history of the town has there been so much interest, as that which prevailed today,' said the Halifax *Herald*, 'and the town is baseball mad.'[43]

Immediately after the First World War, Saint John baseball clubs dominated the provincial scene in New Brunswick. The Saint John St Peter's were the class of the Maritimes, winning the Maritime championship from 1919 to 1924. The St Peter's were led by right-hander Ray Hansen and catcher Joe Dever, both of whom had been scouted by George 'Mooney' Gibson, the famous Canadian-born catcher who had starred for seventeen years in the major leagues and was manager of the Toronto club of the International League after the war. Intrigued by Hansen's explosive sinking curve ball, a pitch that dropped like it had fallen off a table, Gibson arranged a major-league trial for him with the New York Giants after an impressive yet brief stint in a Toronto uniform. Unfortunately for Hansen, his mother's serious illness intervened, and he gave up a chance at a major-league career and returned to Saint John to take care of her. Dever had also been offered a position with Gibson's Toronto club in 1920, but like Hansen he rejected the offer and stayed with the St Peter's squad.[44]

If the St Peter's team dominated the early twenties in New Brunswick, the Saint John Water Department club, assembled in 1925, was the outstanding team of the latter half of the decade. The Watermen were led by pitcher Lloyd Stirling, infielder Aubrey Snodgrass, and by the great Charlie Gorman, one of the finest athletes that the Maritimes ever produced. Gorman, who ran the 100-yard dash in ten seconds flat, was also a world-champion speed-skater who won the 220- and 440-yard and five-mile races at the 1926 world championships held at Lily Lake, New Brunswick. Playing almost every position for the Waterman, Gorman led the club with speed on the base paths and his potent bat. His talents also came to the attention of the New York Yankees, who offered him a contract in 1925 with their Hartford club in the Eastern League, but Gorman declined the offer to retain his amateur status and protect his speed-skating eligibility.[45]

In 1925 Gorman teamed up with Lloyd Stirling to lead the Watermen to the Maritime championship, knocking off the Charlottetown Abbies in a three-game series. Stirling continued to pitch in Saint John for two more years, but signed with the Boston Red Sox organization in 1928, and remained in their system for the next decade. In 1935 Stirling had his best year, winning twenty-four games in twenty-six decisions for the Winnipeg Maroons of the Northern League, fifteen of them in succession. One of the two outstanding pitchers in the minor leagues in 1935, Stirling played for Toronto of the International League in 1936.

The Watermen were not to repeat as Maritime champions after their victory in 1925, although they probably were the best team in the region. Each year from 1926 to 1928, disputes with the Maritime Provinces Amateur Athletic Association resulted in their disqualification from championship play. Although other clubs in the region were no doubt paying some of their players under the table, the Watermen were singled out for scrutiny by the MPAAA. Finally returning to provincial play in 1929, they were nosed out in the finals, losing 2–1 to Moncton in the deciding match. The following year the club turned its back on regional play, and entered the semi-professional Boston Twilight League, playing there until the league collapsed in 1931. After that baseball entered into a period of decline in Saint John, and softball gained increasing prominence in the summer sporting life of the city.[46]

In Nova Scotia, two coal towns, Westville and Springhill, were locked in a bitter rivalry at this time, squaring off in the provincial finals each year fom 1924 to 1928. In addition, Westville won the Maritime championship in 1926, winning two out of three games against the Charlottetown Abbies, and repeated as provincial champion in 1931. (The Abbies were Maritime finalists from 1925 to 1927, and again in 1929 and 1931, but were never Maritime champions.) Springhill took the Maritime title in 1927 and 1928, and were provincial champions once again in 1933 and 1936.

Given that baseball discourse turned less upon notions of class after the war, it is perhaps ironic that two working-class towns carried the banner of provincial baseball in Nova Scotia for most of the twenties. Yet, in the coalfields, class allegiances and community identity were virtually inseparable. In each of these towns most livelihoods were attached in some way to the mining of coal, and the uncertainties, dangers, and collective struggle of coalminers and their families against capitalist exploitation created an intense community solidarity and sense of collective enterprise. Indeed, in Springhill and Westville, the traditions of the workplace suffused other cultural institutions such as the church, the fraternal society, and the sporting club 'to create a distinctive variant of "working class culture."'[47] Ian McKay is right to suggest that 'the intense solidarity of the mining community was the gift of the mine,'[48] but the baseball diamond was an important component of the social fabric of working-class life as well.[49]

The interwar rosters of the Springhill Fencebusters and Westville Miners were dotted with some of the finest sporting talent in the region. Springhill was a rabid baseball town in the early years of the century, and had produced a number of players who starred throughout the region: among them were Charlie Paul, a fire-balling pitcher who not only played on various semi-pro teams in Cape Breton and New Brunswick but had a stint in the Boston Braves' farm system; pitcher Jimmy Trott, who had an equally peripatetic career; catcher-outfielder George 'Brownie' Burden, who played for the Fencebusters during the twenties; and Ackie Allbon, a pitcher and outfielder who first played senior baseball in Nova Scotia at the tender age of sixteen. Paul and Allbon starred on the 1927 Fencebusters team, anchored by big Hank O'Rourke. Squatting behind the plate with only a catcher's mitt and mask, and his socks rolled down, O'Rourke may not have looked like a baseball player, but he was the dominant catcher in Maritime baseball in the 1920s and 1930s. O'Rourke continued to play until the Second World

War, when advancing age and failing eyesight brought an end to his career.

In the 1930s a new generation of stars joined the Fencebuster ranks, including the incomparable second baseman Lawson Fowler, slick-fielding shortstop Jack Fraser, first baseman Leo 'Sailor' Macdonald, and pitchers Tommy Albert Linkletter, Edgar Cormier, Copie LeBlanc, and Stew McLeod. Then there was 'Purney' Fuller, who packed major-league talent in a little-league body. Standing barely five-foot-two, Fuller was probably the smallest player ever to receive a trial with the New York Yankees; the only thing the New Yorkers didn't like about Fuller, said Yankee manager Joe McCarthy later, was his 'lack of poundage.'[50]

Next door in Pictou County, were the Westville Miners, the perennial rivals of the Fencebusters. Led by the pitching of Davey Thompson and Billie Richardson and the fine all-round play of Burns Dunbar, the Miners' finest hour came in 1926 when they won the Maritime title. Thompson was a tough competitor on the mound, and had demonstrated enough talent to be invited to the New York Giants' spring training camp in 1924.[51] Dunbar provided the offensive punch from his lead-off spot in the batting order, and his daring baserunning often unnerved visiting pitchers. The remainder of the line-up was, if not spectacular, at least solid. Rounding out the roster were slugging outfielder Bobbie Williams, pitcher Edgar Cormier, 'Doc' Carrigan, Jack Darroch, Billy McIsaac, Alex Marshall, and 'Red' McLeod.[52]

By 1930 the balance of power in Nova Scotian baseball was shifting south and west, to Halifax, Liverpool, and Yarmouth. In 1930 Sammy Lesser's Halifax St Agnes club knocked off Springhill in the provincial playdowns and proceeded to capture the Maritime championship in a closely fought series with Moncton. Leading the way for Halifax St Agnes – which for years had been the class of the local Twilight League – were pitcher Mellish Lane and outfielder Vince Ferguson. Ferguson was perhaps the most exciting player in the Maritimes at the time, known for his speed and reckless abandon on the base paths and his acrobatic catches in the outfield. He was also a star on the ice, scoring the winning goal in 1935 when the Halifax Wolverines defeated the Montreal Royals for the Allan Cup. 'There have been greater all-round athletes than Ferguson,' Alex Nickerson wrote in 1938, 'better hockey players, smarter ball hawks, but none superior in the dual capacity of hockey star and baseball luminary.'[53] And, to a youthful Robert 'Bun' Foley, who used to haunt the Wanderers grounds with his brothers, Ferguson was 'the player who could do it all, who would get the needed hit or make the big play just when the team needed it. In my mind there was no better ballplayer in the province at that time.'[54]

Halifax's reign as provincial and Maritime champion was short-lived, and as the decade wore on Yarmouth and Liverpool came to dominate the provincial baseball scene. Between 1929 and 1941 Yarmouth won five and Liverpool four provincial championships; Springhill won the title twice, in 1933 and 1936; and Halifax and Westville were one-time winners in 1930 and 1931. The early thirties also witnessed the eclipse of Saint John as a baseball power in New Brunswick, and the rise of the mighty St Stephen–Milltown club. As Halifax and Saint John's baseball fortunes languished, moreover, Maritime baseball in the 1920s became synonomous with small-town life.

In Yarmouth, the Gateways were a small town's pride and joy. Assembled in 1928 by Ernie Grimshaw, a transplanted Haligonian and journeyman second baseman, the Gateways drew upon Yarmouth's rich baseball tradition and established veterans Bobby Forward and Murray Veno. Forward, who began his career in the local town league, played before the war in the Nova Scotia professional league, his strong showing in top-flight competition earning him a couple of major-league trials with the Boston Braves and Pittsburgh Pirates. During the 1920s he was the mainstay of the Yarmouth club's mound corps, both in provincial competition and in the short-lived pro circuit of 1924. Like Forward, Veno learned his baseball in the old Yarmouth Town League, and subsequently honed his skills as a member of the Canadian Army team in England that beat the U.S. Army club in 1918. After playing a year of organized baseball in the United States, where salaries were low, and the road to the majors uncertain, Veno returned to Yarmouth, where he continued to play baseball well into his forties.

Although the Gateways won Maritime titles in 1929 and 1932, the 1935 Maritime championship team was arguably the strongest team Yarmouth assembled between the wars. The leader of the club was shortstop Halley Horton, whose 'somewhat shy manner and infectious grin,' not to mention career batting average in the vicinity of .350, 'made him one of the most popular players in the province.'[55] Halley's brother Doug, at first base, was a long-ball hitter, clever veteran Biss Boyd played a steady game at third base, and in the outfield Murray Veno, 'Red' Goudey, and 'Lightning' Amirault were betimes erratic and spectacular. 'A man remembers Veno for a number of reasons,' Ace Foley once wrote, 'the way he hit and ran and the uncertainty he showed fielding long flies, grabbing them at the last moment as the prayerful fans heaved a great sigh of relief.'[56] Amirault also had great speed afoot and a cannon for a throwing arm, which he obligingly demonstrated to an amazed collection of Boston Braves when they visited Yarmouth in 1935. According to sportswriter Earl Morton, when several of the Braves were demonstrating their skills in a pre-game warmup, the fans urged 'Lightning' to show off the strength of his arm. 'The Yarmouth flash took his place at home plate,' Morton reported, 'and threw the ball over the left field fence, 385 feet away.'[57]

For their mound staff, the 1935 Gateways relied upon 'Copie' LeBlanc, Nate Bain, Cliff Surette, and Ken Veniot. The sometimes sullen and imperious LeBlanc considered himself the best left-hander in the Maritimes, although there were several others – including Cecil 'Lefty' Brownell of St Stephen – who may have disagreed. When he was on his game, though, LeBlanc was virtually unhittable. In one notable outing against the touring House of David club, LeBlanc pitched five no-hit innings and struck out eleven. During these years LeBlanc spurned a number of pro offers in order to maintain his amateur standing, including repeated requests for his services by clubs in the Cape Breton Colliery League. LeBlanc was at his best in the Gateways' victory in the 1935 Maritime championships over the mighty St Stephen Kiwanis club, pitching Yarmouth to an eleventh-inning 3–2 win in the opening game, and a 3–1 triumph in the final game of the series.

After losing to Springhill in the provincial playdowns of 1936, Yarmouth regained the crown in 1937. By this time, however, a powerful rival had emerged in the town of Liverpool. Liverpool's emergence as a baseball power in the 1930s owed much to John 'Pop' Seaman and his four sons' arrival in town after the great stock-market crash of 1929 had wiped out the family business in the United States. Although Liverpool by no means had avoided the aching hardships of the Depression, the establishment of the Mersey Paper Company's mill in 1930 had buoyed the town's economy and helped merchant John Seaman re-establish himself. Pop's boys, Ike, Kal, Garneau, and Danny in turn revived the baseball club's flagging fortunes, while the elder Seaman provided financial backing for the team.

In 1938 the Larruppurs won their first provincial title, with Ike on the mound, Kal at shortstop, and Danny and Garneau in the outfield. The following year the Larrappurs won the first of four consecutive Maritime titles with a line-up that included the Young brothers, Lloyd, Al, and Burton, Clayton Hutchins, Vic Winters, and catcher Nels Deveau. Right-handed flame-thrower Laurie Thorburn, lefty Jim Mont, and Fred

Kenney, 'a mercurial left-hander whose "dipsy-doo" pitch – a quasi knuckleball – caused batters as much anxiety as his drinking caused his teammates,'[58] made up the pitching corps. Garnie Seaman considered this club to be 'the strongest team with which I was ever associated ... If you were to have taken that '39 club and added four pitchers you would have had a team capable of competing in Triple A ball.'[59]

Of all the clubs in the Maritimes between the wars, none could match the record of the St Stephen team, which won eight consecutive New Brunswick titles and six Maritime championships between 1931 and 1938. Lying astride the St Croix River, the border towns of St Stephen, New Brunswick, and Calais, Maine, were in fact a single community separated by an international boundary. The famous St Stephen teams of the thirties reflected that fact, drawing their personnel and crowds from both sides of the river. There was always a good-natured rivalry between St Stephen and Calais, of course. Cries of 'fuck the Queen' from the American side of the border, remembers American pitcher Ken Kallenberg, always invited an indignant and no doubt equally vulgar response from the Canadian side. 'Americans against Canadians, Protestants against Catholics, neighbourhood against neighbourhood,' writes Robert Ashe. 'These shifting allegiances collided for pick-up ball games on sprawling fields with cow flaps for bases and an unravelling sphere for a ball.' Against other Maritime and New England teams, however, these divisions melted away. St Stephen and Calais *lived* baseball together: important games were front-page news in both towns, and the players, wherever they came from, were community heroes.[60]

If the St Stephen ballclub symbolized the connections between baseball in the Maritimes and northern New England, the annual pilgrimage of touring baseball clubs from Maine, Massachusetts, and Connecticut nurtured the attachment of the Maritimes to the 'Boston States.' Usually the New Englanders would enter the region through St Stephen, where they would face the pitching slants of wily veteran 'Lefty' Brownell, right-hander Roy Boles, Howdy Clark, Jim Morell, Mike Calder (who held the Boston Braves hitless and struck out three in two innings of work in 1935), or perhaps the youthful Kenny Kallenberg. Then there was the potent batting line-up, led by Gordon Coffey, a graceful centre-fielder who gradually became the team's best hitter, and Orville Mitchell, the club's cerebral captain. Other stars included smooth-fielding shortstop Phil McCarroll, American-born catcher Theo McLain, Charlie Godfrey, Earl 'Squirrely' Ross, and Harry Boles.

There had been a brief interlude during the First World War when the traditional connection between Maritime and New England baseball had been severed, but a few years after the war the annual northern pilgrimage of teams from Massachusetts, Connecticut, New Hampshire, and Maine resumed. The connection was re-established in July 1921 with the arrival in the Maritimes of Eddie Carr's Auburn baseball team of Cambridge, Massachusetts, and a later tour by Bob Bigney's South Boston All Stars. Carr, who had played professional ball for Stellarton before the First World War, had assembled a club of former high-school and college stars that the Boston *Post* considered 'the fastest amateur team around Boston.'[61] Before leaving on their two-month tour of Maine and the Maritimes, the Auburns had won fifteen of sixteen games from clubs in the Boston Twilight League. On their Maritime tour they swept eleven of fifteen games, but dropped a twin-bill to the region's champions, the Saint John St Peter's by scores of 8–3 and 4–1.

The following year witnessed a veritable invasion by touring clubs from Massachusetts. In addition to Carr's amateur club, another professional team from Auburn managed by Ray Rogers spent the month of August in the provinces. They were joined by Dick Casey's Neponset All Stars. In the previous month, the region had been visited by teams from Arlington, Dorchester, Quincy, Newburyport, and Somerville, Massachusetts, by Bob Bigney's South Boston All Stars, and by a team known as the Boston Travellers. The local teams' schedules had become so crowded, Bigney complained, that his team couldn't get enough games, and was sometimes forced to play against the Travellers. The surfeit of touring teams, however, was a boon for communities usually ignored by visitors. Indeed, for Prince Edward Island clubs in Charlottetown and Summerside, games with New England clubs were the highlight of the season. When the Boston Travellers visited Charlottetown – defeating the local Abegweit Club 5–2 – the town rolled out the red carpet. The Americans were publicly welcomed by Mayor Harold Jenkins, and a band concert was held in their honour in the Public Gardens.

Over the next two decades the flood of New England teams into the Maritimes continued unabated. In addition to those already mentioned, teams from Malden, Salem, Taunton and Attleboro, the James A. Roche club of Everett, Massachusetts, and Frank Silva's Connecticut Yankees were regular visitors to the Maritimes. Occasionally U.S. Navy personnel from the Annapolis Naval Academy, or from warships such as the U.S.S. *Tampa* and the U.S.S. *Milwaukee*, played against local clubs in Halifax. Black barnstorming teams such as the Cleveland Giants, the

Philadelphia Giants, and the Boston Royal Giants, and novelty teams such as the House of David and the New York Bloomer Girls, often visited the region as well. Of these, Burlin White's Boston Royal Giants was the most frequent visitor, playing close to three hundred games against Maritime teams during the 1930s.

The intimate connection between the Maritimes and New England was an important element in the development of community baseball in the Maritimes. The touring clubs provided a standard by which local clubs could judge their abilities, and helped raise the level of play. In many cases, American players who came to the Maritimes returned in later years to play for semi-pro or professional clubs in the region. As they moved from town to town, touring clubs played a more wide-ranging schedule than any single team within the region. As a result, they found themselves in a position to judge the relative strengths of Maritime teams. Those that returned over the years could also assess the progress of Maritime baseball in general. For the most part their judgment was the same. Maritime baseball had improved significantly in the interwar period. By the Second World War teams in Springhill, Yarmouth, Liverpool, St Stephen, Westville, Moncton, Halifax, and Saint John were on a par with the top semi-pro teams in New England.

At the same time, the reaffirmation on the baseball diamond of the traditional connection between the Maritimes and New England between the wars served to emphasize the region's cultural alienation from the rest of Canada. Indeed, while American touring teams looked upon the Maritimes as a northern extension of New England, Canadian teams flatly ignored the region. In the two decades before the war only the Montreal Dow Brewery club ventured east of the Quebec border, and only for a rapid sweep through Nova Scotia and New Brunswick in the summer of 1935. One of the wealthiest and strongest semi-pro teams in the country, the Dows were outfitted in sparkling white and red uniforms and travelled in their own private railway car. Led by the pitching of LaHale and the clutch hitting of Nicky Malfara (who would play in Halifax during the war), the visiting Dows won three games in Halifax and swept doubleheaders against Liverpool and Yarmouth before heading home to Montreal. Although they would later describe the Gateways as the 'best team that they had played in two years,' the Dows left the Maritimes without playing the regional champion St Stephen outfit.[62] Nor did they return to the Maritimes in the future. Robert Ashe has noted the regret that St Stephen ballplayers felt about the isolation of the Maritimes from the rest of Canada. It was a feeling shared by most Maritime ballplayers. 'The most formidable barrier to national recognition was that the St. Stephen club never played a Canadian team from outside the Maritimes,' Ashe writes. 'Surviving players deeply regret this absence of outside competition. Many still feel that a national series of games would have yielded them their due recognition.'[63]

Despite the lack of recognition elsewhere in Canada, Maritime baseball at the end of the thirties was in a flourishing state. Nurtured by the traditional connection with New England, and drawing upon regional and community loyalties, the Maritime baseball championship became the ultimate goal of virtually every significant community in the region. Even in Cape Breton, where class and island loyalties were generally stronger than ties to the greater Maritime mainland, the focus for much of the period was on the Maritime title. The switch from amateurism to professionalism and the subsequent affiliation of the Cape Breton Colliery League with organized baseball in 1937 was only a belated response to years of disappointment in provincial championships. 'Somehow or other,' Gene Connolly observed, 'the best local teams could not cope with the brand of ball produced by such mainland ball centers as Springhill, Westville, Liverpool or Yarmouth, and perhaps it is this fact more than any other that has led the local promoters to go after the pros.'

The transition to professional play actually began in 1935, when the league allowed teams to bring in three imports. New Waterford brought in two pitchers and a catcher, Caledonia two pitchers, Sydney three players from Saint John, and Cumberland County players found their way to Reserve and Dominion. The following year the Colliery League broke with the Nova Scotia Amateur Baseball Association and decided on a policy of unlimited imports. Sydney Mines signed catcher Bob Ayotte, long-time St Stephen star Roy Boles, slugging outfielder George Foster, and the Small brothers, Elliot and Charley from Auburn, Maine. (Charley Small had played for the Boston Red Sox in 1930, and was a familiar figure on ball diamonds in the Maritimes and Maine. He also umpired in the Halifax and District League in the 1940s and 1950s before his death at age forty-eight.) New Waterford, managed by Guy 'Doc' White, a thirteen-year veteran of the major leagues before the war, had a young club anchored by shortstop Lennie Merullo, who later played seven years with the Chicago Cubs. Merullo's second baseman was eighteen-year-old Eddie Gillis, who had broken in with New Waterford the year before, and had been chosen MVP in the 1935 all-star game.[64] The Dominion Hawks were led by George Michaels, formerly of the Boston Royal Giants, and Gene Lumianski, who had pitched for Toronto of the International League; Sydney signed 230-pound left-hander Rube Wilson from South Carolina, and Guido Panciera, who at various times had been owned by the New York Yankees, the Boston Braves, and the Boston Red Sox; and Glace Bay had former major leaguers Del Bisonette, Billy Hunnefield, and Roy Moore in harness.

In 1937 the Colliery League was formally admitted to organized baseball as a Class D circuit, the only league in the Maritimes ever to be affiliated with organized baseball. Under the capable presidency of Judge A.D. Campbell, the league operated for two more seasons, graduating to Class C status in 1939. In the same year the National Association of Professional Base Ball Leagues appointed Campbell to act as chairman of the commission that supervised the 'Little World Series' between the winners of the International League and the American Association. Had the war not intervened, the Colliery, or 'Coal Dust' League as it was sometimes called, would likely have become a Class B operation.

In the Colliery League's three seasons of operation, Cape Breton fans were treated to a number of exciting games and colourful players. A handful of locals like Eddie Gillis, 'Dummy' Jackson (a star rugby player whose nickname came from his ability to fake the 'dummy' pass), and pitcher Murray Matheson secured berths in the league, but most of the players were imports. More than a dozen players had or would play in the major leagues. They included Roy Moore, Billy Marshall, Connie Creedon, Jim Hickey, Eddie Turchin, Charley Small, Fred Maguire, Del Bisonette, 'Doc' White, Billy Zitzmann, Al Smith, Billy Hunnefield, and Lennie Merullo. A number of others – including Dick Baker, all-star shortstop in the International League in 1946, third baseman Jimmy Cullenaine, who would likely have been a Pittsburgh Pirate had he not severely damaged his hand in a run-in with a window pane, slugging first baseman Abe Abramowitz, who led the league in hitting in 1939 with a .326 batting average, and Sydney's pitching ace Bernie Pearlman – had successful careers at the Triple A level. Others would have likely graduated to the majors had not war interrupted their careers, or in some cases taken their lives.

The war, in fact, marked a watershed for baseball in the Maritimes. Not only did it end Cape Breton's experiment with organized baseball, but it once again brought national influence to bear upon the region's sporting culture. Canadian servicemen from across the country flooded into Maritime bases, and as small-town Maritimers left home to serve the country, the deep community allegiances of the interwar years no longer could be expressed with the same vitality on the small-town baseball diamond. In turn, the sporting connection between the Maritimes and New England would be interrupted for a time, and though it would be restored in the late 1940s and the 1950s, when Maritime baseball became increasingly reliant upon American imports, forces were at work that would soon result in the collapse of the community-baseball tradition and the ultimate separation of the New England and Maritime baseball worlds.

9

The 'Others': Race, Ethnicity, and Community Baseball

In the summer of 1936, the Dominion Hawks of the Cape Breton Colliery League, engaged twenty-six-year-old George 'Whitey' Michaels, a native of New Bedford, Massachusetts, as their new coach. A fine all-around ballplayer, and demon on the base paths, Michaels was equally proficient in the field, playing at first or third base, behind the plate, or in the outfield. Well known throughout the provinces as a member of a touring club that visited the Maritimes each year, Michaels was the kind of person, reporter Alex Nickerson of the Halifax *Morning Herald* observed, that 'just seems to fit in anywhere.'[1]

Michaels's appointment was notable in two respects. In the first place, his signing signified the decision of the member clubs of the Colliery League to abandon amateur play and import professional players. Cape Breton had yet to produce a provincial amateur champion, and after the Dominion Hawks were swept in three straight games in the 1935 provincial finals by the Yarmouth Gateways, the league decided to throw its doors open to imports in order to bring the best possible baseball to the island. In addition to Michaels, several players who had or would play in the major leagues graced Cape Breton club rosters in 1936, including Del Bisonette, Freddy Maguire, Billy Hunnifield, Lenny Merullo, and 'Doc' White. The league's decision to play with unlimited imports resulted in the suspension of team executives and players by the Maritime Provinces branch of the CAAU. In 1937 the Colliery League joined organized baseball as a Class D league, and graduated to Class C status in 1939.

Michaels's signing was also significant because he was a black man, and his appointment alarmed some people who favoured a policy of racial segregation in sporting competition. At first, little was said when

Michaels accepted the coaching job, but when he inserted himself in the playing line-up as a replacement for injured catcher Suki Leadbetter, the *Morning Herald* observed that a 'small minority of local fans objected.' These objections were by no means confined to a few vocal grandstand racists. Before a game in Sydney Mines, Michaels was confronted on the field and threatened with bodily harm if he played that day. Summoning as much self-restraint as he could muster, Michaels turned away, walked off the field, and sat on the bench for the rest of the afternoon. Maybe he wasn't going to 'just ... fit in anywhere' after all.[2]

Michaels had appeared in the Maritimes the year before as a member of the Boston Royal Giants, a mixture of veterans from the American Negro leagues and talented young black ballplayers from New England, who spent a month or more each summer barnstorming the Maritimes. Travelling in a rickety old bus, which doubled as their sleeping quarters when rooms were unavailable to them, the Royals, like the members of the fictional 'Bingo Long Travelling All-Stars,'[3] sometimes played as many as three games in a day, splitting the gate with the home club on a 60–40 basis. The manager and star attraction of the club was catcher Burlin White, a veteran of almost a dozen Negro League teams, including the Bacharach Giants, the Cuban Stars, and the Lincoln Giants of the Eastern Colored League. Raised in Boston by a white family, White was a remarkably handsome and affable man who captivated fans, sportswriters, and players alike with his genial personality, his 'toothpaste ad smile,'[4] and his knowledge of baseball. Columnists Alex Nickerson of the Halifax *Herald*, 'Ace' Foley of the rival *Chronicle*, and H.J. Osborne of the Saint John *Telegraph* were particularly fond of him, and when the Royal Giants began their annual month-long swing through the Maritimes, their columns bubbled with praise.

During the dirty thirties the Giants probably played close to three hundred games in the Maritimes, and the players became household names to most ball fans in the region. In addition to catcher White and first baseman Michaels, the team featured speedy outfielder 'Stormy' Faulk, slick-fielding second baseman 'Busky' Johnson, power-hitting outfielder 'Blacky' McKnight, crafty left-handed spitball artist Jim Morrow, and a towering six-foot, four-inch right-hander named 'Babe' Robinson. Of these, Robinson had the most talent: his smooth side-arm delivery and sharp-breaking curve ball was especially tough on right-handed batters. Considered by Alex Nickerson to have been 'one of the finest right hand pitchers ever to show in the province,'[5] Robinson gained notoriety by beating both the St Stephen Kiwanis and one of the

Cape Breton Colliery League teams on the same day in 1935, and re-
peating the feat the same year in a double-header against the Halifax
Willow Parks.

Although the Royal Giants have been described as a second-level
black team, they were probably on a par with the weaker clubs in the
American Negro professional leagues, and provided local clubs with
stiff competition and helpful advice.[6] White, who began his professional
career with the West Baden, Indiana, Sprudels in 1915, and later played
with and against the finest black players in the United States, was
particularly generous with advice for the talented young ballplayers he
played against in the Maritimes. Melvin Sheppard, star full-back on the
famous Caledonia Rugby Club and a catcher for the Glace Bay club in
the Cape Breton Colliery League, recalled a tip he received from White
on how to avoid blinking when batters swung at the ball. 'Practice
ducking your head in a pan of water with your eyes open during the
winter,' was White's advice. Sheppard followed the suggestion, and in
the spring he could follow the ball into his mitt without distraction.[7]
Danny Seaman, whose Liverpool club was one of the first teams in the
province to defeat the Royal Giants, squeaking out a 5–4 victory in
August 1935,[8] also found White's advice invaluable, and credited him
with helping Liverpool to develop a championship-calibre club.[9] Ironically, Seaman had beaten the Giants with a trick they had taught him.
Sliding home with the potential winning run, he kicked the ball out of
White's hand. 'We wanted to help you,' White said later, 'but not to
have you beat us with our own tactics.'[10]

Although players and sportswriters alike remembered the Royal
Giants fondly, barnstorming black teams found themselves caught in the
contradictions of a predominately white market-place. In order to attract
fans, they often had to cultivate an image of 'otherness' that played
upon white racial theories about the different characteristics of the races.
Itinerancy, inconsistent competition, and the need to attract an audience,
moreover, encouraged clowning and buffoonery on touring black teams
that sometimes appealed to the worst racial stereotypes. There was an
ambiguity in these routines, or 'reems' as they were called: for if they
played to white stereotypes, they also exalted the smooth and slick style
that black players brought to the game.[11] Teams such as the Boston
Royal Giants were talented athletes, and their abilities were respected
by both the opponents and the fans, despite the need to showboat.[12]
When taken to extremes, however, clowning was destructive. 'At best,'
Jules Tygiel writes, 'teams and players that engaged in clowning simply

catered to the whims of the fans and added entertainment; at worst, when their performances took on the stereotyped images of a minstrel show or the Stepin Fetchit characteristics portrayed in the movies, the clowns perpetuated the negative perceptions of blacks common among whites, and cast doubts about the quality of the athletes.'[13]

From the beginnings of black baseball in the nineteenth century until after the Second World War, white commentators had difficulty taking black players seriously. Sportswriters delighted in reporting stories in exaggerated black dialect, and emphasized the 'ludicrous' incidents that occurred during the game. In February 1880, for example, the New York *Clipper* reported on a game between the Unique club of Brooklyn and the Excelsiors of Philadelphia for the 'colored championship' of the United States. 'This affair,' it observed, 'was marked with an amount of ludicrousness and comicality that kept the disinterested spectators in almost incessant laughter.'[14] Fifteen years later an article in the *Sporting News* concluded that 'the best negro players are about equal, in caliber, to the Western Association class,' but that the black player was as 'unique on the ballfield as he is on the stage or in everyday life. He is full of original humor, and the best entertainer imaginable. Take nine white men and perhaps one of the lot will amuse the crowd during a game. Take nine coons and you have nine black Arlie Lathams. Their coaching, baserunning, and general play would make a hermit forget his solitary studies and laugh as loudly as anybody.'[15]

Like most touring black clubs, the Royal Giants had their clowns: there was squeaky-voiced 'Stormy' Faulk, an outfielder and catcher, adorned in a cap with a two-foot-long peak, and holding a catcher's mitt five times the normal size,[16] and the incomparable 'King' Tut, included later – along with team-mate Goose Tatum, who began his career as a baseball player before joining basketball's Harlem Globetrotters – in Bill Heward's all-time all-star line-up of clowning players.[17] (Tut may have been a better clown than he was a ballplayer. In 1938 he managed only eight hits in fifty-two at-bats during the Royal Giant's tour through Nova Scotia). White, on the other hand, appeared to have major-league talent, amazing audiences by throwing runners out at second base while sitting in a rocking chair,[18] and bunting the ball with the end of the bat. At first base for the Giants, 'Whitey' Michaels caught the ball between his legs and behind his back, and in a version of the 'ain't lookin' play perfected by 'Chappie' Johnson's touring team, took throws from infielders with his back turned to them.[19] The Royal Giants mastered all the stock-in-trade routines of barnstorming clubs:

the pestering of umpires and opposing players, the 'pepper games,' the ghost- or shadow-ball warm-ups, and the around-the-infield play. On hard-hit balls to the third baseman, the ball was thrown to short, second, and finally to first base to retire the frustrated runner by a step.

While most fans loved the routines, others were often annoyed by them. After the home-town club had lost four games to White's Giants, Alex McLean of St Stephen complained of the distracting nature of clowning, particularly 'Stormy' Faulk's wierd performances on the coaching line, his incessant chatter, and his habit of sneaking up behind players and pulling their socks down. McLean described Faulk as 'the spontaneous star comedian of a well-rehearsed set of buffoons.' If they would only stop their clowning, he suggested, most of the better senior teams in the region would hold their own against them.[20] Laurie Thorburn, a mainstay on the mound for the Liverpool Larrapurs, also wished that the Giants would play ball straight. 'Comedy would offset my pitching,' he has since recalled. 'They'd hold the bat, and instead of tryin' to hit with it, the batter would just point it towards the ball. It looked like he was tryin' to show me up. Once, I threw a close ball to him to see what he was doin', and I split his finger right in two.'[21] Thorburn was probably referring to Burlin White's attempts to bunt the ball with the bat end, since White missed almost a month with a split finger during the Giants' tour in 1936.[22]

The Boston Royal Giants were by no means the only black club to barnstorm the region between the wars. The Cleveland Colored Giants, Detroit Clowns, New York Colored Giants, the Philadelphia Giants, and Chappie Johnson's Philadelphia All-Stars all took swings through the Maritimes. In addition, a team of Hawaiian college stars, with players of Chinese and Japanese descent – known to most sports reporters simply as 'the Japs' – concluded a 1931 North American tour with a series of games in Saint John.[23] Sprinkled through the rosters of the touring clubs were some of the most talented black players of the day. Chappie Johnson's All-Stars featured Bill Jackman, a tall and lanky submarine pitcher from Texas, and Billy Yancey, a right-hand-hitting shortstop and 'sparkplug in the field' for several Negro League clubs during his thirteen-year career.[24] Yancey considered Jackman, when healthy, to be the finest black hurler in the game.[25] For a few years in the late 1920s Jackman toured with Burlin White, but they went their separate ways in 1932 when White established the Boston Royal Giants. Jackman's Philadelphia Giants then hooked up with the Broadway Stars for a series of games in New Brunswick and Nova Scotia that same

July. His team-mates included second baseman Newton Joseph, who later managed the Kansas City Monarchs, Gus Gadsen, who played with the famous Hilldale Club, and Francis Matthews, who played five years in the negro major leagues, including a short stint with White's Boston Royal Giants in 1942.

The success of these clubs at the gate encouraged several other touring clubs to try their luck in the Maritimes. One of these, the Zulu Cannibal Giants, toured the Maritimes in 1936, pushing all of the stereotypes associated with African tribal life to the limit. Dressed in regulation pants and baseball shoes, the Cannibal Giants were stripped to the waist, wore fuzzy head-dresses, and painted their chests and faces 'in the best cinematic presentation of a cannibal.' Particularly talented, the Cannibal Giants had drawn 55,000 people for a three-game series in Montreal the year before, and claimed a season record of 133 victories and 3 ties against only 38 losses.[26] It was rumoured that the team was made up of players from the famous Homestead Grays of Pittsburgh, including the Grays' star catcher and future Hall of Famer Josh Gibson, but this is unlikely.[27]

In the summer of 1936, a second team drawing upon African imagery arrived to do battle with local clubs. The Ethiopian Clowns, who had changed their name from the Miami Clowns to capitalize upon the publicity surrounding Mussolini's invasion of Ethiopia, were one of several touring clubs organized by New York promoter Syd Pollock of Tarrytown, New York. Like the Zulu Cannibal Giants, the identity of the Clowns' players was obscured by disguised surnames, but whoever they were, they were excellent ballplayers.[28] After steamrolling the Moncton club in a three-game series, outscoring them 42–8, the Clowns headed for Liverpool and Yarmouth to take on Nova Scotia's top two amateur teams. They beat Liverpool 2–0 and 4–1 on 13 August and two days later swept a doubleheader from the Gateways by scores of 3–2 and 3–0. In later years this club would change its name to the Cincinnati and then the Indianapolis Clowns, winning nine Negro American League championships, and providing early training to the all-time home-run leader in the major leagues, Henry 'Hank' Aaron.[29]

In addition to the black barnstormers, the famous House of David touring baseball team played upon ethnic and sectarian imagery as it criss-crossed the continent during the 1920s and 1930s. Sporting bushy whiskers and hair that hung to belt level, the team members helped advertise the religious teachings of Benjamin Purnell, the self-proclaimed sixth son of the House of David, who had established a turn-of-the-century religious colony at Benton Harbour, Michigan, to gather together the twelve lost tribes of Israel. Adherents to the faith, attracted to the colony by the promise of eternal life, were asked to contribute their worldly possessions to the colony, and to swear off sex, tobacco, alcohol, and the straight razor. By the First World War, Benton Harbor sported a grand market, greenhouse, hotel, narrow guage railway, amusement park, zoo, and ballpark. Never one to follow too closely the principles of his own teaching, Purnell regularly broke the vow of chastity, seducing hundreds of young female converts into his bed. Indicted for rape in 1922, Purnell went on the lam for four years, but was eventually brought to trial and convicted in 1926. He also had few scruples about hiring ringers to play on his touring ball club. Among the luminaries who played with the club over the years were Grover Cleveland Alexander, Elmer Dean (the brother of Dizzy and Paul), eventual major leaguers Ossie Orwell, Eddie Popowski, Larry Jansen, and Sid Jackucki, and even 'Babe' Didriksen Zaharis, America's greatest female athlete of the day.[30]

The House of David first appeared in the Maritimes in the late summer of 1929, chugging across the border with a portable, gas-powered 100,000-watt lighting system lashed to the roof of the team bus. The team manager, Ernie Gilmore, formerly a talented third baseman and protégé of Connie Mack, was no stranger to Nova Scotia, having led Glace Bay to the Cape Breton championship in 1921. His players, composed of one of three squads assembled at the beginning of the year in a spring camp in Texas, were all entertainers in their own right. 'Flip' Fleming, the catcher, wintered at the Benton Harbor colony as an acrobat; second baseman Denny Williams, although practically the smallest player on the team, was a noted wrestler; and 'Doc' Talley, the star pitcher of the club, his long auburn hair in braids, had already appeared on the Hollywood silver screen in two films with Gloria Swanson. Another who would tour the Maritimes with the House of David during these years was Ed Hamman, a trickster known for throwing behind his back and letting ground balls roll up his legs and into his glove. Hamman later became part-owner and general manager of the Indianapolis Clowns.[31]

When the House of David club first toured the Maritimes in 1929 it found little serious opposition, knocking off all of its opponents and leaving the region undefeated. Over the next decade, however, the calibre of amateur baseball in the region improved dramatically. At the end of the 1939 tour, in which the House of David club won only seven of its twelve games, manager Paul Murray commented upon the great improvement of Maritime baseball over the years, noting that it 'has advanced to a point where it does not have to step back to look up at touring clubs from the States.'[32] Before the opening of the Nova Scotian half of their 1939 tour in Springhill, the 'whiskered wonders' predicted that they would demolish the Fencebusters. One of their players suggested that there would be so many balls hit into the outfield gap that the Springhillers should bring their bicycles, another that the Fencebuster hitters would never adjust to playing under the lights. When Springhill prevailed by an 11–5 score, one of the locals explained that playing night ball was nothing for men used to working in the semi-darkness of the coal mine, with a small lamp as their only light. Burlin White was also impressed with the improvement in Maritime baseball, and felt that pitchers Lefty Brownell of St Stephen, Tommy Linkletter of Springhill, Johnny Harvey in Saint John, and Copie LeBlanc of Yarmouth could have held their own even at the major-league level.[33]

The twenties and thirties were the heyday of barnstorming teams, but during the war many of these clubs folded, the Boston Royal Giants and the House of David included. Revived in 1948, the House of David collapsed once and for all a few years later, when 'Doc' Talley died suddenly at the age of fifty-four. By this time, small-town baseball itself was in decline, and the dramatic encounter of the local community and the eccentric tourist clubs had lost its earlier appeal. During the twenties and thirties, contests between barnstorming teams and community baseball clubs provided a dramatic representation of existing race and ethnic relationships in the Maritimes, and served as unifying events for small towns that transcended, at least temporarily, the divisive forces that undermined civic unity. As Jerry Kirshenbaum later observed, barnstorming was suited to those early days 'before television and sports expansion encouraged the civic boosters of every hamlet to start thinking of themselves in big-league terms.' It was a time 'in which people were still provincial enough to go to the circus to see bearded ladies, or to the ball park to see bearded ball-players.'[34] During the 1950s, as small towns became rapidly integrated into the mainstream of North American culture, itinerant baseball, with its showboating and celebration of racial otherness, appeared increasingly anachronistic, although racial discrimination would, of course, continue to plague sport and society at large until the present day.

Although competition with teams representing racial and ethnic 'otherness' was a popular form of entertainment between the wars, there is another history of sport involving racial and ethnic minorities that is often overlooked. For the black and native people of the Maritimes and New England, baseball addressed admittedly more prosaic but none the less important social needs. On the one hand, the sporting history of these minorities reflects their marginalization and segregation in a society that regarded separation on the basis of colour as a natural 'part of the internationally accepted moral order.'[35] Yet sports such as baseball also served as a resource for minorities, promoting a sense of self-respect and accomplishment to those who took part, and now and then helped those on the economic margin to pick up a few extra dollars to supplement their income.

Although its origins are obscure, black baseball was relatively well entrenched in the Maritimes by the mid-1880s. All-black baseball teams such as the Eurekas, Victorias, Independent Stars, and North-Ends of Halifax, the Royals and Ralph Waldo Emersons of Saint John, the Dartmouth Stanleys, Truro Victorias, Amherst Royals, Woodstock Wanderers, and Fredericton Celestials helped to promote racial solidarity and black self-esteem, but testified to the continuing exclusion of blacks from mainstream white society.[36] Beginning in 1894, a regional championship for black teams took place annually, and usually received coverage in local newspapers. The Eurekas were the dominant club of the decade. Maritime champions in black baseball in seven of the eight years between 1894 and 1902, their only loss in this entire period was to the Amherst Royals in the championship game of 1897. After 1905, the Royals, under the direction of coach and captain A.H. Skinner, took the Eurekas' place as the team to beat in interprovincial championship competitions.

For most black clubs in this period, there was no real possibility of entering organized league play. Except in larger centres such as Saint John and Halifax, there were usually not enough players to form more than one club, and few blacks could afford travelling between communities on a regular basis. Regularly scheduled games were few and far between. Most scheduled games were challenge matches for a money prize arranged through notices in the press. The Fredericton *Gleaner* of 6 June 1890 observed, for example, that the Celestials, under the tutelage of their 'crack catcher' Joe Eatman, were practising each evening from 'tea time to dusk' and hoped to convince a Saint John team to visit Fredericton for a match on the Dominion Day weekend.[37] Believing that there was money to be made by attracting black teams from Saint John and Woodstock to Fredericton, Eatman sent challenges to both clubs, and later to the Halifax Victorias.[38] Eatman's only concern was that the Victorias might bring a pro battery and take away the challenge prize unfairly. 'If they bring Vickery of Truro, the Celestials would not feel him,' said Eatman. 'He can [throw a] curve around a baseball.'[39]

It is hard to know how much money these teams made in challenge matches. Gate receipts depended upon the size of the crowd, the proximity of the field to the centre of town, the calibre of the opposition, and the vagaries of the weather. Bringing in a visiting team was thus a risky business. When the Celestials played the Saint John Royals in July 1890, for example, the game drew a poor crowd even though it was played on the grounds of the Fredericton Amateur Athletic Association. A heavy downpour delayed the match for an hour and a half at the end of the first inning, and when it resumed few were left in their seats. It is unlikely that enough fans showed up to cover more than the expenses of the visiting team.[40] A week earlier, however, when the Celestials had played a challenge match with the 'Fearnaughts,' a white nine from Morrison's Mill, a large crowd congregated at a field a healthy distance from town. The game was won by the Celestials by a score of 33–28, and in the words of the Gleaner, it was 'worth walking some distance to see the playing of Joe Eatman alone.'[41] Although the amount of money made on the game was never disclosed, it probably covered a $25 challenge prize, as was offered in a match between the Ralph Waldo Emerson Colored Club of Saint John and a team of Fredericton journalists earlier that year.[42]

In addition to the supplemental income that players pocketed from challenge matches, black baseball clubs provided a sense of camaraderie and social interdependence similar to that found in other fraternal institutions. For blacks, sport encouraged racial pride and neighbourhood identity. Baseball clubs were part of a network of sociopolitical institutions in black communities, including the church and various mutual-improvement societies, that promoted the community's potential for creativity and self-improvement. For example, in the turn-of-the-century Africville district of Halifax, a black community whose forcible destruction in the 1960s aroused black resistance to the insensitive racism that can accompany experiments in urban renewal,[43] the Seasides sporting club, which fielded baseball teams in the summer and iced hockey clubs in the winter, had a close association with the local African Baptist Church. Black churches also supported teams in Yarmouth, Truro, New Glasgow, Amherst, and Saint John.[44]

After the First World War, black baseball in the Maritimes continued in much the same fashion as it had earlier, largely segregated from the white baseball culture of the region. As before, black teams played white clubs in occasional challenge games, and in some cases black clubs entered leagues with white teams. Only very rarely were black players playing alongside whites on community teams. This was hardly because of a lack of talent, as various games between black and white clubs demonstrated. The Halifax Coloured Diamonds, who had won the provincial coloured championship in 1921, for example, played a hotly contested two-game series the following year against a team of Halifax Old-Timers that included Steve Whalen and Harry Young. Although the Diamonds lost both games, the fact that over 6000 spectators attended the two matches suggests that the Diamonds were a highly skilled and competitive club.[45]

During the 1920s and 1930s, some advances were made in the struggle against segregated play as black activists in Halifax, Saint John, Moncton, Amherst, New Glasgow, and Truro pressed local religious leaders to admit black teams to community leagues throughout the region. During the 1920s the Zion Baptist team of Truro competed against whites in a local church league. In New Glasgow the Colored Wonders were admitted to the town league during the 1920s, and for a brief period in 1932 played in the extremely competitive Pictou County League.[46] In Amherst, Reverend Jeltz of the African Episcopal church organized the Blue Granites baseball club, which regularly played against white teams. Led by star pitcher Carl Izzard, the Blue Granites were a major force in the Amherst church league from 1932 to 1935. A black baseball team also played a regular schedule in the Yarmouth town league between the wars.

As competition between black and white teams became more frequent, a number of black players gained recognition for their baseball talent. In 1931, for example, the pitching of George 'Babe' Whelan and the fine play of catcher Freeman 'Pete' Paris, second baseman Ernest Dorrington, and slugging outfielder Alvin McLean led the Coloured Wonders to the championship of the New Glasgow town league, and earned them an invitation to play in the intermediate Pictou County League the following year. A couple of years later, Paris's heavy hitting earned him a spot on New Glasgow's senior all-white ball club. In addition, touring teams such as the Boston Royal Giants would sometimes schedule games against local black teams on the chance that there might be a prospect waiting to be discovered. After a game in June 1935 between the Giants and an all-star team from Truro that featured both 'white and coloured boys,' Burlin White praised the athletic talent of centre fielder Bob Mentis. The 1931 provincial high-school sprint champion in both the 60- and 100-yard dash, Mentis later accompanied White and the Giants as they toured Nova Scotia, filling in for injured players.[47] Another such discovery was Morton 'Bucky' Berry, a young black pitcher and centre fielder from Yarmouth who toured with the Giants in 1937, hitting .240 in six games and making several fine catches in the outfield.[48]

Of all the black players in the Maritimes during the thirties, none was any better than Vincent 'Manny' McIntyre. A native of Fredericton, New Brunswick, Manny McIntyre began his baseball career with the Devon, NB, junior team in 1938 and was quickly recognized as one of the finest all-around ballplayers in the region. A superb athlete, McIntyre was equally at home on the ball diamond or hockey rink, playing professional hockey in Quebec, Ontario, and the Maritimes. When organized baseball dropped its colour bar with the signing of Jackie Robinson, McIntyre, who had been courted by several Negro League teams in the United States, was one of but six players signed by professional teams for the 1946 season. Suiting up with Sherbrooke of the Class C Border League that June, he hit .310 in thirty games but suffered in the field, and returned to the Maritimes to play for the Middleton club in Nova Scotia's H&D League.[49] In 1949 McIntyre teamed with another black Maritimer, Charlie Pyle, to lead the Fredericton Capitals to the New Brunswick championship over the Moncton Legionnaires. By that time, several other young black players were beginning to make their mark, including Oscar Seale, one of the top hitters in the Cape Breton Colliery League, and Truro native Art Dorrington, who hit .296 for the Saint John Dodgers in 1949.

The accomplishments of black athletes in a less-segregated sporting environment were important to the black community, for in the immediate postwar period many blacks saw an opportunity for improving race relations. Buoyed by the revulsion against Nazi racism, the discrediting of 'scientific' theories about innate racial differences, and new expressions of racial equality in the United Nations charter,[50] black leaders in the Maritimes attacked racial discrimination in housing, education, and employment, and upheld the right to be served in restaurants, hotels, barber shops, and theatres. In 1945 the Nova Scotia Association for the Advancement of Coloured People was established to lead the fight against discriminatory practices. In a celebrated legal case in 1948, Viola Desmond challenged the practice of New Glasgow's

Roseland Theatre to restrict black seating to its balcony. Although Desmond was refused a ticket for the whites-only section of the theatre, she proceeded to sit there and was charged with trying to evade federal taxes in the amount of one cent. This case eventually was decided in Desmond's favour in the Supreme Court of Canada, a landmark decision in the fight for equality of access to public facilities for black people in Canada.[51]

Dr Carrie M. Best's newspaper *The Clarion*, which began publishing in New Glasgow in 1946, was another important black voice in the fight against racial discrimination. This newspaper, which changed its name to *The Negro Citizen* in 1949, followed an editorial policy of promoting education and self-improvement, attacking any incidence of discrimination within Nova Scotia, and emphasizing the accomplishments of successful black men and women, from Jackie Robinson in baseball to internationally acclaimed Nova Scotian contralto Portia White on the stage. Sport was a prominent part of the newspaper's pages, and the columns of associate editor James Calbert 'Cal' Best usually focused on those black athletes who had been able to break the colour bar. Robinson, of course, seemed to embody the qualities necessary to advance the cause of black civil rights. 'Jackie has been one of the greatest ambassadors of good will,' wrote Cal Best. 'He has proven to all concerned that a member of the race can conduct himself with all the decorum and dignity that is necessarily [sic] in the face of the greatest obstacles.'[52]

Although many of Cal Best's stories dealt with American stars such as Robinson, Roy Campanella, Satchel Paige and Larry Doby, he was also careful to point to the accomplishments of those closer to home. One of these was Ontario-born Freddie Thomas, who had played baseball in the wartime Halifax Defence League with the RCAF. Thomas was a remarkable athlete. While at Assumption College in Windsor, Ontario, where he played as a six-foot, two-inch centre, Thomas broke the 2000-point mark during his basketball career, and was invited to join the famous Harlem Globetrotters in 1949. He was also a star football player, courted by both the Montreal Alouettes and the Toronto Argonauts. Thomas refused these offers to play football and basketball, concentrating instead on a professional baseball career.[53] Scouted initially by Abe Saperstein, who in addition to his connection to the Globetrotters served as a baseball bird-dog for the Cleveland Indians, Thomas was Cleveland's first black signee after Larry Doby had joined the club in 1947. Thomas broke in with Wilkes-Barre, Pennsylvania, of the Eastern League in 1948, breaking that loop's colour line.[54]

In addition to Thomas, *The Clarion* acknowledged the contribution of several other black athletes from the region, including Oscar Seale, Charlie Pyle, Manny McIntyre, Doug and Art Dorrington, boxers Percy Parris and Crossley Irvine, and Willie Stroud, 'the great Negro lineman of the Calgary Stampeders,' in breaking down racial barriers.[55] Their accomplishments prepared the way for future black sporting stars such as Halifax's fine infielder Billy Carter, and Willie O'Ree of Fredericton and Stan 'Chook' Maxwell of Truro, both of whom played professional hockey but starred as well on local baseball diamonds.[56]

If the history of blacks in baseball was largely a story of struggling against discrimination and segregation, for native peoples it is one of invisibility. Not surprisingly, the study of native baseball suffers from the general neglect of aboriginal peoples in the existing historiography. Although there has been a recent explosion of attention given to native history in Canada, with native issues becoming a central component in the recent constitutional deliberations, Canadian historians traditionally neglected native peoples.[57] As Bruce Trigger emphasizes, the history of native people in Canada has not been perceived as a study of value in its own right. Native people have appeared in our history as minor players – important only when their actions impacted upon the history of Euro-Canadians. The work of scholars like Trigger, John Reid, Jim Miller, Sara Carter, and others has attempted to redress this neglect and to place native people at centre stage in the development of Canadian history, particularly in the colonial period.[58]

Amongst the practitioners of sporting history, the extensive reliance on 'modernization theory' has also contributed to the neglect of native sport. The modernization model, with its interest in the changing structure of sport, its bureaucratization, increasingly systematic organization, and time-consciousness, tends by its own logic to reify urban sport and to consign hinterland regions and less powerful peoples to the historical dustbin. Modernization theory views history as a linear continuum in which any given circumstance or idea can be labelled 'pre-modern' or traditional, and thus can safely be ignored as something that the seemingly neutral process of 'modernization' has rendered anachronistic.[59] It should come as no surprise, therefore, that historians of the modernization school have shown relatively little interest in recreational sport; recreational games involve fewer of the attributes of modernity than do competitive, organized, and professional sporting competitions. In addition, the sporting life of small communities, hinterland regions, and neglected social groups tends to be given short shrift. Just as sport involves winning and losing, therefore, sport historians interested in the linear race to modernity often glorify the winners and ignore the losers in the process.[60]

For native people modernization theory has exercised a particularly deleterious influence. As Trigger points out, for 'almost three centuries white North Americans had assumed that native peoples were doomed to be culturally assimilated or to perish as a superior European civilization spread inexorably across the continent.' This argument provided a rationale for ignoring the plight of native people: their difficulties were considered to be simply a product of their own inability to adjust to modernization. Tied to this view was the proposition that native societies were static, traditional, and unable to change, but this assumption – made a priori, without any serious investigation and research – contradicts the findings of archaeologists, which demonstrate that most native societies were extremely adaptive and innovative in responding to radical shifts in environmental circumstances and the arrival of Europeans.[61]

The contemporary native peoples of Maine and the Atlantic Provinces are descendants of aboriginal groups within the Wabanaki cluster of the Algonquian peoples. They include the Mi'kmaq people, who are located in all four provinces of the Atlantic region, the Maliseet, who are generally confined to the Saint John River district in New Brunswick, and the Passamaquoddy and Penboscot peoples from Maine.[62] Like native people elsewhere, the people of this region had a long sporting history, in which games of chance, ball games of various sorts (including lacrosse), and contests that emphasized physical skills, such as running or wrestling, or hunting skills, such as spear-throwing and archery, were immensely popular.[63] Anthropological research has told us something of these early pursuits, but the reconstruction of the later sporting history of native peoples, particularly as it relates to games such as baseball, is exceedingly difficult because of the paucity of written sources. The following discussion of the history of native baseball in the Maritimes and northern New England, therefore, relies heavily on the remembrances of native peoples themselves. Although these remembrances are sometimes chronologically imprecise, and even conflicting at times, they provide a way to recover history that has heretofore been lost and ignored.

Although it is difficult to date precisely the point at which native people began to play baseball, there is hard evidence of it being played by Mi'kmaq and Penobscot Indians during the 1870s and 1880s. Harold

Seymour has argued that in the United States the federal government
Indian schools were important in stimulating the development of baseball among native people, and that many of the 113 boarding schools
and 88 reservation schools that had grown up by 1900 encouraged
sports such as baseball as part of the drive towards assimilation and
deracination.[64] This was true of many parts of the United States, but is
less so of the native population in the north-eastern corner of the continent. Douglas Knockwood remembers his experience at the Shubenacadie residential school as one of work and study, without play or
enjoyment. Religious indoctrination, the expunging of the Mi'kmaq
language, and chores around the school stand out in Knockwood's mind
rather than images of childish play and recreation.[65]

In the various native communities in the region it was a different
story. One of the most popular summer games was a variant of baseball
referred to variously as 'old fashion' or 'sponge' or 'raggy' ball, for the
ball was made of either yarn or sponge rubber. The 'old-fashion' game
was being played throughout the region as late as the Second World
War, in addition to the normal scrub games and the ubiquitous 'three
catches and up' involving a batter and a group of fielders.[66] Played by
men and women and boys and girls alike, 'old fashion' has obvious
similarities to the British game of rounders, and may have been taken
up by native people in the middle of the nineteenth century, although
some argue that its roots are indigenous. As in rounders, base runners
ran clockwise, there were no foul lines, and batters were retired by
being struck by the thrown ball. In Knockwood's words, 'there were
many infield hits' in the 'old fashion' game.

What follows are excerpts from three interviews that reflect upon the
'old fashion' game. Wilfrid Prosper, from the Eskasoni Reserve in Nova
Scotia, remembers sponge ball and 'old fashion' in the first of these
conversations:

WP We played sponge ball. You ever hear of that?
Int. No
WP Sponge ball. You could hit that a mile, you know, that sponge ball.
Int. You mean a softball?
WP Soft, spongey.
Int. You didn't play hardball, you played soft ball?
WP Sponge ball, when you were kids cause you couldn't afford to play ball.
    You know you couldn't afford a baseball, you couldn't afford gloves so we
    played sponge ball. And then there is another game that the Indians played.

They called it 'old fashion' game. Now, this is similar to baseball except you don't hit the ball on the first strike and the catcher catches it, you're out, you know. And I believe, is it three outs same as baseball or one out? I believe it's only one out that the team is out. One ... Now if you hit the ball, a fielder doesn't throw to first base. Doing that you can be safe. They have to hit you with the ball, somewhere.

Int. Is this still a soft ball?

WP Sponge ball they call it. They hit it. But I remember one time we didn't have a sponge ball and so we picked up an old, beaten up baseball with the leather off of it. And we used it for that purpose, eh? And by God, one fella hit me in an awful queer place, I tell you. He just about killed me.

Int. Where did this old fashion come from?

WP I dunno where this came from. [The interviewer tries to get the name right, thinking WP is saying 'old possum.'] No, Old Fashion, but they call it pussum because there is no 'f' in our alphabet so you can't say 'old fashion' in Indian, you have to say 'old Pussum. We only got thirteen letter in our alphabet, or fourteen. Those [letters] were real, what you ... real ... what's the word, innovative? So we played this game, I remember playing this game, and there is no such a thing as a foul ball. We have a diamond, the same as baseball, but there is no foul ball. Well, this fella got up to bat and, I think he was a right hand batter, and being a right handed batter, he made out that he was going to bat left handed. He took the other side and said ... like an orthodox, what you call it, like a switch hitter. So he's a right hand batter, he took the left hand stance. When the ball came instead of hitting it back toward the pitcher, he hit it the other way ...

Int. Is this still old fashion?

WP This is old fashion game. Yeah. He hit back toward the catcher, you know. Lucky he didn't hit him flush in the eye.[67]

The two other informants remembered 'old fashion' somewhat differently. Margaret Johnson, who grew up on the Chapel Island reserve (Barra Head), believed the game to be played the same as softball, including foul lines and foul balls:

MJ Old Fashion ball. We used to make the ball out of old rags ... And we played just the same as softball ... but you hit the person, you got to hit the person that she's out ...

Int. Did girls and boys play that together?

MJ No.

Int. Separate?

MJ Yeah.

Int. Do you know where that came from? Was that always around?

MJ I don't know where it came from.

Int. But you were playing it ...

MJ Yeah, when we were small. It was an Indian game. I don't know where it came from. But ever since I remember, they were playing baseball.[68]

John Basque, who like Margaret Johnson grew up on the Chapel Island Reserve, also believed 'old fashion' to be a Mi'kmaq game:

Int. Where did they learn baseball?

JB The way I heard, the Indians are being playing ball for years and years and years and years.

Int. Meaning back to before white people came?

JB Before white people, they used to use their, made their ball by wrapping something, leather or something.

Int. Like leather tongs or something like that?

JB Yeah, and they use the bats, they made the bats with a stick.

Int. There's a game that people keep talking about called 'old fashion' ball. Everyone mentions that they played it around here.

JB I think that's how it started.

Int. You think that's where baseball came from?

JB I think that's where baseball started.

Int. Are you saying that game is the same game that Mi'kmaq played way, way back?

JB I think maybe.

Int. So you don't think that's a white game. It's something Mi'kmaq passed down?

JB No I don't think [it's a white game] ... I think Mi'kmaq passed it down. The 'old fashion' game used to be a good game. We used to be playing 'old fashion game before the season opens ... summer season for ball games. We used to have prayers down below where they had an old school, they used to have prayers there almost every Sunday. And they had a big dish of food of every kind. They spread it among the kids and everybody after prayers [played old fashion] – can't say after mass cause we didn't have mass at that time. But I. It's pretty hard to find out exactly how the baseball game started. I think that's how it started – old fashion game. I think ... you gotta hit the guy with the ball.

Int. Someone was telling me there was not a foul ball, so you could hit the ball anyway [in any direction].

JB No foul ball. We used to play a lot at one time. Then after the season comes, then we start playing the hard ball.

Int. The old fashion ball was around as long as you know?

JB I really don't know exactly how it went or how it came. I know how it went. It's gone for good.

Int. When did that go?

JB When the war was over, the year after I got out, about '45 or '46. I had a team two years, and it died out.[69]

The old fashion game seems to have endured both as a game for younger children and one in which the community could participate as a whole. It had a number of virtues, not the least of which was that it required no equipment. The balls and bats were both home-made and there was no need for gloves or masks; and because the ball was often a rag ball, it could be played on a very small playing field. Old fashion also had the virtue of providing everyone a chance to play, for skill levels were not particularly significant. As Douglas Knockwood pointed out, there were a lot of infield hits, so that weak batters might make a base or two because a more accomplished player missed when throwing at them.

While old fashion persisted primarily as a non-competitive game that everyone could play, baseball was a game exclusively for young boys and men. All of the elders who were interviewed, from reserves at Bear River, Eskasoni, Chapel Island, Shubenacadie (Indian Brook), Milbrook, Membertou, Big Cove, and Lennox Island (PEI) agreed that baseball was being played on each of these reserves by the 1920s. It is likely that baseball was also being played in most of these communities before the First World War. Margaret Johnson remembers that there was a regional championship competition of teams from the various reserves as early as the 1920s, and John Joseph, from the Big Cove Reserve, remembers winning the Maritime Indian championship in 1932 and knocking off teams in Maine and Quebec as well.[70] The existence of these annual championships is also confirmed by a notice in the Halifax *Herald* in 1938 that condescendingly noted that the Sydney Braves were playing at Richibucto, New Brunswick, 'for the Maritime championship scalp. Arrangements are also being made to have the redskins meet the pale faces of the winning intermediate colliery league team this month.'[71] Probably the strongest of these teams in the interwar period was the Barra Head reserve club, led by pitcher Mattie Lewis and a gifted one-armed player, Ben Johnson, who like Ted Gray in the 1940s would catch the ball, throw his glove and ball in the air, catch and throw the ball, and catch his mitt again, all in a split second. Like Gray, Johnson was a strong hitter, with a well-developed right arm, which compensated for a limp left arm injured while a child and left untreated because there were no medical services available on the reserve at the time.[72]

Baseball on the reserve, and between reserves, was often an occasion for a community celebration. The women and old people used to gather around one side of the field, watching the game and often playing a card game called 'seventy five' for a couple of cents a game. At Chapel Island there was a game every Sunday afternoon, and the women would serve food, and sometimes prepare a box social. One old woman by the name of Mary Bernard used to sell molasses candy at a penny a twist. At other times there were community benefit dances to raise money for the team for a new baseball or for transportation costs if the team was travelling off the reserve.[73]

Before the Second World War travelling off the reserve was both costly and difficult. There were few cars or trucks on the reserves, and often it was necessary to rent a bus or a truck with an open back to transport the teams, straining the financial resources of the community in the process. The roads through much of the Maritimes, and particularly on Cape Breton Island, were poor throughout most of the interwar period. Sandy Julian, the last living elder to have played baseball from the Millbrook Reserve near Truro, remembered the difficulty involved in travelling during the twenties and thirties:

SJ I remember we went up to Cape Breton, Sydney [from Truro, a distance of about 250 miles], we played Labour Day tournament up there. And we played there ... We went up in trucks but it used to take about a day to travel there.

Int. About a day by truck? Because it was dirt roads?

SJ Dirt roads and there was no trans-Atlantic. And we used to leave here in the morning and get there about 8:00 at night.

Int. What would you do if it rained? Weren't the trucks open?

SJ Sometimes open, sometimes get newspapers and cover yourself up and that's [laughter] ...

Int. Just huddle down with a newspaper.

SJ I know that's tough one time ... And it only cost us a dollar to go down and back. A dollar return.

Int. Who would take you?

SJ Some truck-drivers in like Brookfield.

Int. Just somebody who had a truck?

SJ He put little benches around.

Int. So you would actually hire him?

SJ Yeah. It used to be open, you know, just sides on the trucks. That's the only time we went there [Sydney], 1934. We got the championship at that time too.

Julian also remembers a rivalry with a team from Springhill Junction, and the mode of travel back and forth for games on Sundays. 'They all hoboed down, and one feller maybe would take a ticket, he get on the train himself, they paid only what 50 cents to come down from Springhill. But one feller he had to pay and the rest of the boys hobo ... old fashioned shunters you know. Shunters, regular big train where they keep the coal. Where they keep the coal, they sit there.'[74]

After the Second World War baseball was eclipsed by softball on most reserves. The war and the postwar policy of the centralizing native people on a few large reserves broke up the old teams and traditions. Gradually softball became the dominant sport on the reserves, and players such as Frank Doucette, Ray Christmas, Alex Denny, and Donald Morrison played throughout the region. Doucette, from the Membertou Reserve, for example, played fastball for three years for the Middle Street Merchants in Portland, Maine. There were also games between Maliseet and Penobscots during the potato-picking season in September in the Aroostook valley. As softball grew in popularity baseball died. By 1960 baseball on the reserves was a thing of the past.[75]

Competition between various reserves in sports such as baseball and softball served then as now to bring native people together, allowing them to discuss matters of common concern in the social moments following the game. Sporting competitions encouraged pride and self-respect in the community. But native involvement beyond the reservation, both at the team and individual level, had far more ambiguous results. In this context, baseball – indeed all sports – reflected the often troubled relationship between native people and the larger community.

The earliest reference to native people competing with non-native teams in regional newspapers is in August 1877, when a team of Mi'kmaqs met a team of 'fat boys' in Halifax.[76] This was one of many burlesque games that characterized the period, including, as we have seen, everything from teams of deaf-mutes to one-legged Civil War veterans. Although on the surface these novelty games might appear only as part of the era's search for entertainment, and as such bear comparison to the development of other popular leisure pursuits such as vaudeville theatres and music-halls, burlesque baseball drew heavily upon racial stereotypes and upon prevailing notions of normality and difference. As Robert Bogdan has observed, the period from 1840 to 1940 was characterized by a fascination with the 'abnormal,' and the exhibition of the odd or the different for amusement and profit.[77] The identification of women, blacks, and native people as the 'other' hindered their involvement in competitive baseball and allowed them to be treated as oddities, while the self-satisfied audience would reaffirm its essential sameness. This was particularly true of black and female barnstorming teams, who were compelled to engage in various forms of clowning that emphasized their difference – and in the community's eyes their gender, race, or ethnic inferiority.[78] This was also true of native people like the one-armed Ben Johnson, who was often hired to play exhibition games because of the attraction of his disability, but despite his physical talent was never signed to play for white teams in regular league play throughout the Maritimes.

It is possible, however, to exaggerate the extent to which ethnic apartheid affected native baseball players in Maine and the Maritimes. During the interwar period native teams in the Maritimes often played against other marginalized groups such as blacks and Acadians, and occasionally against competitive town teams. In addition, players such as Mattie Lewis, Bill Bernard, Frank Doucette, and Joe Paul played beyond the reserve for town teams. At the Bear River reserve in Nova Scotia's Annapolis Valley, the native team played Acadians in Meteghan, black teams in Yarmouth, and town teams such as the Yarmouth Gateways, the amateur champions of the Maritimes in 1935. The team at Chapel Island regularly played teams from Acadian towns such as River Bourgeois, Arichat, Petit de Grat, and L'Ardoise, but now and then ventured farther afield. Wilfrid Prosper remembers a game between the Chapel Island club and the professional club from Reserve Mines in the old Class C Colliery League in the late thirties. 'They had this guy, Smokey Joe Kelly. God Almighty he was awful fast. Fast. I was scared to death he was going to kill somebody with one of those pitches. And this Mattie Lewis use to pitch so ... My God, they did beat that team 1–0, the game I remember. 1–0. He [Lewis] was some pitcher, I tell you.'[79] Somewhat later, in 1951, the team from Lennox Island reserve captured the Intermediate 'B' championship of Prince Edward Island, beating the Peake's Island Bombers in a three-game series.[80]

In Maine, baseball was popular among the Penboscot people in the 1880s and 1890s, and well into the twentieth century. Most famous of all native ballplayers was Louis Francis Sockalexis, a Penobscot from the

Old Town reservation near Bangor, Maine, who was reputedly the first native American to play major-league baseball. Born on 24 October 1871 at the Old Town reserve, Sockalexis grew up playing baseball and other sports. An outstanding physical specimen, standing 5'11" and weighing 185 pounds – one newspaper described him as as a 'mod physically, ... fleet-footed and full of life' – Sockalexis began to play competitive baseball throughout Maine during his late teens. In 1891 the Portland *Eastern Argus* reported that he had played for the Murphy Balsams at the Orphans' picnic, sharing the pitching and catching duties. 'He is a fine thrower, a hard hitter and a general good player,' the newspaper noted. As a result of his performance he was given a trial by the Portland club in the New England League.[81] Rather than playing professional baseball, however, Sockalexis had his eye at that time on a university education, opting for Holy Cross College and later Notre Dame University. In 1897 he joined the National League Cleveland Spiders, where he played outfield for three seasons, compiling a .313 lifetime batting average. Andy Coakley, who pitched in the majors for the Philadelphia Athletics, and later suited up for Fredericton in the New Brunswick League, noted that Sockalexis 'had a gorgeous left handed swing, hit the ball as far as Babe Ruth, was faster than Ty Cobb and as good a baserunner. He had the outfielding skill of Tris Speaker and threw like Bob Meusel, which means that no one could throw a ball farther or more accurately.'[82] Hall of Famers Hughie Jennings and John McGraw both played against Sockalexis and later agreed that he was the finest natural talent they had ever witnessed.[83]

Sockalexis's best year was his rookie season, in which he hit .338, stole sixteen bases, and sparkled in the outfield. In 1898 he stole no bases and his batting average plummeted over a hundred points. The source of the difficulty was alcohol. Hughie Jennings remembers his fall in the following way. According to Jennings, Sockalexis had starred in a series in Chicago during his rookie year, hitting a ninth-inning grand slam to put his club ahead 4–3 and making an almost impossible catch in the bottom of the inning to preserve the victory. After the game the Cleveland fans in attendance rushed onto the field and carried him on their shoulders out of the park and eventually to a local bar. Although Sockalexis supposedly had never touched alcohol before, he was pressured into doing so by the taunts of his intoxicated companions. Thereafter, he descended into serious alcoholism. Released by the Spiders during the 1899 season, he returned to Maine. Over the next decade he played semi-pro ball in Maine and New Brunswick, often as a team-mate of two other Penobscot ballplayers, Henry Mitchell and Joe Neptune. In 1903 he was playing in the semi-pro New Brunswick League, and between 1904 and 1910 for Castine, Maine, paddling down the Penobscot River from Old Town to play ball. He also spent much of his time coaching native youth on the Indian Island reserve. Walter Ranco, a soft-spoken Penboscot who owned a small store in Old Town, remembered Sockalexis as a wonderful coach and teacher. Five of his students, including Teddy Mitchell and Joe Neptune, graduated to the Colonial and the fast New England leagues, then just a step away from the majors. In 1913, at the age of forty-two, Sockalexis was found dead in the woods, where he had been working as a woodcutter for $30 per month. Two years later the Cleveland baseball club took the name Indians in his memory.[84]

In his recently released novel *The Cleveland Indian: The Legend of King Saturday*, Luke Salisbury builds a caricature of Sockalexis in the name of King Saturday.[85] Salisbury's novel is an attempt to capture the colour and rambunctiousness of baseball in the 1890s, which it does well, rather than to portray the particular difficulties native people had in adjusting to white society, which it does not. Although there is reference to the mocking war-whoops that greeted King Saturday from the stands, the novel reinforces the stereotype of the 'worthless Indian.' Saturday is depicted as a hard-drinking, woman-chasing rowdy, with little respect for the game of baseball despite his immense talents, and susceptible to betting on and throwing ball games to fill his own pocketbook. This is not to deny that Sockalexis had his faults: he was expelled from Notre Dame after a brawl in a local bordello,[86] and his alcoholism has been well documented.

What is lacking here, however, is an appreciation of the larger context of native–white relations at the turn of the century,[87] or of the fact that the history of sport 'has been indelibly stamped by the dimensions of race in America.'[88] In the nineteenth century and for much of our own, native peoples, blacks, and ethnic minorities were cast as outsiders, their cultural and supposedly innate racial characteristics setting them off from the mainstream. Stereotypes associated with blacks and native peoples were given quasi-scientific justification in the theory of the different evolution of the 'races,' even though, as Barbara Jean Fields has pointed out, 'race is not an element of human biology ... but an ideology,' that is socially constructed.[89] These stereotypes were used in turn to rationalize de facto segregation in education, housing, employment, and sport.

Sport none the less served important social and community functions in black communities, or for native people on the reserve provided an escape from life's harsh realities and contributed to pride and self-esteem. Sport was also a focal point for cultural and political struggles involving human rights and racial equality. Over time, as talented native and black athletes contributed to the development of sport within their respective communities, they were drawn inexorably into a larger world of sport that at once valued their skills and required them to bear the reputation of their people. For Lou Sockalexis the result was tragic. Even for those who succeeded in challenging the system, like Jackie Robinson, the victory was partial. Whatever the accomplishment of individual athletes, the continuing devaluation of native people and blacks in the larger social order made the road to success for minorities difficult and troublesome. Some simply avoided the challenge and turned to sport within the community as a source of solidarity and pride. That such a tradition of sport exists is admirable: that such choice was often necessary is an enduring testimony to the destructive racism that has plagued our society to the present day.

10

Extra Innings: The Eclipse of Community Baseball

On 1 August 1942 two young boys stood outside the Capitol Theatre in Halifax, waiting patiently for the Saturday matinee. The theatre marquee announced the day's feature film, *Wings for the Eagle*, starring Ann Sheridan and Dennis Morgan, another of Hollywood's characteristic wartime exercises in the patriotic veneration of the American way. On this Saturday, however, the movie lines were noticeably shorter than usual, for across town an even more powerful symbol of America's seeming virtue was readying himself to stride to the batter's box at Halifax's historic Wanderers Grounds. Halfway around the world, on the steamy South Pacific Island of Guadalcanal, Japanese soldiers would soon taunt American marines with the cry 'Babe Ruth is a bum,' but on this day the townspeople of Halifax harboured no such thoughts as they eagerly awaited the appearance of the greatest home-run hitter in baseball history.

For weeks rumours had swirled about Halifax with respect to the Babe's appearance. One had him appearing in a Halifax uniform against Mickey Cochrane's Great Lakes Naval Station baseball team, a collection of former big leaguers now in military service. This team, which included star pitcher Bob Feller, was considered by many to be the equal of the best teams in the talent-drained major leagues.[1] In their flights of fancy Haligonians could envisage the likes of Cochrane, Johnny Lucadello, George Earnshaw, and Bob Feller parading their talents at the Wanderers Grounds. 'It's still not known whether the Babe will take part in whatever game is staged that night or whether he'll just bat a few over the fence in practice,' wrote an exuberant sports columnist for the Halifax *Herald*. 'Just imagine what a spectacle it would be to see him trudge up to the plate and oppose fire-ball Bob Feller on the mound.'

Other rumours had the Babe umpiring the game or suiting up against a college squad from Fordham University.[2]

The fans can be forgiven their disappointment when none of these dreams materialized. They had to be satisfied instead with a somewhat rotund 'Bambino' coming to the batter's box dressed in street clothes and regular dress shoes. A slight drizzle added to the fans' discomfort as Aukie Titus, a young outfielder and occasional relief pitcher for the Navy club in the local Halifax Defence League, took the mound to serve up some batting-practice pitches to the Babe. Probably aware of an earlier trip to the province in 1936 when Ruth was forced to tell fast-baller Dingie McLeod to stop trying to strike him out and to throw one of those 'drug store pitches' down the heart of the plate, Titus avoided giving Ruth anything other than grooved fast balls. It was soon obvious, however, that the Bambino's old magic was gone. The Babe swung weakly at the first two pitches, and then lofted a fly ball to the cinder track in short right field before driving a few line drives down the first-base line. With every pitch the fans waited expectantly for him to muscle a ball out of the park. It was not to be. After popping up to the catcher and swinging and missing the next three pitches, Ruth decided to call it a day, then hauled out a fungo bat and hit a dozen autographed baseballs to an outfield filled with souvenir hunters. When the supply was exhausted he returned to the stands to watch the game of the night, featuring an all-star Toronto Navy team and Halifax Navy.

Ruth had visited the province before on numerous occasions. There were expeditions such as the one that took him in 1936 to Westville, where he gave a hitting exhibition, and hunting trips with friends such as Rufus Sutherland of Lockeport. His attraction to the province, however, had even deeper roots. During his childhood, Ruth had resided at Saint Mary's Industrial School in Baltimore, where, under the tutelage of the Xaverian brothers who administered the institution, he was instructed in the game of baseball. Of all those at the school, Ruth reserved his highest praise for Brother Matthias, who was instrumental in developing his knowledge of the game. At Saint Mary's Matthias had made all the boys learn to play every position on the field, and in this way Ruth developed both his batting and pitching skills.[3] 'He used to back me into a corner of the big yard at Saint Mary's and bunt a ball to me by the hour, correcting the mistakes I made with my hands and feet,' Ruth recalled. 'When I was eight or nine I was playing with the 12-year old team. When I was 12 I was with the 16-year olds, and when

I was 16 I played with the best of the many teams we had in school. All because of Brother Matthias.'[4]

Born and raised in Nova Scotia, Brother Matthias was a towering man, standing six feet, four inches and weighing well over two hundred pounds, and with a personal magnetism that served him well as prefect in charge of discipline at Saint Mary's. Although he had played a little baseball as a youth in Nova Scotia (Ruth remembers him hitting one-handed 350-foot fly balls with a bat in one hand and a small fielding glove on the other), he was less interested in playing the game himself than in using it as a way of teaching young boys self-discipline and good sportsmanship.

Brother Matthias, a native of Lingan, Cape Breton, was born Martin Leo Boutlier on 11 July 1872 to Joseph and Mary Ann Boutlier.[5] After entering the Xaverian brothers in May 1892, he was assigned to Saint Mary's Industrial School in 1894, and remained there until 1931 when he was transferred to Saint John's School in Danvers, Massachusetts. In 1941 he was assigned to the Xaverian juniorate in Peabody, Massachusetts, remaining there until his death on 16 October 1944, just four years before Ruth's own death.[6]

Ruth's appearance in Halifax in 1942 highlighted a gala sports weekend marking the official opening of a new Navy recreation centre at Wanderers Grounds, which Navy brass hoped would provide servicemen with an alternative to less salutary forms of leisure. Unfortunately, wartime Halifax offered little in the way of excitement or hospitality. Not only had the province's temperance forces organized to force the closure of the popular Ajax Club in the spring of 1942,[7] but servicemen and their families were perturbed by the indifference of the city's population to their concerns and by the price gouging tactics of certain landlords, landladies, storekeepers, restaurant owners, and bootleggers.[8]

Throughout its history as a garrison town, Halifax's civilians had ambivalent feelings about the military. Although it depended heavily upon the military presence for its prosperity, the city remained concerned about the indecorous behaviour that often accompanied footloose soldiers and sailors to their town. In contrast to the port of St John's, Newfoundland, which had a reputation among the troops for hospitality, Halifax seemed grimy, drab, and peculiarly Victorian. 'For men on the lower deck,' James Lamb has observed, 'Halifax was a virtual desert ... Swarming ashore from crowded mess decks at the end of a long voyage, they found little to entertain them there, apart from the handful of crowded movies, seedy cafes, and the wet canteen.'[9]

What the city did offer was sport, sport, and more sport. Hardly a day passed without a scheduled game of baseball, football, or hockey. Given its role as the major embarkation point for troops going overseas, Halifax was in a particularly favourable position to deliver high-quality sports entertainment. During the war this city of slightly more than sixty thousand inhabitants swelled to twice that number, as military personnel, their families, and those seeking employment in defence-related industries crowded into the city. Among them were a number of world-class athletes such as National Hockey League stars Bob Goldham, Milt Schmidt, Joe Klukay, Gaye Stewart, Jackie Hamilton, Bob Dill, and George Gee, and major-league ballplayers Dick Fowler, Joe Krakauskas, and Phil Marchildon. The presence of these players contributed to what Paul Thompson, the former general manager of the NHL Chicago Black Hawks, considered the fastest baseball in the country with the exception of Canadian clubs in the International League. Only in Vancouver, Thompson believed, did military baseball compare in quality to that played in Halifax.[10]

If wartime conditions contributed to an elevated level of play on the region's ball diamonds, the excellent standard of baseball during the war owed much to the home-grown players who had grown up in communities throughout the Maritimes during the Great Depression. Many of the stars of the pre-war years were still in the area, but a number had left their town teams to play for service teams or for clubs in the Halifax Defence League. Danny and Garneau Seaman left Liverpool and found themselves on opposite sides of the diamond, Garneau with the Halifax Air Force club and Danny on the Navy team that won two Maritime championships, knocking off the Saint John Ironmen in 1942 and the Saint John Dockmen the following year. Local stars manned all the infield positions on the 1942 Navy club. Cape Bretoners Dev and Gus Vickers made up the double-play combination, Haligonian Billy Hannon was at third base, and Sydney Mines native 'Red' Burchell was at first.

Over the next couple of years Halifax Navy was strengthened by several servicemen from other parts of Canada. Jimmy Heximer, a speedy nineteen-year-old centre fielder from Ontario, joined the club in 1943, and his accurate arm, fine defensive skills, and potent bat soon attracted the attention of major-league scouts. After the war Heximer signed with the Boston Braves and played in the Class C Border and Class A Eastern leagues. Manager Bud Morrison's 1945 club included Manitoban Bob Halloran, formerly of Winnipeg in the Class C Northern

League; Irving 'Peaches' Ruven, who had played for the Montreal Royals in 1932 and later signed as player-manager of the Hackney Wick club in England; Leo Ornest, whose brother Harry was playing with Montreal in the International League; Darrel Ball, who had seen action with the Seattle Rainiers of the Pacific Coast League; and Bobby Porter, a veteran of the Toronto Maple Leafs and Syracuse Chiefs of the International League. Although Porter had been a regular in Triple A ball, he had difficulty breaking into the starting outfield for the Navy club.[11]

During the 1943 season Navy faced tough competition from the Air Force club and a newly formed team at the Halifax Shipyards. Former Cape Breton Colliery League star Art Upper was at the helm of the Air Force nine, which included Garneau Seaman and 'Chic' Charlton, one of the smartest catchers the Maritimes has ever produced. Near the end of the season the airmen added major leaguer Phil Marchildon, a native of Penetanguishine, Ontario, and the Navy acquired Joe Krakauskas of the Cleveland Indians. After a rough initial outing in which he was saddled with a 7–0 loss to Navy, Marchildon began to think that he had lost the effectiveness that had allowed him to win seventeen games for the Athletics the year before, but he settled down and pitched brilliantly after that.[12] In four starts, he won three and lost one, gave up 26 hits, and struck out 52 batters in 35 innings.

While Marchildon's fastball and sharp-breaking curve overpowered many of those who faced him, he had great difficulty getting Danny Seaman out. Seaman had five hits in thirteen at-bats against the major leaguer, including a double and home run, causing Marchildon to grumble that 'Seaman hits the ball too hard and too often to be playing in Nova Scotia.'[13] Krakauskas was unimpressive in his brief stint with the Navy club, giving up eleven hits and seven runs in eight innings, but he did record ten strike-outs.

The 1943 season was also the inaugural one of the Halifax Shipyards club. The driving force behind the team was manager R.J.R. Nelson of Halifax Shipyards Limited, a subsidiary of the Dominion Steel and Coal Company (DOSCO), and a company that for years had regarded the provision of sporting activity as a way to encourage worker productivity and labour compliance. In making application to the league, Nelson noted that sponsoring a ball club at the senior level was 'fully in accord with the policy adopted by our organization towards our employees.' Nelson pointed to the important contribution that Shipyard workers were making to the war effort, producing war materials, supporting the Victory Loan drive, the Aid to Russia fund, and the Red Cross. 'We are anxious,' said Nelson, 'to do anything in our power to maintain their morale at the high standard it is today and we feel that the inclusion of a Shipyards team in the Halifax City League will aid materially in accomplishing this. It will give our shipyards organization something to cheer for.'[14] Shipyard workers may have appreciated having a team to support, but its existence did not ensure labour tranquillity at the Yard. In 1944 workers at the Yard fought a month-long strike to secure the check-off system, which gave them the right to have union dues deducted automatically from their pay cheques.[15]

Over the next few years the Shipyards were a dominant club, and provided an important bridge between the wartime Defence League and the postwar Halifax and District (H&D) Baseball League, which began operation in 1946. The H&D League was a child of the war. The successful policy of mixing locals and imported talent that had been encouraged, even necessitated, by wartime circumstances, meant an end to the pure amateurism that had characterized community baseball in the interwar period. It also inaugurated a process whereby the traditional connection of home-brews to their home town began to dissolve, and where imported players began to squeeze locals off club rosters. One of the native players of the era, Phillip 'Skit' Ferguson, has observed that by the early 1950s 'the average ball player' on most of the semi-pro clubs in the Maritimes 'was no longer a Maritimer, but an American.'[16] Furthermore, when escalating costs and decreasing attendance resulted in the failure of one league after another during the 1950s, and led eventually to the collapse of the H&D League in 1960, the fans who had come to identify good baseball with imported Americans refused to accept a return to the spirited community baseball tradition that had existed between the wars.

The history of the H&D League, which operated for fifteen years before folding before the 1960 season, can be broken into three chronological periods. The first of these was the period 1946–50, in which the league maintained a healthy balance between local and imported players; the second, from 1951–5, in which local players were pushed aside as club teams blended veterans of organized baseball in the United States with American college students; and the last, from 1956–60, when the league became the equivalent of a summer baseball league for American college players who were regarded as prospects by major-league organizations.

The H&D League, like other semi-pro circuits that prospered immediately after the Second World War, capitalized upon the pent-up demand for entertainment among returning war veterans and upon the surplus of baseball talent that existed across North America. In the United States major-league organizations were faced with the enormous task of reassessing the talent of former players in their organizations whose professional careers had been interrupted by military service, and comparing them with those younger players who were on their way up through the minor leagues. As a result, the number of leagues and teams within organized baseball mushroomed. In 1946 there were only twenty-three leagues operating within the National Association of minor leagues; there were forty-two the following year, and fifty-nine by 1949.[17]

Even with the postwar expansion of minor-league baseball, there was room for competitive semi-pro teams outside of the organized baseball operation. The seemingly universal popularity of baseball allowed small towns to offer player salaries that were far more attractive than those in most minor leagues. Semi-pro leagues thus attracted skilled minor-league veterans, who realized that they would never make the major leagues or had lost their jobs when their teams folded. At the same time, they had access to the better college players who were ineligible for minor-league play. Consider the case of left-handed pitcher Gerry Davis, who signed with the Liverpool Larrapurs in 1949 after his club in the Border League folded. In the Border League, Davis played seven days a week, practised daily, and took home less than $100 a week. In Liverpool he made considerably more and played only five times a week. 'I thought I had died and gone to heaven,' Davis remembers. The following year Davis continued his career in the Colonial League, but it collapsed as well, and he returned to Nova Scotia for yet another season.[18]

In eastern Canada and the United States, there was a network of semi-pro leagues that provided a pool of players to draw upon. Among them were the H&D, Central, and Cape Breton Colliery circuits in Nova Scotia, various leagues in New Brunswick and Maine, the long-standing Quebec Provincial League, the Northern League with teams in Vermont and New Hampshire, the Blackstone Industrial League in Massachusetts, the Boston Park League (where the Red Sox and Braves often assessed players on a trial basis), and the Albemarle League in the Carolinas. Players moved freely from one league to another from year to year, seeking out the best offer and hoping to catch the eye of major-league scouts.

The H&D League opened play in 1946 with a mixture of local and imported players. Among the latter were several players from other parts of Canada who had been stationed in Halifax during the war. Leading the roll-call were Peaches Ruven, batting champion in the Halifax Defence League in 1945; catcher Marcel St Pierre, a veteran of four seasons in the Defence League, who had learned his trade in the Quebec Provincial League under the guidance of the old major leaguer Wally Schang; NHL star George Gee, who had the talent to play pro ball, but whose major interest was hockey; and Winnipeg natives Lou Bourbannais and Mike Genthon.

The star of the H&D League, however, was Reserve Mines native 'Skit' Ferguson, a pitcher and first baseman, who won 17 games and batted .438 for the champion Truro Bearcats in 1946, a club that also featured Maritimers Billy McIntyre, Hum Joseph, and Johnny Clark. The following year Ferguson, Clark, and pitcher Clyde Roy left Nova Scotia to play for Drummondville in the Quebec Provincial league. While Clark got homesick and returned home, despite hitting well above the .300 mark, Ferguson stayed and compiled a record of eight wins and seven losses, and hit .306 in 62 at-bats. Plagued by a sore arm, Ferguson stayed home the next year and played briefly for the Halifax Shipyards. Newspaper reporter Harry Fleming contends that Ferguson was the finest left-hander the province has ever produced, but his shortened pitching career makes comparison with those who had lengthier careers impossible.

Over the next three years, clubs throughout the Maritimes turned increasingly towards imported players from the United States. This was particularly true of the H&D League, under its president Harry Butler of Halifax. When Butler declined to run for re-election as vice-president of the Nova Scotia Amateur Baseball Association in 1947 so that he could give 'full attention to top quality ball for Halifax,' local sports columnist Alex Nickerson correctly took this to mean that the league planned to become a high-priced circuit with an emphasis on imported players.[19] In addition to college campuses in New England, the major source of players in the future would be the Northern League (with teams in Vermont and New Hampshire) and the Albemarle League in the Carolinas.

The close association with the Northern League began in 1947 when the Kentville Wildcats of the Central League imported 'Soc' Bobotas, a twenty-two-year-old second baseman from Manchester, New Hampshire, as playing coach. Accompanying Bobotas were a number of his team-mates from the Northern League and from the University of New Hampshire varsity squad. The Wildcats' roster also included seventeen-year-old phenom Art Ceccarelli, a fire-balling left-handed pitcher from New Haven, Connecticut. In just his fifth start with the Wildcats, Ceccarelli pitched a no-hit, no-run game against the Windsor Maple Leafs, striking out twelve and walking just one. After the season Ceccarelli signed with the Brooklyn Dodgers, and eventually played five seasons in the major leagues for Kansas City, Baltimore, and the Chicago Cubs.

In 1948 Hank Swasey, coach of the UNH ball team, took over the reins in Kentville. His club relied heavily upon players from the Northern League, including Bobotas, shortstop Johnny Watterson, speedy outfielders Hal Burby and Jack Kaiser, pitcher-outfielder Chris Tonery, catcher Emil Krupa, and pitcher Jim Arbucho. Swasey also had an informal working arrangement with the Brooklyn Dodgers, who arranged for the signing of Temple university first baseman Dick Gernert (who later played ten years in the majors with the Boston Red Sox, Chicago Cubs, and Cincinnati Reds), Tom McMullen, a seventeen-year-old pitching prospect, and catcher Paul O'Neill, a twenty-seven-year-old, cigar-smoking war veteran who had played three years in the Dodger chain.

The northern exodus of players to the Maritimes swelled appreciably in 1948 because of a decision by the Eastern College Athletic Conference (ECAC) to declare the Northern League a professional league. This meant that players from ECAC schools who signed to play in the Northern League would lose their college eligibility. As a result, Jack Kaiser, Art Raynor, and Jim Arbucho, team-mates of Robin Roberts on the 1947 Northern League's Montpelier club, signed with Kentville rather than returning to Vermont. Roberts was also slated to come north, and would have, had he not signed a Philadelphia Phillies contract in February 1948.

Other clubs were also coming to rely more heavily on imported players. Led by playing coach Burt 'Buster' Pankratz, a former AAA catcher with Jersey City and Columbus, and journeyman ballplayer Bernie Parent, a seven-year veteran of organized baseball, the Middleton Cardinals had a team made up largely of players from the Detroit area. Pankratz, Parent, Jim and John Wingo (sons of former major leaguer 'Red' Wingo), outfielders Paul Bulger and Jack Graham, and pitcher Frank 'Lefty' Lerchen were all from the Motor City, while outfielder Nick Nikita and pitcher Jimmy Dumeah hailed from Windsor, Ontario. Laurence 'Lefty' Letteri was a native of Cambridge, Massachusetts, and shortstop Emmanuel 'Sonny' Senerchia, who graduated to the Pittsburgh Pirates in 1952, hailed from Newark, New Jersey.

The most notable of Middleton's imports was William 'Bucky' Tanner, who had responded to his demotion from the Brooklyn Dodgers to their Montreal farm club in the spring of 1946 by jumping to Jorge Pascual's outlaw Mexican League. Along with major-league stars Sal Maglie, Fred Martin, Max Lanier, Danny Gardella, Mickey Owen, and Lou Klein, Tanner was suspended from organized baseball and not reinstated until 1949. During his exile he pitched for the Mexico City Reds, Alamaderes in the Cuban League, Drummondville in the Quebec Provincial League, and Middleton, in 1947 and 1948.

If some clubs, like Kentville and Middleton, relied almost exclusively on imported talent, most teams throughout the Maritimes were built around a core of local players. The stars of the two Halifax teams, the Citadels and the Shipyards, for example, were local players Johnny Clark, Buddy Condy, Leo Woods, Jimmy Gray, and Skit Ferguson. Condy and Clark, both of whom were major-league-calibre players, finished one-two in the batting race in both 1949 and 1950, far outperforming American team-mates Herb Rossman and Ted Narleski (the son of major leaguer Bill Narleski and brother of Ray Narleski, later of the Cleveland Indians.) Both Rossman and Narleski later played Triple A ball. This is not to denigrate the contribution of the imported personnel, especially pitching stars such as Boston College student Jerry Levinson and Jack Halpin, who had pitched for a couple of years in the Chicago Cubs organization. A big southpaw from Lowell, Massachusetts, Halpin was the H&D League's dominant pitcher from 1948 to 1950, winning forty-seven games while losing only ten.

Across the Bay of Fundy in New Brunswick, town clubs were also turning to imports. Immediately after the war most clubs in the province had relied on local stars, but beginning in 1948 more and more imported players found their way onto New Brunswick rosters. The 1948 Saint John Dodgers brought in second baseman Lou Giammarino from Springfield, Massachussets, and pitchers Charles 'Bud' Hagen and Medo Rios from Westfield in the same state. The Fredericton Legionnaires signed Catcher Fred McOsker from Lowell, shortstop Joe Kuniey of Easthampton, outfielder Art 'Whitey' Weinstock of Newton, and pitcher Bob Bagwell of Watertown, Massachusetts. Moncton signed infielders Ed Juszyk, a veteran of the Northern League, Ed Steitz, a faculty member at Springfield College, and pitcher Bill Nordberg from Mansfield, Massachusetts.

Blending talented local players with imports was a successful strategy, and resulted in baseball of a particularly high calibre. This was indicated by the performance of Maritime teams against three highly regarded touring aggregations, the Brooklyn Junior Dodgers, the New York Equitable Life team, and a group of barnstorming major leaguers performing under the banner of the 'Birdie Tebbetts Major League All-Stars.' In each case the Maritime teams, which drew heavily on local players, played well. The Brooklyn Junior Dodgers visited Nova Scotia in the summer of 1948, taking on a team made up of junior-age players from the H&D league. The parent Dodger organization had taken a serious interest in Maritime baseball, and with scouts Hank Swasey in Nova Scotia and Clem 'Oakie' O'Connor in New Brunswick, Brooklyn kept tabs on players it hoped to sign in the future. A game involving junior prospects from the Brooklyn area and those in Nova Scotia was thus an important way of assessing young talent. The Brooklyn juniors had a powerful line-up, led by pitchers Billy Loes, Don McMahon, and Joe Pignatano, each of whom would eventually graduate to the major-league Dodgers. The H&D league club fielded a mixture of local and imported players, and defeated the Dodgers 3–1 on the strength of a towering home run by Saint John native Joe Breen of the Halifax Capitals. On the mound for the Nova Scotia stars was Stellarton native John 'Twit' Clarke, who held the Dodgers to four hits.

Later in the season the 'Birdie Tebbetts All-Stars' played three games against New Brunswick's Saint John St Peter's and Grand Falls Cataracts. Tebbetts, a native of Burlington, Vermont, and first-string catcher for the Boston Red Sox, had assembled a star-studded squad to barnstorm northern New England and the Maritimes, and whenever possible to do a little hunting and fishing. The infield had Earl Torgeson of the Braves at first base, 'Stuffy' Stirnweiss of the Yankees at second, Boston's Vern Stephens at shortstop, and Eddie Pellagrini of the Cincinnati Reds at third. In the outfield, the All-Stars had Walt Dropo in left, Jimmy Piersall in centre, and another Vermonter, Tony Lupien in right. On the mound, Tebbetts could call upon Ray Scarborough, Carl Scheib, Frank 'Spec' Shea, Joe Coleman, Bob Savage, and Charles 'Red' Barrett, who between them had won seventy-four games in the majors in 1948. In later tours of the region, the All-Stars line-up included such stars as Phil Rizzuto, Al Rosen, Sal Maglie, Johnny Pesky, Vic Wertz, Bob Kennedy, Johnny Groth, Mike Garcia, and Mickey McDermott.

The All-Stars opened their New Brunswick series with a game in Saint John on 21 October, and the following day travelled to Grand Falls for two more games. In Saint John Tebbetts's men faced a team made up entirely of local players, including moundsman Johnny Harvey, a former White Sox chattel who once pitched for Albany of the Class A Eastern League. The major leaguers won 5–1, on the strength of a combined five-hitter by Ray Scarborough and Carl Scheib. For the first five innings, however, the game was a pitchers' duel between Scarborough and Harvey. When Harvey left the game after five innings to allow other players a chance to play, the score was knotted 1–1; he had held the All-Stars to four hits and struck out three. In the next two innings, however, the major leaguers pushed across four runs against reliever Art Wilson. Wilson was replaced by Cecil 'Lefty' Brownell, who held the All-Stars scoreless the rest of the way. At bat, Saint John was led by former Boston Red Sox farmhand and Saint John native Jimmy Fox, who walked, singled, and stole two bases in two plate appearances. In addition to Fox, Aukie Titus went one for two at the plate and stole home for Saint John's only run.

The following day the All-Stars were in Grand Falls for the first of two games against the local Cataracts. The opening game was once again tightly contested, with the All-Stars squeezing out a 4–2 win. 'Spec' Shea and Bob Savage combined for the victory. The Cataracts used four pitchers including starter 'Muck' Carroll, who went four innings that day and then threw six more the next. In the game the following day, the All-Stars completed its three-game sweep of the Maritime clubs, winning 6–1 on Joe Coleman's four hitter and a 400-foot home run by Vern Stephens. Even in defeat, however, the New Brunswick clubs had played well, holding the major leaguers to an average of five runs a game, while playing solid defensive baseball.

The next great test for Maritime baseball came the following year with the visit to Halifax of the New York Equitable Life baseball club. Equitable Life, the National Baseball Congress semi-pro champions of the United States in 1948 and 1949, and the equivalent of a Double A ball club, showed their talent in the first match, pummelling the Shipyards 11–2. Johnny Clark was the only bright light for the Shipyards, with two hits and solid defensive play in the outfield. The final two games, however, rank among the most exciting ever played in Halifax. In the second game, the Halifax Capitals edged the visitors 7–6, led by import second baseman Art West and Cape Breton product 'Red' Burchell. This set the stage for the deciding match, which pitted the Equitable Life squad against a combined Halifax team drawn from the Shipyards and Capitals. The final game was a see-saw affair, with fine plays on both sides, including a superb running catch by Johnny Clark off a drive to deep right-centre field to keep Halifax in the game. After the regulation nine innings the game was knotted at 4–4. Unfortunately for the locals, New York squeezed a run across in the tenth, and went on to win the game and the series. After the game the New Yorkers were lavish in their praise of the Halifax players. One of the most effusive was first baseman Fred Price, who before the Second World War had played for Jersey City in the International League, and at that time was being primed to take over the initial sack for the New York Giants. Price was seriously wounded during the war, however, and by the time he was ready to play ball again the Giants considered him too old to rely upon. After his release he joined the Equitable Life squad. Price's new team-mates had all played in the high minors, and some like Al Mele and Vince Ventura had major-league experience. As a result, they were in a good position to assess the quality of their competition. In coming to Halifax, Price observed, the Americans had expected to play the equivalent of a Class C club, but were surprised to find that the calibre of ball in Nova Scotia was 'as good as anything being played in the Class A leagues in the United States.'[20]

Given the success of local players like Johnny Clark, John Harvey, Jimmy Fox, and Joe Breen against teams of this sort, it is hardly surprising that most of the clubs in the Maritimes during the late 1940s continued to build their rosters around talented local players. In Springhill, Nick Morris, coach of the Keene College (New Hampshire) team, who had coached New Waterford in the Cape Breton Colliery League in the thirties, took over the reins of the club in 1948 and added several imports to a strong roster of locals that included the McLeod brothers, Herb and Claude, Lawson Fowler, Earl and Hilton Boss, and Suki Leadbetter. Charlie Stevens, sportswriter for the New Glasgow *Evening News*, observed that the Fencebusters intended to give baseball more serious attention in the future. 'In past years, time and again we have seen friends come out of the pits, dig in for home, wash, and get into their monkey suits, and be back on the field between four and five o'clock.' Approaching the game more professionally, Stevens believed, would mean a better brand of ball. Nevertheless, 'the old 'Busters did a reasonably fair job, coal dust and all.'[21] In 1949 the Fencebusters increased their import ratio, signing former major-league catcher Bill Cronin as coach, and adding several newcomers to the squad. Each year a new crop of imports arrived in town. Two of those signed for the 1951 season, Richard 'Turk' Farrell and first baseman Jim McManus, would eventually play in the major leagues.

Elsewhere the trend towards imports continued. In Pictou County the

Westville Miners relied heavily on players like Clarkie Wotowicz, Paul Aylward, and Chuck Imhof. Wotowicz would later play Triple A ball in the New York Yankee organization, while Aylward, a 'long, lean, righthanded pitcher, ... built along the lines of Dizzy Dean,' could 'fog the ball past hitters.'[22] In 1952 Aylward, who had grown up around Fenway Park and often worked out with the Red Sox while still in his teens, joined former Maritime league stars Dick Gernert, Bob Atwood, and Hal Buckwalter at Boston's spring training camp. Second baseman Buckwalter had been a member of the 1949 Amherst Ramblers club. While watching Buckwalter hit slashing line drives all over the field during spring training, Boston manager Pinky Higgins came to the conclusion that he could probably hit .300 in any league. In the field, though, Buckwalter caused shudders, especially on pop-ups. The Red Sox could never find a defensive position for Buckwalter, trying him at first, second, and third base as well as in the outfield. Despite his rapid rise to the Triple A level, therefore, he would languish in Boston's farm system and never make the big club.[23]

In Stellarton, manager Stuffy McInnis of the Albions (once a member of the Philadelphia Athletics' famed $100,000 infield) had nine imports in tow when he started the 1949 season in Nova Scotia's Central League. The old major leaguer, head baseball coach at Amherst College, brought six prospects with him, including infielders Ivan Rosedale, Don Mac-Neish, Bob Butters, and Richard Orcutt and pitchers John Lacy and Don Delpierre. Two other imports, big Joe Lamonica and Maine native John Hafenacker, led the club at the plate, hitting .368 and .354 respectively. Hafenacker also led the Central League with eleven home runs. Lamonica later signed with the Boston Red Sox organization, while Hafenacker went on to play in the New York Yankee farm system. McInnis's club also relied heavily on local players Harry Reekie and John 'Twit' Clarke, both of whom worked in the coalmines during the day and played ball at night. '"Stuffy," he couldn't get over it here in Stellarton,' Clarke recalled. 'He said, "I can't figure out how they do it. They work all day in the mines; they come up here; they have a shower and maybe grab a sandwich; and they play ball, and they play *good* ball!"'[24]

By this time as well, imports were flooding into the Cape Breton Colliery League. Third baseman Al Ware, who led the league with a .399 batting average in 1949, later played Triple A ball in the Chicago White Sox organization. Others with professional experience were Al Caprio, playing manager of the Sydney Mines Ramblers, Colonial League grads Johnny Falwell, Dave Barr, and Art Chartier who would later play in the H&D League, and Bob Ayotte, a veteran of the Mexican League who had spent a month as a non-roster player with the Boston Braves in 1944. More than any other league in the province, however, the Colliery League continued to rely upon local players. John 'Brother' Macdonald, second in the batting race to Ware with a .372 batting average, was joined by Bill Marsh and Joe Cormier (formerly of the Kentville Wildcats), Oscar Seale of the Whitney Pier club, Jim O'Dell of the Dominion Hawks, Vince Gouthro of the Glace Bay Miners, and several other local stars.

One community baulked at the trend towards imported players, however. The town of Truro had begun the 1949 season in the six-team Central League, along with Stellarton, Westville, Springhill, Kentville, and Amherst, but dropped out in the middle of June citing low gate receipts and the expense of long road trips. Writing on the team's demise, the editor of the *Truro News* berated the 'phony amateurism' that characterized Maritime baseball, and blamed the team's troubles on the practice of paying salaries of between $50 and $150 per week. In his opinion, baseball in small towns like Springhill survived only because 'the Fencebusters have become more or less a tradition with the miners in a sense somewhat like the Dodgers to the people of Brooklyn. The whole town is interested in the team – there are few other diversions in the way of sport.'[25] Ironically, when Truro returned to the H&D League in 1950 its roster was almost exclusively American, heavily reliant upon players from the old Class B Colonial League, which had folded early in the season.

The increasing reliance on imports was most evident in Dartmouth and Kentville. The Dartmouth club was established in 1948 when two Halifax merchants, Herman and Bob Kaplan, shifted the Halifax Arrows franchise across the harbour to 'Little Brooklyn,' a new park that equalled many Double A parks in seating capacity and other amenities. The 1948 Arrows, under the guidance of 'Peaches' Ruven, relied on local stars Stan Cann, Dev Vickers, Frankie Redmond, and Neil Staples, as well as classy imports Charles 'Bomber' Neal, Stu O'Brien, Johnny Duarte, Tom Dulmage, and Doc Acocella. In 1949 the Kaplans hired playing coach Bob Decker, a veteran infielder who had played in the New York Yankees chain for a decade. Decker was given the responsibility for assembling the team with assistance from the Chicago Cubs organization. Decker's club, which had only one local player, pitcher Howie Martin, was the class of the H&D League that summer. Among the many Americans on the roster were a brash seventeen-year-old outfielder from Greenwich, Connecticut, named John 'Zeke' Bella and a hardbitten pitcher named 'Smokey' Jim Heller, a former team-mate of Decker's in the West Texas League, whose lack of self-discipline and fondness for alcohol had probably kept him from progressing further in professional baseball.

For those who remember the H&D League, Bella and Heller remain among its most memorable characters. Bella was an immensely talented youngster who had all four of the attributes that major-league scouts look for, the ability to hit, hit with power, throw, and run. When Decker had first told Herm Kaplan that he was bringing the young outfielder to Halifax, Kaplan baulked, saying that the club had enough outfielders as it was. 'I'm bringing him anyway,' was Decker's reply. Bella starred in the league in 1949 and 1950 and, after a couple of years of military service, returned to Halifax in 1954, hitting .419 to cop the league's batting championship. After that Bella was caught up in the New York Yankees' stable of talented outfielders. Even though he never hit below .300 in the minor leagues (he hit .327, .317, and .339 in successive years at Triple A), the Yankees were unable to find a place for him, and finally dealt him to Kansas City Athletics in 1959. In his first and only season with the A's, the hard-luck Bella suffered a career-shortening shoulder injury, slamming into the wall while making a running catch. Although Kaplan considered him the finest all-round player ever to play in Nova Scotia, Bella never fully realized his tremendous potential.

Heller was another of Decker's protégés. Unlike Bella, whose career in professional baseball was ahead of him, the hard-to-manage Heller had begun his career in the minor leagues in 1942, and had teamed with Decker on the Borger club of the West Texas League after the war. By the time he arrived in Halifax, his brother George Heller – who would play for the Arrows in 1954 – had already made it to Triple A ball, but most observers considered 'Smokey' Jim the better of the two. Though not an overpowering pitcher, Heller was crafty, keeping hitters off-balance with a delivery that made it difficult to pick up the flight of the ball. Heller delivered the ball 'out of his pocket almost,' Johnny Watterson recalls. 'You just couldn't see it in time.'[26]

Like the Arrows, the 1949 Kentville Wildcats, champions of the Central League, were also import-laden, having dropped former local stars Gordon Troke, Joe Cormier, Leo Fahey, Eddie Gillis, Wilf Anderson, and Bev Buckler, so that rookie pitcher Harris Young was the only Nova Scotian player on the club. When the Wildcats took the field against the H&D League champion Arrows, therefore, two imported delegations, arguably the most powerful teams ever to play in the region to that point, faced each other across the diamond. Perhaps appropriately, the series ended in a 4–4 saw-off; the ninth and intended deciding game, held on Labour Day, was halted by rain and darkness after eleven innings with the score tied at seven all.

That Labour Day game had witnessed a remarkable comeback by the Wildcats. Trailing 7–1 going into the bottom of the ninth inning, they scored six runs to avoid defeat. The goat for the Arrows was none other than their ace left-hander, 'Smokey' Jim Heller, whom Decker called upon to put out a Wildcat rally with the bases loaded. Heller, who was known to have been drinking before the game, served up a grand-slam homer to Jack Kaiser to knot the score. When asked later why he turned to Heller at that time, Decker said without hesitation, 'Heller's my best pitcher, drunk or sober.'[27]

The following year, Johnny Watterson left Kentville in order to take advantage of an offer to coach the Stellarton Albions, a move that led indirectly to a more thorough-going reliance on imported players and the beginnings of a connection between baseball in Nova Scotia and the Carolinas. At the beginning of the 1950 season Watterson received a phone call recommending Bill Brooks, a hulking twenty-six-year-old catcher from Wilson, North Carolina, who had played the year before for the Keene Blue Jays of the Northern League. A veteran of three seasons in the Coastal Plains League and a brief stint with Manchester of the Class B New England League, Brooks had helped lead the Enid Airs club to the United States National Service Championship in 1945. Watterson invited Brooks to join him in Stellarton for the 1950 season. When Watterson received a military-draft notice that took him to Japan in 1951, the club management asked Brooks to put together and coach the Albions during the 1951 season.[28]

With Brooks at the helm the Albions became a powerhouse in Maritime baseball. The semi-pro Albemarle League had collapsed in 1950, leaving Brooks his pick of those players in the Carolinas who had yet to sign with major-league clubs. The majority of the team members were players from the Wake Forest College club in North Carolina, one of the strongest college squads in the United States. Wake Forest reached the finals in the NCAA championships in Wichita, Kansas, in 1949, and in the opinion of one of its star players, Joe Fulghum, had an even stronger club in 1950. Under Brooks, the Albions won three straight league and provincial championships. Stars of the club were Artie Hoch, all-American shortstop in 1946 at Wake Forest (his son Scott is currently a regular on the PGA golf tour); Fulghum, the club's best hitter; shortstop Gair Allie, who was the Pittsburgh Pirates regular shortstop in 1954; speedy second baseman Kent 'Baby' Rogers, and catcher Leroy Sires, who like Hoch and Fulghum was a veteran of the semi-pro Albemarle League in North Carolina. The Albions also signed Duke University star Bill Werber, Jr, who had been playing for the Keene Blue Jays in the Northern League, inaugurating a pipeline of Duke players to the league that eventually included Al Spangler, later a ten-year veteran in the major leagues. Duke shortstop Dick Groat had also been lined up to join the Albions, but signed a pro contract with the Pittsburgh Pirates and jumped directly to the major leagues instead. The same was true of William 'Digger' O'Dell, who had agreed to come to Stellarton in 1954, but was signed as a bonus baby by the Baltimore Orioles, and pitcher Jim Perry, out of Williamston, North Carolina and Campbell College, who signed a contract with the Cleveland Indians.

Brooks's tenure not only established the Carolinian connection to the Albions, but pushed aside local players who by virtue of their talent deserved to be in the line-up. When local management turned team selection over to an American coach like Brooks, it was natural that he would be committed to the players that he had brought north. For local players like Harry Reekie, whom Stuffy McInnis believed would make the major leagues if he went south to play, the result was platooning with weak-hitting North Carolinian Johnny Alford. Reekie, who had led the club at the plate the year before, hit .279 during the 1951 season, while Alford struggled to a .228 average. Similarly, because Brooks had signed Leroy Sires as his catcher, he moved himself to first base at the expense of John 'Brother' Macdonald, who had outshone most of the imports in the Cape Breton Colliery League in 1949. Macdonald was a better hitter and fielder than Brooks, and even though he was by no means a sprinter, he far outdistanced his mentor on the basepaths. Macdonald remembers being taken aside to tell him that he would be sitting on the bench most of the time. 'Now Brother Macdonald,' Brooks began in his jovial southern drawl, 'you know that I'd like to play and play at first base. You wouldn't mind if I played, and we kept you in reserve in case I got hurt would you?' 'What could I say?' Brother later mused. 'I just had to grit my teeth and accept it.'[29]

One local player who continued to play for the Albions at this time was Westville native Syd Roy, who had been, somewhat unexpectedly to Watterson, the team's best pitcher in 1950. The brother of right-hander Clyde Roy, who had a trial with the Memphis Chicks in 1945,

Syd Roy joined the Albions after the failure of the Central League's club in Westville. In four years with Stellarton he won twenty-five games and lost only six. When he came down with pleurisy early in the 1953 season, however, Stellarton released him and replaced him on the roster with an American utility player. The following year, Roy and Harry Reekie left Stellarton for Ontario to look for work. Roy caught on with Guelph of the Ontario Intercounty League and, after beginning as a relief pitcher, worked his way into a starting job.[30]

One of the ironies of the displacement of local players by imports was that it accompanied a gradual waning of fan support. It would be wrong to regard this as a causal relationship, however, for crowds were on the wane everywhere, not just in the Maritimes. Indeed, while the 1940s witnessed a boom in small-town and minor-league baseball across North America, the 1950s saw its contraction. The failure of the New England and Colonial leagues within organized baseball created a surplus of talent for the H&D league to draw upon, as did the collapse of the H&D League's major competitors for semi-pro and college talent. In Nova Scotia the Central League collapsed in 1950 and the Cape Breton Colliery League was no longer importing players after that. Elsewhere, the Albemarle League had died, the Northern League was on its last legs in 1951, and semi-pro ball in Maine, which had seen some prosperous days in the late 1940s, when franchises like the Augusta Millionaires listed such stars as Harry Agganis and Ted Lepcio in their line-ups, was in a weakened state.

By the mid-1950s the H&D League was the premier semi-professional league on the east coast of North America. 'The H&D League has grown in stature over the years,' said the Halifax *Chronicle Herald* in April 1955. 'There was a time when the outstanding college men played in amateur leagues near their home base. Those leagues no longer operate, so the H&D gets the cream of the college crop.'[31] Baseball in New Brunswick was also attracting some of the better college players from the East and South, including future major leaguers Charlie Lau, Mike Roarke, Angelo Dagres, Bill Kunkel, Dave Ricketts, and Ron Perranoski, but players there tended to be a year or two younger than those in Nova Scotia.

Attracting players was one thing, but attracting fans was something quite different. The account books of the Stellarton Albions reveal a steadily declining audience from 1951 through 1958 when the franchise suspended operations (see tables 1 and 2). Season attendance dropped from 46,310 in 1951 to 30,243 in 1954, and then plummeted to 14,742 in 1955. Attendance statistics also suggest the vital importance of post-

TABLE 1
Home attendance, Stellarton Albions, 1951–8

Year	Regular season total	Regular season average	Post season total	Post-season average	Season total	Season average
1951	30,974	1,100	15,516	2,217	46,310	1,323
1952	32,719	1,169	11,575	2,315	44,294	1,342
1953	24,535	909	15,309	2,552	39,844	1,207
1954	24,840	857	5,403	1,801	30,243	945
1955	14,742	567			14,742	567
1956	16,364	584	3,760	1,253	20,124	649
1957	12,520	522	2,939	734	15,459	552
1958	10,569	460	1,429	715	11,998	480

Source: Stellarton Albions club records

season games to the success of a club at the gate. Between 1951 and 1953, when Stellarton won the league and provincial titles, post-season attendance averaged close to 14,000 fans, but in 1954, when the Albions were knocked out in the first round, they drew only 5400 fans. Over the next four years the club would average a mere 2000 fans a year in post-season play.

For club management, the incentive of increased gate revenues in post-season play tended to drive up salaries, as clubs tried to strengthen themselves for the stretch drive. In 1953 the Albions feared that they might not repeat as league champions, and just at the 15 July deadline added pitcher John 'Monk' Raines, who had started the year with Jacksonville of the Double A Southern League. A minor-league veteran, Raines had put up great numbers, winning 20 games in 1949, 21 in 1951, and 26 in 1952. At age twenty-seven, however, he was no longer considered a major-league prospect. Raines's salary of $600 per month was 50 per cent higher than that of most of the players on the Stellarton club. Nevertheless, when he led the club to its third successive league championship, the strategy seemed vindicated.

Not surprisingly, club management repeated the technique the following year when, despite the presence of Raines, the Albions struggled through the first half of the season. The intended saviour this time was John Waselchuck, a journeyman pitcher in the Cincinnati Reds organization, who was hired at a salary in excess of that of Raines. Not only would Waselchuck fail to lift the Albions into the league finals, but the

TABLE 2
Stellarton Albions attendance frequency, 1951–8

	Over 3000	2500– 2999	2000– 2499	1500– 1999	1000– 1499	500– 999	Under 500
1951	1		2	7	17	7	1
1952		2	3	4	15	7	2
1953	1	3	1	1 .	10	14	3
1954		1		2	8	18	3
1955					1	15	9
1956				1	2	21	7
1957					2	15	11
1958						11	14

Source: Stellarton Albions club records

combination of a drop in attendance of almost ten thousand fans and the exorbitant salaries given to Waselchuk and Raines left the Albions in serious financial straits. The club lost $10,000 on its operations in 1954.[32]

Other clubs in the league had been fighting financial difficulties for some time. Kentville had faced financial problems in 1949, when a deficit of $4000 led it to suspend radio broadcasts of its games. In the same year, the provincial champion Dartmouth Arrows lost $2000, causing Herm and Bob Kaplan to decide to sell the club. (Halifax businessman Bill Martin bought the franchise in 1951.) Truro had dropped from the Central League in 1950 because of financial difficulties. In 1953, the same year Stellarton lost $10,000, Halifax had a projected loss of $15,000, caused by an airlift of over fifty players from the United States, most of whom were found wanting. The loss was reduced somewhat when new manager Johnny Clark convinced his players to take a pay cut of $100 per month.

In order to boost revenues, communities turned to night baseball, installing lighting systems. The first to do so was Grand Falls, New Brunswick, which had lights for the 1950 season, causing the editors of the 1950 edition of *Maritime Baseball* to commend the town for its 'progressiveness,' noting that night baseball was 'the only salvation of the game in many centres south of the border and the time is fast approaching when the lights will be equally essential to the life of the game in this area.' Most other communities followed suit over the next three or four years. Of course, the installation costs strained already limited

revenues, demanding considerable community support through donations, bazaars, sport dinners, and lotteries and pools of various sorts.

By 1955 it was clear to most clubs in the H&D League that declining
gate revenues required a change in orientation. Before the season
opened, the league decided to move away from the costly veteran
ballplayer and to concentrate on college prospects. The member clubs
agreed to establish a $300-per-month salary limit and an average player
salary of $250. For the Albions this change meant a significant reduction
in player salaries. In 1954 the monthly salary total for eighteen players
was $7625 (the equivalent of a Class A minor-league club), and $1800
of that went to three players, Waselchuck, Raines, and Brooks. In 1955
the club spent only $4500 per month on player salaries, as the Albions
adhered strictly to the salary limits agreed upon in the spring.

Unfortunately for the Albions, it would appear that not all clubs in
the league were as scrupulous as Stellarton in sticking to the salary
caps. Coached by former major leaguer Stan Benjamin, Stellarton had
the youngest team in the league in 1955, a group of seventeen-year-olds,
most of whom were fresh out of high school or just beginning their
college careers. Before long it was clear that they could not compete
effectively against the other teams in the league. It was not that they
were untalented players – future major leaguer Jack Lamabe was one
of those who played briefly for the 1955 Albions – but they were inex-
perienced and erratic in the field and undisciplined at the plate. Like
most young major league prospects, they could make dazzling plays at
one moment, and throw the ball over the dugout the next. There is little
doubt, however, that fans would have seen a deterioration in the quality
of play as veteran players were phased out. Furthermore, as the Albions
fell behind in the standings the fans deserted the club. Stellarton's total
attendance declined from 30,243 in 1954 to 14,742 the following year.

The irony of this new reliance upon American college players was
that despite a decline in the calibre of play and dropping fan support,
far more H&D League players would graduate to the major leagues in
the second half of league's existence than had done so before. This trend
was already visible in 1953 and 1954. The 1953 Kentville Wildcats' line-
up included catcher Steve Korcheck and pitcher Dave Stenhouse, both
of whom would eventually graduate to the Washington Senators of the
American League; all-American shortstop Don Prohovich, who was
regularly on the Chicago White Sox's forty-man spring roster, but never
broke into an infield dominated by Nellie Fox, Louis Aparicio, Chico
Carrasquel, and Freddy Hatfield; and pitcher Dick Bunker, who was on

the verge of cracking the Philadelphia Phillies' line-up for several years. Liverpool's 1954 club sent pitcher Art Swanson and catcher Tommy Gastall directly to the majors as bonus babies. Halifax's roster included shortstop Tommy Carroll, another bonus baby who jumped directly to the New York Yankees and sat on Casey Stengel's bench for the next two years, as well as outfielders Zeke Bella and Al Spangler and pitcher Bob Davis. Others who would go on to play in the majors from these years were Liverpool pitcher Bill Oster, Truro infielder Grover 'Deacon' Jones, and Stellarton pitcher John Anderson.

The need to cut payrolls meant that henceforth the H&D League would become essentially a summer league for college prospects, similar to the Cape Cod League of the present day. Although there would always be a handful of veteran players such as Johnny Gee, Bob Hooper, Buzz Bowers, Jack Kaiser, Ed Hadlock, and Joe Camacho and a few locals sprinkled across club rosters, most players in the league had been recommended by major-league scouting staffs who wanted to assess their talent among prospects their own age.

By the mid-1950s there were few such leagues left in the eastern United States and Canada, assuring that those who arrived were among the brightest prospects of the day. 'The H&D league was *the* league to play in at the time,' remembers All-American second baseman Don Prohovich who had accompanied Bill Kearns, now a head scout for the Seattle Mariners, to the Maritimes and played there for three years. Major-league scouts kept a close eye on players such as Moe Drabowsky, Ralph Lumenti, Jack Kubiszyn, Jim Bailey, Gordon Massa, Danny Murphy, Moe Morhardt, Lee Elia, Hal Stowe, Norm Gigon, Dale Willis, Ken McKenzie, Vern Handrahan, Ty Cline, Roland Sheldon, Ed Connolly, Jim Hannan, and Purnal Goldy, all of whom were destined for the major leagues.

In retrospect, the phasing out of local and veteran players and the reliance on college prospects came at a heavy price for baseball in the Maritimes, but this was not immediately apparent. Although the shift from community-based amateur play in the 1930s to the mixture of local and imported players during and immediately after the Second World War weakened the attachment of baseball to local community life, before 1950 Maritime baseball rested firmly on the involvement of local players in the game. The high-quality competition that accompanied the mixing of imports and locals, moreover, helped develop the skills of young Maritimers who had the potential to play professional baseball. In addition, many local players demonstrated that they could outperform the imported ballplayer, and thereby commended themselves to professional scouts.

When their talents were discovered at a young enough age, local players such as Billy Harris, Wilson Parsons, Fred Flemming, and Vern Handrahan had a shot at making it to the major leagues. Harris, who had pitched for the Dieppe Juniors and Moncton Cubs in 1949 and 1950, for example, was only eighteen years old when Dodger scout 'Oakie' O'Connor signed him. Armed with a good fastball, a major-league curve, and an occasional slider, Harris quickly ascended the minor-league ladder. After winning 18 games at Valdosta, Georgia, in his first professional campaign, Harris had a remarkable sophomore season at Miami in 1952, pitching 29 complete games, winning 25, and notching an unbelievable 0.83 earned-run average, with 12 shutouts. In his first major league start with the Dodgers in 1957, Harris was beaten 3–2 on a home run by Philadelphia's Willie 'Puddinhead' Jones. Unfortunately for Harris, however, the Dodgers had the finest pitching staff in the majors at that time, and there was no room for him to pitch on a regular basis. Trapped in the talented Dodger system, Harris spent most of his career with the Montreal Royals, which in those days was the equivalent of a second-division major-league club.

Wilson Parsons and Fred Flemming, local players who had developed in the late forties and early fifties, barely missed making the major leagues. Halifax teenager Wilson Parsons came to the notice of Yankee scout Bob Decker in 1951 while pitching for the Dartmouth Arrows of the H&D League. Although Parsons was raw, he had a blazing fastball and reasonably good control and held opposing H&D League batters to a .159 batting average over 70 innings, striking out 55 and walking 41. Like Harris, Parsons moved quickly through the Yankee minor-league system, overpowering batters in the Piedmont League and pitching well in the high minors at Binghampton, Birmingham, and Richmond. Among the organization's brightest prospects, Parsons was invited to a special spring training camp with the Yankees in 1954. In June of that year, Parsons and future Yankee star Ralph Terry combined to hold the parent Yankee club to four hits, as their Binghampton club pulled off a 5–2 exhibition victory. Yet, despite obvious major-league talent, Parsons like Harris found himself trying to break into one of the best pitching staffs in the majors. Although Harris made the grade, Parsons never got his chance, especially after developing arm trouble. After shuttling back and forth between the H&D and International leagues in 1958 and 1959, Parsons finally decided to retire from baseball.

Fred 'Moose' Flemming was a native of Woodstock, New Brunswick, who signed with the Detroit Tigers out of Bowdoin College. He was impressive in a try-out held before Tigers manager Fred Hutchinson in 1952, hitting several balls into the stands at Briggs Stadium off regular Tigers pitchers. In 1954 Flemming went to spring training as a member of the Tigers' forty-man roster, and after a superb training camp in which he hit .426, the young right fielder was assigned to Syracuse of the Eastern League to work on his fielding. Flemming hit over .300 that year and was named the league's all-star right fielder. In 1955 Flemming was promoted to Little Rock and Buffalo, where he hit .288 on the season. In the meantime, however, the Tigers had a budding star in right field named Al Kaline, who would eventually become a member of baseball's Hall of Fame. Seeing little chance of breaking into the Tigers' line-up, Flemming, whose father was premier of New Brunswick, decided to pursue a legal career and retired from professional baseball.

Charlottetown native Vern Handrahan was another Maritimer who was discovered early enough to be considered a major-league prospect. Unlike Flemming, Harris, and Parsons, who played in the period when there were only sixteen major-league teams, Handrahan graduated to the majors after expansion had added four more teams. Handrahan played one season in the H&D League in 1958. Then only nineteen years of age, Handrahan caught the eye of Braves scout Jeff Jones, who signed him to a Milwaukee contract and sent him to Wellsville in the New York–Penn League. Later he would move to the Kansas City organization, breaking in with the Athletics in 1964. Handrahan played two years in the majors, mostly as a reliever, and held major-league batters to a combined .242 batting average.

Other Maritimers had successful trials in the minor leagues, but because of their age or injuries were not regarded as prospects. Spring-hill native Herbie McLeod spent two years tearing up the Florida State League, hitting .340 in 1949 and .354 in 1950 with 106 runs batted in and 24 stolen bases. McLeod's manager, Dipsy Mott, once observed that he had no weaknesses as a hitter. 'He can hit anybody in the National or American League, said Mott, but '[he's a] Lefty O'Doul kind of outfielder,' liable to be hit on the head any time.[33] New Brunswick native Jackie Bowes, an explosive fast-ball pitcher, signed a bonus contract with the Cleveland Indians in 1951 and got as far as the AA level, but was sidetracked by arm trouble. Bowes had a 17 and 3 record in the Class C Quebec Provincial League in 1953, and led the league with a 1.40 earned-run average the following year. Two other Maritime hurlers, Don McLeod and Don Swanson, both of whom came from Prince Edward Island, and played for Liverpool in the H&D League, made it to the Triple A level. Swanson was on the Chicago Cub pre-season roster in 1957, appearing in one exhibition game against the Cleveland Indians.

Then there were those who turned down major-league offers. Johnny Clark, Buddy Condy, Danny Seaman, Stan 'Chook' Maxwell, Don Boudreau, Tommy 'Mountain Boy' Linkletter, and Johnny Mentis all spurned the chance to play organized ball. All of them – with the exception of Mentis, who played only briefly for the Truro Bearcats – had memorable H&D League careers as well. Mentis left Nova Scotia for Quebec in his teens and subsequently compiled the highest lifetime batting average of any player in the Quebec Provincial League. Maxwell played five years in the H&D League, from 1954 to 1959, when it was dominated by American college players, and was one of the better players in the league. In his first season he led the Bearcats with a .283 average, and was third in the league in batting in 1958, outhitting future major leaguers Norm Gigon, Lee Elia, Moe Morhardt, and Ty Cline.

Without question, the finest hitter in league history was Springhill native William 'Buddy' Condy. A left-handed hitter, who hit both for average and with power, Condy terrorized league pitching. Johnny Watterson, who had played with and against major leaguers while in the service, considered Condy the best hitter he had ever seen. Although he had the reputation as a bad-ball hitter, a deficiency that Ted Williams argued would usually turn a .300 into a .200 hitter, Condy rejected the claim. While growing up in Springhill he had spent countless hours hitting rocks and mastering a nine-zone hitting area, which admittedly was wider and deeper than the normal strike zone.[34] In addition to his potent bat, Condy also had incredible quickness in getting down the first-base line, so that shortstops like Watterson didn't know how to play him. 'If you played him back, you couldn't throw him out at first,' remembers Watterson. 'If you played him in tight he'd kill you.'[35] Condy had no weaknesses at the plate, no matter where you threw the ball, remembers left-hander Gerry Davis, the White Sox farmhand who played two years for Liverpool. 'As a left-hander I was supposed to get left-handers out,' recalls Davis. 'But Condy owned me. He was the toughest batter I ever faced.'[36]

While Condy enjoyed baseball, his ambition was to become a medical doctor. He played the 1952 season in Saint John, where he roomed with

Johnny Clark, the two of them emulating the Yankees' Yogi Berra and Bobby Brown – Clark reading comic books while Condy poured over his medical texts. After the season, Condy retired to concentrate on his medical career. In 1955 he made a brief return to the H&D League, hitting .378 in nine games for the Halifax Cardinals. The first pitcher he faced after more than a two-year absence was young Moe Drabowsky, arguably the best pitcher in the league. Condy had a single and walk in three plate appearances that day. After the game Drabowsky visited Condy to tell him that he had hit his 'best stuff' and was as good as his reputation suggested. Had Condy wanted, there is little doubt that he would have been a star in the major leagues. Local baseball historian Burton Russell had this to say of Condy: 'No one ... could hit the ball with the same authority, race down to first base from home plate with such lightning speed, deliver a clothes line throw from rightfield to third base or execute a brilliant grab in the outfield with the consistency of the charismatic Condy.'[37]

Upon reflection, it appears that only the best Maritime players were given a chance to play in the H&D League after 1950. Skit Ferguson's comment that the average player in the league gradually became an American import rather than a home-brew, hits the nail on the head. 'Many locals could've continued to play,' Johnny Clark observed. 'They may not have been stars, but many of those who were brought in from the States weren't stars either.'[38] Clark's observation is supported by the result of the league's all-star game in 1950, which pitted imports against home-brews. The game, which attracted over 5500 fans to the Wanderers Grounds in Halifax, was tightly contested, and while the imports won 5–4 they were held to only five hits. Nevertheless, despite the ability of local players to compete with their American counterparts, fewer and fewer Maritimers were included on the rosters of H&D League teams in the years to follow.

The increasing reliance on imports, especially those with college obligations, alerts one to changing assumptions about the social purpose of baseball in the Maritimes after the Second World War. Between the wars the discourse surrounding baseball had centred upon notions of civic identity and regional pride, and thus mirrored a larger debate about regional integrity that had its political manifestation in the Maritime Rights movement. Committed for the most part to local players playing in their own home communities, interwar baseball clubs in the Maritimes followed a strict definition of amateurism in order to create a level playing field for clubs competing for the coveted Maritime championship. To this end, the amateur baseball associations of New Brunswick and Nova Scotia maintained strict residency requirements, so that the import rule even restricted a player suiting up for a neighbouring town if he had not established residency before the beginning of the season.

This community-based amateurism did not survive the war, however. For one thing, the wartime responsibilities of national service made regional isolation appear anachronistic. The Second World War, Alan Wilson has argued, drew the Maritimes out of its insularity, and brought to it a new cosmopolitanism. Port towns like Halifax and Saint John were flooded with military personnel from all over the world, and their harbours were filled with vessels flying the flags of allied nations.[39] Newspapers emphasized the connection of local endeavour to the international struggle and to far-away places, so that the 1940s, unlike the two preceding decades, would be characterized by the 'absence of a strong sense of regional identity.'[40] In this environment it was difficult to maintain the interwar imagery of a region bypassed by the forces of modernity. Nor would baseball continue to symbolize and validate an avowedly regional allegiance.

Of course, there were those who would turn the clock back, if they could, to an earlier time when baseball expressed a sense of regional identity. Each year between 1946 and 1950 the amateur baseball associations of Nova Scotia and New Brunswick published *Maritime Baseball: Pictorial Year Book*. This glossy magazine reviewed the baseball scene in the Maritimes from the year before, profiled the more prominent players of the day, and outlined the history of baseball in the major centres of the region. Although the annual gave attention to the increasing number of imports who were arriving in the area, its real purpose was to try and revive and restore the primacy of the Maritime championship. The editor of the 1950 edition thus announced his 'conviction that a Maritime Championship series is essential to the welfare of the game. As it is now, Maritime Baseball is like a ship without a rudder – It isn't going any place – except maybe on the rocks. It's like a serial with the last chapter missing. It has no goal.'[41]

As teams relied more and more upon college players from the United States, the likelihood of a regularly contested Maritime championship diminished significantly. Each year, as September approached, American college players were eager to return to their campuses. Because they frequently left for home abruptly, the league, provincial, and regional playoffs were often contested by clubs that fielded makeshift line-ups.

Maritime Baseball thus expressed little sympathy for 'overpaid College players from south of the border, who straggle in when the season is almost half spent and, more important, return home again before even league playoffs have been completed.'[42] This was a common complaint. The *Chronicle Herald* noted after the 1955 playoffs, for example, that 'the game has suffered in most places of late years, and the lack of interest can be traced directly to the fact that the teams were under-manned at playoff time, when admission prices rise and there is more at stake.'[43]

At the same time, while there were difficulties in relying upon American collegians, there was a certain satisfaction in knowing that the Maritime baseball leagues were attracting the brightest college stars of the day. While newspapers complained about the collegians leaving at playoff time, therefore, they also expressed pride that 'Nova Scotia is ... having so many fine young players come this way. The cycle swings this way these years ... Right now the H&D League is getting the talent and the fans are seeing better ball than many larger places where the game once flourished.'[44] The press also made frequent reference to the presence of major-league scouts at league games, and crowed proudly when league players were signed to rich bonus contracts, or jumped directly to the major leagues.

Increasingly, then, baseball was being judged by the ability of the league to produce major-league prospects, rather than by its contribution to civic allegiance or regional identity. Detached from its earlier ties to community and region, Maritime baseball was increasingly enmeshed in a network of play that connected small-town baseball to the major leagues. Earlier, in the twenties and thirties, it had been enough for local communities to put together teams that drew upon local talent, and to assess their abilities in games against touring teams from New England. After the war, however, Maritimers not only came to regard American ballplayers as the epitome of excellence, but in turn tended to devalue the skills of their own local players.

At the end of the decade, semi-pro baseball in the Maritimes was on its last legs. In 1957 the H&D League operated with only four clubs, Halifax and Liverpool having ceased operations before the season opened. Halifax briefly contemplated fielding a team made up exclusively of local players, but was concerned that fans would not support such a club, especially if it was not competitive on the field. When the Stellarton franchise folded in 1959, the league almost collapsed, but was saved at the last minute when Halifax decided to field a team. By this time, however, the league was in a death watch, and attendance during the 1959 season declined sharply. The league would not operate in future years.

The fact that a vibrant, community-based baseball culture in the Maritimes died in the space of a single decade suggests a broader economic and social transformation of small-town life after the Second World War. During the 1950s, communities in the Maritimes were being wrenched out of their insularity, and thrust into a world of consolidated schools, chain stores, shopping centres, and improved highway systems. At the same time, Margaret Conrad has observed, the emergence of mass consumerism 'brought Atlantic Canada into line with the dominant currents of North American culture.'[45] By the end of the decade new forms of leisure, including television and bowling alleys, drew people away from the baseball diamond. In addition, the greater mobility that accompanied the growth of automobile ownership beckoned people to summer cottages or away from the region on extended vacations.

Baseball's failure was also connected to the economic crises faced by most of the region's small towns. Most community clubs in the forties and fifties operated near or at the break-even point and, in order to cover any particular year's deficit, relied upon the community's ability to raise funds through draws, lotteries, bingos, and pools. Even in the days when baseball crowds averaged close to 1500 per game throughout the region, franchise owners rarely made a profit, and were particularly sensitive to declines in attendance. As the 1950s wore on, moreover, the failing prospects of coal towns such as Springhill, Stellarton, Westville, Glace Bay, Reserve Mines, and Dominion, and the precarious condition of communities that served as distribution centres within a struggling primary sector, made it difficult for baseball clubs to continue to operate.

Of course, economic scarcity had also prevailed during the Depression, when baseball had flourished. The difference was in the way the two eras understood baseball's social purpose. Before the Second World War, Maritime baseball was implicated in a discourse about regional solidarity and community integrity. For many, the game seemed to affirm, even amid economic distress, the worth of the town. During the war and after, however, the Maritimes would be inexorably drawn into an emerging mass culture. At the same time, the gradual displacement of local players by imports from the United States required a new way of rationalizing baseball's social meaning. Maritime baseball was increasingly thought of as a feeding ground for professional baseball.

And, as Maritime baseball was structured to serve the purposes of major-league organizations, its roots in the community withered.

When the H&D League, the last remaining semi-pro league in the Maritimes, eventually collapsed, some hoped for a return to the earlier reliance on local players. New leagues sprang up in Nova Scotia and New Brunswick as import-dominated circuits collapsed. Although leagues of this sort have operated from 1960 to the present, and have produced players like Vince Horsman, Rheal Cormier, Matt Stairs, and Paul Hodgson who went on to play major-league ball, the fans have been conspicuously absent. Somewhere along the way Maritimers have come to regard local production as inferior to the exotic products that arrived from elsewhere. As Gary Burrill has pointed out, this is characteristic of regions and peoples who find themselves dominated by more powerful places. It is an idea 'embedded in a culture which has sent off generations of exiles, that everything interesting, important, or worthy of engagement belongs exlusively to the world of "away."'[46] In this sense, the demise of community baseball in the Maritimes at the end of the 1950s was closely related to the triumph of consumer-oriented capitalism (or, put differently, the most recent form of the region's cultural colonization) and to the re-imagining of baseball as but one of many consumer choices in a burgeoning North American market-place of entertainment and leisure.

Post-Game Reflections

Throughout its history, baseball in the Maritimes and New England, as elsewhere, has been deeply implicated in debates about class and gender, race and ethnicity, regionalism and nationalism, amateurism and professionalism, work and play, and the commercialization of leisure. For most of the nineteenth century, discussions about baseball's social value were rooted in the vast renegotiation of class and gender relations that accompanied the development of the new industrial-capitalist order. Those debates, which centred upon prevailing notions of respectability and rowdiness, and upon ideas of appropriate manliness or femininity, reveal that sport was very much part of the constantly shifting interaction of bourgeois and working-class culture, and of the relationship between the sexes.

The baseball diamond, then, was contested terrain, where class, gender, and other antagonisms were continually played out. In the late 1860s and 1870s baseball in the Maritimes was largely the pursuit of the urban bourgeoisie, who regarded sport as a useful educational exercise for young men destined for positions of influence and leadership in the community. After 1870, however, the active involvement of working people in the sport undermined the middle-class hope that baseball could be fashioned into a 'gentleman's game.' During the last quarter of the century, baseball served as a cultural expression of the sharpened class rivalries that accompanied industrial capitalism's penetration of the region. While workingmen – especially the many skilled tradesmen who were attracted to the game – often found that sport offered fraternal camaraderie and an autonomy that was often lacking in the workplace, employers, middle-class journalists, and reform-minded professionals idealized the game as an egalitarian field of play where class antagonisms might be overcome.

Early baseball also mirrored the debate about the appropriate relationship between the sexes, and the place of ethnic and racial minorities in the larger social order. Most people believed that baseball inculcated manly virtue, an assumption that in turn relegated women to observer status. The presence of women in the stands, moreover, was thought to civilize the audience and curb usually aggressive play. Not all women accepted their exclusion from the playing field, of course. Nor did blacks, native people, and other minorities who turned to the game for their own purposes. The extent and nature of their participation may not always have pleased them, but it served notice none the less that baseball was more than the preserve of white middle-class males.

Before the First World War, assumptions about baseball's social purpose underwent a significant metamorphosis. Throughout baseball's early years, Maritime journalists, churchmen, educators, and assorted child-savers such as Charles Cogswell, John Grierson, and Dr A.B. Atherton emphasized that sport could promote or rehabilitate youthful morality. After the turn of the century, reformers were more likely to follow American philosopher William James and anthropologist G. Stanley Hall in arguing that sport was both a useful social technology and a natural expression of biological impulses. During the so-called progressive era, allusions to rowdiness and respectability gave way to those of scientific management and efficient play. Furthermore, as baseball owners tried to divest themselves of the reputation of unsavoury robber-baron capitalists, the game became widely regarded as a wholesome form of exercise for young men and appealed increasingly to an audience that spanned the social spectrum. No longer a social drama that pitted the respectable against the rowdy, baseball in the progressive era became a significant component of an emerging mass culture that venerated scientific management, technological efficiency, and social improvement.

During the First World War baseball's growing appeal was evident even at the battle-front, where it was an important force for rehabilitating battle-weary soldiers and maintaining the efficiency and morale of the troops. As baseball was placed in the service of the nation at war, the imagery of class conflict and social antagonism gave way to the language of national sacrifice. Sport was reconceptualized as a form of war, implying that war was in turn a form of sport, and editorial writers turned to military metaphors to describe hard-fought struggles on the 'battlefield of play.' Baseball was now regarded as a valuable leisure pursuit that encouraged social responsibility and respect for the nation and promoted a willingness on the part of individuals to sacrifice themselves to the victorious cause.

In the postwar Maritimes, this progressive attachment of baseball to the national interest, like the language of class antagonism, receded into memory, succumbing to a rising regional consciousness that manifested itself in the valorization of the regional amateur championship and the connection of baseball to notions of civic identity and pride. Growing out of a postwar disillusionment with national crusades and the bitter reality of postwar de-industrialization, postwar Maritime regionalism was an essentially conservative ideology. It diverted attention from the continuing struggle between workers and their employers, and blamed the region's difficulties on an unsympathetic federal government. Insofar as baseball provided the region and its communities with a sense of purpose and unity in the face of economic and social dislocation, therefore, it acted, like the politically inspired Maritime Rights movement, as a social balm, ignoring questions of class conflict and of gender, ethnic, and racial discrimination that were none the less important aspects of Maritime society. At the same time, baseball in the Maritimes maintained its traditional attachment to New England rather than developing closer sporting ties with other parts of Canada.

The tradition of community-based amateurism in baseball was shattered during the Second World War, as Canada's better players flooded into the Maritimes. Thereafter, Maritime baseball would become increasingly reliant upon the imported ballplayer, at the expense of those local players who had earlier played for their home towns and contributed to vigorous community rivalries. During the 1950s, as local players were pushed aside, interest in baseball began to wane, despite the fact that Maritimers were coming to regard the American as the epitome of the skilful ballplayer. By this time, the social purpose of baseball in the Maritimes had little to do with community or regional identity, but instead concerned the development of prospects who might eventually graduate to the major leagues. It is thus not surprising that, when the semi-pro leagues of the 1950s collapsed, there would be little public support for baseball that relied upon local players.

An emphasis on the shifting discourse surrounding baseball's social utility should not obscure the continuing cultural conflict that was part of the making of the game, and which has since been transferred to the softball diamond. It could conceivably be argued that my concern with the structure of middle-class discourse obscures the place of 'agency' in the foregoing analysis, or even that the eventual demise of baseball in the Maritimes suggests that the history of small-town sport was simply a function of larger social processes. My point, however, is that within the broad structural changes that accompanied the development of the modern capitalist economy – industrialization, de-industrialization and the development of mass consumerism - human action was and continues to be important in shaping the nature of local cultural experience. Not only was this the case with respect to working people, women, and minorities who challenged bourgeois and patriarchal conceptions of how baseball should be organized, but it is also revealed in the relationship between local and imported players and managers. This book's final chapter, which centres upon the role that imported players unwittingly played in devastating the regional roots of the game, suggests that decisions about how baseball should be organized in the Maritimes were as important in shaping the sport's local demise as were the shifting patterns of leisure activity that affected North American society as a whole.

Since 1960 various leagues have operated within the Maritimes, but with minimal fan support. Some local players have graduated to the major leagues and an increasing number of young prospects have been drafted and signed by big-league organizations. Yet most teams receive only minimal support at the gate. Now and then there have been attempts to raise the profile of the leagues by bringing in recognizable players. The Moncton Mets attracted sizeable crowds for a while in the mid-1980s after signing Bill 'the Spaceman' Lee, a colourful and eccentric performer, who had played over a dozen years in the major leagues with the Boston Red Sox and Montréal Expos. Less successful was the New Brunswick Baseball League's more recent 'Coca Cola experiment,' in which former major leaguers U.L. Washington, Glen Gulliver, and 'Pepe' Frias were signed in the hope of rekindling interest in the game, by playing on the rivalry between Pepsi and Coca Cola.

Once an essential component of small-town life, local baseball has since become but one of several available leisure choices in the modern sports market-place. Detached from its community roots, and no longer part of a regional sporting culture that reached across the border into New England, small-town baseball in the Maritimes is now swamped in the continent-wide marketing of major-league baseball. Like other hinterland regions across North America, the Maritimes is awash in commodities bearing the insignias of major-league teams. And in this culture of Blue Jays sweatshirts and Montréal Expos caps, memories of the Springhill Fencebusters, Stellarton Albions, and Yarmouth Gateways understandably, if perhaps regrettably, continue to fade.

Notes

PREFACE

1 Robert W. Malcolmson, *Popular Recreations in English Society, 1700–1850* (Cambridge: Cambridge University Press 1973)

2 Bryan Palmer, 'Discordant Music: Charivaries and Whitecapping in Nineteenth-Century North America,' *Labour/Le Travail* 3 (1978): 5–62; Allan Greer, 'From Folklore to Revolution: Charivaris and the Lower Canadian Rebellion of 1837,' *Social History/Histoire Sociale* 15 (January 1990): 25–43. For an excellent treatment of this transition see Bonnie L. Huskins, 'Public Celebrations in Victorian Saint John and Halifax,' Ph.D. thesis, Dalhousie University, 1991: esp. chap. 8.

3 Samuel Haber, *Efficiency and Uplift: Scientific Management in the Progressive Era, 1890–1920* (Chicago: University of Chicago Press 1964); Samuel P. Hays, *The Response to Industrialism* (Chicago: University of Chicago Press 1957); David Noble, *America by Design* (New York: Oxford University Press 1977); Robert Wiebe, *Businessmen and Reform* (Cambridge: Harvard University Press, 1962); Barton J. Bledstein, *The Culture of Professionalism: The Middle Class and the Development of Higher Education in America* (New York: Norton 1976); George Rosen, 'The Efficiency Criterion in Medical Care, 1900–1920,' *Bulletin of the History of Medicine* 50 (1976): 28–44; Stanley K. Schultz and Clay McShane, 'To Engineer the Metropolis: Sewers, Sanitation, and City Planning in Late Nineteenth-Century America,' *Journal of American History* 65 (1978): 389–411; Colin D. Howell, 'Reform and the Monopolistic Impulse: The Professionalization of Medicine in the Maritimes,' *Acadiensis* 11, 1 (Autumn 1981): 3–22

4 The literature pertaining to the professionalization process is voluminous. See, in particular, Harold Perkin, *The Rise of Professional Society: England*

Since 1880 (London and New York: Routledge 1989) and *The Origins of Modern English Society, 1780–1880* (London: Routledge, Chapman and Hall 1969). Robert Wiebe refers to these reformers as members of the 'new middle class'; see his *The Search for Order 1877–1920* (New York: Hill & Wang, 1967). For a critique of Perkin see Colin Howell, 'Medical Professionalization and the Social Transformation of the Maritimes, 1850–1950,' *Journal of Canadian Studies* 27, 1 (Spring 1992): 5–20. For the impact of progressive reform on the Maritimes see Colin Howell, 'The 1900s: Industry, Urbanization and Reform,' and Ian McKay, 'The 1910s: The Stillborn Triumph of Progressive Reform,' in E.R. Forbes and D.A. Muise, eds, *The Atlantic Provinces in Confederation* (Toronto and Fredericton: University of Toronto Press and Acadiensis Press 1993), 155–229.

5 Ernest R. Forbes, *The Maritime Rights Movement, 1919–1927: A Study in Canadian Regionalism* (Montreal and Kingston: McGill-Queen's University Press 1979). The reconceptualization of Maritime identity after the First World War is the subject of Ian McKay's *The Quest of the Folk: Antimodernism and Cultural Selection in Twentieth-Century Nova Scotia* (Montreal and Kingston: McGill-Queen's University Press 1994).

CHAPTER 1 Laying Out the Field

1 Peter Bailey, *Leisure and Class in Victorian England: Rational Recreation and the Contest for Control* (London: Routledge & Kegan Paul 1978)

2 Robert W. Malcolmson, *Popular Recreations in English Society, 1700–1850* (Cambridge: Cambridge University Press 1973)

3 For a brief sampling of this work in Britain, Canada, and the United States see Allen Gutmann, *From Ritual to Record: The Nature of Modern Sports* (New York: Columbia University Press 1978); Steven A. Riess, ed., *The American Sporting Experience* (West Point, NY: Leisure Press 1984); Paul J. Zingg, ed., *The Sporting Image: Readings in American Sport History* (Lanham, Md.: University Press of America 1988); Wray Vamplew, *Pay Up and Play the Game: Professional Sport in Britain* (Cambridge: Cambridge University Press 1988); Tony Mason, ed., *Sport in Britain: A Social History* (Cambridge: Cambridge University Press 1989); Morris Mott, ed., *Sports in Canada: Historical Readings* (Toronto: Copp Clark 1989); Alan Metcalfe, *Canada Learns to Play: The Emergence of Organized Sport, 1807–1914* (Toronto: McClelland and Stewart 1987).

4 Those who employ the modernization model are indebted to Richard Brown, *Modernization: The Transformation of American Life 1600–1815* (New York: Hill & Wang 1976). Among them are Melvin Adelman, *A Sporting*

Time: New York City and the Rise of Modern Athletics, 1820–1870 (Urbana and Chicago: University of Illinois Press 1986). Adelman argues that 'modern' sport includes the following characteristics: formal organization at the local, regional, and national levels; national and international competition that allows athletes to develop national reputations; the differentiation of the sporting roles of specialist and recreational athletes as well as of players and spectators; the widespread and regular accessibility of public information in newspapers, magazines, and national sports journals; and the statistical measurement of performance and the keeping of records sanctioned by national and international associations. By extension 'premodern' sport is everything that modern sport is not: it involves little formal organization, wide variations in local traditions, the absence of detailed and formalized written rules, and an undeveloped sense of the need to maintain a sport history by collecting statistical information and measuring individual performance. Allen Guttmann, *A Whole New Ball Game: An Interpretation of American Sports* (Chapel Hill and London: University of North Carolina Press 1988) provides a slightly different categorization of 'modern' sport. He emphasizes secularism, equality, bureaucratization, specialization, rationalization, quantification, and the obsession with records as the fundamental characteristics of modernity.

5 Steven A. Riess, *City Games: The Evolution of American Urban Society and the Rise of Sports* (Urbana and Chicago: University of Illinois Press 1989); George B. Kirsch, *The Creation of American Team Sports: Baseball and Cricket, 1838–1872* (Urbana and Chicago: University of Illinois Press, 1989).

6 See, for example, Eric Dunning and K. Sheard, *Barbarians, Gentlemen and Players: A Sociological Study of the Development of Rugby Football* (Oxford: Martin Robertson 1979); and Norbert Elias and Eric Dunning, *Quest for Excitement: Sport and Leisure in the Civilizing Process* (Oxford: Oxford University Press 1986). The most useful theoretical discussion of the notion of a civilizing process is contained in Eric Dunning and Chris Rojek, eds, *Sport and Leisure in the Civilizing Process: Critique and Counter-Critique* (Toronto and Buffalo: University of Toronto Press 1992). Benjamin Rader, *American Sports: From the Age of Folk Games to the Age of Spectators* (Englewood Cliffs, NJ: Prentice-Hall 1983, rev. 1989) also employs modernization theory while emphasizing conflict between the classes. Rader describes a Victorian subculture made up of what middle-class Victorian reformers preaching religious duty, hard work, thrift, sobriety, punctuality, and sexual control considered the 'unproductive rabble' and the 'dissolute aristocracy.' In contrast to the modernizing assumptions of the 'dominant Victorian culture of the nineteenth century, the members of the

subculture wanted to retain preindustrial, pre-urban patterns of life' (p. 25).

7 Roy Rozensweig, *Eight Hours for What We Will: Workers and Leisure in an Industrial City* (London: Cambridge University Press 1983); Tony Mason, *Association Football and English Society, 1863–1915* (New Jersey: Humanities Press 1980); Eileen and Stephen Yeo, *Popular Culture and Class Conflict 1590–1914: Explorations in the History of Labour and Leisure* (Sussex: Harvester Press 1981); John Hargreaves, *Sport, Power and Culture: A Social and Historical Analysis of Popular Sports in Britain* (Cambridge: Cambridge University Press 1986); Stephen G. Jones, *Sport, Politics and the Working Class* (Manchester and New York: Manchester University Press 1988)

8 Jones, *Sport, Politics and the Working Class*, 7–12; Bryan Palmer, *A Culture in Conflict: Skilled Workers and Industrial Capitalism in Hamilton, Ontario, 1860–1914* (Montreal and Kingston: McGill-Queen's University Press 1979) and *Working-Class Experience: Rethinking the History of Canadian Labour, 1800–1991* (Toronto: McClelland and Stewart 1992 revised); Hart Cantellon and Robert Holland, eds, *Leisure, Sport and Working Class Cultures* (Toronto: Garamond Press 1988). See also the essays by Richard Gruneau, Bryan Palmer, and Peter Donnelly in Richard Gruneau, ed., *Popular Culture and Political Practices* (Toronto: Garamond Press 1988).

9 Raymond Williams, *Culture* (London: Fontana 1981), 67

10 Quoted in New York *Clipper*, 26 November 1881.

11 Mary Ann Clawson, *Constructing Brotherhood: Class, Gender, and Fraternalism* (Princeton: Princeton University Press 1989), 10

12 Ibid., 212. Clawson points out the ambiguous nature of the 'cult of domesticity' and of fraternalism, both of which implied a critique of existing capitalism while seeking an accommodation to it. 'The principles of domesticity located the alternative moral dimension within the nuclear family and designated women as the guardians of moral values,' she writes. 'Fraternalism stood as an alternative to domesticity because it identified men as the principal moral actors and proposed to extend the moral economy of kinship beyond the nuclear family to a larger sphere of social relations.'

13 Keith McClelland, 'Masculinity and the "Representative Artisan" in Britain, 1850–80,' in Michael Roper and John Tosh, eds, *Manful Assertions: Masculinities in Britain since 1800* (London and New York: Routledge 1991), 74–91

14 Professional sportsmen constitute a somewhat unique class of professionals in that there is little pressure on them to dispense with personal habits symbolic of the working-class origins of the sport. The curious popularity

of tobacco chewing and spitting among baseball players, not to mention widespread alcoholism, and the physical resolution of disputes on the field or in the clubhouse, contrast sharply with the prevailing social mores of most professional groups.

15 Warren Goldstein, *Playing For Keeps: A History of Early Baseball* (Ithaca and London: Cornell University Press 1989)

16 Gregory S. Kealey, *Toronto Workers Respond to Industrial Capitalism* (Toronto: University of Toronto Press 1980); Palmer, *A Culture in Conflict*; Greg Kealey and Bryan Palmer, *Dreaming of What Might Be: The Knights of Labor in Ontario* (New York: Cambridge University Press 1982)

17 Thomas Bender, *Community and Social Change in America* (New Brunswick, NJ: Rutgers University Press 1978)

18 George A. Hillery, Jr, 'Definitions of Community: Areas of Agreement,' *Rural Sociology* 20 (July 1955): 111–23

19 Harry C. Boyte, *Community Is Possible: Repairing America's Roots* (New York: Harper & Row 1984), argues, for example, that the growth of large-scale institutions and the technology and lifestyle of modern urban man 'has been accompanied by legitimizing ideologies that consciously seek to erode the authority of communal relations' (p. 33).

20 T. Jackson Lears, *No Place of Grace: Antimodernism and the Transformation of American Culture* (New York: Pantheon 1981)

21 See, for example, Adelman, *A Sporting Time*; Metcalfe, *Canada Learns to Play*; Helen Lenskyj, *Out of Bounds: Women, Sport and Sexuality* (Toronto: Women's Press 1986); and Gerald Redmond, 'Some Aspects of Organized Sport and Leisure in 19th Century Canada,' *Society and Leisure* 2, 1 (April 1979): 73–100. For a critique of this urban bias see Michael Smith, 'Sport and Society: Towards a Synthetic History?' *Acadiensis* 18, 2 (Spring 1989): 150–8.

22 Riess, *City Games*, 9

23 This common culture was itself part of a long-term interaction between the two regions, including significant movements of people. Alan A. Brookes, 'Out-Migration from the Maritime Provinces, 1860–1900: Some Preliminary Considerations,' *Acadiensis* 5, 2 (Spring 1976); and 'The "Exodus": Migration from the Maritime Provinces to Boston during the Second Half of the Nineteenth Century,' Ph.D. thesis, University of New Brunswick, 1979; Stephen J. Hornsby, Victor A. Konrad, and James J. Herlan, eds, *The Northeastern Borderlands: Four Centuries of Interaction* (Fredericton: Canadian-American Center, University of Maine, and Acadiensis Press 1989); Margaret Conrad, ed., *They Planted Well: New England Planters in Maritime Canada* (Fredericton: Acadiensis Press 1988)

24 Ernest R. Forbes, *The Maritime Rights Movement, 1919–1927: A Study in Canadian Regionalism* (Montreal: McGill-Queen's University Press 1979). The reconceptualization of Maritime identity also involved the construction of Nova Scotia's 'Scottish' identity. Premier Angus L. Macdonald, Ian McKay argues, 'took a general Nova Scotia sense of regional grievance, merged it with a doctrine of the Scottish essence, and thereby helped transform regional protest from a form of "progressivism" into something that was more like the "conservatism" many scholars have diagnosed.' Ian McKay, 'Tartanism Triumphant: The Construction of Scottishness in Nova Scotia, 1933–1954,' *Acadiensis* 21, 2 (Spring 1992): 43

25 Margaret Conrad, 'The 1950s: The Decade of Development,' in E.R. Forbes and D.A. Muise, eds, *The Atlantic Provinces in Confederation* (Toronto: University of Toronto Press 1993)

26 Many of these studies can be found in P. Buckner and D. Frank, eds. *Atlantic Canada after Confederation: The Acadiensis Reader*, 2 vols (Fredericton: Acadiensis Press 1985), vol. 2.

27 This was the theme of a recent SSHRCC-supported conference in Lunenburg, Nova Scotia, 'Community Level Social Relations' (September 1990), and of my keynote address at that conference, 'A Political and Historiographical Rationale for the Study of Community Life in the Maritimes' See also Larry McCann, ed. *People and Place: Studies of Small Town Life in the Maritimes* (Fredericton and Sackville: Acadiensis Press and Committee for Studying Small Town Life in the Maritimes, Mount Allison University 1987)

28 The important economic contribution of women in the domestic economy has been emphasized by several feminist scholars in particular. See, for example, Martha MacDonald, 'Studying Maritime Women's Work: Underpaid, Unpaid, Invisible, Invaluable,' in Philip Buckner, ed., *Teaching Maritime Studies* (Fredericton: Acadiensis Press 1986), 119–29; Pat and Hugh Armstrong, *The Double Ghetto: Canadian Women and Their Segregated Work*, rev. ed. (Toronto: McClelland and Stewart 1985); Meg Luxton, *More than a Labour of Love: Three Generations of Women's Work in the Home* (Toronto: Women's Press 1980); Patricia M. Connelly and Martha MacDonald, 'Women's Work: Domestic and Wage Labour in a Nova Scotia Community,' *Studies in Political Economy* 4 (Autumn 1980): 99–113. See also Rosemary Ommer, 'Merchant Credit and the Informal Economy: Newfoundland 1918–1929,' *Historical Papers 1989* (Ottawa: Bonanza Press 1989), 167–89.

29 K.R. Bitterman, 'Middle River: The Social Structure of Agriculture in a Nineteenth Century Cape Breton Community,' M.A. thesis, University of

New Brunswick, 1987 and 'Economic Stratification and Agrarian Settlement: Middle River in the Early Nineteenth Century,' in K. Donovan, ed., *The Island: New Perspectives in Cape Breton History* (Sydney and Fredericton: UCCB and Acadiensis Press 1990), 71–87; R. Mackinnon and G. Wynn, 'Nova Scotia Agriculture in the Golden Age: A New Look,' in Douglas Day ed., *Geographical Perspectives on the Maritime Provinces* (Halifax: St Mary's University 1988), 47–59; D.A. McNabb, 'Land and Families in Horton Township, Nova Scotia, 1760–1830,' Ph.D. thesis, University of British Columbia, 1986

30 Guy Debord, *Comments on the Society of the Spectacle* (London: Verso 1990)

31 'New ballparks are actually being scaled down in size and built to resemble their older prototypes (as in Baltimore's much acclaimed Camden Yards),' writes Stephen Jay Gould. 'Artificial turf is in retreat, and those hideous concrete rings, all-purpose and soul-less stadia for the incommensurate sports of baseball and football, will soon be relics of former folly.' Stephen Jay Gould, 'Dreams That Money Can Buy,' *New York Review of Books* 29, 18 (5 November 1992): 45

32 Fredric Jameson, 'Postmodernism, or The Cultural Logic of Late Capitalism,' *New Left Review* 146 (July–August 1984): 53–94; Dan Latimer, 'Jameson and Post-Modernism,' ibid. 148 (November–December 1984): 116–28; Fredric Jameson, *Postmodernism: Or the Cultural Logic of Late Capitalism* (Durham, NC: Duke University Press 1990)

33 Bradd Shore, 'Loading the Bases. How Our Tribe Projects Its Own Image into the National Pastime,' *The Sciences* (May–June 1990): 11–18. Stephen Jay Gould also addresses baseball's undisputed status as America's 'national pastime' in 'Dreams That Money Can Buy.' Gould notes that baseball reflects a central tension between reality and possibility, between the rank commercialism of a distorted marketplace and that beautifully symmetrical game that suggests a gentler, more rational, and egalitarian alternative. Fans support baseball despite its potentially destructive economic arrangements, Gould argues, because it offers 'an equally potent reality played out on the field of dreams – baseball imitating what we would like to be rather than what we are.' (*Washington Post* columnist Thomas Boswell, with tongue firmly in cheek, titled two fine collections of his baseball writings *How Life Imitates the World Series* [New York: Viking Penguin 1983] and *Why Time Begins on Opening Day* [New York: Viking 1984].) While there may be something to this view, one wonders if a somewhat similar judgment could not be made of a number of sports – association football in Britain, ice hockey in Canada or Europe, or basketball in the United States.

34 W.P. Kinsella, *The Iowa Baseball Confederacy* (Toronto: HarperCollins 1986), 29
35 Nicholas Dawidoff, 'Field of Kitsch,' *The New Republic* 207, 8 & 9 (17, 24 August 1992): 22
36 Rick Salutin, 'Rick Salutin wonders if baseball mythology is finally batting zero,' *Globe and Mail*, 10 July 1992, A8

CHAPTER 2 First Innings

1 Halifax *Reporter*, 9 May 1868
2 Robert E. Kroll, 'A Nation's Unity – In a Pig's Ear,' *Halifax* 2, 7 (June 1980): 40–4
3 *Reporter*, 12 May 1868
4 Halifax *Morning Chronicle*, 30 September 1867
5 For a discussion of this idea see Bruce Haley, *The Healthy Body and Victorian Culture* (Cambridge, Mass.: Harvard University Press 1978); Don Morrow, Mary Keyes, Wayne Simpson, Frank Cosentino, and Ron Lappage, *A Concise History of Sport in Canada* (Toronto: Oxford University Press 1989), 69–75.
6 Tony Mason, *Association Football and English Society, 1863–1915* (New Jersey: Humanities Press 1980), 11
7 The officers of the club were Dr A.C. Cogswell, President; Johnathan Grant, commission merchant, Vice-President; W.E. Weir, Secretary; and Jonathan Muir, commission merchant, Treasurer. The field captain was Dr R.H. Carey, a physician from Gay's River, Nova Scotia. The three directors, Archibald Mitchell, Alfred Moren, and Jonathan Strachan Jr all listed their occupations as clerks in the Halifax City Directory of 1869.
8 Cogswell's biography is included in *The Cogswells in America*, 604.
9 *Eastern Argus* (Portland), 21, 27 July; 11, 20, 24, August 1860
10 New York *Clipper*, 28 May 1871
11 *Eastern Argus*, 7, 8, 10 June 1867
12 Ibid., 13 June 1867
13 Ibid., 25 June 1867. The line-up for the Eons was as follows: Broughton p., Evans c., Haggett 1b, Means 2b, McAllister 3b, Eaton ss, Dennis lf, Randall cf, Keazer rf.
14 *Maine Farmer*, 31 August 1869
15 *Eastern Argus*, 1 August 1870
16 Warren Goldstein, *Playing for Keeps* (Ithaca and London: Cornell University Press 1989), 58
17 *Clipper*, 3 May 1879
18 Ibid., 9 August 1879. The older conventions of the game were maintained

by amateur clubs, however. After a game between the 'True Blues' of Halifax and the 'Blue Scarfs' of Waterville in 1876, 'all parties adjourned to the hotel, where they drank one another's health, after which the ball which had been won by the 'True Blue' was presented by the Secretary of the "Blue Scarf" Club, accompanied by a suitable address, which was appropriately replied to.' *Acadian Recorder*, 2 September 1876

19 Melvin Adelman, *A Sporting Time* (Urbana and Chicago: University of Illinois Press 1986), 122-4

20 Harold Seymour, *Baseball: The Early Years* (New York: Oxford University Press 1960), 37

21 Quoted in Adelman, *A Sporting Time*, 122

22 W. Richardson, ed., *The Health of Nations: A Review of the Works of Edwin Chadwick*, 2 vols (London: Longman's, Green & Co. 1887), 1: 185-200

23 J. Austin Fynes, ed., *Athletic Sports in America, England and Australia* (Philadelphia: Hubbard Brothers 1889), 5

24 Chadwick played a particularly important role in cultivating a sophisticated system of baseball statistics, adapting the baseball box score from cricket. His 'untiring industry in collecting and unparalleled ability in so arranging the data of baseball in figures that they furnish a clear and comprehensive grouping,' said an editorial in the *Sporting News* on 13 October 1900, 'have made him the game's greatest statistician.'

25 Robert Smith, *Baseball: A Historical Narrative of the Game, the Men Who Have Played It, and Its Place in American Life* (New York: Simon and Schuster 1947), 80. Not everyone appreciated Chadwick's criticisms of crookedness, especially Harry Wright, who 'thought that baseball would be better off if Chadwick said less about "suspicious play" ... because the public got the impression that all games were dishonest.' Seymour, *Baseball: The Early Years*, 69

26 Fynes, *Athletic Sports in America*, 575-6, contains a brief biography of Chadwick. For a discussion of baseball's origins see ibid., 23-30. See also *The Boy's Own Book, a popular encyclopaedia of the sports and pastimes of youth* (Boston, 1829), 20; James C. Isaminger, ed., *The Reach Official American League Baseball Guide for 1939* (New York, 1939), 11-13; Adelman, *A Sporting Time*, chap. 6; and Steven A. Riess, *City Games* (Urbana and Chicago: University of Illinois Press 1989), 34-42.

27 Henry Chadwick, 'The Evolution of Baseball,' *Spalding Baseball Guide* (1892): 10

28 Robert Henderson, 'Baseball and Rounders,' *Bulletin of the New York Public Library* 43, 4 (April 1939), and *Ball, Bat and Bishop: The Origin of Ball Games* (New York: Rockport Press 1947)

29 Stephen Jay Gould, 'The Creation Myths of Cooperstown: Or Why the Cardiff Giants Are an Unbeatable and Appropriately Named Team,' *Natural History* 11 (1989): 14–24

30 Nancy Bouchier, 'For the Love of the Game and the Honour of the Town: Organized Sport, Local Culture and Middle Class Hegemony in Ontario,' Ph.D. thesis, University of Western Ontario, 1991: 257. See also the discussion by Bouchier and Robert Barney of the reminiscence of an 1838 baseball game played in Beachville, Ontario, witnessed by Adam Ford: 'A Critical Examination of a Source on Early Ontario Baseball,' *Journal of Sport History* 15, 1 (Spring 1988): 75–90.

31 When 'Rube' Waddell, an eccentric country boy from Bradford, Pennsylvania, first broke into the major leagues near the turn of the century, he once knocked a baserunner off his feet by throwing at him as he tried to steal second base. 'That's out where I come from!' explained Waddell to his amused associates. Smith, *Baseball*, 36

32 D.R. Jack, *Centennial Prize Essay on the History of the City and County of St. John* (Saint John: J. & A. McMillan 1883), 124; Brian Flood, *Saint John: A Sporting Tradition 1785–1985* (Saint John: Neptune Publishing 1985); Saint John *Globe*, 14 December 1901

33 Fred G. Lieb, 'History of Baseball,' in *1941 Baseball Register: The Game's 400* (St Louis: C.C. Spink & Son 1941), 6

34 In 1871 Charles Olive of the Saint John Mutuals wrote to the National Association in New York for a rule book to be used in league play during the following season. Flood, *Saint John*, 19

35 *Acadian Recorder*, 15 July 1871

36 *Clipper*, 28 March 1874. The cricketers formed the Germantown baseball nine in March 1874. The players included Dan and Bob Newhall, Van Rensselaer, Shap, Pease, Tiers, McTighe, Fowler, Eckendorff, Fox, and Dixon.

37 *The Halifax Cricket Tournament Visit of the American Twelve of Philadelphia in August, 1874* (Philadelphia: J.B. Lippincott 1874), 7

38 Robert Moss, 'Cricket in Nova Scotia during the 19th Century,' *Canadian Journal of History of Sport and Physical Education* 9, 2 (1978): 58–73; Robert D. Day, 'The British Garrison at Halifax: Its Contribution to the Development of Sport in the Community,' in Morris Mott, ed., *Sports in Canada* (Toronto: Copp Clark 1989), 28–36

39 *Nova Scotia Chronicle*, 17 October 1786

40 Allan Elton Cox, Barbara N. Noonkester, Maxwell Howell, Reet A. Howell, 'Sport in Canada, 1868–1900,' in Maxwell Howell and Reet Howell, eds, *History of Sports in Canada* (Champaigne, Ill.: Stipes Publishing Company 1981), 111

41 Robert D. Day, 'The British Garrison at Halifax,' in Mott, ed., *Sports in Canada*, 30

42 See, for example, Halifax *Herald*, 15 April 1912

43 Robert Moss, 'Cricket in Nova Scotia,' *Canadian Journal of History of Sport and Physical Education* 9, 2 (December 1978): 1–6

44 Keith A.P. Sandiford, 'Cricket in Victorian Society,' *Journal of Social History* 17 (Winter 1983): 303–17

45 *Acadian Recorder*, 14 June 1867

46 *The Dominion Illustrated*, 5 (9 August 1890): 82

47 *Acadian Recorder*, 10 May 1882

48 James C. Whorton, *Crusaders for Fitness: The History of American Health Reformers* (Princeton, NJ: Princeton University Press 1982), 5

49 Stephen Nissenbaum, *Sex, Diet, and Debility in Jacksonian America: Sylvester Graham and Health Reform* (Westport, Conn.: Greenwood Press 1980).

50 The intimate relationship of body and brain, and the ways in which appropriate physical exercise provided a stimulus to the memory, was the prevailing theme of Orson Fowler, *Fowler on Memory: or, Phrenology Applied to the Cultivation of Memory; the Intellectual Education of Children, and the Strengthening and Expanding of Intellectual Powers* (New York: O.S. and L.N. Fowler 1842). Fowler believed that the breaking of the laws of good health and nutrition was a violation of God's law. His physical and dietary regimen included regular exercise, regulation of the bowel function, slow eating and deliberate mastication, periodic abstinence from meat, and frequent sponge baths, sitz baths, and Turkish baths with hartshorn, camphor, whiskey, and cayenne pepper added to the water. Orson Squire Fowler, *Sexual Science; including manhood, womanhood, and their mutual interrelations; as taught by phrenology* (Chicago: National Publishing Company 1870), 695

51 Michel Foucault, *The Birth of the Clinic*, trans. A.M. Sheridan (New York: Vintage Books 1975), 62–4. This emphasis on clinical observation reflected a belief in the possibility of creating a rational or scientific discourse around the individual or the particular circumstance, a belief not unrelated to the veneration of the individual in nineteenth-century political and economic thought.

52 Ibid., 34

53 Roger Cooter, *The Cultural Meaning of Popular Science: Phrenology and the Organization of Consent in Nineteenth Century Britain* (Cambridge: Cambridge University Press 1984); Ann Harrington, *Medicine, Mind and the Double Brain: A Study in Nineteenth Century Thought* (Princeton: Princeton University Press 1987)

54 L.S. Jacyna, 'Somatic Theories of Mind and the Interests of Medicine in Britain, 1850–1879,' *Medical History* 26, 3 (1982): 233–38

55 22nd Annual Report, Medical Superintendent, Nova Scotia Hospital, *Journals and Proceedings of the House of Assembly of the Province of Nova Scotia* (JHA) 1880, app. 3, 5. Colin D. Howell, 'Medical Science and Social Criticism: Alexander Peter Reid and the Ideological Origins of the Welfare State in Canada,' in C. David Naylor, ed., *Canadian Health Care and the State. A Century of Evolution* (Montreal and Kingston: McGill-Queen's University Press 1992), 21

56 S.E.D. Shortt, *Victorian Lunacy: Richard M. Bucke and the Practice of Late Nineteenth-Century Psychiatry* (Cambridge: Cambridge University Press 1982), 145

57 Bruce Haley, *The Healthy Body and Victorian Culture* (Cambridge, Mass.: Harvard University Press 1978); Colin Howell and Michael Smith, 'Orthodox Medicine and the Health Reform Movement in the Maritimes, 1850–1885,' *Acadiensis* 18, 2 (Spring 1989): 55–72; John Harley Warner, *The Therapeutic Perspective: Medical Practice, Knowledge, and Identity in America, 1820–1885* (Cambridge: Harvard University Press 1986)

58 Morris Mott, 'One Solution to the Urban Crisis: Manly Sports and Winnipegers, 1900–1914,' *Urban History Review* 7, 2 (October 1983): 57

59 Charles Rosenberg, 'The Place of George M. Beard in Nineteenth Century Psychiatry,' *Bulletin of the History of Medicine* 36, 3 (May–June 1962): 245–59

60 W.H. Hattie, 'The Care of the Adolescent,' *Maritime Medical News* 18, 12 (December 1906): 456

61 *Acadian Recorder*, 9, 10 May 1882; *Morning Herald*, 10 May 1882

62 Keith A.P. Sandiford, 'Cricket in Victorian Society,' *Journal of Social History* 17 (Winter 1983): 303–17

63 *Clipper*, 19 April 1873

64 *Sporting News*, 16 September 1893

65 Ibid., 28 January 1893

66 Adelman, *A Sporting Time*, 98, 101–14

67 *Acadian Recorder*, 17 June 1867

68 David Scobey, 'Anatomy of the Promenade: The Politics of Bourgeois Sociability in Nineteenth-Century New York,' *Social History* 17, 2 (May 1992): 209

69 *The Halifax Cricket Tournament ... in August*, 1874: 8

70 *Clipper*, 12 September 1874

71 Halifax *Morning Chronicle*, 28 August 1874. Outerbridge also contrasted cricket to other sports and their 'demoralizing' characteristics.

72 Ibid., The Philadelphians needed only one inning to defeat Canada

191–160, and Britain 205–200. The Americans were led by Daniel Newhall, who won the cup for the best average score throughout the tournament.

73 George B. Kirsch, *The Creation of American Team Sports* (Urbana and Chicago: Univesity of Illinois Press 1989), 264

74 Alan Metcalfe, *Canada Learns to Play* (Toronto: McClelland and Stewart 1987), 80–4

75 M. Stephen Kivincich, *A Centennial History of Stellarton* (Antigonish: Scotia Design Publications 1990), 11, 63. Stellarton won the provincial cricket championship in 1905 and again in 1910 (ibid., 90).

76 Stellarton *Trades' Journal*, 19 September 1883

77 Kivincich, *History of Stellarton*, 90

78 *Sydney Record*, 2 August 1906

79 The Alphas took their name from the Greek alphabet, to indicate that they were the first team in the county. They played their first match on 17 May 1876. The competing teams were made up of club members who had paid their one-dollar annual dues. Other games that summer were held with the Intercolonial Baseball Club, a team made up of railway workers, and club minute books refer to an attempt to arrange a 'friendly game' with a ball team in the town of Pictou. See the publication of the Westville Heritage Group and the Grade 12 English Class of Westville High School, *Celebrating Our Heritage: The History of Westville* (Antigonish: Scotia Design Publication 1986); and Halifax *Chronicle Herald*, 16 August 1951

80 H. Charles Ballam, *Abegweit Dynasty: The Story of the Abegweit Amateur Athletic Association 1899–1954* (Charlottetown: Prince Edward Island and Heritage Foundation 1986), chap. 5

81 Charlottetown, *The Patriot*, 16 June 1903

82 *Acadian Recorder*, 19 September 1874. The newspaper attributed Halifax's loss to John Morton, 'a poor player' who took Ryan's place at second base, because the latter was out of town.

83 Colin D. Howell, 'Baseball, Class and Community in the Maritime Provinces, 1870–1910,' *Social History* 22, 44 (November 1989): 270–1

84 Halifax *Morning Chronicle*, 11 September 1876. The Atlantas had been strengthened for this match by adding three players from the True Blues of Halifax. The decision to add these 'outsiders' and leave some of the regular players off the roster resulted in ill feelings on the part of some of the Atlantas.

85 *Acadian Recorder*, 20 August 1877

CHAPTER 3 New Players

1 Alan A. Brookes, 'Out-Migration from the Maritime Provinces, 1860–1900:

Some Preliminary Conclusions,' *Acadiensis* 5, 2 (Spring 1976): 26–56, and 'The Golden Age and the Exodus: The Case of Canning, Kings County,' *Acadiensis* 11, 1 (Autumn 1981): 57–82; Patricia A. Thornton, 'The Problem of Out-Migration from Atlantic Canada, 1871–1921: A New Look,' *Acadiensis* 15, 1 (Autumn 1985).

2 Johnathan Prude, *The Coming of Industrial Order: Town and Factory Life in Rural Massachusetts 1810–1860* (New York: Cambridge University Press 1983), 261. See also Raphael Samuel, 'The Workshop of the World: Steam Power and Hand Technology in Britain,' *History Workshop Journal* 3 (Spring 1977): 6–72, for a discussion of the weakness of the notion of a linear and chronological approach to capitalist development.

3 D.A. Muise, 'The Making of Nova Scotia's Industrial Communities: Yarmouth, Amherst and Sydney Mines, 1871–1921,' paper delivered at Canadian Historical Association meetings, Victoria, June 1990

4 Robert H. Babcock, 'Economic Development in Portland (Me.) and Saint John (N.B.) during the Age of Iron and Steam, 1854–1914,' *American Review of Canadian Studies* 9, 1 (Spring 1979): 3–37

5 Philip Buckner, 'The 1870s,' in E.R. Forbes and D.A. Muise, eds, *The Atlantic Provinces in Confederation* (Toronto: University of Toronto Press 1993), 69

6 *Saint John and Its Business. A History of Saint John and a Statement in General Terms of Its Various Kinds of Business Successfully Prosecuted* (Saint John: H. Chubb & Co. 1875)

7 Buckner, 'The 1870s,' in *The Atlantic Provinces in Confederation*, 63

8 L.D. McCann, 'Staples and the New Industrialism in the Growth of Post-Confederation Halifax,' *Acadiensis* 8, 2 (Spring 1979): 47–79; Ian McKay, 'Capital and Labour in the Halifax Baking and Confectionery Industry during the Last Half of the Nineteenth Century,' *Labour/Le Travailleur* 3 (1978): 63–108

9 Allen Guttmann, *From Ritual to Record* (New York: Columbia University Press 1978), 100–8

10 Steven M. Gelber, 'Working at Playing: The Culture of the Workplace and the Rise of Baseball,' *Journal of Social History* 16, 4 (Summer 1983): 3–22

11 Gelber, ' "Their Hands Are All Out Playing": Business and Amateur Baseball,' *Journal of Sport History* 11, 1 (Spring 1984): 5–27. Gelber contrasts the Doubleday myth to James Fenimore Cooper's description of a ball game on the lawn of his family's Cooperstown home in 1838. That game involved a group of unruly, foul-mouthed apprentices and a 'notorious street brawler.' Cooper's image of the game, Gelber argues, is much more representative than the Doubleday image.

12 Saint John *Progress*, 11 August 1888. In an editorial entitled 'Why We Support Base Ball,' the newspaper expressed the belief that the game was popular because it 'brings into play courage, strength, agility, decision, prudence, foresight – qualities which always compel our admiration; because to witness it involves little loss of time, so that a busy man can gain in two hours on the ball field rest and relaxation that elsewhere he would seek in vain ... The explanation of the absorbing interest which base ball arouses is equally easy. The English-speaking peoples have one characteristic above all others – they work whole-heartedly. It is because we obey the preacher's injunction to do with our might whatever our hands find to do that we set a pattern to the world. It is natural enough that the prevailing attitude of our minds towards business should shape our pleasures. In our offices and shops, we rush and hurry and drive through the day; when we lock the door behind us, it is not surprising that our passion of energy refuses at once to be quieted, and that we seek to gratify it still further.'

13 *Acadian Recorder*, 19 September 1874

14 Dan Cronan was reputed to be the hardest thrower of any of the early Halifax ballplayers. See G.M. Robinson's reminiscenses in 'Baseball Memories,' Halifax *Mail Star*, 30 October 1961

15 Ibid., 22 August 1876

16 Goldstein, *Playing for Keeps* (Ithaca and London: Cornell University Press 1989), 27. 'That so many of baseball's best players were skilled craftsmen, men who, depending on their trade, still retained significant control over their work rhythms, helps to explain how players could have given so much time to baseball practice, ' Goldstein writes. 'Many historians of the game have suggested casually that baseball must have been a middle-class sport because players had to take time off from work, but this description fits relatively few of the fraternity's best and most active players.'

17 *Acadian Recorder*, 11 September 1877

18 Bryan D. Palmer, *A Culture in Conflict: Skilled Workers and Industrial Capitalism in Hamilton, Ontario, 1860–1914* (Montreal: McGill-Queen's University Press 1979), 39

19 *Acadian Recorder*, 7 March 1891

20 Knights of St Crispin, *Proceedings of the 5th Annual Meeting of Grand Lodge, April 1872* (New York: Journeymen Printer's Cooperative Association 1872)

21 Alan Dawley, *Class and Community: The Industrial Revolution in Lynn* (Cambridge, Mass.: Harvard University Press 1976), 180

22 *Acadian Recorder*, 6, 18 September 1877

23 For Great Britain see E. Hopkins, 'Working Hours and Conditions during the Industrial Revolution: A Reappraisal,' *Economic History Review* 35 (1982); for the United States see John Modell, 'Patterns of Consumption, Acculturation and Family Income Strategy in Late Nineteenth Century America,' in Tamara K. Hareven and Maris Vinovskis, eds, *Family and Population in Nineteenth Century America* (Princeton: Princeton University Press 1978); and Clarence Long, *Wages and Earnings in the United States, 1860-1890* (Princeton: Princeton University Press 1960)

24 Roy Rosenzweig, *Eight Hours for What We Will* (London: Cambridge University Press 1983). The development of organized sport, amateur athletic associations, and the YMCA also provided alternatives to the tavern as the focus of leisure activity. See, for example, Peter Delottinville, 'Joe Beef of Montreal: Working Class Culture and the Tavern, 1869-1889,' *Labour/Le Travailleur* 8 (1981): 34-5.

25 Kathy Peiss, *Cheap Amusements: Working Women and Leisure in Turn-of-the-Century New York* (Philadelphia: Temple University Press 1986)

26 *Acadian Recorder*, 8 July 1881

27 Dolphin is first listed in McAlpine's Halifax City Directory in 1874-5, and appears over the next few years variously as an agent of W.K. Lewis Brothers and superintendent of a lobster cannery. Lewis Brothers were lobster canners who also supplied the 'best brands and all varieties of canned goods ... [including] Boston Baked Beans, Borden's Anchor Brand Condensed Milk and Condensed Coffee.'

28 *Acadian Recorder*, 18 July 1857

29 Phyllis Blakely, *Glimpses of Halifax* (Halifax: PANS 1949), 136

30 *Acadian Recorder*, January 13 1892

31 *British Colonist*, August 11 1868

32 The *City Atlas of Halifax* (1878) shows this lot, designated as the Atlantas Baseball Ground and owned by Dr Cogswell.

33 PANS, 'Annual Report,' Halifax Industrial Boy's School (1864), especially the section entitled 'Amusements.'

34 See, for example, *Acadian Recorder*, 15 October 1877; see also Blakely, *Glimpses of Halifax*, 136.

35 *Acadian Recorder*, 19 February 1878

36 Joseph L. Reichler, ed. *The Baseball Encyclopedia: The Complete and Official Record of Major League Baseball*, 5th ed. (New York: Macmillan Publishing Company 1982). See also *Clipper*, 24 May 1879

37 *Acadian Recorder*, 1 July 1878

38 Ibid., 28 May 1878

39 Ibid., 3 June, 1 July 1878

40 Ibid., 11 July 1878
41 Biographical information is drawn from the Halifax city directories for the
   appropriate years. In addition to Morton, the other supplier of sporting
   goods in Halifax at this time was Nicholas Sarre, a Hollis Street merchant
   who specifically advertised baseball goods.
42 Beverly Williams, 'Leisure as Contested Terrain in Nineteenth Century
   Halifax,' M.A. thesis, Saint Mary's University, Halifax, 1991: 28
43 Martin Hewitt, 'Science as Spectacle: Popular Scientific Culture in Saint
   John, New Brunswick, 1830–1850,' *Acadiensis* 18, 1 (Autumn 1988): 114
44 *Clipper*, 15 May 1881
45 Ibid., 28 July 1883
46 Lawrence W. Levine, *Highbrow/Lowbrow: The Emergence of Cultural Hierarchy in America* (Cambridge: Harvard University Press 1988), 68
47 Halifax *Morning Herald*, 17 January 1877
48 Allen Guttmann suggests that professional team sports in the United
   States such as baseball have been less plagued by spectator violence than
   have their counterparts in Europe and 'a host of countries in the process
   of modernization.' A careful study of crowd behaviour in the nineteenth
   century, and of attempts to discipline and control spectator behaviour,
   would be of great value. Guttmann, *Sports Spectators* (New York: Columbia University Press 1986), 111
49 *Acadian Recorder*, 9 September 1878
50 Ibid., 25 September 1878
51 Quoted in Frank Cosentino, 'Ned Hanlan – Canada's Premier Oarsman –
   A Case Study in 19th Century Professionalism,' *Canadian Journal of the
   History of Sport and Physical Education* 5, 2 (December 1974): 7
52 *Acadian Recorder*, 27 September 1888
53 Brookes, 'Out-Migration from the Maritime Provinces,' 26–55
54 St Croix *Courier*, 9 July 1871; quoted in B.J. Grant, *Fit to Print: New Brunswick's Papers. 150 Years of the Comic, the Sad, the Odd, and the Forgotten*
   (Fredericton: Fiddlehead Press and Goose Lane Editions 1987)
55 Tamara K. Hareven and Randolph Langenbach, *Amoskeag: Life and Work in
   an American Factory-City* (New York: Pantheon Books 1978); Tamara K.
   Hareven, *Family Time and Industrial Time: The Relationship between the Family and Work in a New England Industrial Community* (Cambridge: Cambridge University Press 1982)
56 Peter D. McClelland, 'The New Brunswick Economy in the Nineteenth
   Century,' Ph.D. thesis, Harvard University, 1966; T.W. Acheson, 'The
   Great Merchant and Economic Development in St. John 1820–1850,'
   Acadiensis 8, 2 (Spring 1979): 3–27

57 T.W. Acheson, *Saint John: The Making of a Colonial Urban Community* (Toronto: University of Toronto Press 1985), 246
58 *Clipper*, 18 April 1874
59 *New Dominion*, 20 June 1874
60 *Acadian Recorder*, 13 August 1875
61 Acheson, *Saint John*, chap. 12
62 D.R. Jack, *Centennial Prize Essay on the History of the City and County of Saint John* (Saint John: J. & A. McMillan 1883), 151

CHAPTER 4 'Throw 'em Out'

1 Toronto, *The Varsity*, 14 November 1885, 44–5
2 Bangor, *Daily Commercial*, 9 July 1907. The *Eastern Argus*, 6 July 1889, observed that Toole was determined to have a baseball team in Bangor for the 1889 season even 'if he has to sink the Merchants' Hotel to do it.'
3 *Daily Commercial*, 13 July 1889
4 Ibid., 6 July 1885
5 Augie Favazza and Allen Lessels, *Maine Black Bears Baseball: Orono to Omaha* (Portland: Gannett Books 1987), 230
6 *Sporting Life*, 19 April 1890
7 *Daily Commercial*, 23 July 1889
8 *Moncton Times*, 29 April 1878
9 Ibid., 19 July 1879
10 Lloyd A. Machem, *A History of Moncton Town and City 1855–1965* (Moncton: Moncton Publishing Co. 1965)
11 Saint John *Progress*, 17 May 1890
12 Ibid.
13 Bangor *Daily Commercial*, 16 July 1889
14 Quoted in *Acadian Recorder*, 27 July 1889. See also ibid., 3 October 1889.
15 Ibid., 27 July 1889
16 *Halifax Carnival Echo* (midsummer 1889), PANS Microfiche, 9–10
17 *Acadian Recorder*, 14 September 1889. On the Bates College team, see ibid., 8 June 1889
18 Ibid., 5 August 1889
19 Ibid., 3 July 1888
20 Ibid.
21 *Progress*, 11 August 1888
22 *Acadian Recorder*, 8 September 1889
23 On the relationship between team sport and Victorian notions of manli-

ness and the inculcation of ideals of teamwork, patriotism, courage, and respectability, see Morris Mott, 'The British Protestant Pioneers and the Establishment of Manly Sports in Manitoba,' *Journal of Sport History* 7, 3 (Winter 1980): 25–6, and 'One Solution to the Urban Crisis: Manly Sports and Winnipegers, 1890–1914,' *Urban History Review* 22, 2 (October 1983): 57–70; Norman Vance, *The Sinews of the Spirit: The Ideal of Manliness in Victorian Literature and Religious Thought* (Cambridge: Cambridge University Press 1985); Brian Dobbs, *Edwardians at Play* (London: Pelham 1973); and S.F. Wise, 'Sport and Class Values in Old Ontario and Quebec,' in W. Heick and R. Graham, eds, *His Own Man: Essays in Honour of A.R.M. Lower* (Montreal: McGill-Queens University Press 1974). For a contemporary view, see J. Castell Hopkins, 'Youthful Canada and the Boys' Brigade,' *Canadian Magazine* 4, 6 (1905): 551–66. On working-class opposition to bourgeois reformism, see Joe Maguire, 'Images of Manliness and Competing Ways of Living in Late Edwardian Britain,' *British Journal of Sports History* 3 (December 1986): 256–87

24 *Progress*, 31 May 1890
25 Ibid., 22 September 1888
26 *Acadian Recorder*, 20, 21 September 1888
27 Ibid., 30 May 1889
28 Ibid., 24 July 1900. During the 1870s Power had played and umpired games for money, but this was 'when the distinction between amateur and professional athletics was unknown in this city.' Despite subsequent protests that his earlier actions violated his amateur standing, Power was reinstated as an amateur by the Maritime Provinces Amateur Athletic Association's executive committee in 1888. Ibid., 23 May 1888
29 Brian Flood, *Saint John*, (Saint John: Neptune Publishing 1985), 71
30 *Progress*, 10 May 1890
31 Saint John *Globe*, 14 December 1901
32 *Progress*, 31 May 1890
33 Alan Metcalfe, *Canada Learns to Play* (Toronto: McClelland and Stewart 1987), 9
34 *Progress*, 29 March 1890
35 Fredericton *Daily Gleaner*, 15 May 1890
36 *Progress*, 5 April 1890
37 *Globe*, 10 July 1890
38 Ibid., 16 July 1890
39 Ibid., 12 July 1890
40 *Progress*, 7 June 1890
41 Ibid., 24 May 1890

42 *Globe*, 2 July 1890
43 Ibid., 22 August 1890
44 This match is described in lively fashion in Flood, *Saint John*, 71.
45 *Globe*, 22 August 1890
46 *Acadian Recorder*, 8 September 1890
47 Halifax *Daily Echo*, 11 September 1890
48 *Acadian Recorder*, 8 September 1890
49 *Globe*, 8 September 1890
50 Ibid., 4 August 1888

CHAPTER 5 Gendered Baselines

1 *Acadian Recorder*, 4 August 1891
2 Sonya Rose, *Limited Livelihoods: Gender and Class in Nineteenth Century England* (Berkeley: University of California Press 1992), 191
3 Allen Guttmann, *Sports Spectators* (New York: Columbia University Press 1986), 114
4 Kathy Peiss, *Cheap Amusements* (Philadelphia: Temple University Press 1986), 4–5
5 Quoted in Harold Seymour, *Baseball: The Early Years* (New York: Oxford University Press 1960), 91
6 Quoted in Melvin Adelman, *A Sporting Time* (Urbana and Chicago: University of Illinois Press 1986), 158
7 *Sporting News*, 8 August 1895
8 *Sporting News*, 7 April 1896
9 *Clipper*, 1 August 1890
10 *Progress*, 6 September 1890. Franklin had chosen only twelve girls at first, and put a barnstorming team together to compete in New York state. The club scheduled games at Glen Falls, Schenectady, Albany, Troy, Ballston, Saratoga, Whitehall, and Cohoes in August, and in New York City and the surrounding area between 1 and 10 September (*Clipper*, 16 August 1890). Franklin had earlier issued a circular in which he stated that the Young Ladies Base Ball Club of Cincinnati would like to visit Montreal, but there is no indication that any such game was played (*Daily Gleaner*, 18 July 1890).
11 *Clipper*, 6 September 1890
12 Halifax *Morning Herald*, 22 August 1891
13 *Progress*, 6 September 1890
14 The *Globe*, 11 July 1890, reported a game between the ladies of Chatham and Newcastle, in which Chatham prevailed by a score of 51–50.

15 Deborah Gorham, *The Victorian Girl and the Feminine Ideal* (Bloomington: Indiana University Press 1982), 7

16 Kathleen E. McCrone, *Playing the Game: Sport and the Physical Emancipation of English Women 1870–1914* (Lexington: University Press of Kentucky 1988), 13

17 This is similar to the position taken by Edward Shorter, *A History of Women's Bodies* (New York: Basic Books 1982). Shorter argues that until recently women were prisoners of their bodies, and that before the turn of the century real liberation for women was impossible. Shorter sees that liberation emerging from advances in medical knowledge and therapeutic efficiency. In this he is at odds with much of the recent work on the relationship of doctors and women in the nineteenth century. Wendy Mitchinson, *The Nature of Their Bodies: Women and Their Doctors in Victorian Canada* (Toronto: University of Toronto Press 1991); Patricia Vertinsky, *The Eternally Wounded Woman: Women, Exercise and Doctors in the Late Nineteenth Century* (Manchester: Manchester University Press 1990)

18 A. Halliday, 'Hysterical Conditions, with Clinical History of a Case,' *Maritime Medical News*, January 1894: 211

19 Carroll Smith-Rosenberg and Charles Rosenberg, 'The Female Animal: Medical and Biological Views of Woman and Her Role in Nineteenth Century America,' in Judith Walzer Levitt, ed., *Women and Health in America* (Madison: University of Wisconsin Press 1984): 14. The Rosenbergs note the nineteenth-century fear that American women were weaker than their European counterparts, owing to excessive education. Health reformers emphasized physical education and the salutary impact it would have on maternal competence and upon the future development of the race (p. 16).

20 Quoted in Alison Prentice et al., *Canadian Women: A History* (Toronto: Harcourt Brace Jovanovich Canada 1988), 158

21 Gregory Kent Stanley, 'Redefining Health: The Rise and Fall of the Sportswoman. A Survey of Health and Fitness Advice for Women, 1860–1940,' unpublished Ph.D. dissertation, University of Kentucky, 1991)

22 Lois Banner, *American Beauty* (New York: Knopf 1983), chap. 7

23 Patricia Vertinsky, 'Body Shapes: The Role of the Medical Establishment in Informing Female Exercise and Physical Education in Nineteenth-Century North America,' in J.A. Mangan and Roberta Park, eds, *From 'Fair Sex' to Feminism: Sport and the Socialization of Women in the Industrial and Post-Industrial Eras* (London: Frank Cass and Co. 1987), 259

24 *Acadian Recorder*, 16 August 1875

25 Quoted in *Morning Chronicle*, 28 September 1867

26 Debra A. Shattuck, 'Bats, Balls and Books: Baseball and Higher Education for Women at Three Eastern Women's Colleges, 1866–1891,' *Journal of Sport History* 19, 2 (Summer 1992): 91; Gai I. Berlage, 'Sociocultural History of the Origin of Women's Baseball at the Eastern Women's Colleges during the Victorian Period,' in Alvin L. Hall, ed., *Cooperstown Symposium on Baseball and the American Culture* (1989) (Oneonta, NY, and Bridgeport, Conn.: Meckler Publishing, in association with the State University of New York College at Oneonta, 1991), 100, 109

27 Quoted in Betty Spears, 'The Emergence of Women in Sport,' in Barbara J. Hoepner, ed., *Women's Athletics: Coping with Controversy* (Oakland, Calif.: DGWS Publishers 1974), 27. See also Matthew Vassar, 'Matthew Vassar and the Vassar Female College,' *American Journal of Education* 7 (1862): 52–6.

28 McCrone, *Playing the Game*, 53

29 Carole Dyehouse, *Girls Growing up in Late Victorian and Edwardian England* (London, Boston, and Henley: Routledge & Kegan Paul 1981), 58. 'The new institutions were certainly not characterized by any attempt to challenge the sexual division of labour any more than they were by any other kind of social radicalism,' Dyehouse argues. 'The reformers rejected the idea that it was "feminine" to be ignorant and waste one's time in trivial pursuits, and emphasized the desirability of educating women to be cultivated wives and mothers ... The reformers *redefined* the Victorian concept of femininity: they did not (in the main) *reject* it' (58–9).

30 John Reid, 'The Education of Women at Mount Allison, 1854–1914,' *Acadiensis* 12, 2 (Spring 1983): 3–33

31 Quoted in ibid., 15

32 Michael Bliss, '"Pure Books on Avoided Subjects": Pre-Freudian Sexual Ideas in Canada,' in S.E.D. Shortt, ed., *Medicine in Canadian Society: Historical Perspectives* (Montreal and Kingston: McGill-Queen's University Press 1981): 266–71

33 Saint John *Daily Sun*, 6 May 1882

34 W.H. Hattie, 'The Role of Education in the Development of Self Control,' *Maritime Medical News* 14, 8 (April 1902): 281

35 Edward H. Clarke, MD, *Sex in Education; or, A Fair Chance for the Girls* (Boston: James R. Osgood and Co. 1873), 22, 27–8

36 Ibid., 162–7. Clarke also quoted as follows from Harriet Beecher Stowe. 'The race of strong, hardy, cheerful girls, that used to grow up in country places, and made the bright, neat New-England kitchens of olden times, – the girls that could wash, iron, brew, bake, harness a horse and drive him, no less than braid straw, embroider, draw, paint, and read innumerable books, – this race of women, pride of olden time, is daily lessening;

and, in their stead, come the fragile, easy-fatigued, lanquid girls of a modern age, drilled in book-learning, ignorant of common things.' (168).

37 Quoted in Michael Joan Smith, 'Graceful Athleticism or Robust Womanhood: The Sporting Culture of Woman in Victorian Nova Scotia, 1870–1914,' *Journal of Canadian Studies* 23, 1 (Spring 1988): 127

38 *Clipper*, 9 August 1879

39 Ibid., 13 September 1879

40 Howard Seymour, *Baseball: The People's Game* (New York: Oxford University Press 1990), 456

41 *Bridgetown Monitor*, 28 October 1891. See also *Clipper*, 7 January 1893.

42 Seymour, *People's Game*, 455

43 *Daily Gleaner*, 6 August 1891. Burnett's assistant, M.J. Raymond, reported that the club was about twelve years old, and some of its players had been connected with the game for half a dozen years. They had a 'remarkably fast' pitcher, Nellie Williams, but she was not able to play to her potential because their catcher, May Howard, who captained the team, was not able to hold her fastball. The rest of the line-up included Kitty Grant 1b, Angie Parker 2b, Edith Mayves 3b, Edna Mayves ss, Alice Lee lf, Annie Grant cf, and Lottie Livingstone rf. Ibid., 6, 14 August 1891

44 *Daily Gleaner*, 17 August 1891

45 Quoted in *Truro Daily News*, 19 August 1891

46 *Acadian Recorder*, 21 August 1891

47 *Daily News*, 18 August 1891

48 Ibid., 19 August 1891

49 Ibid., 21 August 1891. Over 400 people, 'many of whom were women,' attended the game in Truro. 'The girls can't play ball,' said one reporter, 'but the boys gave them every opportunity to score as many runs as would be consistent without continuing the game too long.'

50 *Eastern Chronicle*, 21 August 1891

51 *Morning Herald*, 14 August 1891

52 *Acadian Recorder*, 4 August 1891

53 *Morning Herald*, 24 August 1891

54 Ibid., 24 August 1891

55 *Acadian Recorder*, 24 August 1891

56 *Clipper*, 19 July 1890. Such an incident occured in Akron, Ohio, where a constable attached the trunks containing all the girls' clothes. The women were obliged to wear their ball suits around the hotel until the matter was settled.

57 *Acadian Recorder*, 25 August 1891

58 *Progress*, 6 September 1890

59 *Clipper*, 7 July 1890

60 Helen Lenskyi, *Out of Bounds: Women, Sport and Sexuality* (Toronto: Women's Press 1986), 95

61 G.J. Barker-Benfield, *The Horrors of the Half-Known Life: Male Attitudes toward Women and Sexuality in Nineteenth-Century America* (New York: Harper & Row 1976)

62 Nancy F. Cott, 'Passionlessness: An Interpretation of Victorian Sexual Ideology, 1790–85,' in N.F. Cott and Elizabeth Pleck, eds, *A Heritage of Her Own: Towards a New Social History of American Women* (New York: Simon and Schuster 1979), 162–81

63 B.S. Talmey (*Genesis: A Manual for the Instruction of Children in Matters Sexual* [New York: Practitioners Publishing Co. 1910]) was concerned that feminism would lead to uncontrolled sexuality in those who supported it. Talmey believed that women, particularly those who aspired to a college education, had to be 'warned against the danger in the sex overvaluation of the most unhealthy sensualists of indulgence, found in the modern literature of the so-called feminists.' The passion there is 'perverted, unsatisfied, masturbatic.' Talmey condemned feminists for 'their intoxication of sensuality as a new religion of the personality' (160). Cesare Lombroso, *The Female Offender* (New York: Appleton 1898); see also Gina Lombroso-Ferrero, *Criminal Man, According to the Classification of Cesare Lombroso* (Montclair, NJ: Patterson Smith 1972).

64 'The Female Twirlers: Women Players Warmly Met in Cuba,' *Sporting News*, 11 March 1893

65 *Daily Post* (Sydney), 30 May 1905

66 Richard Hammond, 'Progress and Flight: An Interpretation of the American Cycle Craze of the 1890s,' *Journal of Social History* 5 (Winter 1971): 235–57; Heather Watts, *Silent Steeds: Cycling in Nova Scotia to 1900* (Halifax: Nova Scotia Museum 1985)

67 *Canadian Practitioner* 21 (November 1896): 848. See also *Dominion Medical Monthly and Ontario Medical Journal* 7 (September 1896): 256. Mitchinson, *The Nature of Their Bodies*, 114

68 See Michael J.E. Smith, 'Female Reformers in Victorian Nova Scotia,' M.A. thesis, Saint Mary's University, Halifax, 1988: esp. chap. 4.

69 The most striking indictment of demanding physical activity for women was that of Dr Arabella Kenealy, 'Woman as an Athlete,' *Living Age* 221 (May 1899): 367. Kenealy thought it inappropriate for women to cultivate muscularity, believing that women lost their charm when they entered into too-active exercise. The bicycle created movements that were 'muscular and less womanly' than were appropriate, and undermined the graceful and quiet bearing of the ideal woman.

70 Smith, 'Graceful Athleticism or Robust Womanhood,' 130, 133
71 *Morning Herald*, 4 June 1910
72 *The Advertiser* (Kentville), 6 December 1988
73 Debra Shattuck, 'Women in Baseball,' in John Thorn and Peter Palmer, eds, *Total Baseball*, 2d ed. (New York: Warmer Books 1989), 617

CHAPTER 6 A Manly Sport

1 Ty Cobb with Al Stumpf, *My Life in Baseball: The True Record* (Garden City: Doubleday 1961), 280
2 Charles Alexander, *Ty Cobb* (New York: Oxford University Press, 1984)
3 Harry Brod, 'The Case for Men's Studies,' in H. Brod, ed., *The Making of Masculinities: The New Men's Studies* (Boston: Allen & Unwin 1987), 40, 46
4 Michael Roper and John Tosh, eds, *Manful Assertions: Masculinities in Britain since 1800* (London and New York: Routledge 1991), 7. To understand the social construction of masculinity, the authors argue, one must delve into the 'mutations of male dominance over time and their relation to other structures of social power, such as class, race, nation and creed.'
5 Joseph Kett, *Rites of Passage: Adolescence in America, 1790 to the Present* (New York: Basic Books 1977)
6 Margaret S. Creighton, 'American Mariners and the Rites of Manhood, 1830-1870,' in Colin Howell and Richard Twomey, eds, *Jack Tar in History: Essays in the History of Maritime Life and Labour* (Fredericton: Acadiensis Press 1991), 143-63
7 See, for example, Murray E. Angus, 'Living in the "World of the Tiger": The Methodist and Presbyterian Churches in Nova Scotia and the Great War, 1914-1918,' M.A. thesis, Dalhousie University, 1993: esp. chap. 2.
8 Anthony Rotundo, 'Body and Soul: Changing Ideals of American Middle-Class Manhood, 1770-1920,' *Journal of Social History* 16 (Fall 1983): 23-38. See also the articles by Rotundo and Roberta Park in J.A. Mangan and James Walvin, eds, *Manliness and Morality: Middle Class Masculinity in Britain and America, 1800-1940* (Manchester: Manchester University Press 1987)
9 Jacksonian democracy is often seen as embodying this self-confident individualism. Edward Pessen points out that European observers saw a rather different reality. Rather than 'an inner-directed American, marching to his own music, living his life according to his own and his family's notions as to how it should be lived,' these observers saw a deficiency of moral independence and an uncommon conformity to prevailing public opinion. Edward Pessen, *Jacksonian America: Society, Personality and Politics* (Georgetown, Ont.: Irwin-Dorsey 1969), chap. 2. quote from p. 20.

10 John L. Thomas, 'Romantic Reform in America, 1815–1865,' *American Quarterly* 17 (Winter 1965): 656–81
11 Rotundo, 'Body and Soul,' 27
12 Ann Douglas, *The Feminization of American Culture* (New York: Knopf 1977)
13 T. Jackson Lears, *No Place of Grace* (New York: Pantheon 1981)
14 Clyde W. Franklin, II, *The Changing Definition of Masculinity* (New York and London: Plenum Press 1984), 8. See also J.H. Pleck and E.H. Pleck, *The American Man* (Englewood Cliffs: Prentice Hall 1980)
15 Roberta Park, 'Physiology and Anatomy Are Destiny!? Brains, Bodies and Exercise in Nineteenth Century American Thought,' *Journal of Sport History* 18, 1 (Spring 1991): 31–62
16 For the craniological tradition in early anthropology, and a discussion of its connections to phrenology, see Paul A. Erickson, 'Phrenology and Physical Anthropology: The George Combe Connection,' *Current Anthropology* 18, 1 (March 1977): 92–3. On cranial measurement and notions of racial inferiority see John Haller, *Outcasts from Evolution: Scientific Attitudes of Racial Inferiority 1859–1900* (Urbana: University of Illinois Press 1971). For a contemporary view of cranial capacity and gender differences, see 'Sex and the Brain,' *Maritime Medical News* 18, 1 (January 1906): 5, which reported the findings of Marchand of Marbourg that the mean weight of the male brain was 3 pounds, 1 ounce, as compared to the female brain at 2 pounds, 10 ounces. 'The disparity, if true,' the report continued, 'is significant with relation to the distinct purposes for which the sexes, respectively are equipped by nature, and with reference to that other and more productive brain centre which distinguishes woman for her office and disposition. The present rage for bringing up the intellectual brain of a woman to a parity with that of man may be successful, but it can be only a transfer of the ... womanly brain from its divine seat to a different place and function. Neither sex is gifted with vital power to grow the other sex upon itself as a double and become mentally bi-sexed.' For an interesting critique of the biological determinism of cranial measurement and intelligence testing see Stephen Jay Gould, *The Mismeasure of Man* (New York: W.W. Norton and Co. 1981). 'What craniotomy was for the 19th century,' Gould observes, 'intelligence testing has become for the twentieth, when it assumes that intelligence (or at least a dominant part of it) is a single, innate, heritable, and measurable thing' (25).
17 Park, 'Physiology and Anatomy,' 48–9; M.J. Smith, 'Graceful Athleticism or Robust Womanhood,' *Journal of Canada Studies* 23, 1 (Spring 1988): 122–3, 128

18 Arthur MacDonald, 'Scientific Study of Baseball,' *American Physical Education Review* 19, 3 (March 1919): 220–41. These measurements bring to mind Dan Sargent's attempts to create the profile of 'typical' male and female students at American colleges, which one medical journal doubted 'contributed anything of value to science. Park, 'Physiology and Anatomy,' 56

19 Havelock Ellis, *The Criminal* (London: Walter Scott 1890); Henry Maudsley, *The Physiology and Pathology of the Mind* (London: MacMillan & Co., 1867); R. von Krafft-Ebing, *Psychopathia Sexualis, With Special Reference to Contrary Sexual Instinct. A Medico-Legal Study*, trans. Charles Gilbert Chaddock (Philadelphia: F.A. Davis Co. 1892); Ruth Friedlander, 'Benedict-Augustin Morel and the Development of the Theory of Degenerescence,' Ph.D. dissertation, University of California, 1973; Enrico Ferri, *Criminal Sociology* (New York: D. Appleton & Com. 1897); Gina Lombroso Ferrero, ed., *Criminal Man According to the Classification of Cesare Lombroso* (New York & London: G.P. Putnam and Sons 1911); Daniel Pick, 'The Faces of Anarchy: Lombroso and the Politics of Criminal Science in Post-Unification Italy,' *History Workshop Journal* 21 (Spring 1986): 60–86

20 A committee of the Nova Scotia Medical Society declared in 1909 that the 'thorough understanding of abnormal conditions requires equally thorough understanding of the normal and the study of the normal as well as the abnormal demands very wide research. We quite accord with Dr. Macdonald's [sic] statement that "As the seeds of evil are usually sown in childhood and youth, it is here that all investigation should commence."' PANS, Nova Scotia Medical Society, Minutes of the Annual Meeting, 7 July 1909

21 MacDonald's views are contained in his *Criminology* (New York: Funk and Wagnall's 1893). See also U.S. Senate Document 187, 58th Congress, 3rd session (Washington: 1905) and U.S. Senate Document 532, 60th Congress, 1st session (Washington: 1908). These latter sources relate to his assumptions about 'man and abnormal man,' juvenile criminals, the stigmata of degeneration, and the prospects for rehabilitation and reform.

22 *Canada Lancet* 2 (October 1901): 158

23 William Krauss, 'The Stigmata of Degeneration,' *American Journal of Insanity* 55, 1 (July 1898): 55–88

24 Eugene S. Talbot, 'Heredity and Atavism,' *Alienist and Neurologist* 19, 4 (October 1898): 628–58; and *Degeneracy: Its Causes, Signs, and Results* (London: Walter Scott Publishing Co. 1909)

25 Woods Hutchinson, 'The Republic of the Body,' *Living Age* 2682, 7th ser., 3 (13 May 1899): 437–44

26 Woods Hutchinson, 'Are There Evidences of Race Degeneration in the

United States?' *Maritime Medical News* 21, 6 (June 1909): 246–7. This paper was first presented to the American Academy of Social and Political Science, 16 April 1909.

27 Mark Dyerson, 'The Moral Equivalent of War: American Ideas of Sport, the State, and National Vitality, 1880–1920,' unpublished paper presented to North American Society of Sport History conference, Albuquerque, NM, June 1993

28 Robert A. Nye, *Crime, Madness, and Politics in Modern France: The Medical Concept of National Decline* (Princeton, NJ: Princeton University Press 1984), 319

29 John Nawright, 'Sport and the Image of Colonial Manhood in the British Mind: British Physical Deterioration Debates and Colonial Sporting Tours, 1878–1906,' *Canadian Journal of History of Sport* 22, 2 (December 1992): 54–71

30 'Moral Degeneration,' *Canada Lancet*, December 1895: 134–5

31 William Bayard, 'The Influence of the Mind on the Body,' presidential address to the Canadian Medical Association, *Maritime Medical News* 6, 9 (September 1894)

32 'Physical Education,' *CMA Journal* 1, 3 (March 1911): 265–6

33 A.B. Atherton, 'Presidential Address to the Maritime Medical Association,' *Maritime Medical News* 19, 8 (August 1907): 292–6

34 P.C. Murphy, 'President's Address to the Maritime Medical Association,' *Maritime Medical News* 21, 9 (September 1909): 345–8

35 Charles Rosenberg notes that the notion that character, disease, and temperament were inherited, and that the individual inherited a constitutional tendency or diathesis, were commonplace ideas throughout the nineteenth century (*No Other Gods: On Science and American Social Thought* [Baltimore: Johns Hopkins University Press 1976]). Until the 1840s, however, these ideas were only rarely used in the rationalization of social problems. Between the 1840s and 1870s, hereditarianism was accompanied by an optimistic confidence that man's most fundamental attributes could be moulded by individual self-control. This was the assumption of health reformers who emphasized the development of the healthful constitution. After 1870 hereditarianism became increasingly entwined with deterministic notions of degeneration, leading to the growing popularity of eugenicist arguments for sterilization and racial 'upbreeding.' At the same time, however, most hereditarians also argued for a reform of the urban environment in order to counter physical degeneracy and social weakness. In this struggle against national debility and decline, sport played a decisive role, encouraging a more robust manhood and national virility.

36 Saint John *City News*, 15 February 1938
37 Sydney *Record*, 26 September 1911
38 'A Sermon by the Rev. Geo. F. Degen of Nashville, Tenn. America's Need of Wholesome Recreation Supplied by Baseball,' *Sporting News*, 16 June 1894
39 Saint John *Progress*, 11 August 1888
40 Norman Vance, *The Sinews of the Spirit: The Ideal of Christian Manliness in Victorian Literature and Religious Thought* (Cambridge: Cambridge University Press 1985), 6
41 Although Kingsley and Hughes may have agreed with the sentiment expressed in American evangelist and former baseball player Billy Sunday's depiction of Christ as no 'dough-faced lick spittle proposition,' but rather 'the greatest scrapper that ever lived,' they would no doubt have been uncomfortable with his ungentlemanly rhetoric. Sunday attacked not only gentle pietistic approaches to Christianity, but the whole framework of institutionalized Protestantism. 'Lord save us from the off-handed, flabby cheeked, brittle boned, weak-kneed, thin-skinned, pliable, plastic, spineless, effeminate, ossified three-karat Christianity,' he declared. Quoted in Michael S. Kimmel, 'Baseball and the Reconstitution of American Masculinity, 1880–1920,' in Alvin L. Hall, ed., *Cooperstown Symposium on Baseball and the American Culture* (1989) (Westport, Conn.: Meckler Publishing, in association with the State University of New York College at Oneonta, 1991): 285
42 Theodore Roosevelt, 'The Value of Athletic Training,' *Harper's Weekly* 37 (December 1893): 156; quoted in Steven Riess, 'Sport and the Redefinition of American Middle-Class Masculinity,' *International Journal of the History of Sport* 8, 1 (1991), 17
43 Quoted in Kimmel, 'Baseball and the Reconstitution of American Masculinity,' 286
44 Herbert Hensdale and Tony London, eds, *Frank Merriwell's 'Father': An Autobiography of Gilbert Patten* (Norman: University of Oklahoma Press 1964), 178
45 John Levi Cutler, 'Gilbert Patten and His Frank Merriwell Saga,' *University of Maine Studies*, 2nd ser., no. 31, vol. 36, 10 (May 1934): 43, 86–7; quote from p. 43
46 Quoted in Cutler, 'Gilbert Patten,' 87
47 This motif can also be found in many subsequent imitators. See, for example, Robert Sherwin's sport series, which included *Strike Him Out* (Chicago: Goldsmith Publishing Co. 1931). The publisher's preface noted that Sherman's 'heroes are the finest examples of sturdy American youth, lovers of sport and sportsmanship without being, in any sense of the

word, "sissies."' Other titles in the series were *Under the Basket*; *It's a Pass*; *Interference*; *Down the Ice*; *Over the Line*; and *The Tennis Terror*.

48 Riess, 'Sport and the Redefinition of American Middle-Class Masculinity.' The *Bangor Commercial* of 8 July 1903 was critical of the college students' veneration of strenuousity. Most college men, it argued, care little for 'artistic music, for painting or sculpture, for poetry or the higher forms of drama ... They know nothing of poetry and deride those who do ... They are all football enthusiasts and they know baseball and rowing. The spirit of college athletics is strong among them and they burn with the flame of the strenuous life.'

49 Charlottetown *Patriot*, 21 March 1903

50 Robin Winks, in Introduction to Ralph Connor, *The Sky Pilot* (Lexington: University of Kentucky Press 1970), 3

51 Quoted in John English, *Shadow of Heaven: The Life of Lester Pearson. Volume One: 1897–1948* (Toronto: Lester & Orpen Dennys 1989), 10

52 Ibid.

53 *Presbyterian Witness*, 'Hustling Boys,' 8 December 1900: 387, col. 2; 'The Boy Who Didn't Care,' 6 April 1901: 110, col. 5; 'A Young Man and His Companions,' 27 September 1902: 310, col. 4; 'Smoking,' 28 May 1904: 32, col. 3; 'The Claims of the Ministry on Strong Men,' 10 August 1907: 254, col. 2–3; 'The Whole Man,' 24 August 1907: 265, col. 4; 'The Boy Who Takes Pride in His Work,' 26 October 1907: 339, col. 3; 'What Is Drink,' 13 June 1908: 187, col. 3; 'A Young Man's Religion,' 22 January 1910: 8, col. 4

54 *Church Work* (Halifax), 22 September 1910

55 See, for example, 'Young Men's Leagues for Small Towns,' *Amherst Daily News*, 4 September 1902. The Young Men's League in Amherst was open to boys from ten to sixteen from 3:30 to 5:30 p.m., and later to young men over sixteen years of age. 'The reading room is filled with young men enjoying the new magazines and games,' the newspaper reported. 'The gymnasium has provided the needed outlet for youthful energies. The young men who had been spending many hours in saloons or pool rooms are now found daily in the quarters of the League.'

56 J. Castell Hopkins, 'Youthful Canada and the Boy's Brigade,' *Canadian Magazine* 4, 6 (1905): 551–6.

57 'The Boy's Brigade,' *Presbyterian Witness*, 11 August 1894: 215, col. 1

58 David I. Macleod, *Building Character in the American Boy: The Boy Scouts, YMCA, and Their Forerunners, 1870–1920* (Wisconsin: University of Wisconsin Press 1983), 35

59 Robert H. MacDonald, *Sons of the Empire: The Frontier and the Boy Scout Movement, 1890–1918* (Toronto: University of Toronto Press 1993), 163

60 John Springhall, 'Building Character in the British Boy: The Attempt to Extend Christian Manliness to Working-Class Adolescents, 1880–1914,' in Mangan and Walvin, eds, *Manliness and Morality*, 60

61 Harvey J. Graff, 'Remaking Growing Up: Nineteenth Century America,' *Histoire Sociale/Social History* 24, 47 (May 1991): 35–59

62 *Amherst Daily News*, 4 September 1902

63 William J. Baker, 'Disputed Diamonds: The YMCA Debate over Baseball in the Late 19th Century,' *Journal of Sport History* 19, 3 (Winter 1992): 257–62

64 Rina Gangemi Spano, 'The Social Transformation of Children's Play and Organized Activities, 1880–1990,' Ph.D. dissertation, City University of New York, 1991: 121

65 Bangor *Daily Commercial*, 9 July 1908

66 Amherst *Daily News*, 2 August 1905

67 *Acadian Recorder*, 3 June 1878

68 W. Goldstein, *Playing for Keeps* (Ithaca and London: Cornell University Press 1989), 50

69 See in particular Gail Bederman, 'Civilization, the Decline of Middle-Class Manliness, and Ida B. Wells's Anti-Lynching Campaign (1892–94),' in Barbara Melosh, ed., *Gender and American History since 1890* (Routledge: London and New York 1993), 207–39

70 See, for example, 'Bane of Baseball. Lushing Has Done the National Game a Great Deal of Harm,' *Sporting News*, 8 February 1896

71 Ibid., 28 March 1898

72 Ibid., 12 October 1895

73 Quoted in Benjamin G. Rader, *American Sports: From the Age of Folk Games to the Age of Spectators* (Englewood Cliffs, NJ: Prentice-Hall 1983), 121.

74 *Sporting News*, 18 July 1895

75 Ibid.

76 *Bangor Commercial*, 11 July 1907

77 Portland *Eastern Argus*, 18 May 1893. In Fall River the electric railway gave $350 in cash, in Brockton, free use of the grounds, in Dover, free grounds, a groundskeeper, and $300 in cash, in Salem $250 in cash, and in Lewiston 'a handsome sum' was presented to the club.

78 Quoted in Lee Lowenfish and Tony Lupien, *The Imperfect Diamond: The Story of Baseball's Reserve System and the Men Who Fought to Change It* (New York: Stein & Day 1980), 31

79 Ibid., 30

80 Joy Parr, *The Gender of Breadwinners: Women, Men and Change in Two Industrial Towns* (Toronto: University of Toronto Press 1990), 142

81 Ibid.
82 Keith McClelland, 'Masculinity and the Representative Artisan in Britain, 1850–80,' in Roper and Tosh, eds, *Manful Assertions*, 77; and Steven Maynard, 'The Social Construction of Masculinity in Working Class History,' *Labour/Le Travail* 23 (Spring 1989): 159–77
83 *Sporting Life*, 9 August 1890
84 *Sporting News*, 11 August 1900
85 New York *Clipper*, 22 April 1876

CHAPTER 7 Reforming the Game

1 Although lacrosse is often referred to as Canada's national game, the claim originated with lacrossists interested in promoting the sport. As Alan Metcalfe has pointed out, 'There is no evidence in the parliamentary debates or Acts to support the contention that it was proclaimed Canada's national game.' Metcalfe, *Canada Learns to Play* (Toronto: McClelland and Stewart 1987), 238
2 Steven A. Riess, *Touching Base: Professional Baseball and American Culture in the Progressive Era* (Westport, Conn.: Greenwood Press 1980). This theme was first advanced in his article 'The Baseball Magnates and Urban Politics in the Progressive Era, 1865–1920,' *Journal of Sport History* 1, 1 (Spring 1974): 41–62.
3 Stephen A. Riess, 'Sport and the American Dream: A Review Essay,' *Journal of Social History* 14, 2 (1980): 295–303
4 Riess, *Touching Base*, 186
5 'The Baseball Outlook,' from the *Boston Advertiser*, reprinted in *Morning Herald*, 26 May 1893
6 *Acadian Recorder*, 13 July 1891. For similar comments see ibid., 25 May and 1, 23 June 1891
7 Halifax *Morning Herald*, 8 August 1891
8 *Acadian Recorder*, 17 May 1895. The Saint John players included Frank White, Thomas Bell, and George Whitenecht of the old professional club, and amateur players Sterling Barker, Samuel W. Milligan, Alex Thompson, Harry DeForrest, James Christie, and A. Holly.
9 Ibid., 20 June 1895
10 Brian Flood, *Saint John: A Sporting Tradition* (Saint John: Neptune Publishing 1985): 124
11 Often games between these clubs came as a result of challenges printed in the local newspapers. The *Acadian Recorder* of 25 June 1898, for example, noted that O.P. O'Sullivan of Taylor's Shoe Factory challenged 'any trade

team' to a match on 9 July, 'combined printers preferred.' Similarly, R. Cooper, captain of the Plant Wharf baseball nine, challenged either Jones' Wharf or Boak's Wharf to a match in April of that year. *Acadian Recorder*, 24 April 1898. For other such challenges see ibid., 23 August 1898, 28 June and 16, 25 July 1900, 14 May 1903, 31 May and 11 June 1904; and *Daily Echo*, 1 August 1895.

12 Saint John *Globe*, 4 September 1896

13 *Acadian Recorder*, 27 August 1900. In 1898 O'Neill had jumped the Roses to play for the Portland baseball club, and in 1901 he broke his contract with his Saint John club to play in Halifax.

14 Saint John *Globe*, 25 June 1901

15 Halifax *Herald*, 26 June 1901

16 Bangor *Daily Commercial*, 9, 22 August 1907

17 Jim Whelly's son Charles tells of his father returning from games on the mound for the Saint John Alerts with his baseball hat full of silver dollars. 'I wasn't old enough to know much about my Dad's ball career but from what I understand he made pretty good money. He was a young man when he owned his first business.' Quoted in Flood, *Saint John*, 124

18 Fredericton *Gleaner*, 3 August 1897

19 Saint John *Globe*, 4 August 1897

20 Ibid., 7 June 1892

21 *Acadian Recorder*, 17 September 1899

22 The Saint John *Globe*, 30 July 1892, noted that 'the unpopularity of baseball was seen Friday when less than a hundred people attended the Moncton versus Saint John YMCA teams' match on the A.A. grounds.' Similary, in May 1894 the *Globe* observed that the interest in baseball that died three years before 'has hardly revived.' A game between Maine State College and the YMCA team, won by the collegians, was very 'poorly attended.' Ibid., 24 May 1894

23 John Thorn and Peter Palmer, eds, *Total Baseball* 2d ed. (New York: Warner Books 1989), 957. Although Hanifin's name is often spelled Hannifin in various baseball encyclopaedias, he is listed in both the Census of 1891, and in Halifax city directories under the name Hanifin.

24 In 1901 the Vancouver team had four Maritimers, 'Billy' Flood of PEI, Walter O'Brien from Saint John, 'Brundle' Pickering from Halifax, and Les Harvie from Dalhousie, NB. Saint John *Globe*, 29 May 1901

25 Amherst *Daily News*, 26 May 1903

26 Halifax *Herald*, 11 April 1910

27 William Humber, *Cheering for the Home Team: The Story of Baseball in Canada* (Erin, Ont.: Boston Mills Press 1983), 90

28 Bangor *Daily Commercial*, 15 July 1903
29 Ibid., 25 July 1907
30 Neil J. Sullivan, *The Minors: The Struggles and the Triumph of Baseball's Poor Relation from 1876 to the Present* (New York: St Martin's Press 1990), 23
31 Will Anderson, *Was Baseball Really Invented in Maine?* (Portland, Me.: Will Anderson Publisher 1992), 19
32 Sydney *Record*, 30 July, 21 August 1906
33 Sydney *Daily Post*, 15 September 1905
34 Ibid., 16, 21 June 1906
35 Flood, *Saint John: A Sporting Tradition*, 128–9
36 Sydney *Record*, 2 August 1906
37 *Acadian Recorder*, 4 August 1906
38 Sydney *Record*, 23 July 1906
39 Springhill *News and Advertiser*, 13 August 1896
40 See, for example, Halifax *Morning Chronicle*, 29 May 1905
41 Don Morrow, 'A Case Study in Amateur Conflict: The Athletic War in Canada, 1906–8,' in Morris Mott, ed., *Sports in Canada* (Toronto: Copp Clark 1989), 215
42 Sydney *Daily Post*, 18 May 1906
43 This was not exclusive to Cape Breton, of course. Amateur athletic clubs in Saint John, Moncton, Fredericton, and Halifax had engaged in the practice for years.
44 Sydney *Daily Post*, 14, 22 June 1907
45 Halifax *Herald*, 11, 14 January 1910
46 Ibid., 25 February 1910
47 Morrow, 'A Case Study in Amateur Conflict,' 204
48 Halifax *Herald*, 19 February 1910
49 Ibid., 3 May 1911
50 Paul Voisey, *Vulcan: The Making of a Prairie Community* (Toronto: University of Toronto Press 1988) 37, 60, 162–4
51 *Acadian Recorder*, 19 September 1888
52 Suzanne Morton has found a similar phenomenon among working men and women in the Maritimes, in a study of bingo, lotteries, and sweepstakes during the interwar years. See her 'Winning Under Capitalism: Luck, Bingo and Lotteries in Canada, 1919–1939,' paper presented to the Canadian Historical Association annual meetings, Charlottetown, June 1992
53 See Ross McKibbon, *The Ideologies of Class: Social Relations in Britain, 1880–1950* (Oxford: Clarendon Press 1990); Wray Vamplew, *Pay Up and Play the Game: Professional Sport in Britain* (Cambridge: Cambridge Univer-

sity Press 1988), esp. chap. 6; James A. Maguire, 'Against the Odds: The Survival of English Working Class Gambling Since 1800,' *Arena Review* 2, 1 (May 1987): 37–43; Ross McKibbon, 'Working Class Gambling in Britain, 1880–1939,' *Past and Present* 82 (1979): 147–78; and David C. Itzkowitz, 'Victorian Bookmakers and Their Customers,' *Victorian Studies* 32, 1 (Autumn 1988): 7–30.

54 For a careful study of the ambiguous response to gambling in a society where risk and rapid gain appeared as essential ingredients in rational capitalist speculation, see Ann Fabian, *Card Sharps, Dream Books and Bucket Shops: Gambling in 19th Century America* (Ithaca and London: Cornell University Press 1990).

55 See, for example, *Daily Echo*, 8, 11 September 1890; and *Acadian Recorder*, 30 August and 19 September 1888, 3 July and 15 August 1890, and 21 July 1900.

56 Sydney *Record*, 23 July 1906

57 Dr E.H. Nichols, 'Discussion of Summer Baseball,' *American Physical Education Review* 19, 4 (April 1914): 292–300

58 'Committee on Ridding College Baseball of Its Objectionable Features,' *American Physical Education Review* 19, 4 (April 1914): 313–14

59 Benjamin G. Rader, *American Sports: From the Age of Folk Games to the Age of Spectators* (Englewood Cliffs, NJ: Prentice Hall 1983), 126–7

60 *Spalding's Official Canadian Base Ball Guide*, 1912 (Montreal: Canadian Sports Publishing Co. 1912), n.p.

61 Halifax *Herald*, 21 July 1911; *Daily Echo*, 8 May 1911

62 Halifax *Daily Echo*, 5 August 1911

63 Halifax *Herald*, 17 June 1911

64 Ibid., 17 June 1911

65 Halifax *Herald*, 16 May 1911

66 *Acadian Recorder*, 17 September 1910

67 Halifax *Herald*, 11 May 1911

68 During the 1912 season, Gordon Isnor and John T. Murphy, both of whom were involved in the operation of the Socials baseball club, announced themselves as candidates for the office of alderman in the Halifax civic elections. 'Two Halifax leading sports promoters are to be candidates for the office of alderman at the coming civic election in that town,' the *Acadian Recorder* noted on 7 April 1912. 'The advancement of the sporting interests is to be one of the planks in their platform ... An appeal to the sporting element would be an excellent card.' The following day, however, Gordon Isnor withdrew his candidacy, 'owing to increased business ties.'

69 Halifax *Morning Chronicle*, 2 August 1912. As of July 29, Daly was hitting .384.
70 Flood, *Saint John*, 131–2; Halifax *Morning Chronicle*, 16 September 1912
71 *Acadian Recorder*, 14, 30 August 1912
72 Ibid., 21 August 1912
73 Ibid., 18 April and 6, 15 May 1914

CHAPTER 8 Baseball as Civic Accomplishment

1 James Weinstein, *The Corporate Ideal in the Liberal State: 1900–1918* (Boston: Beacon Press 1968). For the Maritimes, see Colin Howell, 'The 1900s: Industry, Urbanization and Reform,' in E.R. Forbes and D.A. Muise, eds, *The Atlantic Provinces in Confederation* (Toronto: University of Toronto Press 1993), 155–7.
2 Quoted in Harold Seymour, *Baseball: The Early Years* (New York: Oxford University Press 1960), 265.
3 *Sporting News*, 19 October 1895
4 Quoted in Seymour, *Baseball: The Early Years*, 306
5 See, for example, *Sporting News*, 11 August 1900.
6 Halifax *Herald*, 19 August 1909
7 Barry Cornell, 'Inside Facts about Baseball,' *Technical World Magazine* 15 (1911): 641–9; Hugh Fullerton, 'The Inside Game: The Science of Baseball,' *American Magazine* 70, 1 (May 1910): 3–13
8 S. Leroy Brown, 'Bernoulli's Principle and Its Application to Explain the Curving of a Baseball,' *Popular Science Monthly* 83 (July–December 1913): 199–203
9 Hugh Fullerton, 'The Physics of Baseball,' *American Magazine* 74 (October 1912): 754
10 Edward Lyell Fox, 'What Is "Inside Baseball?"' *Outing* 58 (July 1911): 488–91
11 I am particularly indebted here to Mark Dyerson's brilliant paper 'The Moral Equivalent of War: American Ideas of Sport, the State and National Vitality, 1880–1920,' presented to the North American Society for Sport History annual meeting, Albuquerque, NM, June 1993.
12 Halifax *Herald*, 24, 26 May 1917
13 Ibid., 16 November 1916
14 Paul Fussell, *The Great War and Modern Memory* (London: Oxford University Press 1975), 22
15 All of these phrases can be found in stories relating to the 1917 World Series. See the Halifax *Morning Chronicle*, 10–22 October 1917.

16 Sydney *Record*, 7 August 1914
17 *Acadian Recorder*, 10 August 1915
18 See, for example, Halifax *Herald*, 1 August 1917, announcing a game between the Social and Composite Battalion, the proceeds of which would be turned over to the Red Cross.
19 *Acadian Recorder*, 25 May 1918
20 Sydney *Record*, 4 May 1918
21 Ibid., 12, 13 July 1918
22 *Acadian Recorder*, 17 June 1915
23 Halifax *Herald*, 26 July 1917
24 Sydney *Record*, 20 July 1918
25 Harrington E. Crissey, Jr, 'Baseball and the Armed Services,' in John Thorn and Peter Palmer, eds, *Total Baseball*, 2d ed. (New York: Warner Books 1989), 609–10
26 See, for example, 'Canada Again Beats the U.S. "Bob" Stanley, Toronto Southpaw, Wins at Taplow,' *The Globe* (Toronto), 27 August 1917. Canada won this match 12–3 against an American squad captained by ex–major leaguer Arlie Latham.
27 'W.R. 'Tee' Doyle,' Nova Scotia Sports Hall of Fame citation, Nova Scotia Sport Heritage Centre, Halifax, NS; telephone interview with Mr Tony Doyle, September 1992
28 Halifax *Herald*, 17 May 1917
29 Ibid., 21 May 1919. 'During the past few years baseball has had very little opportunity of developing among the boys of the city, but the sudden boom in the game since the war ceased is wonderful. All ages are playing baseball, among whom are scores of returning soldiers. When attempts were made last season to get the different baseball clubs in the city organized it was difficult to get enough teams to form leagues. This year it is different and the organizers were besieged with applications and many had to be refused.'
30 Halifax *Herald*, 29 June 1920
31 *Acadian Recorder*, 30 June, 13 July 1920
32 The Reserve Mines club folded at the end of July, leaving Dominion and New Waterford to decide the league championship. A dispute over player eligibility, however, meant that the championship series was cancelled without a winner being crowned. *Sydney Record*, 21 August 1920
33 Halifax *Herald*, 14 August 1920
34 Ibid., 24, 27 August 1920
35 Nova Scotia Sports Hall of Fame citations, 'Sammy Lesser' and 'Bill Richardson,' Nova Scotia Sports Heritage Centre

36 Joe D. Willis and Richard G. Wettan, 'Social Stratification in New York City Athletic Clubs,' *Journal of Sport History* 3, 2 (Summer 1976): 45–63

37 The Halifax Wanderers rugby club in 1888, for example, was dedicated to the principles of gentlemanly amateurism, and comprised several doctors, a surgeon, a Member of Parliament, and a Supreme Court Justice. A.J. 'Sandy' Young, *Beyond Heroes: A Sport History of Nova Scotia*, 2 vols (Hantsport, NS: Lancelot Press 1988), 1: 138

38 Amherst *News and Sentinel*, 22 July 1919

39 Kallenberg was not the Kiwanis's best pitcher, but the Braves had wanted him to start the game in order to assess his talent as a major league prospect. He was later signed by the Boston Red Sox, but arm trouble ended his career before he made the major leagues. Robert Ashe, *Even the Babe Came to Play: Small-Town Baseball in the Dirty 30s* (Halifax: Nimbus Publishing 1991), 64–72

40 Ernest R. Forbes, 'The Origins of the Maritime Rights Movement,' in *Challenging the Regional Stereotype* (Fredericton: Acadiensis Press 1989), 100–13; David Frank, 'The 1920s,' in Forbes and Muise, eds, *The Atlantic Provinces in Confederation*

41 Ian McKay, 'Tartanism Triumphant: The Construction of Scottishness in Nova Scotia, 1933–1954,' *Acadiensis* 21, 2 (Spring 1992): 43

42 Ian McKay, 'Helen Creighton and the Politics of Antimodernism,' in Gwendolyn Davies, ed., *Myth and Milieu: Atlantic Literature and Culture 1918–1939* (Fredericton: Acadiensis Press 1993); and '"He Is More Picturesque in His Oilskins": Helen Creighton and the Art of Being Nova Scotian,' *New Maritimes* 12, 1 (September / October 1993): 12–22

43 Halifax *Herald*, 10 August 1920

44 Flood, *Saint John*, 161–4

45 Ashe, *Even the Babe*, 19–21, 36, 90–1

46 Flood, *Saint John*, 161–9

47 Ian McKay, 'The Realm of Uncertainty: The Experience of Work in the Cumberland Coal Mines, 1893–1927,' *Acadiensis* 16, 1 (Autumn 1986): 3–57; quote from p. 5

48 Ibid., 54

49 The experience of leisure activity as part of the rhythm of working-class life and of community culture is a largely neglected field in Canadian historiography. For a useful discussion of the subject in a British context, see Andrew Davies, *Leisure, Gender and Poverty: Working-Class Culture in Salford and Manchester, 1900–1939* (Buckingham & Philadelphia: Open University Press 1992).

50 Halifax *Herald*, 31 July 1939

51 *Morning Chronicle*, 23 August 1924. Upon returning to Nova Scotia, Thompson was suspended by the MPAAA. Thompson was reinstated when Giants manager John McGraw sent a telegram verifying that Thompson was not under contract and received no salary while with the Giants.

52 Burton Russell, *Nova Scotia Baseball Heroics* (Kentville, NS: Burton Russell 1993), 12–13; Westville Heritage Group, *History of Westville* (Westville: Westville High School Publishing Group 1988), 128

53 A.J. 'Sandy' Young and Heather Harris, eds, *Maritime Sports Stars on Parade: Highlighting Nova Scotia's Golden Age of Sports* (Hantsport: Lancelot Press, n.d.), 68

54 Interview with Robert 'Bun' Foley, at Halifax, September 1992. Foley was a member of a family of noted athletes. His father, Tom Foley, had played baseball with Tip O'Neil and Jack McLean at the turn of the century, and gained even greater notoriety in boxing, wrestling, and gymnastics. Brothers Frank and Tommy starred in hockey, baseball, boxing, and track and field; Jimmy was a good ballplayer, but he was an even better hockey player. His hockey career took him to Los Angeles, where he met and socialized with Hollywood stars such as Ida Lupino and Peter Lawford, and then to Europe, where he gained fame as an international referee and coach. At the 1936 Olympics in Berlin, Jimmy organized and umpired an exhibition baseball game in order to showcase the sport as a possible future Olympic event. He also coached the British ice-hockey team, and accepted an offer from Mussolini to develop the Italian ice-hockey program and to coach Italy's team in the following Olympics. This project ended, of course, with the outbreak of the Second World War.

55 Young and Harris, eds, *Maritime Sport Stars*, 58–9

56 Ace Foley, *Ace Foley, the First Fifty Years: The Life and Times of a Sports Writer* (Windsor, NS: Lancelot Press 1970), 27

57 Quoted in Russell, *Nova Scotia Baseball Heroics*, 26

58 Ashe, *Even the Babe*, 138

59 Quoted in Russell and Cameron, *Nova Scotia Sports Personalities*, 38–9. There is little question that the Seaman boys had the talent to play professional baseball. In the late 1930s the four brothers signed to play for New Waterford in the Class C Colliery League, but John Seaman would not let them play, and they were reinstated as amateurs. In 1940 Danny and Garneau accompanied famed baseball and hockey broadcaster Danny Gallivan to spring training with the Red Sox. The two Seamans were offered contracts to play in the Boston farm system, but minor league salaries were hardly attractive at that time, and the brothers returned to Nova Scotia without signing.

60 Ashe, *Even the Babe*, 147
61 Halifax *Herald*, 28 July 1921
62 Ashe, *Even the Babe*, 83
63 Ibid., ii
64 Sydney *Post-Record*, 2 July 1935

CHAPTER 9 The 'Others'

1 Halifax *Morning Herald*, 25 July 1936
2 Ibid., 23 June 1936
3 William Brashler, *The Bingo Long Travelling All-Stars and Motor Kings* (New York: Signet 1973)
4 Halifax *Herald*, 16 June 1937
5 Ibid., 22 July 1939
6 The Boston Royal Giants discontinued their tours of the Maritimes after Canada went to war in 1939. They later joined the short-lived Negro Major Baseball League of America in 1942. Robert Peterson, *Only the Ball Was White: A History of Legendary Black Players and All-Black Professional Teams* (New York: Oxford University Press 1970), 219
7 Interview with Melvin Sheppard, Glace Bay, NS, November 1990
8 The first Nova Scotian club to defeat the Royal Giants was the Stellarton town team, playing errorless ball and winning 2–1 despite garnering only two hits. Halifax *Herald*, 29 June 1935
9 Ibid., 19 May 1936. The *Herald* noted that the Royals also helped the Yarmouth Gateways learn 'a new bag of tricks' that helped them in the championship playoffs.
10 Burton Russell, *Nova Scotia Baseball Heroics* (Kentville, NS: Burton Russell 1993), 29–30
11 Rob Ruck, *Sandlot Seasons: Sport in Black Pittsburgh* (Urbana and Chicago: University of Illinois Press 1987), 121
12 Donn Rogosin has warned against exaggerating the significance of clowning, as was done in the film version of *The Bingo Long Travelling All-Stars*. That film, Rogosin argues, 'trivialized the so-very important experience of life on the road. Life on the road tempered the exuberance of urban black baseball; it deepened the black baseball experience. Negro leaguers gained a perspective on white culture afforded few members of their race. They faced hardship and discrimination, but that was not the whole story. They also were cheered by all-white crowds and admired by white ballplayers less proficient than themselves. In their daily encounters with white players they were usually accorded meaningful respect for their talents.

While they never forgot or forgave the brutal and petty harassments of a society which discriminated on the basis of color, they also experienced the accolades of a culture which celebrated competence and achievement.' Donn Rogosin, *Invisible Men: Life in Baseball's Negro Leagues* (New York: Atheneum 1983), 151

13 Jules Tygiel, *Baseball's Great Experiment. Jackie Robinson and His Legacy* (New York: Oxford University Press, 1983), 19

14 *Clipper*, 21 February 1880

15 *Sporting News*, 29 August 1896

16 Telephone interview with Tom Sweet, Nova Scotia Sport Heritage Centre, Halifax, 5 January 1994

17 Bill Heward with Dmitri V. Gait, *Some Are Called Clowns* (New York: Thomas Y. Crowell Co. 1974), 258

18 This routine had first been developed by Pepper Bassett, catcher for the New Orleans Crescent Stars during the early 1930s. Rogosin, *Invisible Men*, 143

19 John Craig, *Ain't Lookin* (Richmond Hill, Ont.: Scholastic Tab 1983). This book was also published under the title *Chappie and Me* (New York: Dodd Mead 1979), a reference to Chappie Johnson's Travelling All-Stars.

20 Halifax *Herald*, 5 August 1935

21 Quoted in Robert Ashe, *Even the Babe Came to Play: Small-Town Baseball in the Dirty 30s* (Halifax: Nimbus 1991), 119

22 Halifax *Herald*, 26 May 1936

23 Ibid., 3 July 1931

24 Peterson, *Only the Ball Was White*, 235

25 Ibid., 218–9

26 Halifax *Herald*, 25 May 1936

27 It is difficult to know for sure who the players were, for in pandering to contemporary stereotypes about Africa, the Cannibal Giants adopted pseudonyms that suggested African parentage. Upon closer examination, moreover, the names that they chose carried a satirical and somewhat defiant edge. The regular battery included pitcher Mofike (motherfucker) and catcher Ny Ass Ass; at first base stood Limpopo (limp pecker) and at third Taklooie (take a looie). Whether this was an attempt at humour, or a more subtle statement of protest, is impossible to determine; nor can we be certain that the predominately white audiences caught the message. Merritt Clifton, *Disorganized Baseball: The Provincial League from LaRoque to Les Expos* (Brigham, Que.: Merritt Clifton 1982), 4

28 Goose Tatum, Dave Barnhill, Buck O'Neil, and King Tut were members of the club at various times during the late 1930s. Rogosin, *Invisible Men*, 147

29 Heward and Gait, *Some Are Called Clowns*, 79
30 Francis X. Sculley, 'Do You Remember the House of David?' *Leather-stocking Journal*, Summer 1980; Richard E. Derby, Jr, and Jim Coleman, 'House of David – the Bearded Beauties,' unpublished paper, National Baseball Library, Cooperstown, NY
31 Heward and Gait, *Some Are Called Clowns*, 73–9
32 Halifax *Herald*, 23 August 1939; Ibid., 5 August 1939
33 White had great respect for the St Stephen club. At the beginning of its 1939 tour, his Colored Giants lost 5–3 to Brownell and won a squeaker 3–2 over Jim Morrell. Ibid., 15 July 1939
34 Jerry Kirshenbaum, 'The Hairiest,' *Sports Illustrated*, June 1970: 106
35 James W. St G. Walker, *Racial Discrimination in Canada: The Black Experience*, CHA booklet no. 41 (Ottawa: Canadian Historical Association 1985), 16
36 James W. St G. Walker, 'Black History in the Maritimes: Major Themes and Teaching Strategies,' in P.A. Buckner, ed., *Teaching Maritime Studies* (Fredericton: Acadiensis Press 1986), 96–107
37 Fredericton *Gleaner*, 6 June 1890
38 *Acadian Recorder*, 23 May 1891
39 Fredericton *Gleaner*, 10 June, 5 July, 21 August 1890, 20 May 1891
40 Ibid., 8 July 1890
41 Ibid., 2 July 1890
42 Ibid., 20 June 1890. The only other mention in the press of the amount of prize purses, was in ibid., 2 August 1894, when it was reported that Eatman's team won $10. This would suggest that a competitive club like the Celestials, who played a half-dozen prize matches a season and won most of them, would have probably taken home about $50 a season, or approximately $5 per player. Although not a lot, this at least supplemented the income of many players who worked sporadically at several jobs, or in low-paying occupations.
43 Donald H. Clairmont and Dennis W. Magill, *Africville Relocation Report* (Halifax, 1971)
44 On the significance of the Baptist church to Nova Scotia's black community see Frank Stanley Boyd, Jr, ed., *McKerrow: A Brief History of the Coloured Baptists of Nova Scotia, 1783–1895* (Halifax: Afro Nova Scotian Enterprises 1976); and George Elliott Clarke, 'The Death and Rebirth of Africadian Nationalism,' *New Maritimes* 11, 5 (May / June 1993): 24–7
45 Halifax *Herald*, 9, 16 June 1922
46 The Colored Wonders could not afford the travelling costs associated with the league and withdrew in June 1932. Ibid., 10 June 1932

47 Ibid., 24 June, 2 July 1935. On Mentis's track and field abilities see ibid.,
   28 September 1931
48 Statistics compiled by author from various newspaper box-scores
49 Neil Kleinknecht, 'Integration of Baseball After World War II,' Society for
   American Baseball Research (SABR) *Baseball Research Journal*, 1983: 1–6
50 Walker, *Racial Discrimination in Canada*, 17
51 Carman Miller, 'The 1940s: War and Rehabilitation,' in E.R. Forbes and
   D.A. Muise, eds, *The Atlantic Provinces in Confederation* (Toronto: University of Toronto Press 1993), 344
52 *The Clarion*, 1 November 1947
53 Ibid., 23 March 1949
54 Kleinknecht, 'Integration of Baseball,' 1–6
55 *The Clarion*, 12 January 1949
56 See Marty York's column, 'O'Ree knows black can be hell on ice,' *Globe
   and Mail*, 31 October 1990
57 The writing on native sport history includes the following works: Michael
   A. Salter, 'The Effect of Acculturation on the Game of Lacrosse and on Its
   Role as an Agent of Indian Survival,' *Canadian Journal of History of Sport
   and Physical Education* 3, 1 (May 1972): 29–43; Bruce Kidd, 'In Defence of
   Tom Longboat,' *Canadian Journal of History of Sport* 14, 1 (May 1983):
   34–56; Joseph B. Oxendine, *American Indian Sports Heritage* (Champagne,
   Ill.: Human Kinetics 1988); George Eisen, 'Games and Sporting Diversions
   of the North American Indians as Reflected in American Historical Writings of the Sixteenth and Seventeenth Centuries,' *Canadian Journal of History of Sport and Physical Education* 9, 1 (May 1978): 58–85; Victoria Paras-
   chak, 'Native Sport History: Pitfalls and Promise,' *Canadian Journal of History of Sport* 20, 1 (May 1989): 57–64; Charles Ballam, 'Missing from the
   Canadian Sport Scene, Native Athletes,' *Canadian Journal of History of Sport*
   14, 2 (December 1983): 33–43; and John N. Dewar, 'Qu'Appelle Indian
   Residential School, 1884–1990: A 106 Year Sports Perspective,' *North Amer-
   ican Society for Sport History Proceeding and Newsletter*, 1990: 54
58 Bruce Trigger, *Natives and Newcomers: Canada's Heroic Age Reconsidered*
   (Montreal and Kingston: McGill-Queen's University Press 1985); Sara
   Carter, *Lost Harvests: Prairie Indian Reserve Farmers and Government Policy*
   (Montreal and Kingston: McGill-Queen's University Press 1990); John
   Reid, *Acadia, Maine and New Scotland: Marginal Colonies in the Seventeenth
   Century* (Toronto: University of Toronto Press 1981), and *Six Crucial Dec-
   ades: Times of Change in the History of the Maritimes* (Halifax: Nimbus Pub-
   lishing 1987), esp. chaps 1–3; and Jim Miller, *Skyscrapers Hide the Heavens*
   (Toronto: University of Toronto Press 1991). For earlier accounts of na-

tive–white relations see Alfred G. Bailey, *The Conflict of European and Eastern Algonkian Cultures 1504–1700: A Study in Canadian Civilization* (Saint John, 1937); L.F.S. Upton, *Micmacs and Colonists: White Indian Relations in the Maritimes, 1713–1867* (Vancouver: UBC Press 1979); and Harold F. McGee, *The Native People of Atlantic Canada: A History of Indian–European Relations* (Ottawa: Carleton University Press 1983).

59 Tony Judt, 'A Clown in Regal Purple: Social History and the Historians,' *History Workshop Journal* 7 (Spring 1979): 66–94; quote from p. 67

60 Melvin Adelman, Allen Guttmann, and Eric Dunning are among the most respected adherents of the 'modernization' model. See Melvin Adelman, *A Sporting Time: New York City and the Rise of Modern Athletics, 1820–1870* (Urbana and Chicago: University of Illinois Press 1986); Allen Guttmann, *A Whole New Ball Game: An Interpretation of American Sports* (Chapel Hill and London: University of North Carolina Press 1988). Although Guttmann acknowledges native sport, he does so to demonstrate the displacement of traditional sports such as stickball, a native game resembling lacrosse, by more modern forms of sporting activity. In particular, Guttmann emphasizes the centrality of religious ritual to early native games and the extent to which those rituals have been rendered outmoded. 'The force of modernization is such that Indian games no longer exemplify otherness as once they did. The Choctaws still play stickball, but the pre-Columbian rituals have vanished, along with the Great Spirit who called them forth. The teams now have uniforms, and there are officials to enforce the rules. There are boundaries, a clock, and a scoreboard. Medicine men linger on with little to do. Sitting on the sidelines, chanting their magic incantations, they dispiritedly seek to influence the outcome of games in which hardly anyone takes much interest. One can lament the disappearance of traditional games and appeal for the revival of ancient rituals, but there is little likelihood of a tribal return to premodern games' (22). See also Eric Dunning and Chris Rojek, eds, *Sport and Leisure in the Civilizing Process: Critique and Counter-Critique* (Toronto: University of Toronto Press 1992), for a spirited debate about the merits of modernization theory.

61 Trigger, *Natives and Newcomers*, 3, 4–43

62 Andrea Jean Bear, 'The Concept of Unity among Indian Tribes of Maine, New Hampshire and New Brunswick: An Ehnohistory,' thesis presented to Senior Scholars program, Colby College, 1966

63 See Morris Kenneth Mott, 'Games and Contests of the First "Manitobans,"' in M.K. Mott, ed., *Sports in Canada* (Toronto: Copp Clark 1989), 18–27.

64 Harold Seymour, *Baseball: The People's Game* (New York: Oxford University Press 1990), 380

65 Interview with Douglas Knockwood, Halifax, 7 January 1993
66 Interview with Peter Robinson, Shubenacadie, 10 November 1992
67 Interview with Wilfrid Prosper, Eskasoni Reserve, 23 July 1992
68 Interview with Margaret Johnson, Eskasoni Reserve, 21 August 1992
69 Interview with John Basque, Chapel Island Reserve, 24 August 1992
70 Interview with John Joseph, Big Cove, 7 September 1992
71 Halifax *Herald*, 5 August 1938
72 For a useful treatment of medical services available to Mi'qmacs, see Peter Twohig, 'Health and the Health Care Delivery System: The Micmac in Nova Scotia,' MA thesis, Saint Mary's University 1991
73 Interview with Margaret Johnson, 21 August 1992
74 Interview with Sandy Julian, Millbrook Reserve, Truro, 10 November 1992
75 Interview with Frank Doucette, Membertou Reserve, Sydney, NS, 23 January 1992; interview with Raymond Christmas, Membertou Reserve, Sydney, 24 July 1992
76 *Acadian Recorder*, 7 August 1877
77 Robert Bogdan, *Freak Show: Presenting Human Oddities for Amusement and Profit* (Chicago: University of Chicago Press 1988)
78 Heward and Gait, *Some Are Called Clowns*
79 Interview with Wilfrid Prosper, 23 July 1992
80 *Summerside Journal and the Pioneer*, 17 October 1951. I am indebted to John Joe Sark for bringing this item to my attention.
81 *Eastern Argus*, 20, 21 August 1891
82 Bangor Public Library, vertical file, 'Sockalexis, Louis F.' The Worcester *Post*, 29 August 1895, noted that Sockalexis, 'in a recent trial at throwing the ball, made a mark of 404 1/4 feet.'
83 Joseph M. Overfield, 'Tragedies and Shortened Careers,' in John Thorn and Peter Palmer, eds, *Total Baseball*, 2d ed. (New York: Warner Books 1989), 437
84 Frances W. Hatch, 'Maine's All-Time Great Baseball Player,' *Down East*, August 1963: 37–9, 59; Will Anderson, *Was Baseball Really Invented in Maine?* (Portland, Me.: W. Anderson 1992), 18, 28–9, 109–13, 155
85 Luke Salisbury, *The Cleveland Indian: The Legend of King Saturday* (New York: Smith 1992)
86 Overfield, 'Tragedies and Shortened Careers,' 487
87 For an introduction to the relationship of Maliseet peoples to the larger society, see Robert John Cloney, 'Doctor, Lawyer, Indian Chief ... : Dependency among the Maliseet and the Impact of the Indian Act,' MA thesis, Saint Mary's University, 1993
88 Ruck, *Sandlot Seasons*, 206

89 Barbara Jean Fields, 'Slavery, Race and Ideology in the United States of America,' *New Left Review*, 1990: 101

CHAPTER 10 Extra Innings

1 Harrington E. Crissy, 'Baseball and the Armed Services,' 612. In 1944, the sailors pasted the Cleveland Indians 17–4, and completed their 50-game schedule with 48 victories.
2 Halifax *Herald*, July 1942
3 Robert W. Creamer, *Babe: The Legend Comes to Life* (New York: Simon & Schuster 1974), 35–8, 42, 51
4 Babe Ruth, as told to Bob Considine, *The Babe Ruth Story* (New York: Signet 1992), 4
5 The Halifax *Herald*, 31 August 1920, mistakenly identified Brother Matthias as Walter Comeford, who had played baseball for the old Socials at the end of the 1880s.
6 I am indebted to Mr William Kevin Cawley, Associate Archivist, Archives of the University of Notre Dame, for this biographical information.
7 James F.E. White, 'The Ajax Affair: Citizens and Sailors in Wartime Halifax, 1939–1945,' M.A. thesis, Dalhousie University, 1984
8 The extent of such practices may have been exaggerated, particularly in the wake of the VE Day riots in Halifax in May 1945. Editorial writers from across the country often tried to explain the riots as an inevitable result of Halifax's unreasonable treatment of service personnel. See Stanley R. Redman, *Open Gangway: An Account of the Halifax Riots* (Hantsport, NS: Lancelot Press 1981), 76–80.
9 James Lamb, *The Corvette Navy: True Stories from Canada's Atlantic War* (Toronto: Macmillan of Canada 1977), 3
10 Halifax *Herald*, 29 September 1945
11 Burton Russell, *Nova Scotia Baseball Heroics* (Kentville, NS: B. Russell 1993), 40
12 Phil Marchildon with Brian Kendall, *Ace: Canada's Pitching Sensation and Wartime Hero* (Toronto: Viking 1993), 111
13 Quoted in Russell, *Nova Scotia Baseball Heroics*, 38
14 Halifax *Herald*, 6 May 1943. See also ibid., 27 April, 5 May 1943
15 Jay White, 'Pulling Teeth: Striking for the Check-Off in the Halifax Shipyards, 1944,' *Acadiensis* 19, 1 (Autumn 1989): 115–41
16 Phillip 'Skit' Ferguson, address to Nova Scotia Sports Heritage Centre's 'Brown Bag Series,' March 1992
17 Neil Sullivan, *The Minors* (New York: St Martin's Press 1990), 165

18 Interview with Gerry Davis, Halifax, May 1991
19 Halifax *Herald*, 14 May 1947
20 Ibid., 8 July 1949
21 New Glasgow *Evening News*, 6 May 1948
22 *Sporting News*, 27 February 1952
23 Ibid., 7 May 1952
24 Interview with John 'Twit' Clarke, Stellarton, 12 October 1989
25 Quoted in the *Eastern Chronicle*, 30 June 1949; see also ibid., 17 June 1949
26 Interview with John Watterson, Keene, New Hampshire, 20 May 1990
27 Interview with Herm Kaplan, Halifax, 7 January 1990
28 Interview with John Watterson, Keene, NH, 19, 20 May 1990
29 Interview with John 'Brother' Macdonald, Stellarton, 20 January 1990
30 Interview with Syd Roy, Stellarton, 12 October 1989
31 *Chronicle Herald*, 12 April 1955
32 New Glasgow *Evening News*, 3 August 1955
33 Quoted in the New Glasgow *Evening News*, 17 September 1949. Upon his recent induction into the Nova Scotia Sports Hall of Fame, McLeod was asked about the secret of his batting prowess. 'All they ever told me was, if you can't see it don't swing at it,' he replied.
34 Russell, *Nova Scotia Baseball Heroics*, 71
35 Interview with Johnny Watterson, Keene, NH, 19 May 1990
36 Interview with Gerald Davis, Halifax, July 1989
37 Russell, *Nova Scotia Baseball Heroics*, 116
38 Interview with Johnny Clark, Halifax, 29 November 1989
39 I am indebted to Alan Wilson for sharing these insights, which will be included in his forthcoming study *The Mind of the Maritimes.*
40 Carman Miller, 'The 1940s,' in E.R. Forbes and D.A. Muise, eds, *The Atlantic Provinces in Confederation* (Toronto: University of Toronto Press 1993), 306
41 A.S. Foster, ed., *Maritime Baseball. Pictorial Year Book 1950* (Saint John: New Brunswick and Nova Scotia Baseball Associations 1950), 30
42 Ibid., 30
43 *Chronicle Herald*, 12 September 1955
44 Ibid., 12 April 1955
45 Margaret Conrad, 'The 1950s: Decade of Development,' in Forbes and Muise, eds, *The Atlantic Provinces in Confederation*, 419
46 Gary Burrill, *Away. Maritimers in Massachusetts, Ontario, and Alberta: An Oral History of Leaving Home* (Montreal and Kingston: McGill-Queen's University Press 1992), 8

Index

Photo credits

Author's collection Shipyards-Arrows game, H&D League scorecard

John Macdonald 'Brother' Macdonald

Nova Scotia Sports Heritage Centre Halifax Resolutes, Sammy Lesser, Charlie Paul, Babe Ruth, Middleton Cardinals, 'Bomber' Neal, Johnny Duarte, 'Peaches' Ruven and 'Bomber' Neal

Provincial Archives of New Brunswick Chicago Blackstockings, Fredericton Tartars, Saint John Royals

Provincial Archives of Nova Scotia *Tom Conners Collection:* Atlantas club, Young Men's Literacy Association, Socials club, North Commons, Wanderers Grounds, Halifax Coloured Diamonds, Vince Ferguson; *Sports Collection:* Halifax Crescents

Peter Robinson Native players, Bear River

Street & Smith Publishers *Tip Top Weekly* (courtesy Will Anderson)